FROMMER'S

COMPREHENSIVE TRAVEL GUIDE

DENVER, BOULDER & COLORADO SPRINGS

2ND EDITION

by Lois Friedland

PRENTICE HALL TRAVEL

NEW YORK • LONDON • TORONTO • SYDNEY • TOKYO • SINGAPORE

INVITATION TO THE READERS

In researching this book, I have come across many wonderful establishments, the best of which I have included here. I'm sure that many of you will also come across appealing hotels, inns, restaurants, guesthouses, shops, and attractions. Please don't keep them to yourself. Share your experiences, especially if you want to comment on places covered in this edition that have changed for the worse. You can address your letters to me:

Lois Friedland
Frommer's Denver, Boulder & Colorado Springs
c/o Prentice Hall Travel
15 Columbus Circle
New York, NY 10023

A DISCLAIMER

Readers are advised that prices fluctuate in the course of time and travel information changes under the impact of the varied and volatile factors that affect the travel industry. The author and publisher cannot be held responsible for the experiences of readers while traveling. Readers are invited to write to the publisher with ideas, comments, and suggestions for future editions.

FROMMER BOOKS

Published by Prentice Hall General Reference
A division of Simon & Schuster Inc.
15 Columbus Circle
New York, NY 10023

ISBN 0-671-79950-9
ISSN 1042-8763

Design by Robert Bull Design
Maps by Geografix Inc.

Special Sales
Bulk purchases of Frommer's Travel Guides are available at special discounts. The publishers are happy to custom-make publications for corporate clients who wish to use them as premiums or sales promotions. We can excerpt the contents, provide covers with corporate imprints, or create books to meet specific needs. For more information write to Special Sales, Prentice Hall Travel, Paramount Communications Building, 15 Columbus Circle, New York, NY 10023

Manufactured in the United States of America

CONTENTS

LIST OF MAPS

INTRODUCING COLORADO

1. GEOGRAPHY, HISTORY & PEOPLE
• **DATELINE**
• **FAMOUS COLORADANS**
2. ART, ARCHITECTURE & CULTURAL LIFE
3. RECOMMENDED BOOKS & FILMS

Traces of the Wild West are increasingly hard to find in Denver, Boulder, and Colorado Springs—Colorado's Front Range cities framed by the Rocky Mountains. You'll see some in the architecture of the Victorian homes, buildings, and warehouses that have been renovated to house residents, chic shops, galleries, and restaurants. And if you look downward at striding feet, you may discover cowboy boots anchoring an Armani suit on a man walking into Boettcher Concert Hall for an Itzhak Perlman performance.

But it's just a trendy patina for most residents at this point. The three cities today are upbeat, contemporary communities, again on the go after the stagnation of the late 1980s. Denver, in particular, has grown dramatically on the cultural, sports, and business fronts in recent years. For example, the Denver Center for Performing Arts, which houses Boettcher Hall, is now the second-largest performing arts complex in the nation (only Lincoln Center in New York seats more people). The call to "play ball" will start the premiere game of major-league baseball's newest team, the Colorado Rockies, in spring 1993. Currently under construction, the urban, built-for-baseball Coors Field will become the team's permanent home when it opens in 1995.

Boulder, about 30 minutes northwest of Denver and nudging the mountains, is a sophisticated university town, home of the University of Colorado. The generally young, upwardly mobile residents are keen on sports and the environment and are very health-conscious, and love living in a community where deer wander into their yards. Many work in the biotechnology, research, and computer fields.

Colorado Springs, at the base of Pikes Peak and about 1¼ hours south of Denver, was originally developed, in part, as an "open-air cure" for Easterners suffering from tuberculosis and as a resort town. Today it's home to the North American Aerospace Defense Command (NORAD), the U.S. Air Force Academy, and the U.S. Olympic Training Center.

All three cities are truly wonderful places to live, because residents can combine a relaxed lifestyle with big-city pursuits, arts, and culture. Locals live on gentle rolling plains in cities or on the mountainsides within 45 minutes of the downtown sectors. This gives residents easy access to a high-altitude playground rich in sites to explore and peaks to play on, with plenty of snow in the mountains for outstanding winter sports. The climate, however, is surprisingly mild in Denver, despite what you hear from TV weather forecasters on both coasts who are always talking about two feet of snow there—the snow they're talking about is in the mountain ranges. In fact, Denver often enjoys springlike weather in January when the warm, dry chinook wind sweeps across the plains.

Thanks to the opening of $2.7-billion Denver International Airport in October 1993, the area is prepping for an influx of business and tourists directly from foreign countries. Hotels are upgrading facilities, the list of popular and good (versus trendy but so-so) restaurants keeps changing, and visitor-friendly refinements at attractions are constantly being made. In this book, I included the obvious tourist stops, restaurants, and hotels, but also lots of tips about places and things to do that locals love. Consider it a general tour guide, stocked with insider tips from someone who has lived in Colorado for more than a decade.

1. GEOGRAPHY, HISTORY & PEOPLE

GEOGRAPHY

Some 200 million years ago there was a shallow inland sea where dinosaurs roamed in the area that would later be named Colorado (from the Spanish *color rojo,* which described the soil reddened by iron). You can still see their footprints and fossil fragments embedded in the rocky ground from Morrison, Denver's neighbor, westward to Dinosaur National Monument. About 70 million years ago, unimaginable pressures under the earth's crust thrust the land upward, turning the flat seabed into jagged, mountainous terrain, and the Rocky Mountains were born, a chain that stretches from New Mexico into Canada.

Denver is 15 miles east of the "foothills," as Coloradans call the smaller mountains (between 7,000 and 11,000 feet above sea level). Behind those foothills, and about an hour's drive from Denver, is the next ridge of mountains called the Front Range, a crooked line of peaks stretching from Pikes Peak (which looms over Colorado Springs) to the Wyoming border. The Front Range, which stretches westward to the Continental Divide and upward to 14,000 feet, was once under an inland sea, and the Fountain formation, which runs from Wyoming to New Mexico and is still only broken up in a few places (for example, at the cut for Interstate 70), was the beach. The lush red rocks—most beautiful when dampened by rain—that form both the Red Rocks Amphitheatre and the Garden of the Gods are part of that formation. Anyone interested in geology might want to get off at the I-70 Morrison exit and park in the lot just south of the exit. Markers explain the geological history of the region.

Today the Front Range, and the mountain ranges beyond, are

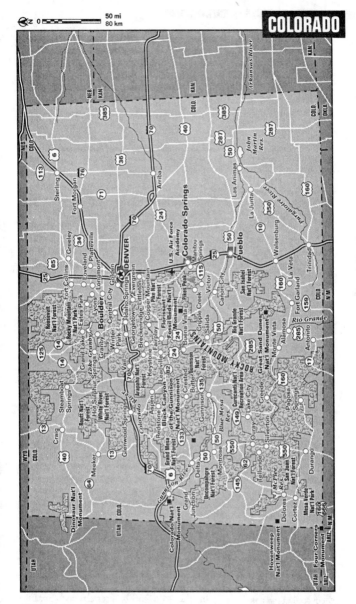

filled with mining towns with intriguing names like Leadville and Breckenridge, as well as such luxurious resort communities as Vail and Aspen. All the mountain communities, whether an hour away or an eight-hour drive from the plains, are surrounded by rugged wilderness areas filled with scenic hiking and horseback-riding trails, old gold mines, and remnants of the Wild West waiting to be explored.

4 • INTRODUCING COLORADO

IMPRESSIONS

"Our sojourn on the peak remains in memory hardly more than one ecstatic gaze. It was then and there, as I was looking out over the sealike expanse of fertile country spreading away so far under these ample skies, that the opening lines of the hymn floated into mind."
—KATHERINE LEE BATES, WHO WROTE "AMERICA THE BEAUTIFUL," 1895

DATELINE

- **50 B.C.–A.D. 1300** The Anasazi live in the Four Corners area of southwestern Colorado, first in caves, then in pueblos, and finally in cliff dwellings, before abandoning the region in the 1300s; Native American tribes move onto the eastern Colorado plains.

- **mid-1500s** French and Spanish explorers arrive.

- **1682** The French claim eastern Colorado.

- **1796** The Spanish claim the western half of the state.

- **1803** The eastern half, included in the Louisiana Purchase, becomes part of the U.S.

- **1848** Mexico cedes its share of Colorado (the western half) to the U.S.

- **1858** Gold is discovered at the confluence of the South Platte River and Cherry Creek, and crude settlements are formed along the streams' banks.

- **1859** Denver is *(continues)*

HISTORY

The first humans arrived approximately 13,000 years ago, wandering across the plains of eastern Colorado hunting bison and mammoths. Early in the Christian era, a group known as the Anasazi lived in the Four Corners area of the Southwest (where the borders of Colorado, Utah, Arizona, and New Mexico meet). These hunters and gatherers, called "basket makers" by archeologists because of their fine basketry, lived in caves from 50 B.C. to A.D. 450. Archeological finds at Mesa Verde National Park indicate that the Anasazi learned to build pit houses and use bows and arrows during the next 300 years. Around A.D. 750 they began building pueblos, villages where south-facing houses were joined together in a curved row. Around the 1100s the Anasazi started using sandstone masonry to build dwellings in rock alcoves on the sides of steep cliffs. (Today, visitors at Mesa Verde can explore the remains of many of those cliffside dwellings mysteriously abandoned in the 1300s.) As the Anasazi were developing a culture in the Southwest, several nomadic Native American tribes were moving around the eastern Colorado plains. The Cheyenne, Sioux, and Arapahoe moved north and south following the buffalo, stopping to gather lodgepole pines for tepees in the area that is now Colorado. The Utes inhabited the mountainous region near today's Colorado Springs.

In the mid-1500s French and Spanish explorers arrived searching for gold and furs. In 1682 the French claimed eastern Colorado; in 1706 the Spanish claimed the western half. But other than a few trappers and Spanish (later, Mexican) military outposts, the area would be virtually uninhabited by European or American settlers for another century and a half. Eastern Colorado became part of the United States in 1803 as part of the Louisiana Purchase, and the rest of Colorado was ceded to the U.S. by Mexico in 1848. The Lewis and Clark expedition and Zebulon Pike's mapping trips (on which he sighted the peak that today bears his name) opened up the territory in the early 1800s.

Settlement began in earnest when people back east heard tales of shiny yellow lumps lying in Colorado streambeds and joined in the "Pikes Peak or Bust!" gold rush. Some trekked along the Santa Fe Trail across the great plains of southeastern Colorado, while others rode on horseback or in covered wagons over the high prairies and past the buffalo herds in the northeastern region, lured by tales of gold in the Rockies.

But while the miners dreamed of quick riches, others dreamed up ways to relieve them of any gold they found. One get-rich-quick scheme was to stake out land claims, lay out city streets, and sell lots to the newcomers. After gold was discovered at the confluence of the South Platte River and Cherry Creek in 1858, as gold-seekers' tents, tepees, lean-tos, and crude log cabins sprang up on both sides of the river, Maj.-Gen. William H. Larimer took over land on the east side of the Platte and, in 1859, laid out a city. He called it Denver, hoping to curry favor with the territorial governor, James Denver (not knowing that the man had already resigned). But while city streets were being staked out, word came that the gold strike had proven to be, literally, a flash in the pan. Many of the 150,000 would-be miners returned east, but most raced on to the mountains when gold was unearthed in Central City. The people who stayed in the fledgling town on the flatland turned it into a supply point for those who headed higher.

In the early days, Bat Masterson and other gamblers, ladies of the night like Mattie Silk, and hucksters like Soapy Smith fought with miners for space in the bars and gambling halls lining the mud-filled streets. The city managed to survive not only colorful characters like these, but also a major fire, a flash flood (which even swept away the city hall), and skirmishes with local Native American tribes (which began avoiding Denver as it grew into a substantial city).

Originally part of the Kansas Territory, Colorado was established as a separate territory by the U.S. Congress in 1861, with its

DATELINE

laid out on the east side of the Platte River.

• **1861** Congress establishes Colorado as a separate territory.

• **1867** Denver becomes capital of the Colorado Territory.

• **1870** A railroad spur south from the transcontinental railroad tracks is completed, linking Denver to the rest of the country.

• **1876** Colorado—the Centennial State—is admitted to the Union.

• **1891–93** Denver's opulent period ends when the price of silver plummets in 1893. Losses are partially offset, however, by a major gold strike at Cripple Creek in 1891.

• **early 1900s** Denver "turns respectable," closing down brothels and gambling halls, cleaning up streets, and building an extensive park system.

• **1910s–1960s** Denver grows into a mid-size city.

• **1970s** An energy boom helps to create a high-rise urban skyline and precipitates an influx of new residents.

• **1980s** The energy boom fizzles out by the middle of the decade; construction dries up and office-vacancy rates reach *(continues)*

DATELINE

unprecedented levels as the city experiences a severe recession; the city's $125-million Colorado Convention Center opens.

- **1991–92** Denver's economy begins to grow again, office space starts filling up, hotel occupancy rates begin climbing, and there is an increase in the number of out-of-state companies moving into the state.
- **fall 1993** The new Denver International Airport opens.

capital first at Colorado City and then at Golden. During the Civil War, in 1862, Colorado was invaded by a Confederate army from Texas sent to seize the gold fields. However, a ragtag volunteer Colorado army fought and defeated the Rebels at the Battle of Glorita Pass.

1864 was the year of the terrible Sand Creek Massacre. Colonel John Chivington led soldiers and volunteers to Sand Creek, south of Denver, where they slaughtered 120 Plains tribes people, mostly children and the elderly. It was a serious blow to the Plains tribes, who were eventually relocated to reservations in other states. For his part in the massacre, Chivington was punished.

Denver, which became the territorial capital in 1867, might have stayed a small, sleepy town when the Union Pacific laid the transcontinental railway tracks far to the north through Wyoming. But local residents, unwilling to see their city fade away, raised $300,000 to construct a railroad spur connecting Denver with the Union Pacific's main line at Cheyenne. Completion of the railroad line in 1870, and the coming of the Kansas Pacific Railroad soon after, produced an immediate boom: Denver's population in 1870 was less than 5,000; only 20 years later it had jumped to more than 100,000.

Although the 1860s were difficult for Colorado, its fortunes began to improve in the 1870s. Ore smelters were built, farming increased, new mining communities were founded, railroad lines were pushed farther into the mountains, and Colorado's population increased fivefold. On August 1, 1876, the state of Colorado—the Centennial State—was admitted to the Union, with Denver as its permanent capital.

In the 1870s and 1880s silver replaced gold as the state's source of great wealth, and Denver prospered. Silver barons arrived to construct fancy mansions on Capitol Hill—and an opera house. This opulent period ended in 1893 when the price of silver plummeted: Mines and smelters closed; banks failed, ruining their depositors; and silver kings became paupers almost overnight. But a major gold strike at Cripple Creek, west of Colorado Springs, in 1891 helped offset Denver's losses from the Great Silver Panic, and prevented a major decline. Throughout the state, farming, cattle and sheep ranching, and commerce began to provide a more stable economy.

At the turn of the century mining fortunes again returned to Denver and the city fathers decided it was time to become respectable. Wild West lawlessness and gunplay were curtailed, brothels were shut down, the streets were cleaned up, the Community Chest plan was developed to finance charities, and huge sums were spent beautifying the city. Thousands of trees were planted along wide boulevards, statues and fountains were placed in parks, and the Capitol with its 24-karat-gold-leafed dome was constructed. The city also purchased 20,000 acres of mountain land, the beginning of today's Denver Mountain Park System, which includes Red Rocks

Amphitheater and Winter Park, one of the state's largest ski areas. (Today, Denver has more parks than any other city in the country.) During those years Denver earned its appropriate nickname: Queen City of the Plains.

During the years between the end of World War I and the 1960s Denver quietly grew into a moderate-size city. Up in the mountains, small towns were beginning to build ski lifts and rustic hideaway lodges, laying the groundwork for today's resort towns. In 1969 there were only three downtown buildings more than 20 stories tall. In the late 1970s there was as much office space under construction as already existed. Cranes poked skyward, altering the city's skyline while developers built badly needed office space for petroleum and other energy companies, plus their supporting banking, accounting, and data-processing industries.

When the energy boom of the 1970s ended, Denver's economy ran out of steam and construction dried up in the mid-1980s. For several years Denver had the unfortunate distinction of having one of the highest office-vacancy rates of any city in the country. However, Denverites, true to their pioneer heritage, reacted aggressively to the slump. In the spring of 1990 the city opened a $125-million convention center with 300,000 square feet of exhibit space and 100,000 square feet of meeting space. In August 1990 the Cherry Creek Mall, one of the top retail centers in the nation, with Lord and Taylor, Saks Fifth Avenue, and Neiman Marcus, opened its doors to a shopping-starved city. And ground was broken in 1989 for a new airport encompassing 53 square miles that is expected to be the world's largest facility when it opens in October 1993. By mid-1992 those vacant offices were filling up with businesses, from a variety of industries this time including many high tech, computer, and cable companies. Houses are being snapped up again, many by Californians disenchanted with their lifestyle in that state, who are moving here in droves. Ground was broken for Coors Field, the new home of the Colorado Rockies, the state's new National League baseball team. Although the stadium, in lower downtown, won't open before the 1995 baseball season, the Rockies will begin playing ball in 1993 at Mile High Stadium. Denver is once again on the move!

FAMOUS COLORADANS

Antonia Brico (1892–1989) Brico bucked the cultural community to become one of the first female, and one of the best, orchestra conductors. She moved to Denver in 1942 to direct the Civic Center Orchestra and founded the Denver Businessmen's Orchestra, which eventually became the Brico Symphony. She stopped conducting in 1984. Her most famous student was former Coloradan singer Judy Collins.

Thomas Chech (1948–) A professor of biochemistry and molecular biology at the University of Colorado, Chech won a 1989 Nobel Prize for genetic engineering. He was applauded for illuminating the way RNA, a basic genetic material, carries information and works as a catalyst within living cells.

Judy Collins (1939–) This folk singer's fame was founded on songs of political protest during the Vietnam War, and her sweet-voiced rendition of folk tunes. Still a popular singer, her repertoire has expanded to include other styles.

Clive Cussler (1931–) A long-time resident of the foothills above Denver, Cussler's books, including *Raise the Titanic!* and *Night Probe,* have sold in the millions. His real love (and the theme of some books) is searching for sunken ships. When his National Underwater and Marine Agency discovers one, Cussler donates the finds to museums and universities.

Thomas Hornsby Ferril   (1896–1988) Robert Frost honored this western poet in one of his verses. During the 42 years Thomas Hornsby Ferril worked for the Great Western Sugar Company, his poems were published in such national publications as *The New Yorker* and *Atlantic.* In 1979 he was named Colorado's Poet Laureate.

William Kreutzer   (1878–1956) Kreutzer was the first U.S. Forest Service ranger in the country. He retired in 1939 after 41 years of service, longer than anyone else in the history of the Forest Service. Mount Kreutzer, near Tincup in Gunnison country, was named for him.

Paul Whiteman   (1890–1967) The world-famous jazz musician was the son of one of Denver's public school music directors. After visiting a jazz spot in San Francisco, he changed his focus from strictly classical to jazz, creating such long-time favorites as "The Japanese Sandman." His stellar career included recordings, performances in the U.S. and Europe, and the position of music director for the Blue Network of NBC (which later became ABC). When he retired, he moved back to Colorado and lived on a ranch until his death.

2. ART, ARCHITECTURE & CULTURAL LIFE

Today's residents of the Mile High City are successfully blending the informality of casual western living with the sophistication of big-city amenities such as quality entertainment and dining. In 1991, the performing arts outdrew Denver's professional sports attendance by almost two to one. The Colorado Symphony orchestra is in the black, theater groups are thriving, and dozens of art galleries line the streets in chic Cherry Creek North and LoDo (as locals call historic lower downtown).

Boulder's lively cultural community supports the Colorado Music Festival and the Shakespeare Festival during the summer, as well as a potpourri of concerts, lectures, and dance performances during the winter months. Colorado Springs also has its own symphony, an arts school in the Fine Arts Center, and a range of cultural events. The largest collection of Van Briggle pottery, by the city's most notable artist, Artus Van Briggle, is in the Colorado Springs Pioneer Museum.

Denver's architecture reflects the key periods in its growth: the Victorian era, during the silver boom in Leadville; the turn-of-the-century, when the many parks were seeded; after World War II, when urban sprawl developed; and the 1970s, when the building crane was virtually the state bird. Walk along the streets around the Molly Brown and the Governor's Mansions for prime examples of Victorian architecture. Just stroll through Civic Park or City Park or visit mountain parks like Red Rocks to see the legacy that astute city promoters left for modern-day city dwellers. The 17th Street business canyon, formed by high-rise office buildings, symbolizes the growth in the '70s. Currently, there's an explosion of loft residences in LoDo, and the units in renovated warehouses and Victorian buildings are being sold almost as soon as they go on the market.

In Boulder, basic wood buildings were the first to go up, followed by Victorian homes, especially around Mapleton Hill. (The historic Carnegie Library at 1125 Pine St. houses many city records.) The early buildings at the University of Colorado reflect Italian Rennaissance style and were constructed from stones from a regional red-rock quarry. Several buildings around town, including the mushroom-shaped Boulder Valley Eye Surgery Center at 2401 Broadway, were constructed with an innovative foam-concrete material by architect Charles Haertling.

Colorado Springs has an eclectic architectural history. Most of the homes at the north end of the downtown corridor, especially on Cascade and Wood avenues around Colorado College, are Victorian, and several are museums. Frank Lloyd Wright assisted in the design and development of the U.S. Air Force Academy.

3. RECOMMENDED BOOKS & FILMS

BOOKS

For background on the state, read Marshall Sprague's *Colorado* (New York: W. W. Norton & Co., 1984), one in a series of popular histories of all 50 states originally published during the Bicentennial celebrations in 1976; and Robert G. Athern's *The Coloradans* (Albuquerque, N.M.: University of New Mexico Press, 1982), which describes the personalities that have shaped Colorado.

James McTighe's *The Roadside History of Colorado* (Boulder, Colo.: Johnson Books, 1989) is a wonderful travelogue, giving bits of history for every place you drive past in the state. And Boyd and Barbara Norton's *Backroads of Colorado* (Chicago: Rand-McNally, 1979) lays out a number of mini-tours around which to plan itineraries.

For additional background information about Denver, read Thomas J. Noel's *Denver: Rocky Mountain Gold* (Tulsa, Okla.: Continental Heritage Press, 1980), an informative, pictoral history of the city. Also Lyle W. Dorsett's *The Queen City: A History of Denver* (Boulder, Colo.: Pruett, 1980), Kay Kane's *Discover Denver* (Aurora, Colo.: Gold Kane Enter, 1983), and Linda Robinson's *Mile High Denver: A Guide to the Queen City* (Boulder, Colo.: Pruett,

IMPRESSIONS

*"Then ho, boys, ho, to Cherry Creek we'll go
There's plenty of gold
In the West we are told
In the new El Dorado."*
—CHERRY CREEK EMIGRANTS' SONG, 1859

1981). *Discover the Heart of Denver,* edited by Ed Natan (Denver, Colo.: Natan and Associates, 1986), a photo-essay of Denver's architecture, also includes a short history of the state; and Marshall Sprague's *Newport in the Rockies* (Athens, Ohio: Swallow, 1981) deals with Colorado Springs.

One of the best "reads" about the Rockies is James Michener's novel *Centennial* (New York: Random House, 1974), a fascinating tale of the settlement of the Rocky Mountain region. And *Colorado,* by Dana F. Ross (New York: Bantam, 1981), is part of a series of novels, with the overall title "Wagons West," that chronicles the conquest and settlement of the American West.

Rex Burns has written several detective stories with a Denver locale, including *The Avenging Angel* (New York: Penguin, 1984) and *The Killing Zone, a Gabe Warner Mystery* (New York: Penguin, 1989). And Jack Kerouac eulogized Denver in his famous novel of the Beat Generation, *On the Road* (New York: Penguin, 1976).

FILMS

Because of Colorado's spectacular scenery and abundance of old mining and Wild West towns, many movies and television shows have been filmed here in whole or in part in order to take advantage of these locales. Parts of the box-office hit *City Slickers,* with Billy Crystal, were filmed in the Durango area, and scenes from *Thelma and Louise* were shot around Grand Junction. *Diehard 2: Die Harder* was partly filmed at Stapleton International Airport and Breckenridge; scenes from *National Lampoon's Vacation* and *Christmas Vacation,* both with Chevy Chase in the lead, were filmed in southern Colorado and Breckenridge; and the opening sequence to *Indiana Jones and the Last Crusade,* starring Harrison Ford and Sean Connery, was done on the Cumbres Toltec railroad in southern Colorado.

Many television shows have also used Colorado as a locale. "Ironsides," with Raymond Burr, was filmed in Denver courtrooms. Segments of "Rescue 911," "America's Funniest People," and "Unsolved Mysteries" were shot in or around Colorado Springs. And the characters Mork and Mindy from the comedy series with the same name, which starred Robin Williams, lived in a house on Pine Street in Boulder.

CHAPTER 2

PLANNING A TRIP TO DENVER, BOULDER & COLORADO SPRINGS

This chapter is devoted to the where, when, and how of your trip—the kind of planning required to get it together and take it on the road. A number of helpful planning tools are provided here, including where to obtain more information about Denver, Boulder, and Colorado Springs.

1. INFORMATION & MONEY

SOURCES OF INFORMATION For information about Colorado in general, contact the **Colorado Tourism Office,** 1625 Broadway, Suite 170, Denver, CO 80202 (tel. toll free 800/COLORAD).

You can get advance information about Denver, Boulder, and Colorado Springs from the visitors bureaus in each city. For Denver (and Colorado in general), contact the **Denver Metro Convention and Visitors Bureau,** 225 W. Colfax Ave., Denver, CO 80202-5399 (tel. 303/892-1112). Ask for the free guidebook to Denver and Colorado, which lists everything from attractions and health services to restaurants and lodging; brochures about individual attractions and lodging properties can also be provided. For information about Boulder, contact the **Boulder Chamber of Commerce,** 2440 Pearl St., Boulder, CO 80302 (tel. 303/442-1044). If you're visiting Colorado Springs, contact the **Convention and Visitor Bureau Visitor Information Center,** 104 S. Cascade Ave., Colorado Springs, CO 80903 (tel. toll free 800/DO-VISIT).

If you have a computer, you may want to sign on with **Colorado TravelBank** for travel and recreation information within the state.

Call 303/671-7669 (modem) or 303/320-8550 (voice) for more information. The parameters are (8, N, 1), 300, 1,200, or 2,400 baud.

MONEY Denver is not a particularly expensive city. One could, of course, find a $400 room and a $40 dinner, but abundant excellent lodging and dining choices exist for far less money. A friend from the East Coast was here on a business trip and was astonished at how well she could eat and still stay comfortably within her travel allotment. Traveler's checks are accepted at most hotels and at many restaurants and stores in the city.

WHAT THINGS COST IN DENVER	U.S. $
Taxi from Stapleton airport to downtown Denver	13.00–15.00
Bus fare	.50
Local telephone call	.25
Double room at the Brown Palace Hotel (expensive)	154.00–194.00
Double room at the Days Inn, Golden (moderate)	56.00
Double room at Motel 6 (budget)	28.00
Lunch for one at Wynkoop Brewpub (moderate)	13.00
Lunch for one at Alternative Gourmet (inexpensive)	5.00
Dinner for one, without wine, at European Café (expensive)	27.00
Dinner for one, without wine, at Hoffbrau Steak (moderate)	12.00
Dinner for one, without wine, at Blue Bonnet (budget)	9.00
Pint of beer	2.75
Coca-Cola	.50–.75
Cup of coffee	.75–1.00
Admission to the Denver History Museum	4.00
Movie ticket	5.50

2. WHEN TO GO — CLIMATE & EVENTS

THE CLIMATE

The rest of the country believes Denver is snowbound when they hear on the weather report that 15 inches of snow has fallen in Colorado. Usually, nothing could be further from the truth. Denver, located just east of a high mountain barrier—the Rockies—receives only 15 inches of precipitation each year (Denver golfers like to boast that they can play more than 300 days a year). Often when the mountain towns located 45 minutes from the city—and 3,000 vertical feet higher—receive a two-foot blanket of snow, Denverites will be walking around in light jackets because it's 50°. Locals in Boulder and Colorado Springs will be doing the same. The Pacific storms moving across the Rockies dump most of their moisture as powder-light snow at the higher altitudes. The wind dries out and warms up as it slides down the eastern slope, sweeping across the rolling plains as a "chinook" wind. Locals love chinooks because they can raise the temperature 40° within an hour or two and produce springlike weather in January.

Average Temperatures for Denver, Boulder, and Colorado Springs

	Jan	Feb	Mar	Apr	May	Jun	July	Aug	Sept	Oct	Nov	Dec
High (°F)	41	46	51	62	70	82	86	85	76	67	52	45
Low (°F)	17	21	26	35	44	54	58	57	48	38	27	20

COLORADO CALENDAR OF EVENTS

The Denver metropolitan area hosts a number of special and often free events and festivals throughout the year—the following are just the highlights—and they have proven so popular that people from all over attend them year after year. Most are scheduled for the same month or holiday period each year, although the exact dates change. For detailed information on specific dates and locations, contact the **Denver Metro Convention and Visitors Bureau,** 225 W. Colfax Ave., Denver, CO 80202-5399 (tel. 303/892-1112), for the annual special events calendar.

Between events in town and happenings at the university, there's almost always something going on in Boulder. Check the Friday entertainment section or the Sunday "Calendar" in the *Boulder Daily Camera* for news of upcoming events. Or stop by the **Boulder Chamber of Commerce,** 2440 Pearl St., Boulder, CO 80302 (tel. 303/442-1044). Contact the **Colorado Springs Convention and Visitors Bureau,** 104 S. Cascade Ave., Suite 104, Colorado Springs, CO 80903 (tel. 719/635-7506, or toll free 800/DO-VISIT), for exact dates on Colorado Springs events.

JANUARY

✪ *NATIONAL WESTERN STOCK SHOW AND RODEO Every January, Denver's streets are filled with ranchers, rodeo riders, and anyone else interested in checking out the world's biggest and richest rodeo and livestock show. About 500,000 spectators and participants from all 50 states and 32 countries show up, so book both* rodeo tickets and lodging in Denver well ahead of your arrival date.

Where: National Western Stock Show Grounds, National Western Livestock Center and Denver Coliseum. **When:** For two weeks in mid to late January. **How:** Call the ticket office at 303/295-1660, or write to National Western Stock Show & Rodeo, 4655 Humboldt St., Denver, CO 80216. Admission is charged for both rodeo and show.

✪ **COLORADO INDIAN MARKET** Well-known and unknown but gifted Native American artists, sculptors, potters, and other craftspeople from more than 90 tribes bring their work to this market. In addition, there are crafts demonstrations, tribal dancing, and other entertainment.

Where: Usually Denver's Currigan Exhibition Hall. **When:** A weekend in mid- to late January, during the National Western Stock Show. **How:** Just show up. Admission is charged.

FEBRUARY

✪ **BUFFALO BILL'S BIRTHDAY BASH** An eagerly awaited annual event for his modern fans, for whom the legendary scout has assumed mythical proportions. Complete with Buffalo Bill look-alikes.

Where: Buckhorn Exchange Restaurant, Denver. **When:** Closest weekend to February 26. **How:** Call 303/534-9505 for information.

MARCH

☐ **St. Patrick's Day Parade.** The Mile High City revels in putting on one of the largest parades and rowdiest celebrations in the country. Colorado Springs also holds an annual blowout along Colorado Avenue that includes floats, bands, clowns, and other entertainers to keep the crowds happy. The Denver parade is held on the Saturday before St. Patrick's Day.

☐ **Pow Wow,** at the Denver Coliseum. An annual gathering of more than 700 dancers and musicians representing 70 tribes from 22 states. There's an accompanying arts and crafts fair. Contact Pow Wow (tel. 303/936-4826) for more information. Admission is charged. Mid-March.

☐ **Program Council Trivia Bowl,** at the University of Colorado at Boulder. Locals claim that this week-long competition for trivia buffs, hosted by the university, is the largest of its kind. To join or just watch, contact Program Council, Campus Box 207, Boulder, CO 80309 (tel. 303/492-7704). Late March or early April.

APRIL

✪ **EASTER SUNRISE SERVICE** This annual rite in the Garden of the Gods renews faith in nature, as worshippers watch the rising sun light the red sandstone formations that are considered sacred ground by the Native Americans who once lived here.

Where: Red Rocks Amphitheatre, Garden of the Gods,

Colorado Springs. ***When:*** *Easter Sunday.* ***How:*** *Just show up.*

✪ ***CONFERENCE ON WORLD AFFAIRS*** *Cosmonauts to witchcraft experts, CIA operatives to bankers—all get their chance to speak at this annual conference. Many of the lectures and sessions are free and open to the public.*
   Where: *University of Colorado at Boulder.* ***When:*** *Early April.* ***How:*** *Contact the Conference on World Affairs, University of Colorado, Campus Box 465, Boulder, CO 80309-0465 (tel. 303/492-2525).*

MAY

☐ **Cinco de Mayo,** Denver. Mexican Independence Day is celebrated at this two-day party, with music, crafts, food, and dancing. There are actually two Cinco de Mayo parties in Denver: One is planned by the local Mexican-American community while the other is organized by the Denver Partnership. May 5.

☐ **The Bolder Boulder,** Boulder. This race attracts up to 30,000 runners each year. You can walk, jog, run, or race-walk the 10km course. Entry forms are available beginning April 1. Send a stamped, self-addressed envelope to Bolder Boulder, 3033 Iris Ave., Boulder, CO 80301 (tel. 303/444-RACE). There is an admission charge for entrants. Memorial Day.

✪ ***THE BOULDER KINETIC FEST*** *This wacky event is a real crowd pleaser. Most years, an average of 70 teams race on land and water in a variety of imaginative human-powered conveyances. The week-long event includes the kinetic parade, kinetic concerts, kinetic kite flying, and the kinetic ball.*
   Where: *At the Boulder Reservoir in Boulder.* ***When:*** *The first Saturday in May.* ***How:*** *For more information about joining in the fun, call 303/444-5600.*

☐ **Old Colorado City's Territory Days,** Colorado Springs. This Colorado Springs neighborhood is transformed into a western carnival, with entertainment, contests, and mock gunfights. Memorial Day weekend.

✪ ***BALLOON CLASSIC*** *You'll use rolls of film photographing the colorful scene as hundreds of hot-air balloons lift off at 6am. One of the most popular spectator events.*
   Where: *Colorado Springs.* ***When:*** *Memorial Day weekend.* ***How:*** *Call the Colorado Springs Visitors Bureau (toll free 800/DO-VISIT) for information.*

JUNE

✪ ***COLORADO RENAISSANCE FESTIVAL*** *This major outdoor Renaissance fair features costumed entertainers speaking Olde English, 200 crafts booths, amusement booths, and medieval-period food.*
   Where: *Larkspur (take I-25 to the Larkspur exit, about*

*halfway between Denver and Colorado Springs). **When:** Weekends and holidays in June and July. **How:** Call the festival headquarters at 303/756-1501.*

○ ***CAPITOL HILL PEOPLE'S FAIR*** One of Denver's most vibrant street festivals. Locals and visitors explore displays in more than 500 arts and crafts booths, and sample food from a variety of restaurant booths. Live entertainment is spread over three stages.
Where: Civic Center Park. **When:** First weekend in June. **How:** Just show up.

☐ **Cherry Blossom Festival,** Sakura Square, Denver. The fragrance of sweet flowers fills the air around Sakura Square, the focal point for the city's Japanese community during this annual event. There are dozens of booths featuring Japanese food and entertainment. Second weekend in June.

☐ **Juneteenth,** Five Points, Denver. This annual neighborhood celebration commemorates the end of slavery in Texas. Festival highlights include the Gospel Extravaganza, a parade, food, and entertainment. Admission is free. Mid-June.

JULY

☐ **Fourth of July Blast,** Denver. Denver's extravagant Independence Day celebration. Highlights include a concert, the "Taste of the West Chili Cookoff," and a spectacular fireworks display. Admission is free; events are listed in the local newspapers.

☐ **Cherry Creek Arts Festival,** Cherry Creek, Denver. In a few short years this has become one of the most popular arts affairs in the city, drawing hundreds of thousands of viewers. More than 170 artists are represented. For more information, call the festival headquarters (tel. 303/355-2787). July 4th weekend.

☐ **Pikes Peak Auto Hill Climb,** Pikes Peak. The nation's second-oldest auto race has drivers racing against the clock on a 12.42-mile gravel course to the summit of Pikes Peak. July 4th.

☐ **Artsfair,** Pearl Street Mall, Boulder. The mall is lined with artists and artisans during this arts and crafts fair, which also features storytellers and free concerts. Events are advertised in the local paper. Mid-July.

☐ **Denver Black Arts Festival,** in City Park. An annual celebration of African American culture, with arts and crafts booths and plenty of food and entertainment. Free admission. Early or mid-July.

☐ **Festival of Asian Arts and Culture,** Denver. Every July the Asian community puts together this weekend celebrating food, music, art, and craftsmanship from various Asian cultures. The atmosphere is alive with exotic colors and sounds. The location changes yearly. For further information, phone the festival headquarters (tel. 303/355-0703).

☐ **Broadmoor Ice Revue,** Broadmoor World Arena, Colorado Springs. World-renowned skaters perform each summer in a production organized by the Broadmoor Skating Club. Many world-class competitive skaters train year round at this ice arena. Call the Broadmoor (tel. toll free 800/634-7711) for performers, dates, and prices. Late July or early August.

AUGUST

- ☐ **Pikes Peak or Bust Rodeo,** Penrose Stadium, Colorado Springs. This is the largest outdoor rodeo in the state and a popular stop on the professional rodeo circuit. For details, call the Pikes Peak or Bust Rodeo Association (tel. 719/635-3547). Early August.
- ☐ **Colorado State Fair,** the State Fair Grounds in Pueblo, about a 2½-hour drive from Denver. Attracting more than a million visitors each year, this traditional state fair boasts a rodeo and a carnival and such headline entertainers as Kenny G and George Strait. There are also demonstrations of quilt-making and cooking, a regional wine tasting, and a fine arts exhibit. Call Ticketmaster or visit any Ticketmaster outlet. From late August through Labor Day.

SEPTEMBER

✪ *FESTIVAL OF THE MOUNTAIN AND PLAIN . . . A TASTE OF COLORADO This very popular end-of-summer celebration attracts some 400,000 people to Denver's Civic Center Park to sample the wide variety of dishes at booths operated by some of the best and most popular restaurants in the city. Top-name acts perform in free concerts, too.*

    Where: Civic Center Park, Denver. When: Labor Day weekend. How: The Denver papers always list the entertainment schedule and details just before the event.

- ☐ **Larimer Square Oktoberfest,** Denver. The 1400 block of Larimer Street is closed to cars for this annual re-creation of Munich's harvest festival, complete with dancing and entertainment in the streets in the evenings. Three weekends in late September and early October.

OCTOBER

- ☐ **The Great American Beer Festival,** at the Denver Merchandise Mart. This annual beer-tasting festival keeps growing and now features the nation's largest beer-tasting exhibit. More than 200 national, regional, micro- and pub breweries offer more than 700 beers for the public to taste. A series of industry seminars are intertwined with the event. Contact the Association of Brewers (tel. 303/447-0816) for admission information and exact dates. Usually during the beginning of October; the public events are scheduled Friday to Sunday.
- ☐ **Denver International Film Festival.** Attracts producers, directors, and actors from around the world. During the festival, films are shown throughout the day for more than a week at theaters around Denver. For more information, call 303/321-FILM. Mid-October.

DECEMBER

- ☐ **Christmas Walk,** Larimer Square, Denver. A Victorian Christmas celebration, with strolling carolers, roasting chestnuts, and

Christmas activities. Weekends from Thanksgiving through Christmas.

□ **Parade of Lights,** Denver. A fully illuminated nighttime Christmas parade through the heart of downtown, with lots of floats, balloons, and marching bands. Usually early December.

3. HEALTH & INSURANCE

HEALTH PREPARATIONS   Although altitude sickness is more common among visitors in the mountain communities, the occasional visitor to Denver (5,280 feet above sea level) Boulder (5,430 feet), or Colorado Springs (6,035 feet) might also be affected. Symptoms include shortness of breath after minimal exertion, fatigue, headache, and difficulty sleeping. If you feel uncomfortable, it's important to slow your pace and rest, particularly during your first days in town. Eating regularly, and avoiding alcohol, especially during the first day or two, will also help. High-altitude pulmonary edema (HAPE) is a less common but potentially life-threatening problem. While high-altitude mountain sickness usually appears and disappears rather quickly, the first signs of HAPE—increasing shortness of breath, feeling of fluid in the lungs, and coughing—show up in roughly three to five days and require immediate medical attention.

In addition, the region's dry air can make you uncomfortable, so drink lots of fluids to avoid dehydration. Because of the low humidity (and because the decreased amount of oxygen at this altitude makes you breathe faster), normal body fluids may be lost more quickly than at sea level. (A headache is one sign that you're dehydrated.) Adults should attempt to drink at least eight glasses of water per day. Alcohol is *not* a substitute: It dehydrates you and is much more potent at this altitude.

INSURANCE   Especially because of the high cost of health care, it's very important to make certain that your medical and accident insurance policies cover you away from home. If they don't, it's a good idea to obtain a traveler's policy before embarking. You should also make sure you're covered for loss of personal possessions and for the cost of trip cancellation. It's also advisable to always carry with you proof of your health and accident insurance when traveling.

4. WHAT TO PACK

Denver, Boulder, and Colorado Springs are casual cities, so you'll only have to dress up for business affairs and special events. Especially during the spring and fall, but also in winter, it's better to layer your clothing so that you can add or subtract a garment when the temperature changes. It's cooler in the evenings here in all seasons, so pack a light jacket or sweater even if it's a warm morning when you start out.

In summer the air is balmy and warm—or downright hot—so cotton clothing is advisable. In the late fall, medium-weight clothing is necessary, with a jacket or topcoat for the evening. On many winter days temperatures can vary from freezing to 60° Fahrenheit, so layering your clothing is again the answer. And although snow rarely sticks to the city streets for a long time, bring boots just in case there's a snowstorm.

If you plan to go to the mountains, warmer clothing is a necessity. Even in the summer—and definitely in the spring and fall—daytime temperatures can vary from hot to crisp to chilly, so take along an extra layer or two of clothing. You might find yourself switching between a sleeveless shirt, a sweatshirt, and a long-sleeve shirt during the same day. Of course, in the winter you must take a warm coat, gloves, a hat, and even warmup pants.

Additional items that could prove very useful on your trip include a Swiss army knife, an alarm clock, a small flashlight, and a travel coffee pot.

5. TIPS FOR THE DISABLED, SENIORS, SINGLES & STUDENTS

FOR THE DISABLED In the city of Denver, meter parking is free with no time limit if you're displaying a handicapped placard or license plate (as long as parking is legally allowed in that space at that time). For more information about parking or access to city buildings, call the Denver Commission for People with Disabilities (tel. 303/640-3056 voice and TDD).

FOR SENIORS Many tourist attractions, movie theaters, and restaurants offer senior-citizen discounts; ask before paying the admission fee. Senior citizens can ride the RTD buses in Denver for 15¢ during off-peak hours. The *Beacon Review,* a free newspaper for adults 40 and older, can be found at more than 400 outlets in Denver, including King Soopers grocery stores.

FOR SINGLE TRAVELERS *Westword* and *Up the Creek,* free newspapers found in stands around Denver, list the most current happenings and usually have advertisements from some of the trendiest nightclubs. I know more than one person who has found a mate through *Westword*'s singles section.

FOR STUDENTS College-age travelers will find peers around the Auraria campus, at the western edge of downtown Denver (west of Speer Boulevard and south of Auraria Parkway), home to Metro State College, the University of Colorado–Denver, and Denver Community College. Students also tend to congregate in the stores and restaurants around the intersection of University Boulevard and Evans Street, by the University of Denver.

6. GETTING THERE

BY PLANE

Each day there are more than 1,100 landings and takeoffs at Denver's **Stapleton International Airport,** located eight miles from downtown. Stapleton maintains a toll-free number for information on just about anything, including flight schedules and connections, parking, ground transportation, current weather conditions, and local accommodations. Call toll free 800/AIR-2-DEN (or 800/688-1333 TDD). This number will be maintained when the new Denver International Airport opens in fall 1993.

Many airlines also offer direct flights or connections to **Colorado Springs Airport,** located at the east end of the city. (See "Orientation" in Chapter 11 for airlines flying into Colorado Springs.) There are no commercial flights to Boulder.

United Airlines and Continental Airlines continue to offer the greatest number of nonstop domestic flights to Denver, and almost all other major domestic airlines have planes touching down here. The only direct international flights are from Canada, Mexico, and London. Stapleton is often subject to flight delays and occasional flight cancellations during inclement weather in the winter. Be sure to allow extra time between your flights connecting in Denver. Denver International is being touted as an all-weather airport, with runways designed to minimize delays caused by bad weather.

On October 29, 1993, Stapleton will yield all operations to $2.7-billion **Denver International Airport.** The total area of the new airport, 53 square miles, is twice the size of Manhattan Island. It's located 23 miles from downtown Denver, so travelers will have to allot additional time to get in and out of the city. On opening day the airport will have five runways and 84 gates ready. A sixth runway will be completed the following year, and the airport may be expanded to 260 gates if needed. The new facility, under a white fiberglass roof that lets in natural light, will be larger than O'Hare and Dallas/Fort Worth airports combined. There will be moving pedestrian walkways and a train that will take passengers from the terminal to the three concourses (on opening day) and back. Even the baggage will be handled by electronic trains.

THE MAJOR AIRLINES   Besides **United Airlines** (tel. 303/398-4141, or toll free 800/241-6522) and **Continental Airlines** (tel. 303/398-3000, or toll free 800/525-0280), other domestic airlines have hubs in Denver, including **America West** (tel. toll free 800/247-5692), **American** (tel. toll free 800/433-7300), **Delta** (tel. 303/696-1322, or toll free 800/221-1212), **Northwest** (tel. toll free 800/225-2525), **TWA** (tel. toll free 800/221-2000), and **USAir** (tel. toll free 800/428-4322). **Continental Express** (tel. 303/398-3000, or toll free 800/525-0280) and **United Express** (tel. 303/398-4141, or toll free 800/241-6522 in Colorado) serve many mountain towns and cities within Colorado.

AIRFARES   The best way to get a budget airfare, whether you're a business traveler or a tourist, is to comparison-shop: Have the airline reservations clerk or your travel agent root through their computer files for the cheapest possible ticket. Unfortunately, most of the cheapest tickets today seem to require advance purchase and are fully or partially nonrefundable. The lowest fares also usually require a Saturday-night stayover.

If you're heading to Denver during ski season, don't expect to get a bargain rate on flights popular with skiers (usually heading into Colorado on Saturday or leaving on Sunday). In fact, if you want to increase the chances of getting bumped (and thus earning a free flight), plan a trip around the Christmas holidays or Presidents' Day weekend.

The lowest domestic fares to Denver are usually Maxi-Savers, most of which require a 14-day advance purchase and a Saturday-night stayover. Next are Super-Savers, most requiring a 7-day advance purchase and a Saturday-night stopover. From time to time an airline may advertise a special fare with only a 3-day advance purchase (although again requiring that you spend a Saturday night in Denver), so keep your eyes open for this kind of deal if you can travel on the spur of the moment. APEX, regular coach-class, business-class, and first-class tickets are considerably more expensive.

BY TRAIN

Amtrak (tel. toll free 800/872-7245) pulls into historic Union Station in downtown Denver. The *California Zephyr* and the *Desert Wind* trains travel through the spectacular Rocky Mountains, offering a special way to view up close these rugged mountain peaks and sheer canyons. One-third of the westbound trains splits off in Denver and goes through Wyoming to Seattle. The **Rio Grande Railroad** (tel. 303/296-I-SKI) runs a special ski train to Winter Park during winter weekends. The train leaves Union Station early in the morning and returns when the lifts close.

There are no passenger trains to Boulder or Colorado Springs.

BY BUS

Unless there's a very special airfare deal, the bus is still the cheapest way to reach Colorado, especially from mid-size and smaller U.S. cities. **Greyhound/Trailways** bus lines (tel. 303/292-6111) has terminals in Denver, Boulder, and Colorado Springs. Call for route information, schedules, and fares.

 FROMMER'S SMART TRAVELER: AIRFARES

1. Shop all the airlines that fly to Denver.
2. Keep calling the airlines, since the availability of cheap seats changes daily. As the departure date nears, you might be able to obtain a seat at a great discount, since an airline would rather sell a discounted seat than fly with it empty.
3. Read the advertisements in newspaper travel sections, since they often offer special deals and packages.
4. Save money by buying your ticket as early as possible, since the lowest fares, such as APEX fares, require that you purchase your ticket in advance (usually 7–21 days).
5. Make sure you understand all restrictions before purchasing your ticket, especially if you're buying a nonrefundable ticket. Depending on the ticket restrictions, you may be able to receive a refund if the fare for your particular route is lowered, so keep an eye on airfares even after you purchase the ticket.

BY CAR

Although Easterners generally consider **Denver** a western city, the Mile High City is actually located only 340 miles west of the exact geographical center of the continental U.S., which is one of the reasons it has become a transportation hub for the Midwest. The major routes into Denver are I-76 from the east, I-25 from the north and south, U.S. 285 from the southwest, I-70 from the east and west, and U.S. 40 from the west.

Boulder is 27 miles northwest of Denver via U.S. 36; **Colorado Springs** is alongside I-25, about 50 miles south of Denver.

CHAPTER 3

FOR FOREIGN VISITORS

Although American fads and fashions have spread across Europe and other parts of the world so that America may seem like familiar territory before your arrival, there are still many peculiarities and uniquely American situations that any foreign visitor will encounter.

---

1. PREPARING FOR YOUR TRIP

ENTRY REQUIREMENTS

DOCUMENTS Canadian nationals need only proof of Canadian residence to visit the United States. Citizens of Great Britain and Japan need only a current passport. Citizens of other countries, including Australia and New Zealand, usually need two documents: a valid **passport** with an expiration date at least six months later than the scheduled end of their visit to the United States and a **tourist visa** available at no charge from a U.S. embassy or consulate.

To get a tourist or business visa to enter the United States, contact the nearest American embassy or consulate in your country; if there is none, you'll have to apply in person in a country where there is a U.S. embassy or consulate. Present your passport, a passport-size photo of yourself, and a completed application, which is available through the embassy or consulate. You may be asked to provide information about how you plan to finance your trip or show a letter of invitation from a friend with whom you plan to stay. Those applying for a business visa may be asked to show evidence that they will not receive a salary in the United States. Be sure to check the length of stay on your visa; usually it's six months. If you want to stay longer, you may file for an extension with the Immigration and Naturalization Service once you are in the country. If permission to stay is granted, a new visa is not required unless you leave the United States and want to reenter.

MEDICAL REQUIREMENTS No inoculations are needed to enter the U.S. unless you are coming from, or have stopped over in, areas known to be suffering from epidemics, particularly cholera or yellow fever.

If you have a disease requiring treatment with medications containing narcotics or drugs requiring a syringe, carry a valid signed prescription from your physician to allay any suspicions that you are smuggling drugs.

CUSTOMS REQUIREMENTS   Every adult visitor may bring in, free of duty: one liter of wine or hard liquor; 200 cigarettes or 100 cigars (but no cigars from Cuba) or three pounds of smoking tobacco; $100 worth of gifts. These exemptions are offered to travelers who spend at least 72 hours in the U.S. and who have not claimed them within the preceding six months. It is altogether forbidden to bring into the country foodstuffs (particularly cheese, fruit, cooked meats, and canned goods) and plants (vegetables, seeds, tropical plants, and so on). Foreign tourists may bring in or take out up to $10,000 in U.S. or foreign currency with no formalities; larger sums must be declared to Customs on entering or leaving.

INSURANCE

Unlike most other countries, there is no national health system in the United States. Because the cost of medical care is extremely high, I strongly advise every traveler to secure health coverage before setting out. You may want to take out a comprehensive travel policy that covers (for a relatively low premium) sickness or injury costs (medical, surgical, and hospital); loss of, or theft of, your baggage; trip-cancellation costs; guarantee of bail in case you are arrested; and costs of accident, repatriation, or death. Such packages (for example, "Europe Assistance" in Europe) are sold by automobile clubs at attractive rates, as well as by insurance companies and travel agencies.

2. GETTING TO THE U.S.

Travelers from overseas can take advantage of the **APEX (Advance Purchase Excursion) fares** offered by all the major U.S. and European carriers.

Some large American airlines (for example, TWA, American Airlines, Northwest, United, and Delta) offer travelers—on their transatlantic or transpacific flights—special discount tickets under the name **Visit USA,** allowing travel between any U.S. destinations at minimum rates. They are not on sale in the U.S., and must, therefore, be purchased before you leave your foreign point of departure. This system is the best, easiest, and fastest way to see the U.S. at low cost. You should obtain information well in advance from your travel agent or the office of the airline concerned, since the conditions attached to these discount tickets can be changed without advance notice.

The visitor arriving by air, no matter what the port of entry, should cultivate patience and resignation before setting foot on U.S. soil. Getting through Immigration control may take as long as two hours on some days, especially summer weekends. Add the time it takes to clear Customs and you'll see that you should make very generous allowance for delay in planning connections between international and domestic flights—an average of two to three hours at least.

In contrast, for the traveler arriving by car or by rail from Canada, the border-crossing formalities have been streamlined to the vanishing point. And for the traveler by air from Canada, Bermuda, and some places in the Caribbean, you can sometimes go through Customs and Immigration at the point of departure, which is much quicker and less painful.

For further information about travel to and arriving in Denver, Boulder, and Colorado Springs, see "Orientation" in Chapters 4, 8, and 11.

3. GETTING AROUND THE U.S.

Flying is the fastest, and most expensive, mode of domestic travel in the U.S. For a list of carriers who service Denver, Boulder, and Colorado Springs from within the U.S., see "Getting There" in Chapter 2.

Travel by car (or perhaps bicycle) is perhaps the best way to see the U.S. if you have the time to really wander. After all, the U.S. is an automobile culture, so the roads here are excellent. But the real adventure is off the interstates, and onto the "blue" highways, the secondary roads, along which the small towns of America are strung like beads on a wire.

Americans on limited budgets often get from city to city or town to town by traveling the "dog," the affectionate nickname for the Greyhound Bus Company (tel. 617/423-5810); Greyhound, as well as other local bus carriers, offers package tours to every region in America, some of which include motel accommodations in the overall price.

Rail travel is another alternative. The **USA Railpass,** available for various lengths of time and in several price ranges, can be purchased from some tour operators, including Thomas Cook in Great Britain, and also from some travel agencies and airlines. Passes may also be purchased at points within the U.S., including Denver; for more information contact the AMTRAK Distribution Center, PO Box 7700, 1549 West Glen Lake Ave., Itasca, IL 60143 (tel. toll free 800-USA-RAIL in the United States). AMTRAK recommends that you make reservations well in advance, since many trains tend to sell out.

 FAST **FOR THE FOREIGN TRAVELER**

Accommodations Most tour operators and travel agencies throughout the world offer package deals on ground arrangements that include hotel accommodations, especially for first-class and tourist-grade establishments. Thus, the room rate you pay as a part of this package—given the fact that travel agencies purchase these rooms at wholesale prices—is likely to be less than you'd pay at the same hotel if you walked in off the street. For accommodations in Denver, Boulder, and Colorado Springs, see Chapters 5, 9, and 12.

Auto Organizations If you're planning an extensive road tour of the U.S., you might want to consider membership in the **American Automobile Association (AAA),** which costs approximately $45. "Triple A," as the organization is known colloquially, will provide you with road service in the event of a breakdown, and also with free maps and marked itineraries, called "trip-tiks," which are themselves worth the price of membership. Contact the office at 4100 E. Arkansas Ave., Denver (tel. 303/753-8800), for information about the office nearest your accommodations.

Business Hours See the "Fast Facts" sections in Chapters 4, 8, and 11.

Climate See "When to Go," Chapter 2.

Currency The U.S. monetary system has a decimal base: one American dollar ($1) = 100 cents (100¢)

Dollar bills commonly come in $1 ("a buck"), $5, $10, $20, $50, and $100 denominations (the last two are not welcome when paying for small purchases and are not accepted in taxis or at subway ticket booths).

There are six coin denominations: 1¢ (one cent or "penny"); 5¢ (five cents or "nickel"); 10¢ (ten cents or "dime"); 25¢ (twenty-five cents or "quarter"); 50¢ (fifty cents or "half dollar"—rare); and the very rare—and prized by collectors—$1 pieces (both the older, large silver dollar and the newer, small Susan B. Anthony coin).

If they're denominated in dollars, **traveler's checks** are accepted without demur at most hotels, motels, restaurants, and large stores. But as any experienced traveler knows, the best place to change traveler's checks is at a bank.

In the U.S., credit cards are the method of payment most widely used: VISA (BarclayCard in Britain), MasterCard (EuroCard in Europe, Access in Britain, Diamond in Japan), American Express, Diners Club, Carte Blanche, Discover, and Transmedia, in descending order of acceptance. You can save yourself trouble by using "plastic" rather than cash or traveler's checks in 95% of all hotels, motels, restaurants, and retail stores. A credit card can also serve as a deposit for renting a car, as proof of identity (often carrying more weight than a passport), or as a "cash card," enabling you to draw money from banks that accept them.

Currency Exchange Stapleton International Airport maintains a currency-exchange booth. In addition, Thomas Cook Currency Services (formerly Deak International) offers a wide variety of services: more than 100 currencies, commission-free traveler's checks, drafts and wire transfers, check collections, and precious metal bars and coins. Rates are competitive and service excellent. There are two branches in Denver: The downtown branch is at 1580 Court Place (tel. 303/571-0808); the other branch is at 5251 DTC Pkwy. (tel. 303/694-2502), in the Denver Tech Center. You can also call toll free 800/582-4496 for information. Many hotels will exchange currency if you're a registered guest.

Note: The "foreign-exchange bureaus" so common in Europe are rare even at airports in the U.S. and nonexistent outside major cities.

Try to avoid having to change foreign money, or traveler's checks denominated in other than U.S. dollars, at small-town banks, or even at branches in a big city; in fact, leave any currency other than U.S. dollars at home—it may prove more nuisance to you than it's worth.

Drinking Laws   The legal drinking age in Colorado is 21.

Electric Current   The U.S. uses 110–120 volts, 60 cycles, compared to 220–240 volts, 50 cycles, as in most of Europe. Besides a 100-volt transformer (sometimes called a converter), small appliances of non-American manufacture, such as hairdryers or shavers, will require a plug adapter, with two flat, parallel pins.

Embassies and Consulates   All embassies are located in the national capital, Washington, D.C.; some consulates are located in major cities, and most nations have a mission to the United Nations in New York City. Many countries maintain consulates in Denver, including Canada, Costa Rica, the Dominican Republic, Finland, France, Honduras, Germany, Italy, Korea, Mexico, the Netherlands, Norway, Sweden, and Switzerland. Check the *US West Yellow Pages* to see if your country has a consulate in Denver.

Listed here are the embassies of the major English-speaking countries—Australia, Canada, Ireland, New Zealand, and Britain. If you're from another country, you can get the telephone number of your embassy by calling "Information" in Washington, D.C. (tel. 202/555-1212).

The Australian embassy is at 1601 Massachusetts Ave. NW, Washington, DC 20036 (tel. 202/797-3000).

The Canadian embassy is at 501 Pennsylvania Ave. NW, Washington, DC 20001 (tel. 202/682-1740).

The Irish embassy is at 2234 Massachusetts Ave. NW, Washington, DC 20008 (tel. 202/462-3939).

The New Zealand embassy is at 37 Observatory Circle NW, Washington, DC 20008 (tel. 202/328-4800).

The British embassy is at 3100 Massachusetts Ave. NW, Washington, DC 20008 (tel. 202/462-1340).

Emergencies   Call **911** for fire, police, and ambulance. See the "Fast Facts" sections for each city in Chapters 4, 8, and 11 for further information.

Holidays   On the following legal national holidays, banks, government offices, post offices, and many stores, restaurants, and museums are closed: January 1 (New Year's Day), third Monday in January (Martin Luther King Day), third Monday in February (President's Day, Washington's Birthday), last Monday in May (Memorial Day), July 4 (Independence Day), first Monday in September (Labor Day), second Monday in October (Columbus Day), November 11 (Veteran's Day/Armistice Day), last Thursday in November (Thanksgiving Day), and December 25 (Christmas Day).

Legal Aid   If you are stopped for a minor infraction (for example, of the highway code, such as speeding), never attempt to pay the fine directly to a police officer; you may be arrested on the much more serious charge of attempted bribery. Pay fines by mail, or directly into the hands of the clerk of the court. If accused of a more serious offense, it's wise to say and do nothing before consulting a lawyer. Under U.S. law, an arrested person is allowed one telephone call to a party of his choice. Call your embassy or consulate.

Mail   If you aren't sure of your address, your mail can be sent to you, in your name, c/o General Delivery at the main post office in

Denver, Boulder, or Colorado Springs. (See the "Fast Facts" sections in Chapters 4, 8, and 11 for addresses and telephone numbers.) The addressee must pick it up in person, and must produce proof of identity (driver's license, credit card, passport, and so on).

Mailboxes These are blue with a red-and-white logo, and carry the inscription U.S. MAIL. Domestic postage (including Canada and Mexico) currently costs 29¢ per ounce. Mail to foreign destinations costs 50¢ per ounce.

Medical Emergencies You may call an ambulance by dialing 911; no coin is necessary. For additional information on hospitals and clinics, see the "Fast Facts" sections in Chapters 4, 8, and 11.

Newspapers and Magazines The *New York Times,* the *Denver Post,* and the magazines *Newsweek* and *Time* cover world news. The Newsstand Café (see Chapter 6) and the Tattered Cover Bookstore (see Chapter 7) both sell papers and magazines from cities around the world.

Post Offices See "Mail," above.

Radio and Television See the "Fast Facts" sections in Chapters 4, 8, and 11.

Safety Whenever you're traveling in an unfamiliar city or country, stay alert. Be aware of your immediate surroundings. Wear a moneybelt and don't flash expensive jewelry and cameras in public. This will minimize the possibility of your becoming a crime victim. Be alert even in heavily touristed areas.

Taxes In the U.S. there is no VAT (Value-Added Tax) or other indirect tax at a national level. Every state, and each city in it, is allowed to levy its own local tax on all purchases, including hotel and restaurant checks, airline tickets, and so on. See the "Fast Facts" sections in Chapters 4, 8, and 11 for specifics.

Telephone, Telegraph, Telex, and Fax Pay phones can be found on street corners, as well as in bars, restaurants, public buildings, stores, and service stations. Local calls cost 25¢.

For **long-distance or international calls,** stock up on a supply of quarters; the pay phone will instruct you when you should put them into the slot. For long-distance calls in the U.S., dial 1 followed by the area code and number you want. For direct overseas calls, first dial 011, followed by the country code (Australia, 61; Republic of Ireland, 353; New Zealand, 64; United Kingdom, 44; and so on), and then by the city code (for example, 71 or 81 for London, 21 for Birmingham) and the number of the person you wish to call.

Before calling from a hotel room, always ask the hotel operator if there are any telephone surcharges. These are best avoided by using a public phone, calling collect, or using a telephone charge card.

For **reversed-charge or collect calls,** and for **person-to-person calls,** dial 0 (zero, not the letter "O") followed by the area code and number you want; an operator will then come on the line and you should specify that you are calling collect, or person-to-person, or both. If your operator-assisted call is international, ask for the overseas operator.

For local **directory assistance** ("Information"), dial 411; for long-distance information dial 1, then the appropriate area code and 555-1212.

Like the telephone system, **telegraph** and **telex** services are provided by private corporations like ITT, MCI, and above all, Western Union. You can bring your telegram to the nearest Western Union office (there are hundreds across the country), or dictate it over the phone (tel. toll free 800/325-6000). You can also telegraph money, or have it telegraphed to you, very quickly over the Western Union system.

Most hotels have **fax** machines available to their guests (ask if there is a charge to use it). You will also see signs for public faxes in the windows of small shops.

Time The U.S. is divided into six time zones. From east to west, these are: eastern standard time (EST), central standard time (CST), mountain standard time (MST), Pacific standard time (PST), Alaska standard time (AST), and Hawaii standard time (HST). Always keep the changing time zones in mind if you're traveling (or even telephoning) long distances in the U.S. For example, noon in New York City (EST) is 11am in Chicago (CST), 10am in Denver (MST), 9am in Los Angeles (PST), 8am in Anchorage (AST), and 7am in Honolulu (HST). When it's noon in London (GMT, or Greenwich Mean Time), it's 7am in New York.

Daylight saving time is in effect from 1am on the first Sunday in April until 2am on the last Sunday in October, except in Arizona, Hawaii, part of Indiana, and Puerto Rico.

Tipping The standard rates for tipping are 15% (before tax) to waiters for a well-served meal; 15% of the fare for a cab ride; $1 to the bellhop for carrying one or two bags ($1 per additional bag); and a couple of dollars for maid service when you check out.

Toilets Often euphemistically referred to as "restrooms," public toilets are nonexistent on the streets of most American cities. They can be found, though, in bars, restaurants, hotel lobbies, museums, department stores, and gasoline stations—and will probably be clean (although ones in the last-mentioned sometimes leave much to be desired). Note, however, that some restaurants and bars display a notice that "Toilets are for use of patrons only." You can ignore this sign, or better yet, avoid arguments by paying for a cup of coffee or a soft drink, which will qualify you as a patron. The cleanliness of toilets at railroad stations and bus depots may be questionable; some public places are equipped with pay toilets that require you to insert one or two dimes (10¢) or a quarter (25¢) into a slot on the door before it will open. In restrooms with attendants, leaving at least a 25¢ tip is customary.

Yellow Pages The local phone company provides two kinds of telephone directory. The general directory, called the "white pages," lists subscribers (business and personal residences) in alphabetical order. The inside front cover lists emergency numbers for police, fire, and ambulance, and other vital numbers (like the Coast Guard, poison control center, crime-victims hotline, and so on). The first few pages are devoted to community-service numbers, including a guide to long-distance and international calling, complete with country codes and area codes.

The second directory, the "yellow pages," lists all local services, businesses, and industries by type, with an index at the back. The listings cover not only such obvious items as automobile repairs by make of car, or drugstores (pharmacies), often by geographical location, but also restaurants by type of cuisine and geographical location, bookstores by special subject and/or language, places of worship by religious denomination, and other information that the tourist might otherwise not readily find. The *Yellow Pages* also includes city plans or detailed area maps, often showing postal ZIP Codes and public transportation.

THE AMERICAN SYSTEM OF MEASUREMENTS

LENGTH

1 inch (in.)	=	2.54cm				
1 foot (ft.)	=	12 in.	=	30.48cm	=	.305m
1 yard	=	3 ft.	=	.915m		
1 mile (mi.)	=	5,280 ft.	=	1.609km		

To convert miles to kilometers, multiply the number of miles by 1.61 (for example, 50 mi. × 1.61 = 80.5km). Note that this conversion can be used to convert speeds from miles per hour (m.p.h.) to kilometers per hour (km/h).

To convert kilometers to miles, multiply the number of kilometers by .62 (for example, 25km × .62 = 15.5 mi.). Note that this same conversion can be used to convert speeds from kilometers per hour to miles per hour.

CAPACITY

1 fluid ounce (fl. oz.)	=	.03 liters		
1 pint	=	16 fl. oz.	=	.47 liters
1 quart	=	2 pints	=	.94 liters
1 gallon (gal.)	=	4 quarts	=	3.79 liters
	=	.83 Imperial gal.		

To convert U.S. gallons to liters, multiply the number of gallons by 3.79 (for example, 12 gal. × 3.79 = 45.48 liters.)

To convert U.S. gallons to Imperial gallons, multiply the number of U.S. gallons by .83 (for example, 12 U.S. gal. × .83 = 9.95 Imperial gal.).

To convert liters to U.S. gallons, multiply the number of liters by .26 (for example, 50 liters × .26 = 13 U.S. gal.).

To convert Imperial gallons to U.S. gallons, multiply the number of Imperial gallons by 1.2 (for example, 8 Imperial gal. × 1.2 = 9.6 U.S. gal.).

WEIGHT

1 ounce (oz.)	=	28.35 grams		
1 pound (lb.)	=	16 oz.	=	453.6 grams
			=	.45 kilograms
1 ton	=	2,000 lb.	=	907 kilograms
	=	.91 metric tons		

To convert pounds to kilograms, multiply the number of pounds by .45 (for example, 90 lb. × .45 = 40.5kg).

To convert kilograms to pounds, multiply the number of kilos by 2.2 (for example, 75kg × 2.2 = 165 lb).

AREA

1 acre   =   .41 ha
1 square mile =   640 acres   =   2.59 ha   =   2.6km

To convert acres to hectares, multiply the number of acres by .41 (for example, 40 acres × .41 = 16.4ha).

To convert hectares to acres, multiply the number of hectares by 2.47 (for example, 20ha × 2.47 = 49.4 acres).

To convert square miles to square kilometers, multiply the number of square miles by 2.6 (for example, 80 sq. mi. × 2.6 = 208km).

To convert square kilometers to square miles, multiply the number of square kilometers by .39 (for example, 150km × .39 = 58.5 sq. mi.).

TEMPERATURE

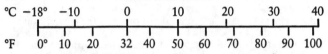

°C −18° −10   0   10   20   30   40

°F   0° 10   20   32 40   50   60   70   80   90 100

To convert degrees Fahrenheit to degrees Celsius, subtract 32 from °F, multiply by 5, then divide by 9 (for example, 85°F − 32 × 5/9 = 29.4°C).

To convert degrees Celsius to degrees Fahrenheit, multiply °C by 9, divide by 5, and add 32 (for example, 20°C × 9 ÷ 5 + 32 = 68°F).

GETTING TO KNOW DENVER

Denver is growing by leaps and bounds. Only a decade ago the outer edge of the metropolitan area was marked by a lone house that stood in a flat, barren field on the western plain; today it's climbing up the foothills of the Rockies. The urban sprawl is extending in all directions—to the west dotting the mountainsides, to the north two-thirds of the way to Boulder, and to the south and east to the flat fields where the native yucca proliferates.

This chapter aims to help you orient yourself and find your way around the Mile High City. And the "Fast Facts" section will give you those little bits of information that can make the difference between an enjoyable visit and a disaster.

1. ORIENTATION

ARRIVING

BY PLANE From **Stapleton International Airport,** visitors can take taxis, airport shuttle limousines, private limousines, or RTD buses to their hotels, depending on location. There's a transportation information booth on the lower level near Door 6. Many of the rental-car and limousine services have counters on Stapleton's lower level; taxis are available outside several doors on the lower level as well. The RTD bus stop is located outside Door 11.

Note: Stapleton International will cease operations when the new Denver International Airport opens on October 29, 1993.

BY TRAIN Amtrak arrives at Union Station, at 17th Street and Wynkoop Street, in the lower downtown historic district. The station is within easy walking distance of the 16th Street Mall's free shuttles, which will take you close to many downtown hotels.

BY BUS The bus station is at 1055 19th Street, near some of the downtown hotels and three blocks from the 16th Street Mall, where free shuttles will ferry you close to other downtown hotels.

TOURIST INFORMATION

The **Denver Information Center,** 225 W. Colfax Ave. (tel. 303/892-1112), across from the U.S. Mint, has staff prepared to answer visitors' questions. General information about the city as well as maps and brochures on attractions and restaurants are available. Ask for the free guidebook to Denver and Colorado that lists everything from attractions and health services to child care and

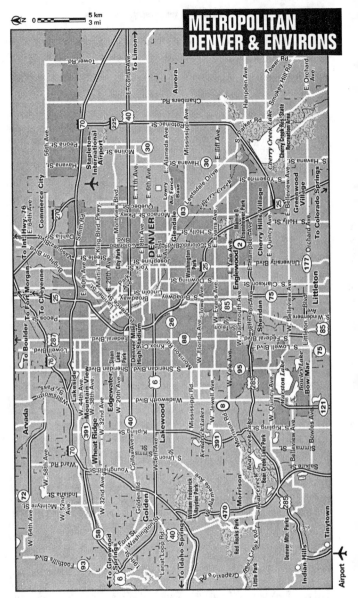

METROPOLITAN DENVER & ENVIRONS

lodging. It's open in summer, Monday through Saturday from 8am to 5pm and on Sunday from 10am to 2pm; in winter, Monday through Friday from 8am to 5pm and on Saturday from 9am to 1pm.

The **Stapleton Information Center,** located between Concourses C and D at Stapleton International Airport, also provides brochures and visitor information. The booth is staffed daily from 8am to 5pm. **Colorado Ski Country USA** maintains a booth at Stapleton during the winter months and has literature and information available on the different ski areas in the state. There will of course be information booths at Denver International Airport when it opens, too.

CITY LAYOUT

In 1859, when Denver was just a collection of tents and the first streets were being laid out, those streets parallel to Cherry Creek were numbered, the cross streets were named, and it was hard to get lost. But as the tent town grew into a city, a new north-south and east-west grid pattern was imposed around the existing streets (now the downtown area), leaving the streets of the oldest area of Denver at an angle to the rest of the city. Today this grid pattern extends past the nearby suburbs to include virtually all the four counties around the city of Denver.

Even knowing this, finding your way around today can be a bit daunting, since the metropolitan area has grown to include several additional interesting neighborhoods as well as number of rapidly growing suburban communities on the outskirts. There's even a small incorporated city completely within Denver! But if you get lost, do what the locals do—look to the mountains in the west to orient yourself.

MAIN ARTERIES & STREETS **Downtown** encompasses an area of about 1½ square miles, roughly bounded by West 13th Avenue on the south, Speer Boulevard (which follows Cherry Creek) on the west, the South Platte River on the north, and Grant Street on the east. There are 16 main **named streets** (running parallel to the South Platte River) through downtown, stretching from Wynkoop Street to Cleveland Place. The main **numbered streets** (running parallel to Cherry Creek) are 14th Street, 15th Street, 17th Street, 18th Street, and 19th Street. In addition, there's **Broadway,** which runs north-south through the downtown streets. You should also know that 16th Street has been turned into the **16th Street Mall,** for pedestrians only.

FINDING AN ADDRESS **North-South Streets** All north-south streets are named, and are generally called "streets" or "courts," although some may be called "boulevards," "parkways," "drives," etc.—but *not* "avenues." **Broadway,** which runs from the old section of downtown south into the suburb of Englewood, divides "avenues" into east and west. (North of downtown, heading out into the northern suburbs, **Washington Street** divides addresses into east and west.) Addresses increase east and west from Broadway, and each block adds 100 to the "avenue" address. Thus "1630 East 14th Avenue" is on 14th Avenue a little more than 16 blocks east of Broadway.

The **major north-south cross streets *east* of Broadway** include Logan Street (400 block), Downing Street (1200 block), York Street (2300 block), Colorado Boulevard (Colo. 2; 4000 block), and Monaco Parkway (6500 block), going out as far east as Gun Club Road (23300 block) past the suburb of Aurora. The **major north-south cross streets *west* of Broadway** include Santa Fe Drive (U.S. 85; 1000 block), Pecos Street (1600 block), Zuni Street (2400 block), Federal Boulevard (Colo. 88; 3000 block), and Sheridan Boulevard (Colo. 95; 5200 block), going out as far west as Quaker Street (16400 block) past the suburb of Arvada.

East-West Streets All east-west streets are called "avenue" (either named or numbered) or "place." Running straight through the city, and forming the southern boundary of the downtown area, **Colfax Avenue** (also known as Business Route I-70, U.S. 40/287, and Colo. 40) is the primary east-west thoroughfare. And although it does not divide streets into north and south, it has become such an important route that maps usually show distances measured from Colfax.

The avenue that divides north-south streets into their southern extensions is **Ellsworth Avenue,** a comparatively minor street about 1½ miles south of Colfax Avenue. The east-west streets north of Ellsworth are generally numbered (although a few have names; for instance, Colfax Avenue is actually 15th Avenue), beginning with 1st Avenue and progressing northward up to 168th Avenue in the northern suburbs; south of Ellsworth, virtually all east-west streets are named. South of Ellsworth Avenue, north-south cross streets bear the designation "South"; however, since these are considered southern extensions of existing streets, no "North" designation is needed north of Ellsworth. Street addresses increase north and south from Ellsworth Avenue, with each block adding 100 to the street address. Thus "1530 Downing Street" is on Downing Street a little more than 15 blocks north of Ellsworth, while "1130 South Downing Street" is on Downing Street just a little more than 11 blocks *south* of Ellsworth.

The **major east-west streets *north* of Ellsworth Avenue** include 1st Avenue (100 block), 6th Avenue (U.S. 6 heading west; 600 block), Colfax Avenue (1500 block), Montview Boulevard (2000 block), 26th Avenue (2600 block), Martin Luther King Drive (which runs into the Stapleton Airport entrance; 3200 block), going out as far north as 168th Avenue (16800 block) at the Weld County line. The **major east-west streets *south* of Ellsworth Avenue** include Alameda Avenue (Colo. 26; 300 block), Mississippi Avenue (1100 block), Florida Avenue (1500 block), Evans Avenue (2100 block), Yale Avenue (2700 block), and Hampden Avenue (which is U.S. 285 and Colo. 30; 3500 block), going out as far south as County Line Road (8300 block) at the southern edge of suburban Littleton.

Diagonal Streets   There are a few important streets in Denver that run diagonally across the grid plan, generally in a northwest-southeast direction. These include **I-25, Speer Boulevard,** and **Leetsdale Drive.**

STREET MAPS   Maps of the city and state are available at the

---

IMPRESSIONS

"This town, 'Denver City,' is situated at the mouth of Cherry Creek where it forms its confluence with the South Platte. This is the point where the Santa Fe and New Mexico road crosses to Fort Laramie and Fort Bridger, also the great leading road from the Missouri River: in short, it is the center of all the great leading thoroughfares and is bound to be a great city."
—GENERAL WILLIAM LARIMER, TO THE MAYOR OF LEAVENWORTH
AFTER CROSSING FOUR COTTONWOOD STICKS TO STAKE OUT A TOWN,
1858.

Denver Information Center, 225 W. Colfax Ave. across the street from the U.S. Mint. The best free maps for tourists are in a pull-out section of the *Official Visitors Guide to Denver,* available at the information center. You can also get city maps at many hotels. Members of the **American Automobile Association** can get free maps from the eight local offices; contact the office at 1400 E. Arkansas Ave. (tel. 303/753-8800) for information about the office nearest your accommodations.

NEIGHBORHOODS IN BRIEF

Lower Downtown   LoDo, as the locals call it, is a 22-block sector of turn-of-the-century warehouses and National Historic Landmark Victorian buildings, many housing shops, restaurants, and businesses behind 10-foot doors and elegant exteriors. This neighborhood, centered around Larimer Square, which is the oldest part of the city, stretches from Wynkoop Street southeast to Market Street, and from 20th Street southwest to Speer Boulevard.

Central Business District   This section consists of skyscrapers built after 1977, strung along 16th, 17th, and 18th Streets. This section of town has the skyline visitors see as they approach the Mile High City from any direction.

Civic Center Park   This park is a two-square-block oasis of trees and greenery, surrounded by state and local government buildings, the Denver Art Museum, the U.S. Mint, and the Colorado History Museum.

Uptown   Denver's oldest residential neighborhood, this section of town stretches from Colfax Avenue to 23rd Avenue between Broadway and York Street and boasts 17th Avenue's Restaurant Row. Some of the Queen Anne– and Victorian-style homes have been turned into bed-and-breakfasts.

Capitol Hill   Bordering the southeastern end of downtown, the Capitol Hill area is a collection of mansions from the gold-boom days, many converted into modern apartments and offices. There are no old wooden buildings here, because after Denver burned to the ground in 1863, city officials decreed that structures must be constructed of brick or stone (the law remained in force until after World War II).

Cherry Creek   This neighborhood, a few miles southeast of downtown, is home for many of Denver's old wealthy families who live in the Denver Country Club area. The chic boutiques and stores along 1st, 2nd, and 3rd Avenues east of York Street comprise a shopping area known as Cherry Creek North that is, along with Cherry Creek Mall, a shopaholic's dreamland.

Washington Park   A half-mile south of 1st Avenue, this residential section surrounds a formal English-style park containing two lakes, flower gardens, and jogging and biking paths.

Five Points   The cultural and commercial center of Denver's African American community, Five Points is one of the city's oldest and most diverse neighborhoods. It stretches from the Platte River to Downing between 20th and 38th Streets.

Far East Center   This thriving section of Denver is the focal point and commercial center of the city's Asian community. If you like Vietnamese or Thai food, you'll find many restaurants to choose from in the strip malls located along Federal Avenue from Alameda Avenue south to Mississippi Avenue.

Tech Center   The Tech Center area, at the southeastern end of the metropolitan area and approximately a 25-minute drive southeast of downtown, is the newest part of town. Roughly bounded by the Tech Center and the County Line Road exits of I-25, it evolved around the Denver Tech Center and has expanded over the years to include many technological centers and business parks. Several international and national companies have their headquarters here.

Glendale   This is an incorporated city, about a square mile in area, that's completely surrounded by Denver. It goes east from South Colorado Boulevard and south from East Alameda Avenue, straddling Cherry Creek. There are several nightclubs here.

The Suburbs   The metropolitan Denver area includes the city of Denver, with a population of 470,000, and several adjacent or neighboring suburbs that push that total to more than 1.8 million. The western suburbs, nudging the foothills of the Rockies, include Lakewood, Wheat Ridge, Arvada, and Westminster. The major eastern suburb is Aurora, the fastest-growing city in the region. Sheridan, Englewood, Littleton, Cherry Hills Village, and Greenwood Village are south of Denver, and Commerce City, Northglenn, and Thornton lie to the north.

2. GETTING AROUND

BY PUBLIC TRANSPORTATION [BUS]

The **Regional Transportation District (RTD)** (tel. 303/299-6000 for route and schedule information) runs the buses that service metropolitan Denver, Boulder, and some of the foothills communities. You should be aware that buses begin operation between 4 and 5am and some stop as early as 6pm, but most go until midnight or 1am. Only the East Colfax Avenue bus runs 24 hours. During off-peak hours on certain busy routes, such as East Colfax Avenue, West Colfax Avenue, and Broadway, for example, some buses go only part of the way along the route. (For example, during the midafternoon some West Colfax Avenue buses go only as far as Wadsworth Boulevard while others travel all the way to Golden.) So when asking for route information (or reading the schedule), be sure to ask for the hours of operation and check how far the bus goes.

The local **bus fare** is $1 during peak hours (6 to 9am and 4 to 6pm), 50¢ during off-peak hours, and exact change (in coins or dollar bills) is required. The cost of regional and express rides varies according to the route; for example, the Denver–Boulder, Denver–Evergreen, and Denver–Conifer routes are $2.50. Children 5 and younger travel free. Senior citizens with identification pay 15¢ for local rides during off-peak hours, but the regular fare during peak times. The driver can provide you with a transfer (at no charge) that's valid for approximately one hour after the issuing bus reaches its final destination.

BY TAXI

You'll find a taxi stand outside the lower doors at the airport terminal, and the bell captains at major hotels can hail a cab within a few minutes, but you'll have to call for one anywhere else in the city. Allow 10 minutes if you're calling from the downtown area, 15 minutes for most other sections of Denver, and at least 20 minutes from an outlying area. Try **Yellow Cab** (tel. 303/777-7777), **Zone Cab** (tel. 303/861-2323), or **Metro Cab** (tel. 303/294-9204).

Fares begin at $1.40, and increase another $1.40 for each mile. There's a 40¢ charge for each extra passenger when there are two or more passengers, except for children under 12 years of age. The trip from the airport to downtown will cost approximately $13 plus a $1 gate fee that drivers must pay to leave the airport grounds. You can pay some taxi companies by credit card.

BY CAR

Unless you're staying in the downtown area, it's a lot easier and faster to move around this sprawling metropolitan area by car than by bus or taxi, which can get expensive.

RENTALS   Most major car-rental companies have offices in Denver. Those with booths at Stapleton International Airport, or shuttle service between the airport and their in-town offices, include (in alphabetical order): **Advantage Rent-a-Car** (tel. 303/399-6600, or toll free 800/777-5500), **Alamo Rent-a-Car** (tel. 303/321-1176, or toll free 800/327-9633), **Avis** (tel. 303/398-3725, or toll free 800/331-1212), **Budget Rent-a-Car** (tel. 303/341-2277, or toll free 800/527-0700), **Dollar Rent-a-Car** (tel. 303/398-2323, or toll free 800/800-4000), and **Hertz** (tel. 303/355-2244, or toll free 800/654-3131). Per-day rentals range from $31 to $45 for a midsize car. Car rentals may be less expensive on weekends. Call for exact prices and specials.

Enterprise Leasing, 6030 Smith Rd., near the airport (tel. 303/320-1121, or toll free 800/325-8007), is a good company to rent from, but office hours are limited. Most of the cars are less than a year old, have low mileage, and cost less than at many other rental agencies. Drivers get unlimited mileage within the state.

A Note on Mountain Driving: If you intend to drive into the mountains during the winter, it's wise to rent a four-wheel-drive vehicle if you can afford it (about $70 per day). If you're on a budget, at least rent a front-wheel-drive car, because they tend to perform better in the snow. For all rental cars, be sure that there are chains in the trunk, because local law requires snow tires and/or chains on cars traversing many mountain passes during snowstorms.

Visitors can arrange for airport transfers, local use, or trips to mountain resorts through several companies. **Admiral Limousine,** 8055 E. Tufts Ave. (tel. 303/741-6464, or toll free 800/828-8680), has luxury to Grand Wagoneer stretch limos. **Barrons International/Sterling Limousine** (tel. 303/366-5466, or toll free 800/366-5416) has chauffeur-driven sedans and luxury limos.

PARKING   Rates at the downtown parking lots range from 50¢ per half hour to $9 for a day, depending on the lot's proximity to the 16th Street Mall and the 17th Street office building corridor. There is also some on-street parking, but you should have change available for meters. Note that the red meters around downtown are for shorter periods and take quarters only.

Outside downtown it's usually possible to find space in the free parking lots or on the side streets.

DRIVING RULES   Everyone in the front seat of a car must wear a seat belt, according to Colorado law. There's also a state child-protection law: Any child under 4 years old and weighing 40 pounds or less must be in an approved child seat.

In Colorado, drivers can make a right turn at a red signal, after making a complete stop, unless posted otherwise.

Colorado is a mandatory-insurance state, so drivers in their own vehicles must have proof of insurance with them.

When it's snowing on the Front Range, the city streets and highways become slippery. Allow extra driving time to reach your destination in these conditions, reduce your speed, and leave more space than usual between your vehicle and the car in front. When the weather is very bad, the state will announce an "accident alert" in effect for specific counties. Drivers involved in minor accidents in those counties must exchange information at the scene (without calling police), and call local police within 48 hours. When parking during the winter, watch for snow removal route signs. These are tow-away zones when it's snowing.

ON FOOT

You probably won't have much trouble getting around downtown. It's a comparatively small area, so you can walk most places. But you can also use the convenient **free shuttles** that travel back and forth on the 16th Street pedestrian mall.

Outside downtown, of course, walking is another matter— Denver is a big city. Those of you who enjoy walking should know before you set out for a destination that there are about 16 east-west (street) blocks to the mile and approximately 10 north-south (avenue) blocks to the mile.

 DENVER

Airport   See "Orientation," above.

Altitude   Denver isn't called the "Mile High City" for nothing—it's literally a mile high, 5,280 feet above sea level. And this can occasionally cause some distress for visitors (see "Health and Insurance" in Chapter 2).

American Express   There are several American Express Travel offices in Denver. The downtown office (tel. 303/298-7100) is located at 555 17th St.

Area Codes   The telephone area code for Denver and Boulder is 303.

Babysitters   The front desk or concierge at your hotel may well be able to provide information on babysitters. The hourly cost may vary by day and time, as well as by the age of your children, and there may be an additional charge for transportation.

Banks   Most banks are open Monday through Friday, but hours vary. Some banks open as early as 8:30am and close inside services as late as 6pm. Rocky Mountain BankCard System's automated Plus System provides automated banking (tel. toll free 800/THE-PLUS for locations) at more than 600 ATMs. Money Express,

907 E. Colfax Ave. (tel. 303/830-CASH), has a 24-hour check-cashing service, including personal and out-of-state checks. Many hotels will cash checks for guests.

Business Hours   Shopping hours vary widely. Most malls open at 9:30 or 10am and close at 9pm Monday through Friday and at 5 or 6pm on Saturday. Many malls are also open from 11am or noon to 5 or 6pm on Sunday.

Car Rentals   See "Getting Around," above.

Climate   See "When to Go" in Chapter 2.

Currency Exchange   Foreign-currency exchange services are provided by several banks as well as Thomas Cook Currency Services, in the downtown area. Thomas Cook has two locations: 1580 Court Place, downtown (tel. 303/571-0808, or toll free 800/332-6357 inside Colorado), and 5251 DTC Pkwy. in the Denver Tech Center, near the intersection of I-25 and Belleview Ave. (tel. 303/694-2502). Both are open Monday through Friday from 9am to 5pm for currency exchange. There's also a currency-exchange service booth at Stapleton International Airport.

Doctor/Dentist   For medical and dental referrals, call Pro-logue (tel. 303/443-2584). Med-Search (tel. 303/866-8000), run by St. Joseph Hospital, is also a free physician-referral service; when it's closed, there's a recording telling you where to call for emergency service.

Documents Required   See "Entry Requirements" in Chapter 3.

Driving Rules   See "Getting Around," above.

Drugstores   There are drugstores at many King Soopers and Safeway grocery stores. Family Pharmacy, 1724 S. Chambers Rd. (tel. 303/695-1702), is open daily from 9am to 10pm; you can also get 24-hour emergency service by calling the same number. (A recorded message will tell you how to contact the pharmacist on duty, and arrangements will be made so that you can obtain needed medicine, even if it's 3am.)

Embassies/Consulates   See Chapter 3, "For Foreign Visitors."

Emergencies   Dial **911** for police, ambulance, and fire emergencies; for non-emergency police assistance, call 303/575-3127.

Eyeglasses   You can replace lost or broken glasses in about one hour at one of the five Lenscrafters stores, located at Cinderella City Shopping Center, 701 W. Hampden Ave. (tel. 303/761-3423); Buckingham Square Shopping Center, 1343 S. Joliette (tel. 303/745-9700); Villa Italia Mall, 7200 W. Alameda Ave. (tel. 303/936-4117); Cherry Creek Mall, 3000 E. 1st Ave. (tel. 303/321-8331); and Westminster Mall, 5491 W. 88th Ave. (tel. 303/429-2950).

Hairdressers/Barbers   Michael of the Carlyle (tel. 303/757-5445) has 13 salons in the Denver area. All appointments are made through that central number. Cuts cost $18–$22 for men and $22–$25 for women. Fantastic Sams has more than 20 haircutting salons in the metropolitan area offering cuts for approximately $9.

Holidays   See Chapter 3, "For Foreign Visitors."

Hospitals   There are several hospitals in Denver. For emergency service, try Rose Medical Center, 4567 E. 9th St. (tel. 303/320-2455); Swedish Medical Center, 501 E. Hampden Ave. (tel. 303/788-6911); or St. Anthony Hospital, 4231 W. 16th Ave. (tel. 303/629-3721).

Hotlines   The Battered Women's Support Group/Safehouse has a 24-hour crisis line (tel. 303/830-6800). The Poison Control Center number is 303/629-1123. For the State Patrol, call 303/239-4501. And for Travelers Aid, call 303/832-8194. The hotline number for the Rape Assistance and Awareness program is 303/443-7300.

Information   The Gay and Lesbian Community Center of Colorado is located at 1245 E. Colfax Ave. (tel. 303/831-6268). Senior Answers and Services, 3006 E. Colfax Ave. (tel. 303/333-3482), primarily geared for local residents, has information and counseling on problems facing seniors.

For general information about Denver, see "Orientation," above.

Laundry/Dry Cleaning   If your hotel doesn't have a laundry service, ask at the front desk for a reliable cleaners or the location of the nearest laundrette. Colorado Lace is a reputable chain with 20 locations in the metropolitan area. Check the *Yellow Pages* for the location most convenient to you.

Libraries   Anyone can use the citywide network of libraries, but a local card is needed to check out material. The main library is located at 1357 Broadway (tel. 303/640-8800), on the edge of downtown. Copy machines, faxes, and typewriters are available for a fee. The main library has one of the best collections of books and materials on western history and art in the country and also has strong children's, genealogy, and business collections. The library sponsors events, exhibits, and activities throughout the year. Open Monday through Wednesday from 10am to 9pm, Thursday through Saturday from 10am to 5:30pm, and on Sunday from 1 to 5pm.

Liquor Laws   Alcoholic beverages may be served in restaurants, lounges, and bars Monday through Saturday from 7am to 2am, from 8am to 8pm on Sunday and Christmas Day (bars and restaurants with extended-hours licenses can serve until midnight on Sunday and Christmas). The legal drinking age is 21—proof of age is required. Alcoholic beverages are sold in liquor stores, open Monday through Saturday from 8am to midnight. The 3.2% beer is sold in supermarkets and convenience stores Monday through Sunday from 5am to midnight.

Luggage Storage/Lockers   There are lockers and a luggage-storage area at Stapleton International Airport and the downtown bus station.

Maps   See "Orientation," above.

Newspapers/Magazines   The *Denver Post* and the *Rocky Mountain News* are the major local papers. The "Weekend" section in Friday's *Denver Post* and the "Happenings" section in Friday's *Rocky Mountain News* list weekend events, movies, shows, museum exhibits, and restaurants.

Westword, a free weekly newspaper, lists many of the current "in" restaurants, nightclubs, and local events. You can find it in wire stands on many street corners and businesses around town, including supermarkets. *Up the Creek* is another free weekly newspaper, aimed at singles and focusing on events at the southern end of town.

Photographic Needs   Pallas Photo Labs, 700 Kalamath St. (tel. 303/893-0101), and The Pro Lab, 1200 W. Mississippi Ave. (tel. 303/744-6126), are both used by many professional photographers in this town. Each offers a full range of photographic services.

Post Office   Denver offers 24-hour full postal service at two locations. The Downtown Station (tel. 303/296-2920) is located at

951 20th St., and has the largest philatelic stamp section in the city. The Terminal Annex at 1595 Wynkoop St. (tel. 303/297-6815) in lower downtown next to the train station, has 24-hour window service, including Express Mail dropoff. The General Mail Facility Finance Station, 7500 W. 53rd Place (tel. 303/297-6456), also offers all postal services 24 hours daily.

Radio   There are a couple dozen local radio stations. KVOD (99.5 FM) offers classical music, MAJIC (100.3 FM) has light rock, MIX (107.5 FM) plays adult contemporary, KDHT (92.5 FM) croons country music, and KBPI (105.9) blasts hard rock.

Religious Services   Most religious faiths are represented in this town. Denver's oldest church, the lovely Trinity United Methodist Church, 1820 Broadway (tel. 303/839-1493), is open for tours and welcomes visitors for Sunday worship. Services at the Holy Ghost Catholic Church, 19th and California Streets in downtown (tel. 303/292-1556), are open to the public. The First Baptist Church of Denver, 1373 Grant St. (tel. 303/861-2501), also welcomes guests. See the *Yellow Pages* for a complete list.

Road Conditions   For information on road conditions on the major highways throughout the state, call 303/639-1234; for road conditions within a two-hour driving radius of Denver, call 303/639-1111.

Safety   Whenever you're traveling in an unfamiliar city, stay alert. Be aware of your immediate surroundings. Wear a moneybelt, and don't sling your camera or purse over your shoulder. It's your responsibility to be alert even in the most heavily touristed areas. In particular, avoid walking around the West Colfax Avenue area near the capitol and the Five Points section after dark.

Shoe Repairs   You can have certain repairs done while you wait at Molinaro Cobblers, in Writer Square at Lawrence and 16th Streets (tel. 303/534-2034), across from the Tabor Center, downtown.

Taxes   The sales tax varies from county to county. In Denver County (including all of the city of Denver) it's 3.5% (a total of 7.3% for city and state), but lower in suburban Lakewood and the foothill communities of Jefferson County to the west.

Denver has a hotel tax of 12%, which is added to the room rate.

Taxis   See "Getting Around," above.

Telephones   Since deregulation, several different telephone companies operate the pay phones in the Denver metropolitan area. A local call from a pay phone is usually 25¢, depending on the telephone company. At this time, U.S. West local information is free; however, other telephone companies charge 40¢ per call. Some companies keep your money, even if no one answers.

Local directory assistance is 1-411; long-distance directory assistance is 1 + the area code + 555-1212.

Television   There are 10 television stations, including four major ones: Channels 2 (KWGN, an independent station), 4 (NBC), 7 (CBS), and 9 (ABC). Channel 6 is the public television station (PBS). Cable is available at most hotels.

Time   Denver is on mountain standard time, two hours behind eastern standard, one hour behind central standard, and one hour ahead of Pacific standard time. When it's noon in Denver, it's 2pm in New York City and 11am in San Francisco. Daylight saving time is in effect from April to October.

Tipping Suggested amounts for tipping are in line with those in other major U.S. cities: 15%–20% for service in restaurants and lounges. Accepted tipping for taxis is 10%–15%. A tip of 50¢–$1 per bag is appropriate for hotel porters, 75¢ per bag for airport porters. If you're staying longer than a night or two in a hotel, you might tip the cleaning person $1 or $2 a night.

Transit Information See "Getting Around," above. Denver has a $70-million light-rail system under construction which is expected to be completed by the end of 1993. The three-mile track will run from the Auraria campus, past the convention center, over the 16th Street Mall, and out through the eastern part of downtown to 30th and Welton Streets. This is expected to be the first leg of a citywide system.

Weather To hear the forecast for the Denver metro area (which includes Boulder), call 303/398-3964.

DENVER ACCOMMODATIONS

Denver has hundreds of hotels—in clusters strung alongside each main access road to the city, along the main thoroughfares, and in the downtown sector. So how do you choose? In this section, I've listed hotels downtown, around town, by the airport, and along most of the major routes into the city. The key criterion was quality—from cleanliness to service—for the bucks involved. (As savvy travelers know, two hotels in the same price range often don't offer the same quality of accommodations.) The choices offered in this chapter provide the most quality commensurate with the dollars you're willing to spend.

Since the opening of the Colorado Convention Center in downtown Denver, hotel occupancy rates have climbed steadily. While room rates haven't gone up as fast, one can no longer plan on just walking into a downtown hotel and finding a room, let alone one at a bargain rate. These days, the safest approach is to book a room *before* leaving home.

When planning for your accommodations, keep in mind that the Denver Metro Convention & Visitors Bureau runs a program called "Mile High Lights," which combines special cultural performances and events with lodging at a discounted price. Hotel packages can be booked independently of theater tickets. For more information, call Denver Vacation Packages (tel. toll free 800/489-4888; fax 303/892-1636).

In addition, many chain hotels have their own "clubs," and membership confers discounts on room rates, among other benefits such as coffee in the morning or even free rooms. (The Days Inn Inn-Credible Club and the Hyatt Regency Gold Passport Club are two examples.) If you don't already belong to such a club, you might consider joining one before making your reservations.

For those who would prefer the coziness of bed and breakfast accommodations over hotel rooms, staying in such private homes or inns can be a relatively inexpensive way to go.

The location of your hotel will no doubt be a prime concern for you. If you're traveling on business and operating under time constraints, you'll probably be looking for lodging downtown, near the airport, or at the Tech Center; fortunately, there are many good hostelries to choose from in each of these areas.

If you're on vacation, however, you have many more options. If you have a car and intend to spend most of your time exploring the Rocky Mountains, I'd suggest a hotel on the west side of the city, where you'll be only 20 minutes from downtown but beyond the traffic congestion. Thanks to the Colo. 470 expressway that follows the foothills, it's only an 8- to 10-minute ride between I-70 and U.S. 285, the two main routes into the mountains. If you prefer city entertainments, and you intend to spend time in Colorado Springs, stay on the south side of the city or in the Denver Tech Center area. Visitors who enjoy nightlife should locate themselves in the center of the city, near the downtown nightspots and theaters. And if you're staying an hour's drive from the airport and catching an early-morning flight home, consider spending the last night at an airport hotel.

Because location will be important to you, I've listed the accommodations by geographical area, with each area divided into four categories: "Very Expensive" ($140 or more per night, double occupancy), "Expensive" ($100–$140), "Moderate" ($45–$100), and "Budget" (less than $45).

Please be aware that all prices quoted were in effect at the time this book went to press and, of course, may change. Also, note that most of the rates quoted here do *not* include the 12% city hotel-room tax.

1. DOWNTOWN

VERY EXPENSIVE

BROWN PALACE HOTEL, 321 17th St., Denver, CO 80202. Tel. 303/297-3111, or toll free 800/321-2599, 800/228-2917 in Colorado, direct to the hotel, or 800/323-7500 to Preferred Hotels Worldwide. Fax 303/293-9204. 205 rms, 25 suites. A/C TV TEL

$ Rates: $159–$184 single or double; $249 Regal Weekend (including a suite and dinner at the Palace Arms). AE, DC, DISC, JCB, MC, V. **Parking:** $10 per day.

A favorite hostelry for the rich and famous since 1892, the Brown Palace is still a very special place to spend a night. Each of the rooms is decorated with fine antique furniture, lamps, and mirrors, and with decorative artifacts and original art. Because the hotel has an unusual triangular shape, edging against the corner of 17th Street and Broadway in the central business and financial district, many of the rooms have interesting angles. (Some of the corner rooms have long marble bathrooms.) There are 25 suites, each decorated differently. In particular, the Beatles Suite (so named for its famous former occupants) has a Victorian ambience with its four-poster bed in one of the two bedrooms, swagged drapes, mirrored ceilings, chandeliers, remote-control televisions, and plush robes.

Dining/Entertainment: Its atmosphere and the well-prepared fresh seafood and Colorado prime rib make the Ship Tavern Bar one of my favorites. Once inside the swinging tavern doors, you'll see a marvelous model clipper-ship collection and porcelain Jamaican rum casks made in 1820 (see Chapter 6, "Denver Dining," for a complete

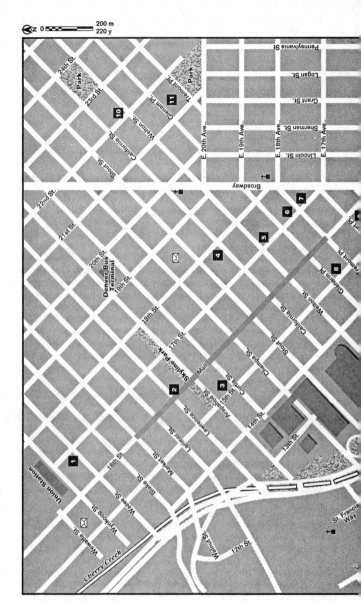

description). The other two restaurants in the hotel are Ellyngton's, open for breakfast and lunch and famous for its Dom Perignon Sunday brunch (see Chapter 6), and the Palace Arms, which presents formal dining at its best in an elegant room highlighted by stained glass and antiques from the Napoleonic era. Even if you don't stay at the Brown Palace, stop by for a traditional English afternoon tea (with finger sandwiches, scones, and pastries) in the atrium lobby served Monday through Saturday from 2 to 4:30pm.

Services: Concierge, 24-hour room service, valet.

DOWNTOWN DENVER ACCOMMODATIONS

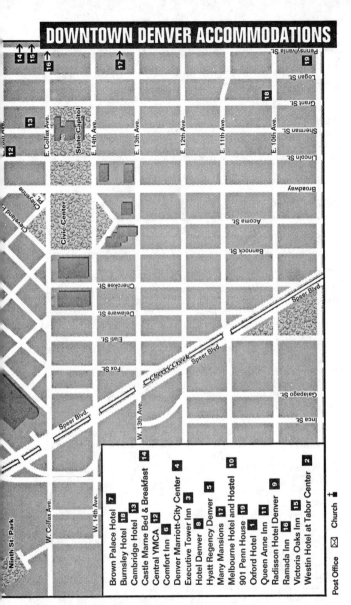

Brown Palace Hotel **7**
Burnsley Hotel **18**
Cambridge Hotel **13**
Castle Marne Bed & Breakfast **14**
Central YMCA **12**
Comfort Inn **6**
Denver Marriott-City Center **4**
Executive Tower Inn **3**
Hotel Denver **8**
Hyatt Regency Denver **5**
Many Mansions **17**
Melbourne Hotel and Hostel **10**
901 Penn House **19**
Oxford Hotel **1**
Queen Anne Inn **11**
Radisson Hotel Denver **9**
Ramada Inn **16**
Victoria Oaks Inn **15**
Westin Hotel at Tabor Center **2**

Post Office ⊠ Church ✝■

Facilities: United Airlines desk, art gallery, florist, barber, apparel shop, gift shop, newsstand; meeting facilities for 1,000.

CAMBRIDGE HOTEL, 1560 Sherman St., Denver, CO 80203. Tel. 303/831-1252, or toll free 800/877-1252. Fax 303/831-4724. 27 suites. A/C TV TEL
$ Rates (including continental breakfast): Sun–Thurs, $150–$210 suite. Fri–Sat, $89–$140 suite. Ask about holiday specials and romance packages. AE, DC, MC, V. **Parking:** $5 per night.

★ Down the block from the Capitol building, the Cambridge Hotel offers 27 suites, all individually decorated in styles ranging from French provincial to Oriental. The formal amenities list—continental breakfast brought to your suite, turn-down service, and chocolates—doesn't sound like a lot, but the real key here is "If a service isn't listed, ask for it." The fact that 80% of the guests are repeat customers should tell you that service is exceptional.

Dining/Entertainment: The neighboring Profile, a good continental restaurant, can be reached directly from the hotel. Sherry is served in the living room/lobby every evening.

Services: Concierge, room service, turn-down service.

DENVER MARRIOTT—CITY CENTER, 1701 California St., Denver, CO 80202. Tel. 303/297-1300, or toll free 800/228-9290. Fax 303/298-7474. 612 rms, 15 suites. A/C TV TEL
$ Rates: $145 single; $165 double. Weekends (including breakfast for two) $69 single or double. AE, MC, V. **Parking:** $12 per day, valet.

The Marriot, in the heart of Denver's downtown, is a busy hotel set in a 42-story building. The comfortable guest rooms are popular with groups because there is more than 25,000 square feet of meeting space on site. The concierge level has a private lounge serving complimentary continental breakfasts, afternoon cocktails, and evening desserts.

Dining/Entertainment: Charms offers light fare and snacks, accompanied by live piano music. Marjolaine's serves three meals daily and laden buffets in a Victorian setting.

Services: Room service, babysitting (upon request).

Facilities: Health club with indoor swimming pool, weight room, whirlpool, and saunas.

HYATT REGENCY, 1750 Welton St., Denver, CO 80202. Tel. 303/295-1234, or toll free 800/233-1234. Fax 303/292-2472. 511 rms, 25 suites. A/C MINIBAR TV TEL
$ Rates: Sun–Thurs, $150 single; $175 double; Regency Club, $165 single; $190 double. Fri–Sat, $65 single or double ($77 including breakfast for two). AE, CB, DISC, MC, V. **Parking:** $12 per day.

The rooms and suites at this hotel, located on the 17th Street business corridor, all exude a feeling of luxury, with fabric wall coverings, long drapes, white bedspreads, wing chairs at a table, a desk, and marble-top oak dressers. Standard amenities at this four-diamond AAA-rated hotel include electric shoe polishers, special soaps, and oversize bathtowels.

Gold Passport members (call the Hyatt toll-free number above for information about joining this "frequent user" club) get special amenities, including a room on a limited-access floor, free morning newspaper, express check-in/checkout, and late checkout upon request. Guests on the Regency Club floors (the Hyatt version of a concierge floor) stay in rooms with king-size beds or oversize twin beds and such upgraded amenities as makeup mirrors, hairdryers, robes, and snacks. In the Regency Room, where a concierge is on duty, guests can enjoy a complimentary breakfast buffet and complimentary hors d'oeuvres with beer, wine, champagne, or soft drinks later in the day.

Dining/Entertainment: McGuire's restaurant is a casual restaurant with an eclectic menu; there's also a lobby bar.

Services: Twice-daily maid service, room service, babysitting (available upon request).

Facilities: The Sky Court, a fourth-floor outdoor fitness facility, with sunbathing, swimming, and tennis in the summer.

WESTIN HOTEL, 1672 Lawrence St., Denver, CO 80202. Tel. 303/572-9100, or toll free 800/228-3000. Fax 303/572-7288. 403 rms, 13 suites. A/C TV TEL

$ Rates: $145–$180 single; $165–$199 double. Ask about weekend packages. AE, DC, MC, V. **Parking:** $8 per day.

Located in the Tabor Center complex in the heart of downtown, the Westin offers rooms decorated in restful mauve, gray, and ivory tones. Each has a bay window, a desk with a telephone, a telephone by the bed, and voice mail. Other standard amenities at this well-run hotel include remote-control television, VCRs, and video checkout. The standard and deluxe rooms are similar here; you pay a premium to spend the night on a higher floor. The top three floors are the Executive Club, where the rooms have access to the Executive Club Lounge and upgraded amenities, including a telephone and a television in the bathroom, robes, a daily fruit basket, and a complimentary newspaper.

Dining/Entertainment: Both the Tabor Grill and Augusta's are excellent (see Chapter 6, "Denver Dining," for complete descriptions). A walkway connects the hotel to the Tabor Center, a two-block, indoor complex housing 70 shops and eateries (most are situated in a food court). The Tabor Center fronts on the 16th Street Mall, so Westin guests can use the shuttle system to move around downtown.

Services: 24-hour room service, daily maid service.

Facilities: Health club with a hot tub and a pool long enough to swim laps (it's half indoors and half outdoors, stretching onto a balcony exactly one mile above sea level), racquetball courts, and an exercise room; guests can obtain passes to a nearby full-service health club.

EXPENSIVE

BURNSLEY HOTEL, 1000 Grant St., Denver, CO 80203. Tel. 303/830-1000, or toll free 800/231-3915. Fax 303/830-7676. Telex 510 100 0140. 82 suites. A/C TV TEL

$ Rates: $95–$135 suite. Weekend packages, $150 Sat night with Sun brunch, $180 Sat night with dinner and Sun brunch. Ask about long-term corporate rates. AE, DC, DISC, MC, V. **Parking:** Free.

A quiet hotel on the edge of downtown, the Burnsley is a member of the Small Luxury Hotels group and the service lavished on guests is of the appropriate level. These pleasant suites, each with a kitchen and lots of closet space and drawers, are designed for long-term stays. The Denver and Colorado suites have separate bedrooms. The Colorado suites on the higher floors have an upgraded decor, terrycloth robes, and other amenities. It's the hotel of choice for local TV stations housing visiting celebrities, and for many long-term corporate clients.

Dining/Entertainment: An elegant restaurant for fine dining; an intimate lounge offering jazz on weekend nights.

Services: Business services, concierge, room service (until midnight).

Facilities: Seasonal outdoor pool; access to health clubs.

EXECUTIVE TOWER INN, 1405 Curtis St., Denver, CO 80202. Tel. 303/571-0300, or toll free 800/525-6651. Fax 303/825-4301. 336 rms. A/C TV TEL

$ Rates: $107–$122 single; $117–$132 double. Ask about corporate rates and other special rates. Children under 16 stay free in parents' room. AE, MC, V.

★ One of the best buys for your money in the downtown area, the Executive Tower is an older but very recently renovated hotel located across the street from the PLEX and two blocks from the 16th Street Mall. The rooms are a bit larger than in most of the downtown hotels; some have a view of the mountains and some look down into the PLEX galleria.

Dining/Entertainment: Two restaurants and a cocktail lounge; fine dining as well as buffets are offered.

Services: Room service, valet, complimentary hors d'oevres.

Facilities: Health club with an indoor Olympic-size pool, tennis courts, squash and racquetball courts, weight room, running track, and sauna.

OXFORD HOTEL, 1600 17th St., Denver, CO 80202. Tel. 303/628-5400, or toll free 800/228-5838 outside Colorado. Fax 303/628-5413. 81 rms, 2 suites. A/C TV TEL

$ Rates: $110–$155 single or double. Call about corporate and special weekend rates. AE, MC, V. **Parking:** $10 per day.

A block from the railroad station and a few blocks from the 16th Street Mall, the historic Oxford is one of Denver's loveliest hotels. When it opened in 1891, guests could safely watch the frenetic street activity—horses, hacks, streetcars, delivery wagons, and pedestrians—from the hotel's lobby. The action is different today, with dozens of art galleries, shops, and restaurants within walking distance. Each room in the hotel is decorated with English, French, or American antique furnishings collected when the hotel was renovated and reopened in 1983. Most rooms have lovely old armoires (which also conceal modern television sets), two comfortable armchairs, and burnished-wood desks with period lamps. Several rooms have canopy beds, a few have decorative fireplaces (which don't work), and the outside rooms have tall windows. The lobby, with its original brass chandeliers, is a relaxing setting for afternoon sherry, served daily from 4 to 6pm.

Dining/Entertainment: The public areas on the main floor include a sitting area in the lobby, two lounges, and McCormick's Restaurant. It's always fun to while away a few hours sitting at the highly polished, art deco Cruise Room bar. It opens at 4:30pm and patrons can order off the Oxford Front Room bar menu. The Oxford Front Room bar, which looks as if it had been pulled intact from a Boston waterfront saloon, has a $1.95 snack menu during the happy hour.

Services: 24-hour room service, turn-down service, complimentary coffee, overnight shoeshine, newspaper delivery, 24-hour limousine service from the Oxford to any location in downtown Denver.

Facilities: Oxford Club Fitness Center, spa/beauty salon.

RADISSON HOTEL, 1550 Court Place, Denver, CO 80202. Tel. 303/893-3333, or toll free 800/333-3333 for Radisson national reservations. Fax 303/623-0303. 717 rms, 22 suites. A/C TV TEL

$ Rates: $120–$140 single or double. AE, DC, DISC, MC, V. **Parking:** $7 per day.

The Radisson, in the heart of downtown, underwent a recent $20-million renovation. The rooms are comfortable and attractively decorated.

Dining/Entertainment: The hotel has three restaurants: Windows Café; the informal Katie's Ice Cream Parlor; and Finnegan's Irish Pub, a lively spot for Irish and American fare.

Services: Limited room service, voice messaging.

Facilities: Health club with an outdoor heated pool and whirlpool, business center with secretarial and fax services, beauty/barber shop, florist, print shop.

MODERATE

There's a limited number of good, moderately priced accommodations in the heart of downtown. Two of them—the Hotel Denver and the Comfort Inn Downtown—are right in the center of the city, just a block or two off the 16th Street pedestrian mall. Others are located at the edge of the downtown sector.

COMFORT INN, 401 17th St., Denver, CO 80202. Tel. 303/296-0400, or toll free 800/237-7431, 800/631-2050 in Colorado. Fax 303/297-0774. 229 rms. A/C TV TEL
$ Rates (including continental breakfast): Sun–Thurs, $55 single, $65 double; Fri–Sat, $49, based on availability. AE, DC, MC, V. **Parking:** $7.50 per day.

This hotel is ideally located if you want to be near the downtown business district, the Denver Art Museum, and the U.S. Mint. At one time this property was part of the posh Brown Palace Hotel. The two hotels are connected by an overhead walkway, and the Brown Palace ballroom is located in the Comfort Inn. Both hotels are owned by the same company, but the amenities, style of rooms, and pricing are at opposite ends of the spectrum. Although the rooms aren't fancy, you get good value for your money when you consider that a room across the street, or in the other luxury hotels a few blocks away, is double or triple the price—without breakfast. Guests may use the Brown Palace restaurant and charge the bill to their rooms.

HOLIDAY INN DENVER SPORTS CENTER, 1975 Bryant St., Denver, CO 80204. Tel. 303/433-8331, or toll free 800/HOLIDAY. Fax 303/455-7061. 167 rms. A/C TV TEL **Transportation:** Free shuttle from the airport.
$ Rates: $49–$65 single; $49–$75 double. AE, DC, DISC, MC, V. **Parking:** Free.

This is a 14-story round building located just off I-25 Exit 210B, next to Mile High Stadium, home of the Broncos. It's reasonably priced and centrally located, but it may be difficult to negotiate the traffic when there's an event at the stadium or the neighboring McNichol's Sports Arena. There are comfortable rooms, a restaurant, and an outdoor swimming pool.

HOTEL DENVER, 1450 Glenarm Place, Denver, CO 80202. Tel. 303/573-1450, or toll free 800/423-5128. Fax 303/572-1113. 400 rms, 2 suites. A/C TV TEL
$ Rates: $80–$95 single; $90–$105 double; $250 suite. Corporate rate, $80 single; $90 double. Ask about the $49 weekend rate. AE, DC, DISC, MC, V. **Parking:** Free in hotel's garage.

Units in this 21-story hotel include economy rooms (facing the next-door parking lot), standard rooms (with a limited view), rooms with king-size beds, junior suites, and one- and two-bedroom executive suites. Most rooms have a standard decor of cream walls, a desk and drawers along one wall, beds covered with patterned spreads, and a night stand; the suites are more elaborately decorated. The Skyline Grill serves breakfast, lunch, and dinner, and drinks are served in the adjacent Lobby Lounge. There's a rooftop pool open during the summer, and guests can work out at the International Athletic Club, two blocks away.

RAMADA INN, 1150 E. Colfax Ave., Denver, CO 80218. Tel. 303/831-7700, or toll free 800/524-8603. Fax 303/894-9193. 146 rms. A/C TV TEL

$ Rates: $45 single or double. AE, DC, MC, V. **Parking:** Free.
On the edge of downtown in a changing neighborhood, the Ramada is one of the nicest of the moderate hostelries within a mile of downtown. The comfortable, nicely decorated rooms are reached from inside corridors or from the courtyard with a pool (open in season). Rooms have coffee makers. There's a casual restaurant, a lounge, and shuttle service to designated areas.

BUDGET

CENTRAL YMCA, 25 E. 16th Ave., Denver, CO 80202. Tel. 303/861-8300. 190 rms (some with bath).
$ Rates: $16–$18 single, $29–$31 double. MC, V.
The YMCA offers simple rooms with a bed, chair, dresser, and telephone. Rooms have private baths, shared baths, or baths down the hall. There are many parking lots in the area.

MELBOURNE HOTEL, 607 22nd St., Denver, CO 80205. Tel. 303/292-6386. 16 rms (none with bath).
$ Rates: $18 single; $24 double. No credit cards. **Parking:** Free.
If you're a backpacker, this international hostel may be for you. On the edge of downtown, it has clean rooms with ceiling fans and refrigerators, a full kitchen, and a self-service laundrette. There are private rooms for couples, family-style rooms with double beds and bunk beds, and dorm rooms.

2. NORTH, WEST & SOUTHWEST DENVER

EXPENSIVE

DENVER MARRIOTT WEST, 1717 Denver West Marriott Blvd., Golden, CO 80401. Tel. 303/279-9100, or toll free 800/228-2990. Fax 303/271-0205. 307 rms. A/C TV TEL
$ Rates: $119 single or double; corporate rate, $114 single or double. This Marriott is experimenting with an airline-style rate structure: $104 if you book 7 days in advance, $84 if you book 14 days in advance, and $74 if you book at least 21 days in advance. AE, DC, DISC, MC, V. **Parking:** Free.
The Marriott West, just off I-70, about 15 minutes from downtown, is located in a quiet part of the Denver West Office Park in the foothills. Because of its location and the indoor swimming pool and health club, it's as popular with vacationers as it is with business travelers. The guest rooms are decorated with plush, textured fabrics in rust, beige, and light tan, and are accessible by electronic key cards.
Dining/Entertainment: You can get breakfast, lunch, and dinner in the casual Meadows restaurant. Complete meals during the "early bird" dining hours (5 to 8pm) cost $8.95–$12.95. Goldfields is the type of bar where you can play backgammon, pente, cocktail-hour–style football, or dance.
Services: Room service, turn-down service, fax service.

Facilities: The large, glass-enclosed indoor pool, surrounded by deck chairs and tables, is popular with families year round. The outdoor pool, set on a landscaped deck, is a busy place in the summer; also available are a whirlpool, two saunas, and an exercise room. Arrangements can be made to use nearby tennis courts and golf courses.

DOUBLETREE HOTEL, 137 Union Blvd., Lakewood, CO 80228. Tel. 303/969-9900, or toll free 800/222-TREE. Fax 303/989-9847. 168 rms, 2 suites. A/C TV TEL **Directions:** From the Sixth Avenue freeway, head 5 blocks south on Union Boulevard.

$ Rates (including breakfast): $99 single; $109 double. Ask about seasonal rates and packages. AE, DC, DISC, MC, V. **Parking:** Free.

The Doubletree Hotel has attractive rooms, but the real lure is the lovely, oversize living room with chairs and sofas sectioned into private socializing areas, making this a popular place for friends and groups to meet. There's a library with newspapers, current periodicals, and books that guests can take to their rooms. Coffee and tea are always on tap. Every morning guests get a full breakfast, a hosted Director's Reception in the afternoon, and late-night snacks. Light dinners are available in the club room. The guestrooms are nicely decorated in quality fabrics and have a full-size work desk with phone, an additional bedside phone, a remote-control cable television, and a sitting area.

Services: Limited room service, business services.
Facilities: Library, outdoor pool, whirlpool, weight room.

MODERATE

COMFORT INN, 3440 S. Vance St., Lakewood, CO 80227. Tel. 303/989-5500, or toll free 800/221-2222. Fax 303/989-2981. 112 rms, 8 suites. A/C TV TEL

$ Rates (including continental breakfast): $42 single; $48 double; $70 suite. Ask for weekly and corporate rates. AE, DC, DISC, MC, V. **Parking:** Free.

This is another good midway location (at Hampden Avenue and Wadsworth Boulevard) for vacationers who want to explore the mountain towns off U.S. 285 or I-70 and visit Colorado Springs. Some of the rooms with king-size beds have lounge chairs and small writing desks; others have queen-size beds. The eight two-room suites have microwave ovens and refrigerators. There's a complimentary manager's reception with open bar and hors d'oeuvres Monday through Thursday from 5 to 6:30pm, an outdoor swimming pool and Jacuzzi, and access to the Lakewood Sports Club, within walking distance.

DAYS INN, 15050 W. Colfax Ave., Golden, CO 80401. Tel. 303/277-0200, or toll free 800/325-2525. Fax 303/277-0209. 145 rms, 25 suites. A/C TV TEL **Directions:** Take the Colfax Avenue exit from I-70 and head east a few hundred yards.

$ Rates: $48 single; $56 double. Corporate Connection members, $41 single or double; $70 one-bedroom suite. Children 17 and younger stay free in parents' room. AE, DC, DISC, MC, V. **Parking:** Free.

This is located at the western edge of town, so it's easy to head for the mountains. The rooms are standard Days Inn: clean, comfortable,

🄵 FROMMER'S COOL FOR KIDS: HOTELS

Cherry Creek Inn *(p. 63)* It's a convenient spot for parents of children old enough to send to Celebrity Sports alone. It's also next to one of Denver's most popular walking and jogging pathways, and near the Cherry Creek Shopping Center, which has a movie theatre and a Disney Store. There's also an outdoor seasonal pool.

Denver Marriott West *(p. 53)* The glass-enclosed pool surrounded by deck chairs is popular with families year-round.

Embassy Suites *(p. 61)* Both parents and kids love this place because the suites have private bedrooms, so kids sleep in the living room—with their own television and refrigerator for snacks. There's an indoor pool, and a full breakfast comes with the room rate.

Many Mansions *(p. 66)* In this apartment complex, children can have their own room plus a living room to roam in, and there's a full kitchen to house their favorite foods.

nicely decorated, and compact. There's an outdoor pool and a guest laundry. The moderately priced Daybreak Restaurant attached to the inn is open for breakfast, lunch, and dinner. Every time I've called this Days Inn, they've always had a "special" rate to offer me, so don't be afraid to ask for a better rate. If you're on a business visit, ask about a Corporate Connection membership, which includes rooms with desks, free local calls, express checkout, free breakfast, and a free newspaper. Families of Corporate Connection members can stay free in the room.

HAMPTON INN, 3605 S. Wadsworth Blvd., Lakewood, CO 80235. Tel. 303/989-6900, or toll free 800/HAMPTON. Fax 303/985-4730. 148 rms. A/C TV TEL
$ Rates (including continental breakfast): $46–$48 single; $52–$54 double. AE, CB, DC, DISC, MC, V. **Parking:** Free.
South of U.S. 285, on the southwest side of the metropolitan area and at the edge of the foothills, this is a good midway location for vacationers who want to explore Colorado Springs and the mountain towns off the U.S. 285 and I-70 corridors. This Hampton Inn offers very comfortable rooms for a most reasonable price. There's a continental breakfast available daily from 6am to 10pm, and complimentary cocktails and hors d'oeuvres Monday through Thursday from 5 to 6:30pm. Bennigan's restaurant is next door and a Denny's is across the street.

LA QUINTA, 3301 Youngfield Service Rd., Golden, CO 80401. Tel. 303/279-5565, or toll free 800/531-5900. Fax 303/279-5841. A/C TV TEL **Directions:** From I-70, exit on West 32nd Avenue/Youngfield Street.
$ Rates (including free local phone calls): $44–$47 single; $53 double. AE, DC, DISC, MC, V. **Parking:** Free.

The rooms in this La Quinta are wrapped around a courtyard with a large pool. They're comfortable and nicely decorated; the sink is in an alcove, outside the bathroom. There's a bottomless pot of coffee in the lobby, and laundry facilities are onsite.

REGENCY HOTEL, 3900 Elati St., Denver, CO 80216 Tel. 303/458-0808, or toll free 800/525-8748. Fax 303/477-4255. 378 rms, 22 suites. A/C TV TEL

$ Rates: $55–$65 single; $65–$75 double. Ask about corporate rates and special packages. AE, DC, DISC, MC, V.

Located at the northern edge of the city, 10 minutes from Stapleton Airport and 10 minutes from downtown, the Regency has some rooms with updated decor and some older rooms as well, but all are comfortable. The hotel has two restaurants, a lounge, health club facilities, and both outdoor and indoor pools.

BUDGET

There are lots of choices in town for travelers on a tight budget. Among the most reliable are the eight Motel 6 lodgings (tel. 505/891-6161 for central reservations) in the Denver area. Each offers the clean, compact rooms and free local telephone calls the radio ads have led us all to expect. All have air conditioning, and all except one have pools. Some of the motels have only showers in the rooms. Kids 12 and under stay free in parents' room at most of them. Rates may be slightly lower in the summertime at several of these motels.

MOTEL 6, 6 W. 83rd Place, Thornton, CO 80221. Tel. 303/429-1550. 121 rms. A/C TV TEL **Directions:** Get off I-25 at Exit 219, proceed west to Acoma Way, turn left on Acoma Way, and left again on West 83rd Place.

$ Rates: $24.35 single. Additional person $6 extra. AE, MC, V. **Parking:** Free.

Located at the northern edge of the Denver metropolitan area, this 121-room Motel 6 is 15 minutes from downtown, but close to Water World, the largest publicly owned water park in the U.S. and the kids' favorite spot for keeping cool during the summertime.

MOTEL 6, 10300 S. I-70 Frontage Rd., Wheat Ridge, CO 80033. Tel. 303/467-3172. 113 rms. A/C, TV, TEL

$ Rates: $21.95 single. Additional person $6 extra. AE, MC, V. **Parking:** Free.

This motel is at the northern edge of Denver, just minutes from the mountains on a superhighway, and eight miles from downtown Denver.

MOTEL 6, 480 Wadsworth Blvd., Denver, CO 80226. Tel. 303/232-4924, 119 rms. A/C TV TEL

$ Rates: $21.95 single. Additional person $6 extra. AE, MC, V. **Parking:** Free.

Midway between downtown and the foothills, just off the Sixth Avenue freeway, this is a good choice if you're planning on dividing your time between exploring the museums and sites in Denver, and visiting mountain towns. Downtown is nine miles away, and you're one block off I-70, the main expressway to the mountains.

VALLI-HI MOTEL HOTEL, 7320 Pecos St., Denver, CO 80221 Tel. 303/429-3551. 55 rms. A/C TV TEL

$ Rates: $19.95 single; $29.95 double. AE, DISC, MC, V.
A family-run, independently owned motel north of downtown on the Boulder Turnpike (U.S. 36) at Pecos, the Valli-Hi has clean, comfortable rooms, free local phone calls, and a seasonal pool.

WHITE SWAN MOTEL, 6060 W. Colfax Ave., Lakewood, CO 80214 Tel. 303/238-1351, or toll free 800/257-9972. 20 rms. A/C TV TEL
$ Rates: $27–$35 single or double. AE, DC, DISC, MC, V. **Parking:** Free.
Located on Colfax Avenue about 10 minutes west of downtown, this independently owned budget motel has regular rooms and eight rooms with kitchenettes. It's right on the Denver city bus line. The swimming pool is seasonal.

3. AIRPORT HOTELS

Many of these hostelries have shuttle buses to take you to and from Stapleton International Airport. If you're vacationing in the Rocky Mountains and taking an early-morning flight, consider spending the night at one of the hotels near the airport. Compare the ease and price of turning in your rental car a day early and letting the hotel's van shuttle you to the airport with getting up at 4am and driving down from the resort and through Denver during rush hour. If you call, many of these hotels will pick you at the car-rental office, instead of the airport pickup locations.

EXPENSIVE

The most expensive hotels, at the edge of the airport, have the same level of amenities one would expect to find at major hotels in the heart of the city. The lobbies and restaurants in several are popular and convenient meeting spots for those who must fly in for a quick meeting. When making reservations at the more expensive hotels, always ask if there are any "special" rates the nights you'll be in Denver. Most of these hotels have flexible pricing structures, and offer corporate rates.

(*Note:* There will be no hotels at Denver International Airport when it opens in October 1993. At the time this was written, several hotels around Stapleton Airport were discussing running shuttles for their guests for the 15- to 20-minute ride.)

EMBASSY SUITES DENVER AIRPORT HOTEL, 4444 N. Havana St., Denver, CO 80239. Tel. 303/375-0400, or toll free 800/EMBASSY. Fax 303/371-4634. 212 suites. A/C TV TEL **Directions:** Take I-70 three miles east of the airport to the Havana Street exit.
$ Rates (including full breakfast and cocktail hour): $120 single; $130 double. Corporate rate, $105 single; $115 double. Weekend special, $89 up to four people. Children 12 and younger stay free in parents' room. AE, DC, DISC, MC, V. **Parking:** Free.
The 212 two-room suites on seven levels overlooking the atrium are typical of the chain. Each suite has a private bedroom with a telephone, comfortable chair, TV, and sink, and a living room with a

sofa bed, second telephone, wet bar, TV, and dining room table. The glass elevator opens up to well-lit, open hallways overlooking the atrium.

Dining/Entertainment: The atrium, with its lush green foliage, houses a café, where guests eat a cooked-to-order breakfast in the morning and enjoy a complimentary cocktail hour every afternoon. The restaurant, Giatt's, features Italian and American cuisine.

Services: Room service, 24-hour shuttle to the airport.

Facilities: The pool, whirlpool, exercise bikes, and steam room are in a glass-enclosed area behind the atrium.

RED LION HOTEL, 3203 Quebec St., Denver, CO 80207. Tel. 303/321-3333. Fax 303/329-5233. 576 rms and suites. A/C TV TEL **Transportation:** Free shuttle to/from the airport.
$ Rates: $95–$135 single; $105–$145 double. Corporate rate, $90 single; $100 double. Weekend special, $69 single or double. AE, DC, DISC, MC, V. **Parking:** Free.

An upscale hotel, the Red Lion is at the very entrance to the airport. The guest rooms are attractively decorated, and each has two direct-dial phones with data ports for computers. The public areas include a marble lobby accented with rich woods, two restaurants, the Lobby Bar, and Characters Sports Bar, where hors d'oeuvres are served Monday through Friday from 5 to 7pm. The Red Lion has an Executive Level floor where guests get upgraded amenities, including continental breakfast, after-work hors d'oeuvres, and robes in the room.

Dining/Entertainment: The Café is for informal dining, Rosso's Ristorante serves northern Mediterranean cuisine, and there are two lounges.

Services: 24-hour room service, laundry and valet service, coffee in the lobby each morning, free airport shuttle service, concierge floor.

Facilities: Health club with 60- by 24-foot indoor swimming pool, hot tub, and sauna.

STOUFFER CONCOURSE HOTEL, 3801 Quebec St., Denver, CO 80207. Tel. 303/399-7500, or toll free 800/HOTELS-1. Fax 303/321-1986. 400 rms & suites. A/C MINIBAR TV TEL **Transportation:** Free shuttle to/from the airport.
$ Rates: $99–$160 single; $109–$170 double; $165–$600 suite. AE, DC, MC, V. **Parking:** $4 per day.

The guest rooms in this pyramid-shaped building are decorated in blends of peach, tan, straw, and lime green. Guests staying on the three club floors pay more for such amenities as the assistance of a full-service concierge, robes, hairdryer, bathroom scale, and access to the Club Lounge. They also get a complimentary continental breakfast each morning, and complimentary appetizers every afternoon (and an honor bar), in the lounge with its large-screen television.

Dining/Entertainment: The Concorde Lounge in the 12-story atrium is a pleasant backdrop for relaxing with friends or an informal meeting. The Concorde Restaurant in the atrium, filled with greenery sectioning off tables with comfortably cushioned benches and chairs, offers a continental cuisine. There's piano entertainment each night, too.

Services: Room service, complimentary coffee and a newspaper with your wake-up call, 24-hour airport shuttle; arrangements can be made for secretarial services. The Stouffer Concourse allows guests to receive faxes free of charge and will send a fax for a flat $5 (domestic) or $10 (international) fee that includes the telephone line charges.

Facilities: Indoor and outdoor pools, two whirlpools, an exercise room with Universal equipment and computerized bikes, steam room, car-rental desk, enclosed parking for guests.

MODERATE

If you usually head straight for the lowest-priced lodges, first check into reserving the lowest-priced room at some of these moderately priced places. Your cost per night could be very close to the price of that budget room, and you might get a continental breakfast tossed into the deal.

COMFORT INN, 7201 E. 36th Ave., Denver, CO 80207. Tel. 303/393-7666, or toll free 800/221-2222. Fax 303/355-6545. 117 rms. A/C TV TEL
$ Rates (including continental breakfast): $42.95–$47 single; $48.95–$53 double. AE, DC, DISC, MC, V. **Parking:** Free.
This Comfort Inn is located on a side street, just behind the bigger hotels across the street from the airport. It's a two-story building without an elevator, housing compact but adequate rooms, and offering the most reasonable rates of any hotel three minutes from the airline check-in counters. The complimentary continental breakfast is served early, from 6:30 to 8am daily, and there are restaurants in the other nearby hotels. The inn has coin-operated laundry facilities, an exercise room with a rowing machine and some free weights, and a swimming pool open during the summer.

COURTYARD MARRIOTT, 7415 41st Ave., East Denver, CO 80216. Tel. 303/333-3303, or toll free 800/321-2211. Fax 303/399-7356. 145 rms, 12 suites. A/C TV TEL **Transportation:** Free shuttle to/from Stapleton.
$ Rates: $85 single; $95 double. Children 18 and younger stay free in parents' room. AE, DC, DISC, MC, V. **Parking:** Free.
This classic Courtyard Marriott property, specifically designed for business travelers, is less than five minutes from Stapleton's terminal. The rooms have such practical amenities as an extra-long telephone extension cord (so you can use the telephone at the large desk or while sitting on the couch), a remote-control television, and in-room coffee and tea service. There's a restaurant and lounge, a swimming pool, whirlpool, and exercise room.

DAYS HOTEL, 4590 Quebec St., Denver, CO 80216. Tel. 303/320-0260, or toll free 800/228-2000. Fax 303/320-7595. 195 rms. A/C TV TEL **Transportation:** Free shuttle to/from the airport.
$ Rates: $52–$59 single; $57–$74 double. AE, DC, DISC, MC, V. **Parking:** Free.
The Days Hotel has attractive rooms and a lot of big-hotel amenities. There's a 24-hour free airport shuttle available for the five-minute ride. The hotel has a restaurant and lounge, an outdoor heated pool, and an exercise room. Some of the rooms have coffee makers. Pets are welcome.

DRURY INN, 4400 Peoria St., Denver, CO 80239. Tel. 303/373-1983, or toll free 800/325-8300. Fax 303/373-1983.

138 rms. A/C TV TEL **Transportation:** Free shuttle to/from the airport.

$ Rates (including continental breakfast): $49 single; $56 double. AE, CB, DC, DISC, MC, V. **Parking:** Free.

Just off I-70, this chain member offers some of the nicest rooms in the moderate price range. The guest rooms at this Drury Inn have rust-colored carpeting, tan walls, patterned spreads on the two double beds or the king-size bed, two chairs by a small table, and a desk. There's also an outdoor pool.

HAMPTON INN, 4685 Quebec St., Denver, CO 80216. Tel. 303/388-8100, or toll free 800/HAMPTON. Fax 303/333-7710. 138 rms. A/C TV TEL **Transportation:** Free shuttle to/from the airport.

$ Rates (including continental breakfast and local phone calls): $51–$75 single; $59–$75 double. Extra-large "king" room $5 extra. AE, CB, DC, DISC, MC, V. **Parking:** Free.

This hotel is a business traveler's favorite. The pleasantly decorated rooms have a king-size bed or two double beds, plus two comfortable armchairs on wheels pulled up to a table. The executive "king" room also has a sitting area with a couch and chair. A shuttle bus leaves for the airport every half hour. The hotel is located next door to a Denny's restaurant on a quiet street set off the superhighway.

BUDGET

There's a cluster of budget motels located off the I-70 Peoria exit, about three miles from the airport. At this busy intersection you'll also find a number of fast-food havens—including Pizza Hut, Bennett's Bar-B-Que, Taco Bell, and the International House of Pancakes. There's also a Denim Broker Inn, for those who want a nice meal that always begins with a large bowl of shrimp.

MOTEL 6, 12033 E. 38th Ave., Denver, CO 80239. Tel. 303/371-0740, or 505/891-6161, the Motel 6 central reservations number. 93 rms. A/C TV TEL

$ Rates: $25.70 single. Additional person $6 extra. AE, MC, V.

The Motel 6 on 38th Street is two miles from the airport and five miles from downtown. It has an indoor pool, tubs in some rooms (in addition to showers), and an elevator. This motel has free local phone calls and HBO.

MOTEL 6, 12020 E. 39th Ave., Denver, CO 80239. Tel. 303/371-1980, or 505/891-6161, the Motel 6 central reservations number. 137 rms. A/C TV TEL

$ Rates: $20 single; $26 double. AE, MC, V. **Parking:** Free.

Neat and clean, this motel, located just off I-70, has the compact rooms with showers that have become this chain's hallmark. The rooms are air-conditioned and there is a pool. The Motel 6 listed above is a block away.

TRAVELERS INN, 3850 Peoria St., Denver, CO 80239. Tel. 303/371-0551, or toll free 800/633-8300. Fax 303/371-2328. 132 rms. A/C TV TEL

$ Rates: $27.95 single; $34.65 double; $39.15 triple; $43.60 quad. AE, MC, V. **Parking:** Free.

Located just off I-70, this Travelers Inn has clean, compact rooms with run-of-the-mill economy furnishings. The inn offers queen-size beds, free local phone calls, free coffee, a pool, 24-hour fax services, and a coin-operated laundry.

4. SOUTH & SOUTHEAST DENVER & THE TECH CENTER

When Denverites refer to the "Tech Center area," they're really talking about the southeastern edge of town and the neighboring suburb of Englewood. The actual Denver Tech Center, off I-25 and Belleview Avenue, where high-tech businesses proliferated during the last decade, is primarily an office district, with some hotels and restaurants. Today there are many tech centers in that region, stretching from the Denver Tech Center to the County Line exits of I-25 and including several expensive and moderate hotels, restaurants, and shopping districts. The Tech Center area is approximately 15 miles southeast from downtown Denver and 10 miles south from Stapleton International Airport.

EXPENSIVE

EMBASSY SUITES, 10250 E. Costilla Ave., Englewood, CO 80112. Tel. 303/792-0433, or toll free 800/654-4810 outside Colorado, or 800/EMBASSY to Embassy Suites national reservations. Fax 303/792-0432. 236 suites. A/C TV TEL **Directions:** Take the Arapahoe Road exit and go one mile east of I-25.
$ Rates (including continental breakfast and cocktail): $119 suite Sun–Thurs, $89 Fri–Sat; Ambassador floor $20 additional. Children 12 and younger stay free in parents' room. AE, DC, DISC, MC, V. **Parking:** Free.
The suites on the nine floors overlooking the atrium are what you'd expect from this chain. Each suite has a private bedroom with a telephone, comfortable chair, and sink, and a living room with a sofa bed, a second telephone, a wet bar, and a dining room table. Suites on the Ambassador floor have additional amenities, including robes and breakfast brought to the room. The atrium, with its lush, green foliage, houses the café, where guests eat a cooked-to-order breakfast in the morning and enjoy a complimentary cocktail hour every afternoon.

Dining/Entertainment: The New West Grill is a casual restaurant serving sandwiches, salads, and food with a Southwestern flair. Dinner entrees range from $8 to $12, lunch from $5 to $7.

Services: Room service, courtesy van service within six miles of the hotel.

Facilities: Indoor pool, whirlpool, exercise room.

HYATT REGENCY TECH CENTER, 7800 Tufts Ave., Denver, CO 80237. Tel. 303/779-1234, or toll free 800/233-1234. Fax 303/850-7164. 450 rms and suites. A/C TV TEL
$ Rates: Sun–Thurs, $105–$130 single; $130–$155 double; $140–$165 Regency Club rooms. Fri–Sat, $59 single or double; $84 Regency Club rooms. AE, MC, V. **Parking:** Free.
Located in the heart of the Denver Tech Center, the Hyatt Regency's attractive rooms and suites, in wings off the 11-story atrium lobby,

exemplify the quality expected from this luxury chain. The rooms, decorated in bright colors, have a Southwestern flair. The executive king rooms are a bit larger than the regular ones.

Dining/Entertainment: Centennial, the rooftop restaurant, serves continental fare. The Café, a casual restaurant in the atrium with an eclectic menu, is open for three meals daily. Garrity's is a lively sports bar.

Services: Room service, concierge floor, free valet parking, free shuttle within a 5-mile radius.

Facilities: Fitness center with an indoor pool, outdoor tennis court; bike rental during the summer.

LOEWS GIORGIO HOTEL, 4150 E. Mississippi Ave., Denver, CO 80222. Tel. 303/782-9300, or toll free 800/223-0607. Fax 303/758-6542. 179 rms, 18 suites. A/C MINIBAR TV TEL **Transportation:** Free shuttle to/from the airport.

$ Rates (including continental breakfast): $125 single or double; from $175 suite. Ask for corporate rates. AE, DC, DISC, MC, V. **Parking:** Free.

The Giorgio, located about 10 minutes southeast of downtown, has an Italian flair and a continental approach to hospitality. The striking public rooms are decorated in European antiques, and the guest rooms have an Italian decor with comfortable furniture and marble bathrooms. There's a lovely, quiet library on the main floor. Tuscany is an elegant four-diamond AAA-rated restaurant.

Dining/Entertainment: The Tuscany restaurant, featuring northern Italian cuisine, is popular with the city's affluent set. (The lunchtime pasta bar is popular with the business crowd.)

Services: Room service, free shuttle to/from the airport.

Facilities: Library on main floor, use of Cherry Creek Sporting Club, executive board room on the 10th floor.

SCANTICON, 200 Inverness Dr. W., Englewood, CO 80112. Tel. 303/799-5800, or toll free 800/346-4891. Fax 303/799-5874. 302 rms and suites. A/C MINIBAR TV TEL

$ Rates: $125 single; $135 double. Concierge floor, $139 single; $149 double. Weekends, from $69 single or double. AE, MC, V. **Parking:** Free.

At the Scanticon, there are 302 deluxe guest rooms and suites and a concierge floor off the dramatically designed, soaring wood-and-glass lobby, a PGA golf course on site, and indoor and outdoor pools. The Scanticon is in the Inverness Business Park at the south end of the Tech Center area.

Dining/Entertainment: There's elegant dining in the Black Swan restaurant, or more casual dining in the Garden Terrace restaurant, which features a weekend seafood buffet and a lavish Sunday brunch.

Services: Room service, turn-down service.

Facilities: On-site golf course with a pro shop in the lobby, indoor and outdoor swimming pools, tennis courts.

SHERATON, 4900 Denver Tech Center (DTC) Pkwy., Denver, CO 80237. Tel. 303/779-1100, or toll free 800/552-7030. Fax 303/779-1100 and ask for fax extension. 625 rms. A/C MINIBAR TV TEL

$ Rates: $107 single or double. Concierge level, $124 single or double. AE, DC, DISC, MC, V. **Parking:** Free.

Located in the Denver Tech Center area, just off I-25, this hotel offers some rooms overlooking a large indoor atrium (you can faintly hear some of the noise), with the rest in a connecting tower. The pleasant rooms around the atrium have a tiny table, a chair, and a sofa, while most of the rooms in the tower have desks. The Embassy Level is a concierge floor with upgraded amenities, including a full breakfast and cocktail hour.

Dining/Entertainment: The hotel has an excellent northern Italian restaurant, Compari's; a casual café; and a 24-hour deli.

Services: Room service.

Facilities: Health club with racquetball and handball courts.

MODERATE

CHERRY CREEK INN, 600 S. Colorado Blvd., Denver, CO 80222. Tel. 303/757-3341. Fax 303/756-6670. 323 rms. A/C TV TEL

$ Rates: Weekdays, $68 single or double; weekends, $55 single or double. AE, DC, DISC, MC, V. **Parking:** Free.

The Cherry Creek Inn is conveniently located in south-central Denver, 5 minutes from the Cherry Creek shopping area, 10 minutes from downtown, and 15 minutes from the airport. United Airlines books many of the rooms, long-term, for personnel staying in Denver temporarily. The rooms, decorated either with mint green and peach or with blue and beige decor, have queen-size beds and refrigerators. The restaurant, Maxie's, has a nice soup-and-sandwich bar at lunch (see Chapter 6, "Denver Dining," for a complete description). There's limited room service, an outdoor pool, and an exercise room. Guests may use Bally's Health Club next door.

DENVER TECH COURTYARD, 6565 S. Boston St., Englewood, CO 80111. Tel. 303/721-0300, or toll free 800/321-2211. Fax 303/721-0037. 154 rms. A/C TV TEL **Directions:** Exit I-25 east on Arapahoe Road.

$ Rates: Sun–Thurs, $69 single; $79 two or more people. Fri–Sat, $48–$58 per room. AE, DC, DISC, MC, V. **Parking:** Free.

This small hotel designed specifically for business travelers is located in a cluster of medium-priced lodges and restaurants. When Marriott decided to create a separate chain of small, moderately priced hotels for business travelers, market surveys of potential guests helped create a standard for such hotels around the country. The results show up here in rooms with such practical amenities as an extra-long telephone extension cord (so you can use the telephone at the large desk or while sitting on the couch), a remote-control television, and a faucet with boiling water and packets of instant coffee. Both the regular bedrooms and the one-bedroom suites have either a king-size bed or two double beds. The suites have mini-refrigerators. There's a restaurant serving breakfast only, a swimming pool, whirlpool, and exercise room.

DENVER SOUTH RESIDENCE INN, 6565 S. Yosemite St., Englewood, CO 80111. Tel. 303/740-7177, or toll free 800/331-3131. Fax 303/740-7177. 96 studios; 32 penthouses. A/C TV TEL **Directions:** Take the Arapahoe Road exit off I-25.

$ Rates (including breakfast and cocktails during the week): $103 studio for one or two; $130 penthouse suite. Ask about corporate and special rates. AE, DC, DISC, MC, V. **Parking:** Free.

Friendliness, along with lots of valuable suggestions, appear to be the official approach here. Guests stay in units that look more like private apartments than hotel rooms. A member of Marriott's Residence Inn chain, this inn offers studios and penthouses. In the studios the bed is set against the back wall and the front section of the room has a tiny living room area in front of a fireplace, plus a full kitchen. The two-story penthouse suites with vaulted ceilings have a sitting room (with a Murphy bed) on the main floor, which can be closed off by a curtain from the living room, kitchen, and bathroom. There's a second bedroom in an upstairs open loft and an upstairs bathroom at the top of the stairs. Amenities include limited free shuttle Monday through Friday to nearby business parks.

HAMPTON INN DENVER/AURORA, 1500 S. Abilene St., Aurora, CO 80012. Tel. 303/369-8400, or toll free 800/ HAMPTON. Fax 303/369-0324. 132 rms. A/C TV TEL **Directions:** Take the Mississippi Avenue exit (Exit 7) off I-225; the hotel is located on South Abilene Street between Mississippi and Iliff Avenues.

$ Rates (including continental breakfast and local phone calls): $49–$64 single; $57–$72 double. Children 18 and younger stay free in parents' room; the third and fourth adults in a room stay free. Ask about the special program for guests age 50 and older. AE, DC, DISC, MC, V. **Parking:** Free.

Hampton Inns are excellent buys in the moderate range for value-conscious travelers and business travelers on a strict expense account who want a conventional hotel. The rooms are comfortable and pleasantly furnished. Rooms with double and king-size beds, and with king-size bed and study rooms, which have a pull-out couch and desk, are available. Half the rooms are no-smoking.

There's another Hampton Inn located at 9231 E. Arapahoe Rd., Englewood, CO 80112 (tel. 303/232-4924), which also has a seasonal pool and offers a complimentary beer-and-wine cocktail hour.

BUDGET

MOTEL 6–DENVER SOUTH, 9201 E. Arapahoe Rd., Englewood, CO 80112. Tel. 303/790-8220. Fax 303/799-3405. 139 rms. A/C TV TEL **Directions:** Head east of Exit 197 off I-25.

$ Rates: $28.60 single. Additional person $6 extra. Children 17 and younger stay free in parents' room. AE, DC, DISC, MC, V. **Parking:** Free.

This Motel 6 has larger rooms than most in the chain. The comfortable guest rooms have two double beds or a queen-size bed and recliner chair or sofabed. There's a seasonal heated swimming pool.

TRAVELERS INN, 14200 E. Sixth Ave., Aurora, CO 80011. Tel. 303/366-7333, or toll free 800/633-8300. Fax 303/344-1536. 147 rms. A/C TV TEL **Directions:** Take the Sixth Avenue exit off I-225.

$ Rates: $25.95 single; $31.95 double. AE, DC, MC, V. **Parking:** Free.

This is a clean, economical hotel on the east side of the metropolitan area. Located 25 minutes from downtown, it has a pool and is near a Denny's restaurant.

5. BED & BREAKFASTS

If you are willing (and able) to pay more, you can find accommodations in rooms or suites in luxurious mansions, mini-castles, or historic homes with such amenities as outdoor hot tubs, pools, and tennis courts. In recent years, I've noticed many more working professionals choosing the B&B inns instead of hotels, especially women in town for extended business stays. In this type of accommodation, guests may visit with the hosts and other travelers in the public rooms over breakfast and in the evening instead of sitting in a hotel room or visiting bars and lounges alone.

In addition to the B&Bs I have listed below, **Bed & Breakfast Inns of Colorado,** 1102 W. Pikes Peak Ave., Colorado Springs, CO 80904 (tel. toll free 800/83-BOOKS), a referral and reservation service for B&Bs throughout Colorado, has listings ranging from ordinary private homes to mansions in Denver, the suburbs, and the nearby foothill communities.

CASTLE MARNE, 1572 Race St., Denver, CO 80206. Tel. 303/331-0621. Fax 303/331-0623. 9 rms (all with bath). A/C (Air-cooled), TEL

$ Rates (including gourmet continental breakfast): $70–$155 single; $80–$155 double. Additional person $10 extra. Corporate and long-term rates available. AE, DC, DISC, MC, V. **Parking:** Free.

This stunningly furnished lava-stone house was turned into a luxurious urban bed-and-breakfast inn about four years ago.

The owners, Diane and Jim Peiker, completely refurbished this mansion built with rectangular blocks of lava rock. The guest rooms are furnished with a combination of period antiques, family heirlooms, and carefully chosen reproductions. Cherry four-poster beds, original claw-foot tubs, queen-size brass beds, an armoire with French beveled-glass mirror, twin sleigh beds, and a Victorian writing desk are just a sampling of the surprises in these wonderfully decorated rooms. The two-room Presidential Suite has an alcove sitting area surrounded by windows, a king-size tester bed, and a solarium with a modern whirlpool bath. The corner Balcony Room, with its iron-and-brass bed, has a large but private stone balcony overlooking the residential area.

The public rooms are filled with furnishings one sees in house tours of late 19th-century homes—only here everything is used. Castle Marne, listed on the National Register of Historic Structures, is most famous for its Peacock Window, a 104-year-old circular stained-glass work of art on the landing between floors.

QUEEN ANNE INN, 2147 Tremont Place, Denver, CO 80205. Tel. 303/296-6666. Fax 303/296-2151. 10 rms (all with bath). A/C TEL

$ Rates (including continental breakfast): $75–$135 single or double. Corporate rates available. Children over 12 welcome. No pets. AE, DC, DISC, MC, V. **Parking:** Free.

A restored Victorian home at the edge of downtown in the Clements Historic District, on Tremont Place between 21st and 22nd Streets, this inn hosted by Tom King is popular with both corporate travelers and urban dwellers who want a "getaway" overnight. The Skyline Room, with its five windows opening on both city and mountain views, for example, has an antique brass queen-size bed and a carved-walnut love seat and armchair. The Garden Room has stained-glass windows, a brass bed, an antique walnut-and-ash armoire, and an antique walnut library table and armchair. Continental breakfast is served buffet style. Wine and tea are served every afternoon. No smoking is permitted inside the inn.

The owner is planning to open four new two-room suites, some with Jacuzzis, in an adjacent landmark Victorian home in 1993.

VICTORIA OAKS INN, 1575 Race St., Denver, CO 80206. Tel. 303/355-1818. 9 rms (1 with bath). TEL

$ Rates (including continental breakfast, laundry, and kitchen privileges): $39–$49 single without bath, $69 single with bath and fireplace; $49–$59 double without bath, $79 double with bath and fireplace. Ask about weekly rates. AE, DC, DISC, MC, V.
Parking: Free on the street.

The blond oak floors and trim, accented by green carpeting, create a very different feel in this bed-and-breakfast located one mile east of downtown Denver in a residential area across the street from Castle Marne. Run by Clyde Stephens and Richard Bowling, who spend many evenings visiting with their guests, the inn has individually decorated guest rooms with shared baths on the upper two floors. There's a lovely Victorian-era room with a fireplace and private bath on the main floor. The public rooms in this circa 1896 home are sparsely but attractively furnished, and have original tile fireplaces.

6. LONGER-TERM STAYS & CAMPING

APARTMENT RENTALS If you're going to stay for at least four nights and you'd like to settle in someplace that's more like home than a hotel room, **Metropolitan Suites,** 2000 S. Colorado Blvd., Denver, CO 80222 (tel. 303/759-8577), has one-, two-, and three-bedroom apartments in several locations around town. The agency manages comfortable to luxurious apartments at the Terrace at Cherry Creek at the Denver Tech Center, and the Highline Terrace at Hunters Run and the Atrium, both in southeastern Denver. Some buildings have health clubs and other athletic facilities. Rates run $45–$65 per night for a one-bedroom apartment, climbing up to $90–$105 per night for a three-bedroom. Free local telephone calls and daily or weekly maid service is included in the price, and a four-night minimum stay is required.

Many Mansions, 1313 Steele St., Denver, CO 80206 (tel. 303/355-1313, or toll free 800/225-7829 outside Colorado), is a building located 10 minutes from downtown filled with comfortable apartments for the traveler. Amenities include 24-hour message service, 24-hour security, daily maid service, and complimentary transportation to locations within 15 minutes of the hotel during early mornings and late afternoons. Rates (including full breakfast Monday through Friday and continental breakfast on Saturday and Sunday), for a one-bedroom are $90 single and $105 double; a two-bedroom apartment, triple occupancy, is $145. Ask about corporate rates.

As an alternative to a luxury hotel, some visitors choose **901 Penn House,** 901 Pennsylvania Ave., Denver, CO 80202 (tel. 303/831-8060). There are two apartments in this 1893 mansion set back from a quiet street by manicured lawns and an ornamental iron fence, which is a block from the Governor's Mansion and minutes from downtown. The five-room Quality Hill Suite has hints of 18th-century England in the 28-foot living room, two large bedrooms, and dining room. The three-room Tree Top Suite is a one-bedroom, 1,800-square-foot, third-floor flat with southwestern accents. Both units have full kitchens, stocked with breakfast ingredients and snacks. Included are daily linen and hand-laundry service, evening turn-down, and one-day valet. Guests gain access by key and use of a security code; parking is indoors. Prices are $335 for the Quality Hill Suite and $215 for the Tree Top Suite during peak periods, 15% less off-season (parts of September and October, and February through May).

RV PARKS & RESORT CABINS Those who travel in RVs and take their homes with them, needing only a suitable place to park and hook up to local services, as well as those who seek resort-cabin accommodations, will find several good choices in the Denver area.

The **Colorado Association of Campgrounds, Cabins & Lodges,** 5101 Pennsylvania Ave., Boulder, CO 80303 (tel. 303/499-9343), describes 249 commercial campgrounds (both KOAs and independents) and lists 1,702 cabins and lodge rooms for rent at more than 200 resorts throughout Colorado in its annual directory, including several ranches and campgrounds in the Denver environs. Write or phone for a free copy of their *Colorado Directory of Camping, RVs, Cabins, and Fun Things To Do* (allow three weeks for delivery; if you want it sent by first-class mail, send $2 for postage and handling). This is not a booking agency, so even though the directory has detailed information about each listing, you must contact the establishment directly for prices and reservations. Sites in RV parks cost $12–$20 per night, depending on the number of people, the length of your stay, and the amenities available. Hilton and Jenny Fitt-Peaster, who have been publishing the directory for 10 years, have visited most of the places listed and can be relied on to give valid comparisons.

DENVER DINING

Denverites like to eat well—whether it's chateaubriand, burgers, fajitas, or mesquite-grilled fish—and good restaurants abound. Most of the restaurants listed below have been around for at least a year, and many for much longer. The list is, quite frankly, a collection of perpetual winners in the local newspaper "favorite restaurant" contests, my favorites, choices from friends' lists, and a few that consistently win awards. I've categorized the restaurants by geographical area and then by price: for this edition, "Very Expensive" indicates that a meal will cost over $35; "Expensive," $20–$35; "Moderate," $10–$20; and "Budget," under $10.

Keep in mind that the restaurant sales tax is 7.9 percent. It's generally acceptable to tip 15 to 20 percent for good service; some restaurants automatically add a service charge for large dining groups.

Most Denver restaurants offer eclectic menus—a combination of American and continental fare, for example. So read beyond the "cuisine" label, especially in the "American" listings, for a broader understanding of the chefs' culinary efforts. You'll find a number of places that include a few southwestern or Tex-Mex dishes on their menus—cuisines that are popular here.

Even though Denver is far from either coast, there are several excellent seafood restaurants, and many places offer a "fresh catch of the day." Thanks to an excellent pipeline that brings in fresh fish from around the country, Denverites have come to expect high-quality fresh fish in both supermarkets and restaurants. However, if the menu doesn't specify "fresh" or "fresh frozen" (a technique for freezing fish on the boat, which many restaurateurs claim ensures freshness for fish that takes up to four days to get to your plate), always ask before you order.

Vietnamese and Thai food are very popular in Denver, thanks to an explosion of restaurants opened by refugees in recent years. Many are located in small shopping mall strips along Federal Boulevard, south of Alameda Avenue.

Another phenomenom has been the proliferation of espresso bars; the Mile High City is now vying for honors with Seattle for most espresso bars. Denver's coffee drinkers have been swinging by the Market on Larimer Square for years, but now there are dozens of other choices.

In recent years, as people have become more health conscious, the better restaurants in Denver (and not just the expensive ones) have cut back on the use of fats, replacing them with cholesterol-free oils, and now offer at least one or two Healthmark-rated dishes (dishes prepared in accordance with guidelines issued by Denver's Healthmark Institute for a low-fat, low-cholesterol meal).

Keep in mind that many fine restaurants change their menus several times a year, if not daily. Thus it is possible that some dishes described in this book might not be available when you visit; the prices listed for each restaurant were, however, accurate at press time.

1. DOWNTOWN

VERY EXPENSIVE

CLIFF YOUNG'S RESTAURANT, 700 E. 17th Ave. Tel. 303/831-8900.
   Cuisine: CUISINE COURANTE. **Reservations:** Recommended.
$ **Prices:** Appetizers $7.50–$12.50; main courses $18–$29. AE, DC, DISC, MC, V.
   Open: Lunch Mon–Fri 11:30am–2pm; dinner Sun–Thurs 5–10pm, Fri–Sat 5–11pm.

Cliff Young's has sent a steady stream of satisfied diners out the door for years. The simple decor and contemporary art on the walls form a backdrop to the beautifully presented and formally served regional American cuisine. The menu changes seasonally, and is likely to include such entrees as pan-roasted venison chop with ragoût of fresh plums or pan-roasted quail with cabernet and soy glaze, peach chutney, foie gras, and puff pastry. The restaurant's trademark is its Colorado rack of lamb roasted with apricot mustard and brioche crust. The wine list contains more than 300 selections, 100 of them by the taste.

EUROPEAN CAFE, 1515 Market St. Tel. 303/825-6555.
   Cuisine: FRENCH/AMERICAN. **Reservations:** Recommended.
$ **Prices:** Appetizers $6.95–$8.95; main courses $12.95–$22.95; lunch $6–$10. AE, DC, DISC, MC, V.
   Open: Lunch Mon–Fri 11am–2pm; dinner Sun–Thurs 5:30–10pm, Fri–Sat 5–11pm.

The European Cafe is located in a renovated brick warehouse in lower downtown, where tables are spread over three floors filled with antique carved-oak paneling transported from Lloyds of London. The owner/chef, Radek Cerny, creates an imaginative variety of dishes, using herb-infused oils and vegetable purées to create lighter fare with exquisite tastes. For example, he creates dishes such as veal au citron, filet mignottee "monsieur Louis" (a filet of beef tenderloin sautéed with Madagascar pepper and topped with a sauce with Hennesey brandy), and pasta served with fresh salmon, cream, and chives.

EXPENSIVE

AL FRESCO, 1523 Market St. Tel. 303/534-0404.
   Cuisine: NORTHERN ITALIAN. **Reservations:** Recommended.
$ **Prices:** Appetizers $4.95–$6.95; main courses $9.95–$15.95. AE, DC, DISC, MC, V.
   Open: Lunch Mon–Fri 11:30am–2pm; dinner Mon–Thurs 5:30–10pm, Fri–Sat 5–11pm.

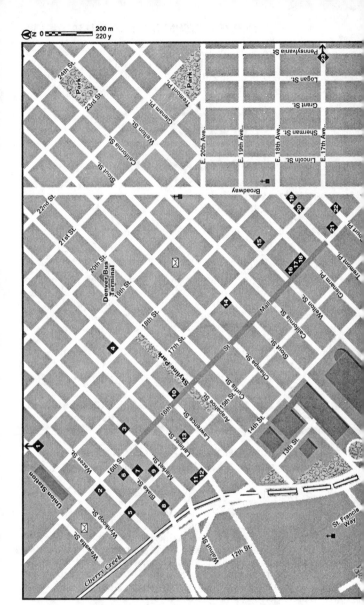

Al Fresco is popular for fast service before a play or after an early concert for a delicious and light—but filling—dish of pasta, an entree, or a pizza. In the northern Italian style, the chef uses less tomato sauce and more olive oil and garlic in the pasta dishes. The menu lists a variety of oven-roasted and wood-grilled seafood and meat. Ask about the express lunch. Al Fresco is in the same renovated brick warehouse that houses European Cafe and is under the same management. Booths line the narrow mezzanine which overlooks the

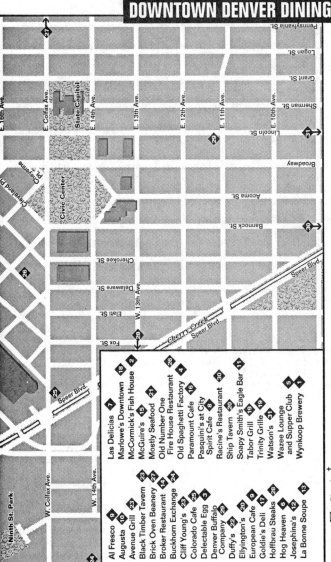

Las Delicias 7
Marlowe's Downtown 18
McCormick's Fish House 2
McGuire's 15
Mostly Seafood 1
Old Number One
Fire House Restaurant 4
Old Spaghetti Factory 16
Paramount Cafe 8
Pasquini's at City
Spirit Cafe
Racine's Restaurant 30
Ship Tavern 20
Soapy Smith's Eagle Bar 11
Tabor Grill 19
Trinity Grille 31
Watson's
Wazee Lounge
and Supper Club 5
Wynkoop Brewery 1

Al Fresco 9
Augusta 10
Avenue Grill 22
Black Timber Tavern 23
Brick Oven Beanery 27
Broker Restaurant 14
Buckhorn Exchange 24
Cliff Young's 25
Colorado Cafe 21
Delectable Egg 3
Denver Buffalo
Company 29
Duffy's 20
Ellyington's 9
European Cafe 17
Goldie's Deli 28
Hoffbrau Steaks 6
Hog Heaven 12
Josephina's
La Bonne Soupe 13

Post Office ✚ Church ⊠

massive pizza and calzone oven that stretches up one wall, as well as the second and third floors of this narrow Baltimore-style row building. The decor is casually elegant, more akin to New York chic than Denver casual, making this place a popular choice for the sophisticated set. The smell of warm pizza puts your tastebuds into gear, and the five booths opposite the wood-burning pizza oven stay open from lunch through dinner so guests can order selected pastas and pizzas.

THE BROKER RESTAURANT, 821 17th St. Tel. 303/292-5065.

Cuisine: AMERICAN. **Reservations:** Recommended.

$ **Prices:** Appetizers $3–$6; main courses $18–$30. AE, DC, DISC, MC, V.

Open: Lunch Mon–Fri 11am–2:30pm; dinner Sun–Thurs 5–10pm, Fri–Sat 5–10:30pm.

Every meal begins with a generous bowl of peel-and-eat shrimp at the Broker, located on the lower floor of the Women's Bank building, built at the turn of the century. One room is a converted bank vault, and all dining areas are furnished with dark woods and solid furniture for an elegant look. The menu features well-prepared conventional choices, including steaks, lobster, veal, lamb, and Rocky Mountain trout amandine. In addition to the shrimp, dinners include soup, salad, and dessert. If you drive, use the valet-parking service after 6pm, because parking can be a problem in that area.

BUCKHORN EXCHANGE, 1000 Osage St. Tel. 303/534-9505.

Cuisine: AMERICAN/WESTERN. **Reservations:** Recommended.

$ **Prices:** Main courses $16–$29; lunch $4.95–$12.50. AE, DC, DISC, MC, V.

Open: Lunch Mon–Fri 11am–3pm; dinner Mon–Thurs 5–10:30pm, Fri–Sat 5–11pm, Sun 5–10pm.

For a quick immersion in the Wild West, head for the Buckhorn Exchange. This saloon—which obtained Denver's first liquor license—opened in 1893 alongside the railroad tracks. The founder, Henry H. Zeitz, was a member of Buffalo Bill's band of scouts and was nicknamed "Shorty Scout" by Chief Sitting Bull. The original clientele—cowboys packing six-guns, silver barons, shifty-eyed roustabouts, and con men—are long gone, but reminders of that era adorn the walls. Although the western dishes are the big lure, every first-time diner prowls around the rooms to study the Zietz collection of Native American and Old West memorabilia and hunting trophies that crowd the walls. Start with a drink in the comfortable upstairs Victorian lounge with its 120-year-old hand-carved oak bar. Many of the tables in the main dining room, surrounded by bentwood chairs, are old poker tables from Germany. The decorative metal ceiling is a wonderful example of its kind. If you're in town around February 26, stop by for the annual Buffalo Bill birthday bash featuring look-alikes of the showman, held during the closest weekend.

For lunch, the bean soup is popular, and you can even get a sarsaparilla with your pot roast, huge sandwich, or salad at lunch. At dinnertime, try a slab of buffalo or a T-bone; light eaters might prefer the pheasant or Rocky Mountain trout. Entrees include soup, salad, and potato.

DENVER BUFFALO COMPANY, 1109 Lincoln St. Tel. 303/832-0880.

Cuisine: AMERICAN/WESTERN. **Reservations:** Not required.

$ **Prices:** Appetizers $4.95–$6.95; main courses $11.95–$28.95; lunch $5.95–$10.95. AE, DC, DISC, MC, V.

Open: Lunch Mon–Fri 11am–2pm; (limited lunch menu in the saloon on Sat); dinner Mon–Sat 5–10pm.

As much an experience as a place to eat, the Denver Buffalo Company houses a restaurant, a saloon, a deli and a market (selling buffalo meat and jerky, plus deli sandwiches and espresso), as well as a trading post and an art gallery. Native American beaded dresses, traditional masks, a massive stuffed buffalo, and other western memorabilia are part of the decor. Country bands are featured on weekends. You can mail-order buffalo products (call toll free 800/BUY-BUFF outside Colorado).

And the food, by the way, is excellent. Try the trio of buffalo sausages for an appetizer; each one has a distinctive taste. Stir-fry assumes a novel taste, with its lean buffalo, fresh vegetables, and spicy black-bean sauce. Other choices include buffalo ribs and buffalo steak; Santa Fe chicken and almond fried shrimp are available for those not up for buffalo.

MARLOWE'S DOWNTOWN, 511 16th St. Tel. 303/595-3700.

Cuisine: AMERICAN. **Reservations:** Recommended.

$ Prices: Appetizers $3.50–$6.95; main courses $7.25–$19; lunch $6.95–$10.95. AE, DC, MC, V.

Open: Mon–Thurs 11am–11pm, Fri 11am–midnight, Sat 5pm–midnight.

This trendy saloon and eatery on the 16th Street Mall is filled with natural woods, brass rails, tables on balcony, and glass walls revealing the mall scene. When it's warm outside, doors are opened and tables are pulled out onto the mall. During pretheater hours the wood tables are filled with folks having a glass of wine prior to the opening curtain at the adjoining historic Paramount Theatre. The eclectic menu lists pasta platters, salads, soups, seafood, and beef.

MOSTLY SEAFOOD, 303 16th St. Tel. 303/892-5999.

Cuisine: SEAFOOD. **Reservations:** Recommended.

$ Prices: Appetizers $2.25–$5.95, main courses $4–$11 at lunch, $10–$17 at dinner. AE, DC, MC, V.

Open: Lunch Mon–Fri 11am–5pm; dinner Mon–Thurs 5–9pm, Fri–Sat 5–10pm.

At Mostly Seafood, located in the Republic Plaza on the 16th Street Mall, the menu changes daily to reflect the freshest of the catch flown in from both coasts and a few inland lakes. You can have your fish—ahi, salmon, snapper, catfish, or trout—grilled, blackened, steamed, or fried. A stew of the day is also offered. Appetizers include steamed New Zealand cockles and succulent green-lip mussels, Cajun-fried fish fingers, and seafood gazpacho soup. Daily specials always consist of a pasta, a stir-fry, and a fried fish. At lunchtime, appetizers average $4–$5 and entrees cost $6–$12. Desserts such as key lime pie, chocolate bread pudding, and carrot cake go for $3.

MODERATE

DUFFY'S, 1635 Court Place. Tel. 303/534-4935.

Cuisine: AMERICAN. **Reservations:** Not required.

$ Prices: Breakfast $3.50–$4.50; lunch $2.80–$4.55; dinner $4.55–$10.95. AE, MC, V.

Open: Mon–Fri 7am–2am, Sat 8am–2am, Sun 11am–2am.

Even if you don't have a trace of Irish in you, you'll enjoy this lively spot in the heart of downtown for a casual meal. Burgers, Braunschweiger, steaks, Healthmark salads and fish dishes, chili, and, of course, corned beef and cabbage are staples of the menu.

HOFFBRAU STEAKS, 1301 Santa Fe St., at 13th Ave. Tel. 303/629-1778.

Cuisine: AMERICAN. **Reservations:** Not required.
$ Prices: Appetizers $2–$5.25; main courses $5–$14. AE, MC, V.
Open: Mon–Sat 11am–11pm, Sun 3–11pm.

The Hoffbrau delivers tender, aged, juicy steaks for surprisingly low prices. The expansive menu at this casual restaurant also includes burgers and sandwiches.

IMPERIAL, 1 Broadway. Tel. 303/698-2800.

Cuisine: CHINESE. **Reservations:** Recommended.
$ Prices: Appetizers $1.50–$6.95; main courses $7.95–$14.95; Imperial dinner $14.95–$25; lunch $6. AE, DC, MC, V.
Open: Mon–Thurs 11am–10pm, Fri 11am–10:30pm, Sat noon–10:30pm, Sun 4–10pm.

My tastebuds believe that there's no better Chinese restaurant in Denver than the Imperial. It offers both classic and innovative Szechuan, Mandarin, and Cantonese dishes. You can argue about the best dishes, but my meals always seem to start with cold noodles with a wonderful hot chili-sesame sauce. You might also fight over the last drop of hot-and-sour soup. My favorite choices: seafood bird's nest, with its collection of fresh seafood and vegetables sautéed in a wine sauce; sesame chicken; and sweet-and-sour pork (the Imperial bags the pork and sauce in two separate containers for take-out, so the meat doesn't get soggy). If you're feeling adventurous, try Johnny's seafood gumbo, a delicious Chinese version of the Cajun-spiced dish. Other specialties include Dungeness crab stir-fried with scallions and ginger, Peking duck, sea bass, and tea-smoked duck. The Imperial dinner is a delectable soup-to-dessert collection of Chinese dishes.

JOSEPHINA'S, 1433 Larimer St. Tel. 303/623-0166.

Cuisine: ITALIAN. **Reservations:** Recommended.
$ Prices: Appetizers $2.25–$9.95; main courses $8.95–$18.95; lunch $6–$9. AE, DC, DISC, MC, V.
Open: Sun–Thurs 11am–10:30pm (pizza served until 11pm), Fri–Sat 11am–11:30pm (pizza served until midnight).

At Josephina's the tables are packed with people who enjoy dining on good food in a casual atmosphere. You can get gourmet pizzas and well-prepared northern Italian fare. Sharing an antipasto salad, with its blend of tastes, is a great way to start your meal, but don't forget to order the mouth-watering garlic bread with mozzarella cheese. You might also try toasted ravioli, fried calamari, or the pesto—tomato-basil fettuccine with pesto-cream sauce. Entrees range from pizza to chicken Cinzano (marinated in olive oil and spices and sautéed with vermouth). Dinner entrees come with soup or salad and fresh bread. Josephina's, located in a historic brick-walled Victorian-era building in Larimer Square, is filled with antiques and rich woods. At night, you may have to fight your way through the lively bar crowd to reach the dining area. At lunchtime, meals are less, but soup or salad is not included.

There's another branch on 17th Avenue (see "North Denver," below).

LA BONNE SOUPE, 1512 Larimer St., in Writer Sq. Tel. 303/595-9169.
   Cuisine: FRENCH. **Reservations:** Not required.
$ **Prices:** Appetizers $3–$5; main courses $7–$18; lunch $6–$7.50. AE, DC, MC, V.
   Open: Mon–Thurs 11am–10pm, Fri–Sat 11am–11pm, Sun noon–8pm.

A French bistro set in the heart of the American West, La Bonne Soupe is run by Shep Brown, who grew up in Paris. Typical offerings are escargots baked in butter, white wine, and garlic, and assorted pâtés and fondues. On a nice day, it's fun to people-watch on the patio while enjoying a glass of wine.

PARAMOUNT CAFE, 511 16th St. Tel. 303/893-2000.
   Cuisine: AMERICAN. **Reservations:** Recommended.
$ **Prices:** Appetizers $1.95–$4.95; main courses $3.95–$9.95. AE, DC, MC, V.
   Open: Mon–Sat 11am–midnight.

At this restaurant in the restored lobby of the historic Paramount Theatre, on the 16th Street Mall, the clientele is usually a mix of casually dressed locals, young adults, tourists, and conventioneers. The original decor, with handcrafted giltwork on the walls and a terazzo tile floor, is typical of so many movie theaters of the 1940s and '50s. The history of Paramount Pictures is displayed on the walls in movie stills and pages of print. The music is always loud, but that doesn't seem to bother the diners working on baby back ribs, roasted chicken, Tex-Mex dishes, buffalo burgers, salads, and sandwiches. You can wash your food down with an all-American malt or milkshake and then indulge in Sweetie (the ice cream pie). There's lots of action around the big, black Linoleum-top bar after working hours. For children 12 and younger, there's a kiddie menu.

RACINE'S RESTAURANT, 850 Bannock St. Tel. 303/595-0418.
   Cuisine: ECLECTIC. **Reservations:** Recommended for parties of seven or more.
$ **Prices:** Appetizers $3–$7; main courses $5.75–$9.95. AE, DC, DISC, MC, V.
   Open: Mon–Fri 7am–midnight, Sat 8am–midnight, Sun 8am–11pm.

This is one of those comfortable-but-noisy, perpetually popular places, especially so at lunchtime and after the theater. (In recent years it has also become a hotspot for "business breakfasts.") The chef puts an imaginative twist on most dishes. For example, sandwiches include smoked gouda cheese and turkey, tuna and Swiss cheese grilled on sourdough bread, and New York strip steak with boursin cheese on French bread. Pastas range from ziti and vegetables to linguine romano to chicken Alfredo. The menu also lists Mexican dishes plus the likes of rosemary chicken breast and scallops San Felipe served with black beans. It's a pleasant stop at the end of an evening out for cappuccino and the chocolate-mousse torte—so rich it's hard to finish—or one of Racine's giant chocolate brownies. (How about a German chocolate, peanut butter, or white-chocolate raspberry brownie?) Sandwiches average $5.75, pastas cost $6.95–$11, Mexican fare is $5.95–$7.95, and desserts are $1.95–$2.95. The menu includes an unusual breakfast salad.

SOAPY SMITH'S EAGLE BAR, 1317 14th St. Tel. 303/534-1111.

Cuisine: AMERICAN. **Reservations:** Required for large parties.

$ Prices: Appetizers $1–$7.50; main courses $4.95–$14.95; lunch $4.95–$6.95. MC, V.

Open: Mon–Sat 11am–2am, Sun 1pm–2am (burgers and appetizers only after 10pm).

The crowd is often loud but always friendly at Soapy Smith's, named after a con man who fleeced miners in the 1880s. This historic three-story saloon, located at one end of Larimer Square, is equally popular with tourists, businesspeople, and families. After you order, you'll want to saunter around the building to see the photos of Soapy Smith, old Denver, and mining towns hanging on the brick walls with intricately carved wood paneling. The dinner menu lists burgers, chicken, Mexican dishes, and steak; at lunch, you'll find burritos, salads, green chili, and burgers. A band plays on weekends and the pool hall is packed.

THE TRANSALPIN, 416 E. Seventh Ave., between Logan and Pennsylvania Sts. Tel. 303/830-8282.

Cuisine: ECLECTIC. **Reservations:** Recommended.

$ Prices: Lunch grills and main courses average $6; dinner $8–$12. MC, V.

Open: Lunch Mon–Fri 11:30am–2pm; dinner Mon–Sat 5–10pm, Sun 5–9pm.

The TransAlpin, located behind the governor's residence, features dishes from many countries. The menu changes with the seasons. At press time, for example, it included a curry-and-ginger stir-fry with chicken from Sri Lanka, clams and spinach fettuccine with a Puttonesca sauce from Sicily, and blackened Pacific snapper with a ginger-cilantro pesto from Hawaii. The decor is simple but attractive, and the staff friendly and helpful in describing the different dishes. Wine specials, many offered by the glass, are chosen to complement various entrees.

TRINITY GRILLE, 1801 Broadway. Tel. 303/293-2288.

Cuisine: AMERICAN. **Reservations:** Accepted for dinner only.

$ Prices: Appetizers $4.50–$7.95; main courses $10.95–$22.95; sandwiches $6.50–$12. AE, DC, MC, V.

Open: Lunch Mon–Fri 11am–2:30pm; limited menu Mon–Fri 2:30–5:30pm; dinner Mon–Thurs 5:30–10:30pm, Fri–Sat 5:30–11pm.

Sparsely decorated, the Trinity Grille attracts the business crowd from the surrounding high-rises. You can order anything from tuna salad to blackened prime rib or veal chops off the menu, where most choices are prepared without lots of fancy sauces. Try the steakburger with cheese or grilled onions, or the large center-cut veal chop with rosemary-and-sage butter.

WAZEE LOUNGE AND SUPPER CLUB, 1600 15th St. and Wazee St. Tel. 303/623-9518.

Cuisine: AMERICAN. **Reservations:** Not required.

$ Prices: Sandwiches $3.10–$5.65; pizzas $3.95–$16.95. MC, V.

Open: Mon–Sat 11am–1:30am.

This urban bar sits in a part of lower downtown that's less than fashionable, but locals keep coming. The black-and-white tile floor anchors Depression-era wainscoting and is illuminated by gas lights. The bleached mahogany burl bar is pure 1930s art deco. The pizzas are good, and the sandwiches range from buffalo burgers to stromboli to Philadelphia cheesesteak.

WYNKOOP BREWING COMPANY, 1624 18th St. Tel. 303/297-2700.

Cuisine: PUB FARE. **Reservations:** Accepted only for parties of six or more.

$ Prices: Appetizers $2.25–$5; main courses $8.95–$13.95. AE, MC, V.

Open: Lunch Mon–Sat 11am–3pm; dinner Sun–Thurs 5–10pm, Fri–Sat 5–11pm; brunch Sun 11am–2pm.

You don't have to be a beer lover to like the food at Denver's oldest microbrewery, although many of the moderately priced dishes include beer as a seasoning. This working brewery, with pressed-tin ceilings, ancient maple floors, and oak paneling is located in the renovated 1898 J. S. Brown Mercantile Building. The Wynkoop offers pub favorites—bangers and mash (sausage fitted with breadcrumbs) and shepherd's pie—anytime. At lunchtime you can also get salads and sandwiches. Try the Gorgonzola ale soup, a delicious beer-cheese soup with a pungent flavor that's a bit spicier than most cheese soups. The pub favorites and other lunch dishes average $5. At dinnertime you can order off either the lighter menu or the dinner menu, which lists trout, salmon, beef, and chicken. There's also a limited late-night menu. If you're a beer drinker, order a taster set: six four-ounce glasses of different brews for $4.25. This noisy but attractive brewery always has six beers on tap. Plan lunch here on Saturday; then take a brewery tour offered between 1 and 5pm. There's a first-rate pool hall on the second floor with billiards, snooker shuffleboard, and darts.

BUDGET

BAYOU BOB'S, 524 17th St. Tel. 303/573-6828.

Cuisine: CAJUN. **Reservations:** Not accepted.

$ Prices: Po-Boys (subs) $4.35–$7.80; main courses $3.80–$8.25.

Open: Mon–Sat 11am–10pm.

New Orleans's transplants eat here, where jambalaya, fried catfish, and shrimp étoufée are served up. Authentic Cajun cooking at its best.

BLUE BONNET LOUNGE, 457 S. Broadway. Tel. 303/778-0147.

Cuisine: MEXICAN. **Reservations:** Accepted only for parties of six or more.

$ Prices: Appetizers $3.25–$5; main courses $3.95–$5.75. No credit cards.

Open: Summer, Mon–Sat 11am–11pm. Winter, Mon–Thurs 11am–10pm, Fri–Sat 11am–11pm.

Just south of downtown, the Blue Bonnet is a small, noisy Mexican restaurant where one wall is papered with newspaper clippings of rave reviews and awards for the food and the margaritas. You can get enchiladas, tacos, tostadas, rellenos, burritos, steaks, and combination platters.

BREWERY BAR II, 150 Kalmath St. Tel. 303/893-0971.
Cuisine: MEXICAN. **Reservations:** Not accepted.
$ Prices: Appetizers $1.50–$3.75; main courses $4–$5. No credit cards.
Open: Mon–Thurs 11:30am–7:45pm, Fri 11:30am–8:45pm, Sat 11:30am–4:40pm.

Plan on arriving before 11:45am if you want to beat the lunchtime crowd that packs this Mexican restaurant. Nothing fancy here, just basic fare from knock-'em-dead chili rellenos to a variety of burritos and enchiladas, and some basic sandwiches, at great prices.

GOLDIE'S DELI, 511 16th St. Tel. 303/623-6007.
Cuisine: DELI. **Reservations:** Not accepted.
$ Prices: Main courses $3–$6. AE, DC, MC, V.
Open: Mon–Sat 11am–4pm.

If you're running around downtown Denver and want to grab a fast, tasty sandwich, this is the place to stop. The behind-the-counter staff is efficient, so you shouldn't have to wait too long, even if the line is out the door. You can order a full or half hot pastrami on rye, or a corned beef sandwich with cole slaw and Swiss cheese at the counter. Or just ask the staff to put together a sandwich of any deli fixings you can name, because they're sure to be available at this New York–style Jewish deli. This is also my favorite downtown frozen yogurt stop.

HOG HEAVEN, 1525 Blake St. Tel. 303/572-7828.
Cuisine: AMERICAN. **Reservations:** Accepted only for parties of eight or more.
$ Prices: Appetizers $3.95–$9.95; main courses $4.60–$15.95. AE, MC, V.
Open: Mon–Thurs 11am–11pm, Fri–Sat 11am–midnight (lounge open later on weekends).

Stuffed pigs, pictures of pigs, faces of pigs in the burnished-steel restaurant-front, and "pig" sandwiches. Get the "pig"ture?! Burgers and sandwiches, rib and chicken combos, smoked sausage links, southern fried chicken, and more are available. At least stop by for a drink just to see this place.

LAS DELICIAS, 1530 Blake St. Tel. 303/629-5051.
Cuisine: MEXICAN. **Reservations:** Not accepted.
$ Prices: Appetizers 60¢–$3.75; main courses $1.50–$7. MC, V.
Open: Mon–Fri 7am–9pm, Sat 8am–9pm, Sun 9am–9pm.

People who really know good Mexican cooking come to Las Delicias for authentic Mexican dishes. The menu includes tamales, burritos, enchiladas, tacos, combination platters, carne adobada, and carnitas estilo Michoacán (pork marinated in a special sauce).

NEWSSTAND CAFE, 630 E. Sixth Ave., at Washington St. Tel. 303/777-6060.
Cuisine: DELI. **Reservations:** Not accepted.
$ Prices: 75¢–$5.95. MC, V.
Open: Sun–Thurs 7am–10pm, Fri–Sat 7am–midnight.

Readers of *Westword*, a popular free weekly, called the Newsstand the best hangout for middle-aged folks who want to read periodicals and hometown newspapers while munching on a bagel or a pastry and sipping a cappuccino. Two potato knishes or a bagel and lox will make a full meal for some folks, but the café also has soups and deli sandwiches. Get a cup of plain coffee (50¢) and start reading. The café stocks 1,100 magazines and newspapers, and books on tape.

OLD NUMBER ONE FIRE HOUSE RESTAURANT, 1326 Tremont Place. Tel. 303/892-1436.

Cuisine: AMERICAN. **Reservations:** Accepted only for large parties.

$ Prices: $3.75–$5. No credit cards.

Open: Lunch only, Mon–Fri 11am–2pm.

Survey old fire engines and other memorabilia from early fire-fighting days as you walk through the museum to reach the second-floor restaurant. Basic sandwiches and soup, an unlimited salad bar, and some Mexican dishes are the fare here.

OLD SPAGHETTI FACTORY, 1215 18th St., at Lawrence St. Tel. 303/295-1864.

Cuisine: ITALIAN. **Reservations:** Accepted only for lunch for parties of eight or more.

$ Prices: Main courses $4.50–$9.10. MC, V.

Open: Lunch Mon–Fri 11:30am–2pm; dinner Mon–Thurs 5–10pm, Fri–Sat 4:45–11pm, Sun 4–10pm.

You can get an inexpensive and tasty spaghetti dinner at the Old Spaghetti Factory, in the old Tramway Cable building with its 195-foot-high chimney. In addition to a plate of pasta, every meal comes with salad; fresh-baked bread and garlic butter; coffee, tea, or milk; and spumoni ice cream. But don't stagger out before eyeing the old-fashioned booths (if you're not in one), antiques, and memorabilia in and around the building.

PASQUINI'S AT CITY SPIRIT CAFE, 1434 Blake St. Tel. 303/575-0022.

Cuisine: PIZZA/HEALTH FOOD. **Reservations:** Accepted only for parties of six or more.

$ Prices: Appetizers $2–$5.50. MC, V.

Open: Mon–Thurs 11am–midnight, Fri–Sat 11am–2am.

This casually upbeat restaurant offers "urban fare," a collection of healthy and innovative, reasonably priced dishes, plus pizzas and calzones. You can get sandwiches, healthy dishes such as steamed vegetables and brown rice, and southwestern fare. The daily specials include imaginative items like mulligatawny soup, city pizza, and lamb pisole soup. There's usually chamber music in the background, and live jazz and blues bands play once a week. The café has nightly tarot card and palm reading.

WATSON'S, 900 Lincoln St. Tel. 303/837-1366.

Cuisine: AMERICAN. **Reservations:** Not accepted.

$ Prices: $1.75–$3. AE, MC, V.

Open: Mon–Thurs 8am–10pm, Fri 8am–midnight, Sat 10am–midnight, Sun noon–6pm.

Belly up to the soda bar and order a "black cow" (root beer), a "muddy river" (chocolate Coke), or an ice-cream float. This drugstore, a throwback in looks, style, and service to the old-fashioned drugstores, also serves hot dogs and sandwiches.

2. NORTH DENVER

In Denver, the line of restaurants strung along East 17th Avenue is called Restaurant Row. It stretches from just outside downtown eastward almost to Colorado Boulevard. Several restaurants "on the row" are listed here, as well as a variety of other dining experiences in the north, northeast, and northwest sectors of the city.

VERY EXPENSIVE

AIRPORT DENIM BROKER, 12100 E. 39th Ave., just off the Peoria St. exit of I-70. Tel. 303/371-6420.
  Cuisine: AMERICAN. **Reservations:** Recommended.
$ Prices: Main courses $16.95–$30.95. AE, DC, DISC, MC, V.
  Open: Lunch Mon–Fri 11am–2pm; dinner Mon–Sat 5–10pm, Sun 5–9pm.
At the Airport Broker, east of the airport, you'll begin your meal with an immense bowl of shrimp (included with all entrees) and move on to choices like steak, lobster, chicken Wellington, and Rocky Mountain trout amandine, with all dinners including soup, salad, vegetables, and dessert. It's a casual place with candles on the tables, stained-glass panels from Liverpool, England, and a 100-year-old bar from St. Louis.
    There's another restaurant of the same chain, the **Country Broker,** 10151 W. 26th Ave., at Kipling Street (tel. 303/232-3461). The lovely dining room in the Country Broker also has stained-glass windows, plus a brick fireplace and bookcase-lined walls.

TANTE LOUISE, 4900 E. Colfax Ave. Tel. 303/355-4488.
  Cuisine: CONTEMPORARY FRENCH. **Reservations:** Recommended.
$ Prices: Appetizers $4–$8.50; main courses $16.50–$24.95. AE, DC, DISC, MC, V.
  Open: Lunch Fri only, 11:30–2pm; dinner Mon–Sat 5:30–10pm.
Intimate dining in a renovated bungalow with glowing fireplaces, candlelit tables, and classical music in the background is the draw at Tante Louise. Chosen one of the city's best restaurants by many critics and magazines, including *Bon Appétit* and *Gourmet,* Tante Louise is the place for a special evening. The contemporary French menu changes seasonally and features locally grown products and scrumptious pastries. The wine list is extensive. Valet parking is available.

WUTHERING HEIGHTS DINNER HOUSE, 7785 W. Colfax Ave., a block west of Wadsworth Blvd. Tel. 303/238-7774.
  Cuisine: ECLECTIC. **Reservations:** Not required.
$ Prices: Complete dinners from $19.95. AE, CB, CH, DC, DISC, MC, V.
  Open: Dinner only, daily 4–9:30pm.

FROMMER'S SMART TRAVELER: RESTAURANTS

1. Visit the more expensive restaurants at lunchtime if you're on a moderate budget but want to sample some fine dining.
2. Some restaurants offer less expensive "early bird" dinners, if you're willing to eat an early-evening meal.
3. Some fine-dining restaurants offer chef's specials or fixed-price menus which may prove cheaper than ordering à la carte.
4. Denver's "brewpubs" offer excellent meals at surprisingly low prices.
5. Watch those appetizers, side dishes, and desserts; they always run up the bill.
6. You can make a meal off the laden tables at some happy hours!
7. Both young and old get price breaks at many restaurants in Denver. Always ask if there's a children's menu, and if there are discounts for senior citizens.

When you enter the waiting area at Wuthering Heights it's like walking into an old-fashioned parlor. Meals are served in several cozy rooms, many with fireplaces. The menu lists steak, prime rib, filet of beef Wellington, veal, and seafood dishes. Dinners include soup or salad, vegetables, dessert, coffee, and a cordial.

EXPENSIVE

MIKE BERARDI'S, 2115 E. 17th Ave. Tel. 303/399-8800.
   Cuisine: ITALIAN. **Reservations:** Not required.
$ Prices: Appetizers $2.50–$4.95; pastas $6.95–$10.95; main courses $7.95–$16.95. AE, MC, V.
   Open: Lunch daily 11:30am–2pm; dinner Sun–Thurs 5:30–10pm, Fri–Sat 5:30–11pm.

This small Italian eatery serves a variety of classic Italian dishes. The pastas are excellent and the sausage is outstanding. Pastas range from lasagna and pasta with simple marinara sauce to tagliatelli with prosciutto and peas sautéed with whole cream, or spaghetti with sautéed sea scallops with basil pesto. Many regulars seated in the 11 booths or at the wood tables in this simply decorated room come for the specials, which change nightly.

STRINGS, 1700 Humboldt St., at 17th Ave. Tel. 303/831-7310.
   Cuisine: ECLECTIC. **Reservations:** Recommended.
$ Prices: Appetizers $5.50–$8.25; main courses $11.25–$19.50; lunch $5.55–$10.50. AE, DC, MC, V.
   Open: Mon–Thurs 11am–11pm, Fri–Sat 11am–midnight, Sun 5–10pm.

Strings remains one of this city's most popular places. The food at this elegant restaurant is best described as contemporary cooking with a California-style focus on fresh pasta, mesquite-grilled seafood, and innovative appetizers.

MODERATE

AVENUE GRILL, 630 17th Ave., at Washington St. Tel. 303/861-2820.

Cuisine: AMERICAN. **Reservations:** Not required.

$ **Prices:** Appetizers $5.95–$6.95; main courses $6.95–$15.95. AE, CB, DC, MC, V.

Open: Mon–Thurs 11:30am–11pm, Fri 11am–midnight, Sun 5–10pm.

Set in an older brick building, the Avenue Grill seats its guests in a spacious dining room with a high ceiling, green pillars, and cream-colored walls. There's also a long wooden bar against one wall. Both down-home cooking and subtly sophisticated fare are served up, including chicken wings and carpaccio as appetizers, and half-pound burgers, broiled and marinated pork tenderloin sandwiches, blackened porterhouse pork chops, and linguine with clam sauce.

BEAU JO'S GREAT AMERICAN PIZZA, 7805 Wadsworth Blvd., Arvada. Tel. 303/420-8376.

Cuisine: PIZZA. **Reservations:** Not accepted.

$ **Prices:** Pizza $1.95–$25.19. AE, DISC, MC, V.

Open: Sun–Thurs 11am–9:30pm, Fri–Sat 11am–10:30pm.

For years, skiers stopped for mountain pies at the Beau Jo's in Idaho Springs on their way home from the slopes. Management finally got smart and opened several restaurants in the flatlands. Pizza is treated irreverently at these casual restaurants: You buy mountain pies by weight—one-, two-, three-, or five-pounders. You'll have to tell the waiter the type of bread you want (white, whole wheat, or sesame wheat) and the thickness, as well as the type of sauce, cheese, and ingredients you want on top. If you're too lazy to go through the ordering process, choose one of the house specialties, like the Conestoga, topped with Canadian bacon, zucchini, artichoke hearts, and fresh sliced tomatoes and baked with provolone cheese under a second crust. There are conventional "prairie pies" for the less adventurous. You can order a plate from the salad tub, with its good array of veggies, to eat with your pizza. Come early, as it can get busy during prime dinner hours, especially on weekends.

Beau Jo's has three other restaurants: at 2700 S. Colorado Blvd. (tel. 303/758-1519) in Denver, at 1517 Miner St. (tel. 303/573-6924 or 567-4376) in Idaho Springs, and at 1600 28th St. (tel. 303/444-5135) in Boulder.

BENNETT'S PIT BAR-B-QUE, 3700 Peoria St. Tel. 303/375-0339.

Cuisine: BARBECUE. **Reservations:** Not accepted.

$ **Prices:** Lunch $4.80–$7; dinner $7–$12. AE, CB, DC, DISC, MC, V.

Open: Sun–Thurs 11am–9:30pm, Fri–Sat 11am–10:30pm.

You won't be able to resist the beef or pork smothered in the smoky, pungent barbecue sauce at Bennett's Pit Bar-B-Que, located just south of I-70 off the Peoria Street exit. The beef and pork, basted and smoked over hickory logs for up to 14 hours, are so tender you can cut them with a fork. Barbecued pork, beef, chicken, sausage, and rib dinners come with garlic bread, coleslaw, and beans, fries, or baked potato. You can also order sandwiches, steaks, and salads.

There are three other restaurants around town, at 695 Kipling St.

(tel. 303/233-5516) in Lakewood, at 6730 S. Lima (303/799-6668) in Englewood, and at 7490 W. 52nd Ave. (tel. 303/424-0318), just north of I-70 off Wadsworth Boulevard. Bennett's also has stalls in the food courts at Tabor Center, Southwest Plaza, Cinderella City, and Villa Italia.

BLACK TIMBER TAVERN, 538 E. 17th Ave. Tel. 303/839-5390.

Cuisine: AMERICAN. **Reservations:** Not required.
$ **Prices:** Appetizers $4–$6; main courses $4.50–$13. AE, MC, V.
Open: Mon 11am–11pm, Tues–Thurs 11am–midnight, Fri–Sat 11am–2am.

Brick and wood walls, a ceiling-high rock fireplace, hardwood floors, and Native American rugs create a pleasant dining atmosphere. The casual fare includes smoked turkey or pastrami sandwiches, salads, burgers, and barbecued baby back ribs. Try the Jack Daniels chocolate pecan pie for dessert.

DARIO'S, 2011 E. 17th Ave. Tel. 303/333-5243.

Cuisine: SWISS/ITALIAN. **Reservations:** Recommended.
$ **Prices:** Appetizers $3–$5.50; main courses $6.25–$13.50; lunch $4.25–$6.50. MC, V.
Open: Lunch Mon–Sat 11am–2pm; dinner Sun–Thurs 5–9pm, Fri–Sat 5–10pm.

Don't expect to get a plate of spaghetti in a hurry—the chefs get upset if you ask them to rush the food, because it takes time to properly prepare dishes from scratch. The menu lists such classic Italian dishes as veal parmigiana, saltimbocca, and veal scaloppine. Consider starting your meal with an antipasto misto or carpaccio and following that with a tasty pasta marinara loaded with shrimp, scallops, and clams, and spiced with fresh herbs. Save room for chocolate cheesecake or tiramisu.

GOODFRIENDS, 3100 E. Colfax Ave., at St. Paul's St. Tel. 303/399-1751.

Cuisine: ECLECTIC. **Reservations:** Accepted, especially for parties of seven or more.
$ **Prices:** Main courses $5.95–$9.95. AE, DC, DISC, MC, V.
Open: Mon–Fri 11am–midnight, Sat 10am–midnight, Sun 10am–11pm; brunch Sun 9:30am–3pm.

Goodfriends is a comfortable place, perfect for those times when you just don't feel like cooking dinner. House specialties include spicy Aztec chicken, stir-fried chicken and vegetables, and English fish and chips. There are Mexican dishes, soups, salads, sandwiches, and burgers. The kitchen prepares stocks, soups, sauces, and salad dressings from scratch, and uses "pure" ingredients, including natural beef, grown on the hoof without hormones. Leave room for the mouth-watering chocolate amaretto pie, layers of dark and light chocolate laced with brandy and amaretto.

JOSÉ O'SHEA'S, 385 Union Blvd., Lakewood. Tel. 303/988-7333.

Cuisine: MEXICAN. **Reservations:** Accepted only for parties of eight or more.
$ **Prices:** Appetizers $3.95–$5.95; main courses $4.95–$8.25; lunch $3.95–$7.95. AE, DC, DISC, MC, V.
Open: Mon–Thurs 11am–11pm, Fri–Sat 11am–midnight, Sun 11am–10pm.

The servings are large and the food is tasty at José O'Shea's, a few blocks south of U.S. 6. There are small rooms and alcoves for dining on several levels of this colorful adobe building. The classic Mexican menu lists everything from burritos to fajitas.

JOSEPHINA'S, 1037 E. 17th Ave. Tel. 303/860-8011.
  Cuisine: ITALIAN. **Reservations:** Recommended.
$ Prices: Appetizers $3.50–$9.95; main courses $7.50–$17.95. AE, DC, MC, V.
  Open: Mon–Fri 11am–10pm, Sat–Sun 11am–11pm; brunch Sun 9am–3pm.

The tables fill up quickly at this casually elegant uptown restaurant. The light, airy space has lots of large windows and a greenhouse room with colorful blue and white accents, from the floor tiles to the painted walls. There's another branch downtown on Larimer Street; see "Downtown" above, for details on the menu offerings at both spots.

TRAIL DUST STEAK HOUSE, 9101 Benton St., Westminster. Tel. 303/427-1446.
  Cuisine: AMERICAN. **Reservations:** Accepted only for parties of seven or more.
$ Prices: Appetizers $2.50–$4.30; main courses $8–$12. AE, DISC, MC, V.
  Open: Dinner only, Mon–Thurs 5–11pm, Fri 5pm–midnight, Sat 4pm–midnight, Sun noon–10pm.

At this restaurant near the Westminster Mall, they'll cut off your necktie, tack it on the wall, and exchange it for a free drink. (You can take off the tie and stuff it in your pocket if it's a favorite one, but you won't get the drink.) The mesquite-grilled steaks (either beef or buffalo), served in 9- to 50-ounce portions, come with salad, country-style beans, and ranch bread. Ribs, chicken, chops, fish, and kid-size dishes are also available. On Wednesday, $9 buys all the top sirloin you can eat; on Sunday, all the ribs you can eat. The action on the dance floor is usually lively, with diners shuffling to country-music tunes played by a live band.

There's another Trail Dust Steak House (tel. 303/790-2420) in south Denver on South Clinton Street off the Arapahoe Street exit of I-25.

BUDGET

ACAPPELLA'S, 17th Ave. and Humboldt St. Tel. 303/832-1479.
  Cuisine: AMERICAN. **Reservations:** Not required.
$ Prices: Appetizers $2.25–$4; main courses $3.75–$8.50. MC, V.
  Open: Mon–Thurs 11am–10pm, Fri–Sat 11am–11pm (bar stays open later).

Acappella's is a very casual, noisy hangout, and the only place in town where acappella singers perform (call ahead for the schedule of live entertainment). You can get burgers, sandwiches, soup and salad, cheesesteaks, seafood baskets, pasta, hot dogs, and munchies here.

BAGEL DELI, 6217 E. 14th Ave., at Krameria St. Tel. 303/322-0350.

Cuisine: DELI. **Reservations:** Not required.
$ Prices: Main courses $4.95–$8.50; dinner platter $5.95–$8.95. MC, V.
Open: Daily 8am–8pm.

Corned beef on rye is the most ordinary deli sandwich available at the Bagel Delis. Pastrami, tongue, brisket of beef, and salami can all be stuffed into sandwiches with a smear of mustard, or you can have the staff mix a variety of deli meats, cheeses, and trimmings in any combination you desire. The menu lists traditional deli foods, including chopped liver, whitefish, and salmon salads, as well as potato latkes, knishes, and stuffed peppers.

BLACK-EYED PEA, 7095 W. 88th St., Westminster. Tel. 303/425-4442.

Cuisine: AMERICAN. **Reservations:** Not accepted.
$ Prices: Appetizers $2.65–$3.65; main courses $4–$10.95. AE, DC, MC, V.
Open: Daily 11am–10pm.

Black-Eyed Pea is a chain of family restaurants, where you can order thick, delightfully rich cheese-broccoli soup as well as burgers, chicken sandwiches, chicken-fried steak, mom's meatloaf, or juicy pot roast. The cobbler of the day is a delicious warm concoction of fruit and crust. Soup is $2.25 a bowl, sandwiches are $4–$4.95, entrees average $5.95, and all side dishes—including black-eyed peas—are $1.10. There's a separate children's menu.

There are eight Black-Eyed Peas spread around the Denver metropolitan region. All are casual restaurants with old frying pans, popcorn poppers, and other old items or antiques on the walls.

BRICK OVEN BEANERY, 1007 E. Colfax Ave. Tel. 303/860-0077.

Cuisine: AMERICAN. **Reservations:** Not accepted.
$ Prices: Appetizers $2.95–$3.25; main courses $3.95–$5.95. MC, V.
Open: Daily 11am–10pm.

Arguably the best fast-food place in town, where you get sit-down–quality meals going through a cafeteria line. The inside of the Beanery resembles the old places around Boston's wharves, but the soup is Louisiana Créole gumbo. Sandwiches are made to order with a choice of crusty French or natural-grain bread, half a chicken with sage-nut stuffing and other trimmings is only $5.95, and you can get wild-rice meatloaf. Dishes of pickles and hot peppers sit on the counter. Wash your food down with an old-fashioned malt or shake.

CASA BONITA, 6715 W. Colfax Ave. Tel. 303/232-5115.

Cuisine: MEXICAN. **Reservations:** Not accepted.
$ Prices: Main courses $5–$8.50; kids' meals $3; complete dinner less than $10. AE, MC, V.
Open: Sun–Thurs 11am–9:30pm, Fri–Sat 11am–10pm.

With divers leaping off a high platform into a tiny pool, roving bands, and mock gun fights, this is a great place to take the kids. At Casa Bonita, one of the most popular tourist attractions in the state, diners go through a cafeteria line to pick up the Mexican fare. The many dining rooms hold 1,100 people, as well as an arcade and two gift shops. If you're a hearty eater, try the all-you-can-eat combination plate ($8.30). Also, you might want to try the tasty sopaipillas, brought warm to your table.

DAVIES' CHUCK WAGON DINER, 9495 W. Colfax Ave. Tel. 303/237-5252.

Cuisine: AMERICAN. **Reservations:** Not accepted.

$ Prices: Breakfast/lunch $1.45–$4.45; dinner $2–$5. No credit cards.

Open: Daily 5:30am–9pm.

This fully equipped diner was hauled in from New Jersey in the mid-1950s and the cheerful waitresses have been serving the inexpensive food ever since. You can get stomach-filling breakfast specials all day, as well as sandwiches and pork chops, fried shrimp, and roast beef dinners with soup, salad, potatoes, and a roll. Prices range from $2 for breakfast specials to around $5–$6 for a complete dinner.

HOFFBRAU BAR AND GRILL, 7699 W. 88th Ave., at Wadsworth Blvd., Arvada. Tel. 303/422-7755.

Cuisine: AMERICAN. **Reservations:** Not required.

$ Prices: Appetizers $1.75–$5; main courses $4.65–$12.95. AE, MC, V.

Open: Sun–Thurs 11:30am–10pm, Fri–Sat 11:30am–11pm.

The Hoffbrau Bar and Grill is the epitome of the neighborhood tavern, with the television over the bar, a friendly bartender, and a reasonably priced menu. The steaks are aged, cut in-house, and grilled. You can also order salads, burgers, sandwiches, fajitas, and southern fried chicken.

JUANITA'S UPTOWN, 1700 Vine St., at 17th Ave. Tel. 303/333-9595.

Cuisine: MEXICAN. **Reservations:** Accepted only for large parties.

$ Prices: Appetizers $2.95–$5.95; main courses $5.95–$10.95. AE, MC, V.

Open: Sun–Thurs 11:30am–10pm, Fri–Sat 11:30am–11pm.

A vast wooden barn of a room usually filled with casually dressed folks at lunch and, later on, with the after-work crowd munching nachos and sipping beer or gorging on large plates of Mexican fare. Hang around for a game of pool in the popular back room.

LICKETY SPLIT ICE CREAM AND FROZEN YOGURT, 2039 E. 13th Ave., at Vine St. Tel. 303/321-1492.

Cuisine: DESSERT.

$ Prices: $1.50–$5.

Open: Daily 11am–11pm.

On a scorching-hot day, it's a worthwhile detour to get rich-tasting, all-natural ice cream or yogurt from here. They also have specialty coffee drinks and pastries at the espresso bar.

3. CHERRY CREEK

Some of the best and most popular restaurants are clustered in Cherry Creek North and Cherry Creek Mall. It's a wonderful area for browsing and window-shopping. Here are a few of the many good restaurants in this wealthy section of the city.

EXPENSIVE

BISTRO ADDIE BREWSTER, 250 Steele St. Tel. 303/388-1900.
   Cuisine: AMERICAN. **Reservations:** Recommended.
$ Prices: Appetizers $4.50–$7.25; main courses $5.75–$15.25.
   Open: Mon–Thurs 11:30am–10pm, Fri–Sat 11:30am–11pm.

Bistro Addie Brewster, a perennially popular restaurant in Cherry Creek North, serves fat burgers topped with caramelized onions (or chili aioli if you want) and such entrees as steak au poivre with four-peppercorn–brandy sauce. It's a prime spot to see a mix of locals, from ladies-who-lunch to businesspeople setting up deals. Soft lighting and a decor of textured mustard-colored walls, dark woods, and white tablecloths create a friendly background that combined with the high quality of the food ensures repeat business.

CACHE-CACHE, 265 Detroit St., Tel. 303/394-0044.
   Cuisine: FRENCH PROVINCIAL. **Reservations:** Recommended.
$ Prices: Appetizers $3.95–$5.95; main courses $9.95–$16.95; lunch $4.95–$8.95. AE, MC, V.
   Open: Lunch Mon–Sat 11:30am–2pm, Sun 11:30am–3:30am; dinner Sun–Thurs 5:30–10pm, Fri–Sat 5:30–10:30pm.

The focus is on dining in this quiet restaurant, a sister to the chic Cache-Cache in Aspen. The sophisticated menu includes appetizers such as wild-mushroom ragoût with phyllo layers and pastas like angel hair with basil, tomato fondue, chèvre, sun-dried tomatoes, and olives. Entrees range from duck confit with honey-lavender sauce to ribeye steak grilled with a burgundy sauce.

SFUZZI, 3000 E. 1st Ave., in Cherry Creek Mall. Tel. 303/321-4700.
   Cuisine: ITALIAN. **Reservations:** Recommended.
$ Prices: Appetizers $4.50–$6.75; main courses $9.25–$16.25; lunch $6.25–$10.75. AE, DC, MC, V.
   Open: Lunch Mon–Sat 11am–4pm; dinner Mon–Wed 5:30–11pm, Fri–Sat 5:30pm–midnight, Sun 5–10pm; brunch Sun 10:30am–3pm.

My personal favorite, this Italian bistro stays fashionable because of the unfailingly well prepared food and the lively atmosphere. It's not just for the trendy—it's for anyone who wants creative Italian cuisine in an attractive setting with brick walls and an open kitchen. The lounge area is always packed after working hours.

MODERATE

IT'S GREEK TO ME, 165 Steele St. Tel. 303/333-4553.
   Cuisine: GREEK. **Reservations:** Not required.
$ Prices: Appetizers $3–$4; main courses $5.95–$12.95. AE, MC, V.
   Open: Mon–Thurs 10:30am–11pm, Fri–Sat 11am–2am.

You can get hearty, reasonably priced meals, including many Greek dishes, at this family-run restaurant and bar in Cherry Creek North.

The Greek specialties include gyros, pasticcio, and moussaka, as well as grilled steaks and chops. The Greek sandwiches are served in fresh, warm pita bread with a side of delicious tzatziki (cucumber and garlic in sour cream) and good crispy fries. There's live music and dancing on Friday and Saturday nights.

SOREN'S, 315 Detroit St. Tel. 303/322-8155.
   Cuisine: CONTINENTAL. **Reservations:** Not required.
$ **Prices:** Appetizers $4.75–$5.50; main courses $9.75–$17.50; lunch sandwiches and entrees $6.25–$9.60. AE, DISC, MC, V.
   Open: Lunch Mon–Sat 11am–5pm; dinner Wed–Thurs 5–9:30pm, Fri–Sat 5–10pm; brunch Sun 10:30am–2:30pm.

Soren's is a pleasant place to eat, especially on the outdoor patio when the weather is nice. The food is an eclectic collection of dishes like cobb and duck salads, Maryland crabcakes, classic eggs Benedict, and chicken fettuccine at lunchtime. During the dinner hour, you'll find Black Angus New York steaks, lamb loin noisette, fresh grilled salmon, and cheese tortellini among the menu offerings. A classical guitarist plays on Friday and Saturday evenings and during Sunday brunch.

BUDGET

GOURMET ALTERNATIVE, 300 Fillmore St. Tel. 303/355-6137.
   Cuisine: SANDWICHES/PASTRIES. **Reservations:** Not accepted.
$ **Prices:** Sandwiches $4–$5; desserts $1–$3. MC, V.
   Open: Mon 7am–6pm, Tues–Thurs 7am–10pm, Fri–Sat 7am–midnight, Sun 9am–5pm.

You order at the counter and take your food to tables inside or outside this storefront restaurant which has a tasty variety of mouth-watering pastries and sandwiches made with tasty breads and better-than-average fillings.

4. SOUTH DENVER & THE TECH CENTER

South of the Cherry Creek area, you'll find many good restaurants along such main streets as Colorado Boulevard and farther south all the way to the business parks, including the Denver Tech area, and the Arapahoe Street exit of I-25 on the southeast end of the metropolitan area, and to the popular Southwest Mall on the southwestern edge.

VERY EXPENSIVE

CHATEAU PYRENEES, 6538 S. Yosemite Circle. Tel. 303/770-6660.
   Cuisine: FRENCH CONTINENTAL. **Reservations:** Recommended. **Directions:** Take the Arapahoe Road exit of I-25; Château Pyrenees is on the west side.
$ **Prices:** Appetizers $5.50–$11.50; main courses $12.75–

Ⓕ FROMMER'S COOL FOR KIDS: RESTAURANTS

Casa Bonita (see p. 85) Lots of action—from divers leaping off a high platform into a tiny pool to roving bands and mock gun fights—keeps kids entertained at this immensely popular Mexican cafeteria-style restaurant.

Red Robin (see p. 93) Children love the bottomless glasses of pop, the "rookie Magic" mocktails, and the video machines lining one wall.

The Brick Oven Beanery (see p. 85) The made-to-order sandwiches and blue-ribbon dinners make this cafeteria a great spot to take lively kids with picky appetites.

Buckhorn Exchange (see p. 72) Kids will love any place once frequented by cowboys, con men, and the one and only Buffalo Bill. The walls are crowded with Old West memorabilia and big-game hunting trophies. 1001 W. Hampden Ave., Englewood (tel. 303/761-8638).

$26.50; fixed-price five-course dinner $22–$49. AE, DC, DISC, MC, V.
Open: Lunch Mon–Fri 11:30am–2pm; dinner Mon–Sat 5:30–10pm.
Château Pyrenees strives to provide "total elegance," and they succeed, having won top awards for years. An evening here is always memorable for the service, the food, and the old-world ambience. Guests sit on plush banquettes or around beautifully set tables lit by glittering chandeliers listening to soft tunes played on a 120-year-old replica Louis XVI piano. The à la carte continental menu includes many classics, such as chateaubriand bouquetière, fresh salmon or swordfish, and rack of lamb provençal. Beluga molossal caviar is available.

EXPENSIVE

WELLSHIRE INN, 3333 S. Colorado Blvd., at Hampden Ave. Tel. 303/759-3333.
   Cuisine: ECLECTIC. **Reservations:** Recommended.
$ Prices: Appetizers $6.75–$10; main courses $14–$23.50; lunch $7–$11.75. AE, DC, MC, V.
   Open: Breakfast Mon–Fri 7–10am; lunch Mon–Sat 11:30am–2:30pm; dinner Mon–Sat 5:30–10pm, Sun 5:30–9pm; brunch Sun 10am–2pm.
At the Wellshire, reminiscent of an old Tudor inn, the service is excellent and the food is exceptional. The menu changes regularly, but at dinnertime there's always a range of artfully presented entrees, such as rack of Colorado lamb, charcoal-grilled swordfish, aged beef, and Wellshire chateaubriand. The luncheon menu's tasty dishes include orange-flavored roast chicken salad, maple-grilled duck breast, and a three-cheese burger. The chow chow (fresh vegetables

stir-fried with beef, pork, or chicken over pan-fried noodles) is perpetually popular. The chocolate torte and the black-bottom pie vie for top honors from chocoholics. The Wellshire Supper Club offers lighter fare from 4:30 to 6:30pm daily.

MODERATE

In the southeast sector of the city, you'll find a **Beau Jo's Great American Pizza** at 2700 S. Colorado Blvd. (tel. 303/758-1254), a **Bennett's Pit Bar-B-Que** at 11300 E. Arapahoe Rd. (tel. 303/799-6668), and a **Trail Dust Steak House** at 7107 S. Clinton St., off the Arapahoe Road exit of I-25 in Englewood (tel. 303/790-2420). For all of these chain restaurants, see the listings under "North Denver," above, for complete details.

BENNIGAN'S, 3601 S. Wadsworth Blvd., Lakewood. Tel. 303/969-9955.
  Cuisine: ECLECTIC. **Reservations:** Not required.
$ **Prices:** Appetizers $3.75–$5.65; main courses $4.75–$10.95. AE, DISC, MC, V.
  Open: Mon–Sat 11am–2am, Sun 10am–2am.
It's hard to go wrong at Bennigan's—they consistently deliver large plates of well-prepared, reasonably priced dishes. The quilting-bee menu starts with a "Great Beginnings" section listing fried cheese, peel-and-eat shrimp, and a dozen other choices, including Mexican munchies. The warm parmesan breadsticks smeared with garlic butter are scrumptious. Bennigan's offers regular and warm salads (like Oriental chicken salad), quiche, sandwiches, burgers, fried fish, chicken prepared several ways, pastas, Oriental dishes, steaks, and baby back ribs you'll gnaw on for the last taste. "Death by Chocolate" ($3.45) is the only way to end a meal. There's also a children's menu. These restaurants have a variety of $4.95 lunch specials on a separate menu, and an express lunch (served in 15 minutes or it's free). The decor is similar in these casual restaurants—dark woods, plants, tables on different levels wrapped around a big bar—and they're all popular after-work hangouts.

You'll find other southern locations for Bennigan's at 9281 E. Arapahoe Rd., Englewood (tel. 303/792-0280), two blocks east of I-25; 1699 S. Colorado Blvd., Glendale (tel. 303/753-0272); 13950 E. Mississippi Ave., Aurora (tel. 303/671-5040), one block east of I-225; and 2710 S. Havana St., just south of Iliff Avenue, Aurora (tel. 303/750-7822). There are locations up north at 7605 W. 88th Ave., Westminster (tel. 303/431-1696), and 7425 W. Alameda Ave., Lakewood (tel. 303/233-5090). Reservations policies and hours may vary.

COMPARI'S, in the Sheraton Denver Tech Center, 4900 Denver Tech Center (DTC) Pkwy. Tel. 303/779-8899.
  Cuisine: ITALIAN. **Reservations:** Recommended. **Directions:** Take the Belleview exit off I-25 to the Sheraton Denver Tech Center.
$ **Prices:** Appetizers $2.75–$7.95; main courses $10.25–$19. AE, DC, MC, V.
  Open: Lunch Mon–Fri 11:30am–2pm; dinner Sun–Thurs 6–10pm, Fri–Sat 6–11pm.
At Compari's, menu choices include a variety of imaginatively

prepared pasta, sausage, chicken, shrimp, and meat entrees, as well as fresh fish and such specialties as cioppino.

FRESH FISH CO., 7800 E. Hampden Ave. Tel. 303/740-9556.
Cuisine: SEAFOOD. **Reservations:** Sun–Mon not required, Tues–Sat accepted only for parties of five or more.
$ Prices: Appetizers $3.25–$12; main courses $12–$25. AE, DC, DISC, MC, V.
Open: Lunch Mon–Fri 11:30am–2:30pm; dinner Mon–Sat 5–11pm, Sun 5–10pm; brunch Sun 10am–2pm.

This place is usually busy after 6:30pm because of the variety of fresh fish available and the careful way it's cooked. Menus change daily at this restaurant in the Tiffany Plaza, and the choices usually include about 30 different types of seafood. There's a lobsterbake on Sunday nights.

H. BRINKER'S, 7209 S. Clinton St., Englewood. Tel. 303/792-0285.
Cuisine: AMERICAN. **Reservations:** Not required. **Directions:** Take the Arapahoe Road exit off I-25.
$ Prices: Appetizers $1.75–$6.25; main courses $7.95–$18; lunch $6.50–$10.95. AE, DC, DISC, MC, V.
Open: Lunch Mon–Fri 11am–4pm; luncheon buffet Mon–Fri 11am–1:30pm; dinner Mon–Sat 4–10pm; brunch Sun 9am–3pm.

The big windmill and the slowly revolving water wheel signify that you've found H. Brinkers. Although it specializes in mesquite-grilled steak, fresh fish, and prime rib, you can also get salads and sandwiches. For a fast lunch, try the $6.50 luncheon buffet from 11am to 1:30pm Monday through Friday. There's music in the piano bar Wednesday through Saturday evenings.

LAS BRISAS, 6787 S. Clinton St., Englewood. Tel. 303/792-3212.
Cuisine: SOUTHWESTERN. **Reservations:** Not required.
$ Prices: salads and main courses $6.50–$14.95. AE, MC, V.
Open: Lunch Mon–Sat 11am–4pm; dinner Mon–Thurs 4–10pm, Fri–Sat 4–10:30pm.

The dried peppers hanging from the ceiling and the cool white-and-blue interior hint at the style of food served: dishes from Mexico, South America, and Spain. Paella and a selection of fajitas and enchiladas are just a few of the southwestern and Spanish items on this menu. Many of the beef and seafood entrees also have southwestern flavorings, from tenderloin medallions in a delicate jalapeño-cream sauce to pollo con cilantro.

OFF BELLEVIEW GRILL, 8101 E. Belleview Ave., in Marina Sq. Tel. 303/694-3337.
Cuisine: ECLECTIC. **Reservations:** Not required.
$ Prices: Appetizers $5–$6; main courses $7–$15. AE, DC, DISC, MC, V.
Open: Mon–Thurs 11am–10pm, Fri 11am–11pm, Sat 5–11pm.

A trendy restaurant with a southwestern decor, the Off Belleview Grill specializes in spit-roasted chicken and duck, fresh fish, fresh pastas, and gourmet pizzas cooked in a wood-fired oven visible from the dining room.

PANDA CAFE, 1098 S. Federal Blvd. Tel. 303/936-2500.

Cuisine: CHINESE. **Reservations:** Not required.
$ Prices: Appetizers $2.40–$16. AE, DISC, MC, V.
Open: Sun–Thurs 11am–11pm, Fri–Sat 1–10:30pm.

⭐ Visitors walk past a brace of hanging, glistening barbecued ducks and a tank of live crabs to reach the dining area in this simply decorated restaurant that consistently gets raves for its superb Chinese fare. Local food critics praise the Cantonese-style seafood dishes. The Crystal prawns, sautéed with hints of ginger, scallions, and a dash of vinegar, are good, as is the house special lo mein. Vegetarians might want to try the deep-fried tofu, stuffed with shrimp and pork and covered with oyster sauce.

RED LOBSTER, 5656 S. Wadsworth Blvd., Littleton. Tel. 303/978-1416.
Cuisine: SEAFOOD. **Reservations:** Not accepted.
$ Prices: Appetizers $2.65–$5.65; main courses $8–$15.65. AE, DISC, MC, V.
Open: Sun–Thurs 11am–10pm, Fri–Sat 11am–11pm.

Red Lobster is a nationwide chain you can usually count on to provide fresh fish prepared in a variety of ways and, often, a fairly priced lobster in a town where it's usually out of sight. In addition to the regular menu, a list of fresh fish is written on a chalkboard. Most Red Lobsters in the Denver region are very popular, so expect to wait a bit (perhaps in the lounge) on weekend nights.

Red Lobster restaurants on the north and east sides of the city are at 1350 W. 104th Ave., Northglenn (tel. 303/457-9298), half a mile west of I-25; 4455 Wadsworth Blvd., Wheat Ridge (tel. 303/420-4210), half a mile south of I-70; 264 Union Blvd., Lakewood (tel. 303/987-3789), a few blocks south of Sixth Avenue; 10854 E. Alameda Ave., Aurora (tel. 303/343-6161), just east of the intersection of Havana St. and Alameda Ave.; and 9595 E. Arapahoe Rd., Englewood (tel. 303/790-7925), one mile east of I-25. Hours may vary.

BUDGET

In this area, you'll find branches of **Bagel Deli** at 6439 E. Hampden Ave. (tel. 303/756-6667). Also a **Hoffbrau Bar and Grill** at 3355 S. Wadsworth Blvd. (tel. 303/980-6200). For complete descriptions see "North, Northeast, and Northwest Denver," above.

COUNTY LINE BARBEQUE, 8351 Southpark Lane, off County Line Rd. Tel. 303/797-3727.
Cuisine: BARBECUE. **Reservations:** Accepted only for 10 or more.
$ Prices: Sandwiches $4.50–$6.95; main courses $7.45–$13.95. AE, DC, DISC, MC, V.
Open: Lunch Mon–Fri 11am–2pm, Sat–Sun 11am–4pm; dinner Mon–Thurs 5–9pm, Fri–Sat 5–10pm, Sun 4–9pm.

A casual place for barbecue that has been smoked-cooked for 18–20 hours before it gets to your plate. Pork, beef, and baby back ribs, as well as sausage, beef brisket, and sandwiches, are on the menu. It gets busy some nights, so expect to wait in the bar.

HEALTHY HABITS, 865 S. Colorado Blvd. Tel. 303/733-2105.
Cuisine: AMERICAN. **Reservations:** Not accepted.

$ Prices: Salad bar $5.95; salad and pasta $6.95. AE, MC, V.
Open: Daily 11am–9pm.

S This cafeteria-style restaurant, just south of Exposition Street, delivers the best 70-item salad bar, the freshest pasta bar, and the tastiest just-out-of-the-oven muffins and cookies in town— and all for an extraordinarily low price. First-timers make the mistake of loading their chilled plates with basic salad fixings, leaving little room for when they get to the section loaded with pasta salads (vegetarian to seafood), herring, tuna, hearts of palm, and chunks of fresh fruit. The separate pasta bar offers a choice of pastas and four fresh sauces. The last stop before heading for the dining room is the bakery for wonderful poppy-seed or banana–chocolate-chip muffins (whole-wheat bran and sugarless banana-blueberry muffins are also offered). The price includes dessert: big, crispy chocolate-chip, peanut-butter, and oatmeal-raisin cookies, brownies, and frozen yogurt with fresh fruit. Drinks, including beer and wine, are extra.

RED ROBIN BURGERS AND SPIRITS EMPORIUM, 3333 S. Wadsworth Blvd., Lakewood, a block north of U.S. 285. Tel. 303/989-8448.

Cuisine: ECLECTIC. **Reservations:** Accepted Mon–Fri only.
$ Prices: Burgers and main dishes $3.95–$7.45. AE, DC, DISC, MC, V.
Open: Mon–Thurs 11am–10pm, Fri–Sat 11am–11pm.

Fat, juicy hamburgers and pure chicken burgers keep locals returning to the Red Robin. Some 19 different types of burgers come with toppings such as guacamole, bacon, Swiss cheese, red onion, barbecue sauce, and Cheddar cheese. If you're not a red-meat eater, choose a Cobb salad, a chicken burger, or a vegetable stir-fry. The Red Robin serves bottomless pop and unlimited fries with burgers.

The Red Robin gets busy at dinnertime, so go early or expect to wait in the bar. If you have kids with you, bring lots of quarters so they can busy themselves at the video machines. An entire side of the menu is filled with appetizers and drink suggestions ranging from fruity boozie smoothies to java royale. Teens love the non-alcoholic version of Cookie Magic that blends vanilla ice cream and Oreo cookies. The same menu (with a "tiny tots" section) is available at lunch and dinner. The bar stays open an hour later. There's another Red Robin in Arvada.

T-WA TERRACE, 6882 S. Yosemite St. Tel. 303/741-4051.

Cuisine: VIETNAMESE. **Reservations:** Not required. **Directions:** Take I-25 to the Arapahoe Road exit, go west a block to Yosemite Street, and turn left.
$ Prices: Appetizers $5–$8; main courses $6.95–$10.50; lunch $4.95–$8.50. AE, DC, MC, V.
Open: Sun–Thurs 11am–8:30pm, Fri–Sat 11am–10pm.

The dishes in this Vietnamese restaurant are lighter and more delicate than Chinese food (because the chef uses less cornstarch), and all are made from fresh ingredients. I particularly enjoy the light Vietnamese eggrolls and deep-fried jumbo shrimp wrapped in crabmeat and rice paper. The big bowls of soup, with huge chunks of shrimp, crab legs, and pork piled on rice noodles, are more than filling. There are many spicy dishes with shrimp and other seafood, as well as pork, beef, and chicken.

5. OUT OF TOWN

EXPENSIVE

THE FORT, 19192 Colo. 8, Morrison. Tel. 303/697-4771.
   Cuisine: AMERICAN. **Reservations:** Recommended.
$ **Prices:** Appetizers $3.95–$12; main courses $12–$24. AE, DC, DISC, MC, V.
   Open: Dinner only, Mon–Fri 6–10pm, Sat 5–10pm, Sun 5–9pm.

Owner Sam Arnold likes to boast that his restaurant serves 9,000 Rocky Mountain oysters, 40 pounds of Texas rattlesnake, and 300 pounds of elk medallions each week! It's no wonder that out-of-towners in search of "Wild West" cuisine go to the Fort, located at the junction of Colo. 8 and U.S. 285, 20 minutes southwest of downtown. It's a full-scale replica of Colorado's fur-trading post, Bent's Fort, which is built on the side of a foothill overlooking Denver. It's hard to beat the nighttime view of the plains dotted with twinkling lights. Past the massive doors, diners find hand-hewn beams, beehive fireplaces, period furniture, and a collection of western Americana on the adobe walls. If you start dinner with a cocktail, order one of the period drinks, such as the Hailstorm, made with instructions bartenders have used since 1812. If you're feeling adventuresome, try the Historian's Platter, filled with roast buffalo marrow bones with sea biscuits, boudies, and buffalo tongue with Sam's sauce. The pumpkin muffins, which come in the bread basket, are delightful. If you've never had buffalo, sample a steak— it's tasty and has half the calories of beef and one-third the cholesterol. If you like game, the elk medallions are well prepared and the broiled quail is delicious. Personally, I like the Taos trout, a fresh mountain trout broiled and basted in a mint sauce and topped with bacon bits. "The bowl of the Wife of Kit Carson," a spicy sort of chili, gets rave reviews. All entrees come with muffins, salad, a vegetable, and rice or potatoes. Fellow chocoholics must leave room for a negrita, a sinfully rich chocolate-rum cup. Buffalo goes for market price.

MODERATE

BEAU JO'S GREAT AMERICAN PIZZA, 1517 Miner St., Idaho Springs. Tel. 303/567-4376.
   Cuisine: PIZZA. **Reservations:** Not accepted. **Directions:** Get off at either I-70 Idaho Springs exit and head into the center of town.
$ **Prices:** Pizza $1.95–$25.19; AE, DISC, MC, V.
   Open: Sun–Thurs 11am–9:30pm, Fri–Sat 11am–10pm.

On weekends, especially in the winter, you might have to wait for a table at Beau Jo's, located in one of the historic old buildings on the main street. For more information, see the description in "North Denver," above.

BUCK SNORT SALOON, 15921 Elk Creek Rd., Pine. Tel. 303/838-0284.
   Cuisine: AMERICAN. **Reservations:** Not accepted. **Directions:** Head out U.S. 285 to Conifer, go 6½ more miles to Schaffers Crossing, and turn left onto Elk Creek Road for 6 miles

(it becomes gravel for the last 3½ miles to the rustic Buck Snort Saloon).
$ Prices: Sandwiches and burgers $3–$6; steaks $14. No credit cards.
Open: Summer, daily noon–9pm. Winter, dinner only, Wed–Fri 5–9pm, Sat–Sun noon–9pm. Bar, Sat–Sun 4pm–midnight, Mon–Fri it depends on the business.

If you're ready to explore the boondocks, head for the Buck Snort Saloon. Go during the daylight hours so you can enjoy the wonderful views of the high country. Once at the saloon, you can sink your teeth into big fat burgers, BLTs, GLTs (guacamole, lettuce, and tomato), tacos, taco salad, or a 16-ounce-minimum T-bone steak. There's live music every Saturday night, and the locals head here for the annual Halloween party.

EL RANCHO, just off I-70 West at Exit 252 or I-70 East at Exit 251. Tel. 303/526-0661.
Cuisine: AMERICAN/WESTERN. **Reservations:** Recommended.
$ Prices: Appetizers $4–$6; main courses $10–$19; complete dinner $7.95–$21. AE, MC, V.
Open: Mon–Fri 8am–9pm, Sat 8am–10pm, Sun 8am–8pm.

Visit El Rancho for lunch with a spectacular mountain view, or for a good dinner on the return trip to the flatlands after a day in the high country. The panoramic view of mountain peaks from this family-owned restaurant is breathtaking. Don't fill up on the freshly made cinnamon rolls, because the tasty American fare includes broasted chicken, beef, and seafood combinations, steaks, Colorado Mountain trout, and range-fed buffalo. On a cold day you can warm yourself at one of the seven fireplaces in the many rooms of this log cabin–style building. Dinners include rolls, soup, salad, potatoes, and dessert. If you're heading into the mountains for a day, get a brown-bag lunch from the Sweet Shoppe on the lower level.

TIVOLI DEER, 26300 Hilltop Dr., Kittredge. Tel. 303/670-0941.
Cuisine: SCANDINAVIAN. **Reservations:** Recommended.
$ Prices: Appetizers $2.50–$6.75; main courses $6.50–$13; fixed-price dinner $33.50. AE, MC, V.
Open: Mon and Wed–Sat 11am–10pm, Sun 10am–10pm.

Combine a spectacular drive with lunch at this wonderful Scandinavian restaurant in the center of this tiny town. Take the breathtaking 20-minute drive during daylight hours along Colo. 74 (Bear Creek Road), which follows a winding creek from Morrison to Kittredge. (You could continue two miles to Evergreen and then take the highways back to Denver.)

The restaurant has a menu in the more informal Wine Garden, and serves the fixed-price meal in the formal dining room. It's hard to choose an appetizer, so order a few and share. I particularly enjoy the herring salads (three types of herring and sauces) and the smooth, subtle-tasting gravlax (salmon marinated Swedish style and served with mustard-dill dressing). You can get sandwiches or entrees like boeuf Lindstrom and Copenhagen stew—my favorite—a creamy, rich combination of oysters and mussels.

The fixed-price dinner includes several appetizers, including a wonderful smoked-game sausage and the gravlax; salad; a choice of entree; cheeses; and dessert.

BUDGET

T-WA INN, 1153 Colo. 74, Evergreen. Tel. 303/674-0778.
Cuisine: VIETNAMESE. **Reservations:** Not required. **Directions:** Get off I-70 at the El Rancho exit and take Colo. 74 to the King Sooper's Shopping Center.
$ Prices: Appetizers $3.95–$4.95; main courses $6.95–$11.95. MC, V.
Open: Mon–Sat 11am–8:30pm.
If you're exploring mountain towns, detour two miles down a winding, scenic local highway into Evergreen and stop at the T-Wa Inn. You'll find traditional Vietnamese dishes in an informal setting.

6. SPECIALTY DINING

HOTEL DINING

AUGUSTA, in the Westin Hotel Tabor Center, 1672 Lawrence St. Tel. 303/572-7222.
Cuisine: ECLECTIC. **Reservations:** Recommended.
$ Prices: Appetizers $6.25–$9.25; main courses $14.75–$24.50; lunch $7.25–$11. AE, DC, MC, V.
Open: Lunch Tues–Fri 11:30am–2pm; dinner Tues–Sat 5:30–10pm.
Westin's award-winning gourmet restaurant is run by an imaginative chef with a delicate hand for saucing and spicing dishes. The menu lists pastas; seafood, such as poached Dover sole topped with shrimp and crabmeat and glazed with chardonnay mousseline; and specialties such as grilled veal chop with morel mushrooms simmered in Calvados cream. Some nights, Augusta offers a "chef's creation" fixed-price dinner ($35). Certain nights, the restaurant also offers a three-course, fixed-price dinner for theater patrons seated before 6pm. (And free shuttle service to the Denver Performing Arts Complex.)

Augusta's ebony walls are a perfect backdrop to the etched-glass dividers placed throughout the two-tiered room, and broad windows offer a view of downtown Denver.

If you can't afford the dinner tab, stop by for lunch when diners can order a variety of light dishes and expect to be out within an hour. The lighter menu emphasizes salads, pasta, seafood, and items from the rôtisserie. Complimentary valet parking is available for dinner guests.

MAXIE'S, in the Cherry Creek Inn, 600 S. Colorado Blvd. Tel. 303/757-2435.
Cuisine: AMERICAN. **Reservations:** Not required.
$ Prices: Appetizers $4.25–$6.75; main courses $6–$16.95; lunch $4.95–$8.95. AE, DC, MC, V.
Open: Daily 6am–10pm; brunch Sun 10am–2pm.
Professionals in the area know that the luncheon buffet here is a tasty bargain. For $5.95 you can get soup and salad—or soup and a sandwich you make yourself from a variety of fixings. Maxie's serves healthy-size portions for the money, whether it's an Oriental stir-fry

or the pasta-Cobb salad. The menu lists sandwiches, burgers, a variety of salads, and entrees, including fresh fish, pasta, and chicken fried steak. At dinnertime, entrees also include chops, steak, and chicken.

MCCORMICK'S FISH HOUSE, in the Oxford Hotel, 1659 Wazee St. Tel. 303/825-1107.

Cuisine: SEAFOOD. **Reservations:** Not required.

$ Prices: Appetizers $4.95–$8.95; main courses $9.95–$22.95. AE, DC, DISC, MC, V.

Open: Breakfast Mon–Fri 6:30–10am; lunch Mon–Fri 11:30am–2:30pm; dinner Sun–Thurs 5–10pm, Fri–Sat 5–11pm; brunch Sat–Sun 7am–2pm.

McCormick's has an incredible variety of fresh seafood for a restaurant in a landlocked city and serves one of the best clam chowders I've ever tasted (and I lived in an East Coast state for 10 years): thick, buttery, and filled with big clams. There's a new menu each day, featuring a couple dozen fresh seafood items ranging from four different types of oysters to fish from the waters off Massachusetts and Oregon. One evening I started with giant, succulent emerald mussels from New Zealand, followed by a cup of New England-style clam chowder and a fresh, steamed Dungeness crab from Oregon. In addition to seafood, McCormick's also offers burgers, fish and chips, and fresh pastas. If you order selectively, you could easily leave here with a moderate bill. Best bets are the $1.95 specials—fish and chips, corned-beef sandwich, and smoked trout pâté—served in the front bar from 3 to 6pm and 9 to 11pm daily.

MCGUIRE'S, in the Hyatt Regency, 1750 Welton St. Tel. 303/295-1200.

Cuisine: ECLECTIC. **Reservations:** Not required.

$ Prices: Appetizers $2.50–$4; main courses $5–$14. AE, DC, MC, V.

Open: Daily 6am–midnight.

This informal restaurant has a tasty something for everyone. The sandwiches and clubs come in all varieties, from roast beef to reubens. French onion soup, New York steak, Rocky Mountain trout, and pasta dishes are also offered.

SHIP TAVERN, in the Brown Palace Hotel, 321 17th Ave. Tel. 303/297-3111.

Cuisine: AMERICAN. **Reservations:** Accepted only for parties of six or more.

$ Prices: Appetizers $5.25–$8.50; main courses $7.25–$21. AE, DC, DISC, MC, V.

Open: Daily 11am–11pm (happy hour Mon–Fri 4:30–6pm).

The Ship Tavern has long been one of my favorites for its casual atmosphere, perfectly cooked fresh fish, and Colorado prime rib. Once inside the swinging tavern doors, you'll see a marvelous model clipper ship collection from the 1850s and '60s, and porcelain Jamaican rum casks made in 1820. Check out the replica of the *Flying Cloud*, the fastest of the clippers, while walking to and from the happy-hour appetizer table that's loaded with goodies. It's basic fare here: tender prime rib; fresh fish, steamed, broiled, or sautéed; chicken and lamb chops; and hot and cold sandwiches. The one drawback is the noise level, attributable to the high-ceilinged open room.

TABOR GRILL, in the Westin Tabor Center, 1672 Lawrence St. Tel. 303/572-7292.
    Cuisine: AMERICAN. **Reservations:** Not required.
$ Prices: Appetizers $2.75–$4.50; main courses $3.50–$14. AE, DC, MC, V.
    Open: Daily 6am–10pm.
The Tabor Grill is the place to go if you want good food served in a sophisticated setting, but don't want to pay big bucks. You can get breakfast anytime, as well as pasta, salads, sandwiches, and down-home cooking, including southern-style chicken fried steak and grilled chicken breasts.

LIGHT, CASUAL & FAST FOOD

The **Plaza Court Food Emporium,** located downstairs in Republic Plaza, 370 17th St., has Cozzoli's Pizzeria, Le Petit Boulangerie, All-American Hero, and other fast-food outlets spread around the perimeter of a colorful room of red-topped tables and white wire chairs.

    You can get Chinese, hot chocolate-chip cookies, falafel, burgers, and much more at the 18 booths in the **Shops at Tabor Center Picnic Court.** It's located on the upper level of the Tabor Center, 1201 16th St., at the end of the mall between Lawrence and Larimer Streets. There's plenty of seating.

BREAKFAST/BRUNCH

In addition to the establishments listed below, there's **Racine's Restaurant,** 850 Bannock St. (tel. 303/595-0418), a popular place for power breakfasts (see "Downtown," above).

THE DELECTABLE EGG, 1642 Market St. Tel. 303/572-8146.
    Cuisine: AMERICAN. **Reservations:** Recommended for parties of six or more.
$ Prices: Main courses $2.95–$5.75. DC, DISC, MC, V.
    Open: Mon–Fri 6:30am–2pm, Sat–Sun 7am–2pm.
Eggs prepared dozens of different ways and served with pancakes, waffles, French toast, or in pockets, are some of what's available at this casual restaurant in lower downtown. You can also order a variety of sandwiches and salads. Egg dishes run $4.50–$5.75, pancakes are $2.95, and sandwiches and salads cost $3.95–$5.50.

    The **Delectable Egg** has another location at 16th Street and Court Place (tel. 303/892-5720), at one end of the 16th Street Mall.

ELLYNGTON'S, in the Brown Palace Hotel, 321 17th St. Tel. 303/297-3111.
    Cuisine: AMERICAN. **Reservations:** Recommended.
$ Prices: Basic brunch without champagne $21.95; champagne brunch $27.95–$89.95. AE, DC, MC, V.
    Open: Breakfast Mon–Fri 6:30–11am, Sat 7–11am, Sun 7–10:30am; brunch Sun 10:30am–2pm.
The Dom Perignon champagne Sunday brunch at Ellyngton's, which is also open for breakfast and lunch the rest of the week, is a rare treat. On Sunday the tables are filled with delicious hot and cold dishes, pastas, salads, cheeses, fruits, and pastries you'd expect to find at one of Denver's poshest hostelries. However, the Dom Perignon is the real draw, although Ellyngton's offers three tiers of champagne,

recognizing that there are brunchers not on a deluxe champagne budget.

LATE-NIGHT/24-HOUR DINING

COLORADO CAFE, 740 W. Colfax Ave. Tel. 303/825-5443.
   Cuisine: AMERICAN. **Reservations:** Not accepted.
$ Prices: $3.30–$7.
   Open: Daily 24 hours.
This coffee shop, located on one edge of downtown, serves breakfasts, burgers, sandwiches, and other basic fare.

PICNIC FARE & WHERE TO EAT IT

Denver is filled with big parks as well as small park spaces in the downtown sector. If you want to sit on the grass while picnicking in the downtown area, head for the Civic Center or Confluence Park. There's a more complete listing of parks in Chapter 7.

Stop at **Goldi's** (See "Downtown," above), the **Market** (see "Espresso Bars," below), or a **Bagel Deli** (see "North Denver," above), or one of the food courts to get sandwiches.

ESPRESSO BARS

I've listed several popular espresso bars and stands here, but so many are opening up that it's unlikely all will do well. Most are small, with a few tables covered with current newspapers and magazines and the rich fragrance of gourmet roasted beans wafting in the air. You can get a cup of fresh-brewed java—either the house brand or the day's "special" regular and decaffeinated choices and, of course, the ubiquitous biscotti. Hours vary, but most are open from early morning to late evening.

The Market, 1445 Larimer Sq. (tel. 303/534-5140), is the granddaddy of coffee bars in this city. The line forms to the left, just inside the door, for the espresso/coffee counter. If you want a full meal, just go farther into this food emporium. You'll find a treasure trove of gourmet salads, the makings for interesting sandwiches, and a pastry-lover's nirvana at the various counters. The tables—both inside and out—are the spot for the best people-watching in town.

There are five downtown **BRIO** locations, small outlets where you can get coffee, fresh juice, and pastries. They are located in the Prudential Plaza at Arapahoe Street and the 16th Street Mall; in the Petroleum Club Building, at the 16th Street Mall and Cleveland Place; in the Equitable Building, at 17th and Stout Streets; One Denver Place, at 18th and Champa Streets; and in the 17th Street Plaza at 1225 17th Street.

You can't walk a block in Cherry Creek without seeing one. **In Peaberry Coffee** is located at 3031 E. Second Ave., the **Starbucks Coffee Company** is at 2701 E. Third Ave., and the **Coffee Bean and Tea Leaf** is at 2432 E. Third Ave. **Java Creek,** 287 Columbine St., is larger than most. At **The Gourmet Alternative Cafe,** 300 Fillmore St. you can get mouth-watering pastries too.

CHAPTER 7

WHAT TO SEE & DO IN DENVER

There are so many things to see and do in Denver—sights, museums, amusements, special events, sports, shopping, nightspots—that you'll have to be selective. In this chapter I've tried to highlight what is most special about each major attraction, as well as passing on a few suggestions for places locals love to visit or frequent. Once you get out and start exploring Denver, you're sure to discover many more things of interest on your own.

SUGGESTED ITINERARIES

IF YOU HAVE ONE DAY The lure of gold is as irresistible today as when miners flooded Denver, so most visitors rate a tour of the Denver Mint high on their list of things one "must do." Afterward, walk over to the Denver Art Museum and examine the Native American collection of art and artifacts. Take a free shuttle down the 16th Street Mall to lower downtown (LoDo) and stroll around the renovated Victorian buildings filled with shops, galleries, and restaurants in Larimer Square and LoDo. Stop at a brewpub or one of the many restaurants in this area for lunch. If you're up for another museum, visit the Museum of Western Art and/or the Black American West Museum. As you moved up and down the mall, did you stop by the Ticket Bus to see what special events, concerts, and activities are happening in town that night?

IF YOU HAVE TWO DAYS For your first day, follow the suggestions above.

On the second day, head for the Denver Museum of Natural Science to see the dioramas and dinosaurs, and catch an IMAX film or a planetarium show. If you have children along, you may want to head for the zoo. Stop by the Denver Botanic Gardens or the Molly Brown house afterward. Check the local papers to see if there's an evening event that sounds appealing; otherwise, try one of the jazz or comedy clubs.

IF YOU HAVE THREE DAYS Follow the suggestions above for the first two days.

On your third day, head for the mountains. If you have a car, try one of the day excursions listed at the end of this chapter. Otherwise, consider signing up for a tour (see "Organized Tours," below). If you like sports, rent a bike and challenge some of the bike paths in the city if you're moderately athletic, or the off-road mountainbikes in

- The Colorado State
  Capitol dome is
  covered with 200
  ounces of 24-karat
  gold, but the really
  valuable material
  used in its
  construction was
  rose onyx—the
  entire world's supply
  was used as
  wainscoting in the
  building.
- The Museum of
  Western Art is
  housed in the
  Navarre—a gem of
  a Victorian building
  that was Denver's
  swankiest bordello
  and gambling hall.
- The U.S. Mint is the
  second-largest
  storehouse of gold
  bullion in the nation
  (after Fort Knox),
  and produces more
  than five billion coins
  each year.
- Golda Meir attended
  high school in
  Denver before
  becoming a prime
  minister of Israel (the
  home she grew up in
  is preserved on the
  Auraria campus in
  downtown Denver).
- Denver originally had
  three different
  names, but for the
  price of a barrel of
  whiskey all other
  names were
  dropped.
- Denver is truly a mile
  high! (The 15th step
  of the State Capitol
  building is exactly
  5,280 feet above sea
  level.)

the foothills if you're in good shape. If
you're a shopper, stop by the Cherry Creek
Mall and browse Cherry Creek North,
stopping for lunch along the way. If you
have kids along, head for the Children's
Museum, the Funplex, or Celebrity Sports
in the afternoon.

**IF YOU HAVE FOUR DAYS OR
MORE** After visiting the attractions suggested above, if you have more time, visit
the U.S. Air Force Academy—the state's
most visited "man-made" attraction, and
the "natural" Garden of the Gods in Colorado Springs. If it's summertime and you'd
rather head north, head to Rocky Mountain National Park and stop at Boulder's
Pearl Street Mall on the way home. If it's
wintertime and you're a skier, talk to the
Denver Ski Lift about renting equipment
and winter clothing and about a ride to the
slopes.

1. THE TOP
ATTRACTIONS

Denver's **Cultural Connection Trolley,**
at the munificent cost of $1 per day for
unlimited travel, will set you at the door-
step of many of the museums and attractions listed below. Hopping on and off the
trolley is a lot easier than maneuvering
through city streets, especially during rush
hour, and finding parking spaces. The
trolley's route includes stops at the Colorado Convention Center, U.S. Mint, Denver Art Museum, the PLEX, Molly Brown
House, Denver Botanic Gardens, Denver
History Museum, and the Colorado State
Capitol. The full route runs every half
hour between 9am and 6pm daily. It runs a
more limited route in the evenings. You
can buy a ticket at the Denver Visitor's
Bureau, 225 W. Colfax Ave.; the Ticket
bus, 511 16th Street Mall; RTD's Market
Street Station, 1601 Market St.; and other
locations. For more information, call 303/
299-6000.

**DENVER MUSEUM OF NATURAL
HISTORY, 2001 Colorado Blvd.,
in City Park at Colorado and**

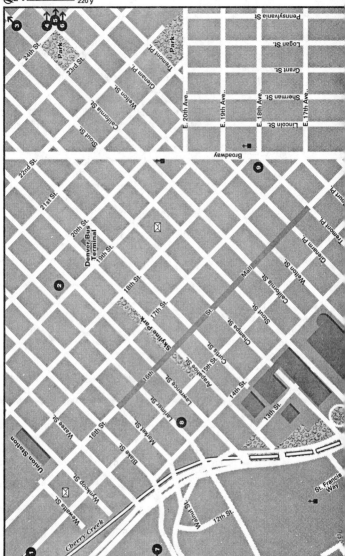

Montview Blvds. Tel. 303/322-7009 or 303/370-8257 for hearing impaired.

⭐   Arguably, the most popular exhibit at this museum is the wildlife diorama called "The Watering Hole." Life-size zebras, wild boars, antelope, and other animals roam an African plain in a scene so detailed that footprints are etched into the earth and the animals standing around the waterhole cast shadows on the sand. (And there's no glass between you and the scene to remind you that it's just an exhibit.) This tableau in the Botswana African Hall is just

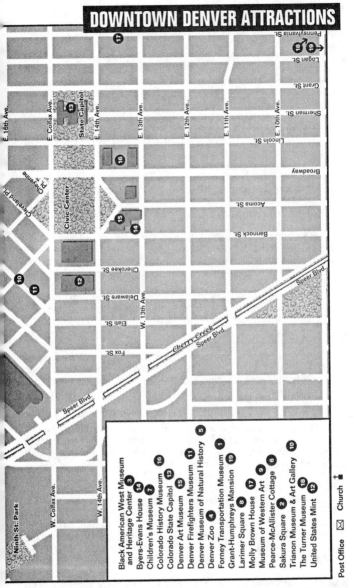

DOWNTOWN DENVER ATTRACTIONS

Black American West Museum and Heritage Center **3**
Byers-Evans House **14**
Children's Museum **7**
Colorado History Museum **16**
Colorado State Capitol **13**
Denver Art Museum **15**
Denver Firefighters Museum **11**
Denver Museum of Natural History **5**
Denver Zoo **4**
Forney Transportation Museum **1**
Grant-Humphreys Mansion **19**
Larimer Square **8**
Molly Brown House **17**
Museum of Western Art **9**
Pearce-McAllister Cottage **6**
Sakura Square **2**
Trianon Museum & Art Gallery **10**
The Turner Museum **18**
United States Mint **12**

✚ Post Office   ⊠ Church

one in an exceptional collection of almost 90 dioramas displaying flora and fauna from four continents. In the Alaskan diorama, the life-size moose and caribou are surrounded by three million leaves that were hand-cut and tied by volunteers.

The Hall of Life has permanent interactive exhibits about how life begins, genetics, the five senses, and human anatomy; also nutrition, fitness, stress management, and substance abuse. When you enter, you'll get a magnetic "Life" card, which activates various exhibits. For example, in the "senses" area, when you enter a sound-clues booth and activate the exhibit with your Life card, sounds begin filtering into the booth (you can choose your audio environment—beach, traffic, etc.). In the "genetics" area there's a computer board game that lets you create a person by choosing various options shown by the computer. How you respond to questions about illnesses will determine how long you play the game. If you choose to see a doctor to improve your health, it opens up additional options. If you make poor health choices, the game will end quickly. At the end, you'll receive a printout of all your answers.

Kids of all ages will enjoy the Dinosaur Hall, where seven fossil creatures are on display, including a stegosaurus, a cast of *Tyrannosaurus rex,* and a diplodocus. Some 91 other prehistoric mammals are displayed in the Fossil Mammal Hall. The Coors Mineral Hall features an exotic grouping of gems, minerals, and Colorado gold, including the largest nugget ever found in the state, the 8½-pound Tom's Baby. The American Indian Hall displays artifacts from the Florida Seminoles to the Alaskan Eskimos.

The museum also presents such blockbuster special exhibits as "Aztec: The World of Moctezuma" and "Ramses II," which have lured in thousands of visitors. The lines for some of the special exhibits are long, but you can circumvent them by ordering tickets for a specific time slot in advance.

The museum also houses an **IMAX theater.** You don't need to sit close to the screen, which climbs 4½ stories skyward and is 6 stories wide—the screen's size and the surround-sound system really put you in the center of the action. And the cinematography is always stunning, whatever the subject. The films vary widely, from a bird's-eye view of the Grand Canyon to a fast trip through the human body inside the blood vessels or an explosive view of an active volcano's fury. There are showings several times each day, but since hours vary, you should call ahead for the schedule. A separate admission is charged.

The **Gates Planetarium,** inside the museum, offers both star programs and laser-light shows. If you're interested in the stars, call the planetarium (tel. 303/370-6351) for information on the current show. A separate admission is charged. The laser-light shows, which change often, combine rock music with spectacular laser effects. A separate admission is charged; call 303/370-6487 for further information.

Admission: Museum, $4 adults, $2 seniors and children 4–12. IMAX theater, $5 adults, $4 seniors and children 4–12. Planetarium, star shows, $3.50 adults, $2.50 seniors and children; laser-light shows, $3.50 before 6pm, $6 after 6pm. Combination tickets for the museum and either IMAX or the planetarium are available.

Open: Daily 9am–5pm. **Closed:** Christmas Day.

COORS BREWERY, 13th Ave. at Ford St., Golden. Tel. 303/277-BEER.

The free tour of the largest single-site brewery in the U.S. is both entertaining and informative. Children are as welcome as adults to see the malting of the barley, beer brewing in massive copper vats, and the packaging process. If the sight of hundreds of cans of beer moving around on clanking assembly lines in the packaging room at the Coors Brewery makes you thirsty, know that at the end of the line there's beer tasting in the brewhouse for visitors of legal drinking age (and a non-alcoholic brew for everyone else). Visitors should allow

1–1½ hours for the 30-minute walking tour, shuttle ride through historic Golden, and stops in the hospitality lounge and gift shop. Advance notice is appreciated for groups of 15 or more. With advance notice, Coors can arrange special tours for the hearing-impaired and the physically disabled, as well as some non-English-speaking guests.

Admission: Free.

Open: Mon–Sat 10am–4pm. **Closed:** Hols.

DENVER ART MUSEUM, 100 W. 14th Ave. Tel. 303/640-2793.

★ This futuristic building, just south of the Civic Center, contains an internationally acclaimed collection of Native American art and artifacts. Uniquely carved totem poles are set in a special two-story gallery. Other rooms display exquisite examples of handcrafted silver jewelry, pottery, woven blankets and baskets, and weavings. The museum is a treasure house of art objects, both in the American art collection and from around the world, spanning many centuries. The six floors house galleries containing a contemporary collection, African and South Pacific art, pre-Columbian and Spanish colonial art, art of the American West, classical European art, Asian art, and a textile collection including painstakingly stitched handmade quilts. In addition to the permanent collection, the museum hosts special art and photographic exhibits, and high-quality traveling shows. Call for the current list of exhibits. Whichever galleries you choose to explore, don't leave before viewing *Linda,* a sculpture by John DeAndrea so lifelike that you'll expect her to stand up and walk away.

Stop at the information desk to ask about free tours of the museum. The museum's café is a nice place for lunch, and there's an excellent gift shop with an impressive display of art books. The popular "Top of the Week," Wednesday jazz/conversation/meet-with-friends evenings run at various times of the year. Call and see if one is scheduled when you're in town.

Admission: $3 adults, $1.50 students and seniors, free for children under 5; free for everyone Sat.

Open: Tues–Sat 10am–5pm, Sun noon–5pm.

MOLLY BROWN HOUSE MUSEUM, 1340 Pennsylvania St. Tel. 303/832-4092.

★ This Victorian home, guarded by stone lions, was once owned by the "Unsinkable" Molly Brown, a heroine during the *Titanic* disaster. The Browns bought the house in 1894, made many changes and additions, then leased it out during the first decade of the 1900s while they traveled in Europe and the Far East. They were legally separated in 1909, but Molly Brown continued to travel and, of course, booked passage on the *Titanic.* Her language skills made her a national heroine when she helped women and children onto lifeboats during that fateful night of April 15, 1912, and later raised money to help these survivors. By the 1920s she had converted her home into a rooming house, maintained by the Browns' housekeeper. It was sold after Molly's death in 1932. Under threat of demolition, it was purchased by Historic Denver in 1970 and restored and furnished in a 19th- and early 20th-century style. The tour is fascinating both for the intriguing stories told about this flamboyant woman and for the look into the upper-middle-class lifestyle of the period. The furnishings and decorative art objects, all faithful to the era, include many possessions from the Brown family. There's a gift shop in the carriage house, behind the main house, where you purchase tour tickets.

On your way to or from the Molly Brown House, walk or drive around the surrounding streets to view the many huge mansions in the Capitol Hill area that were built by wealthy miners as wintertime residences. Today some are still private homes, while others have been turned into condominiums or apartment houses, or filled with white-collar businesses. The **Grant-Humphreys Mansion,** at Pennsylvania Street and Seventh Avenue, and the neighboring **Governor's Mansion** are two of the most outstanding examples.

Admission: $3 adults, $2 senior citizens, $1.50 students and children 6–17, free for children under 6.

Open: Sept–May, Tues–Sat 10am–4pm, Sun noon–4pm; June–Aug, Mon–Sat 10am–4pm, Sun noon–4pm. The last tour starts at 4:30pm. **Closed:** Major hols.

UNITED STATES MINT, 320 W. Colfax Ave. (tour entrance around the corner on Cherokee St.). Tel. 303/844-3582 (tours) or 303/844-5588.

Seeing dull-colored metal blanks turned into coins seems to fascinate both adults and children. During the tour you'll see the stages by which approximately 32 million coins of all denominations are minted each day! Presses punch out blank discs from metal coils, stamping up to 530 coins per minute, and vibrating machines shake the coins and drop the ones that aren't the proper size through a screen. The last stop is the entrance to the room holding six gold bars, each weighing 400 troy ounces. The Denver Mint, which opened in 1863, is one of four in the country, and the second-largest gold depository in the U.S., after Fort Knox.

To take the tour, which leaves every 15–20 minutes, line up outside the entrance. If the line is long and you don't have the patience to wait, walk around the block to the exit door and explore the gift shop. There are interesting displays, such as the old weight scales. The shop also has numismatic items, medals, and coin sets for sale, including some unusual ones, and even some at "vault clearance" prices. Visitors can stamp their own Denver Mint Souvenir Medal on an old press.

Admission: Free; children under 14 must be accompanied by an adult.

Open: Mon–Fri 8am–3pm (tours begin at 9am Wed). **Closed:** Hols.

2. MORE ATTRACTIONS

HISTORIC BUILDINGS & SIGHTS

Larimer Square, the oldest section of Denver, situated on the 1400 block of Larimer Street, is a gas-lit street of Victorian buildings now housing boutiques, stores, and restaurants. Stop in one of the shops and pick up a free walking-tour brochure and trace the steps of the early miners, gamblers, and ladies of the night along the street and through the arcades and courtyards. (You can also hop in a horse-drawn carriage for a ride around this section of town.) Many

FROMMER'S FAVORITE DENVER EXPERIENCES

Watching the Fiery Sunsets At the moment just after the sun sinks below the peaks, flashes of gold, orange, and pink sear through the high cumulus clouds overhead. It's a scene locals and tourists alike pause to watch. You can see it from almost any open spot in Denver or upper-floor west-facing windows, but especially from a bench in City Park.

Examining One of the "Maria" Black Pottery Bowls at the Denver Art Museum Native American women are responsible for reviving the special art form of creating these bowls—such perfectly smooth, graceful pieces. They're just one of many masterpieces in the museum's world-acclaimed collection of Native American art and artifacts.

People-Watching in Larimer Square It's best while sipping espresso between bites of a sinfully rich dessert at the Market in Larimer Square. Join in the swatch of life passing by the Market's outdoor tables on a sunny day. Toward the end of the day, watch tourists, students, and power-dressed women and men pour into the brewpub across the street.

Sitting on a Bench in Red Rocks Ampitheatre This is especially nice during a concert, when your eyes wander beyond the stage down to flatlands which seem to stretch to Kansas. As the singer struts her stuff and the natural light dims, a sea of lights flicker on in Denver homes, hundreds of feet lower and miles away.

Visiting the Cherry Creek Shopping Center One of the top retailing malls in the country, the upmarket Cherry Creek Shopping Center is always busy. Window-shopping at such stores as Neiman Marcus, Gucci, and the Disney Store is almost as much fun as buying.

Visiting the U.S. Mint During the tour, one can't help wondering how much fun it would be to walk out with some of that brand-new "change" jingling in your pockets.

shops are open until 9pm Monday through Saturday and until 6pm on Sunday.

Bounded by 19th Street and Lawrence Street, **Sakura (Cherry Blossom) Square** contains Asian restaurants, shops, Japanese gardens, and a Buddhist temple. This is the site of the annual Cherry Blossom Festival in June, when there are exhibitions and demonstrations of Japanese arts and a Japanese food bazaar.

COLORADO STATE CAPITOL, at Broadway and Colfax Ave. Tel. 303/866-2604.

Walk up the west steps of the State Capitol building to exactly one mile above sea level and take a deep breath. The air is thinner here than at sea level. The building, with its 24-karat gold-plated dome, was modeled after the U.S. Capitol in Washington, D.C. More than 200 stonecutters were employed to construct the five-foot-thick granite exterior walls, and it took seven years to complete the Colorado rose onyx wainscoting. On the first-floor rotunda are eight wall murals by artist Alan True, and verse by poet Thomas Ferril, celebrating the state. The attention to detail can be seen in the brass doorknobs featuring the state seal, the elevators with bronze panels depicting events in the state's history, and the grand staircase encrusted with oak leaves and acorns. If you have the stamina, climb to the top of the 180-foot-high dome for a spectacular panoramic view of the Rockies and flatlands.

Admission: Free.

Open: Tours approximately every 30 minutes Mon–Fri 9am–2:30pm.

GRANT-HUMPHREYS MANSION, 770 Pennsylvania St. Tel. 303/894-2505.

This 42-room turn-of-the-century mansion is furnished with period pieces. It was built by former governor James B. Grant and remodeled by wildcat oil industrialist Albert E. Humphreys in 1917.

Admission: $2 adults, $1 seniors and children 6–16.

Open: Tours conducted Tues–Fri 10am–2pm.

MUSEUMS

ARABIAN HORSE CENTER, 12000 Zuni St. Tel. 303/450-4710.

Arabian horse fans might want to stop at this center in suburban Westminster, with its small art gallery, museum, and library dedicated to research on Arabian horses.

Admission: Free.

Open: Mon–Fri 8:30am–4:30pm.

BLACK AMERICAN WEST MUSEUM AND HERITAGE CENTER, 3091 California St. Tel. 303/292-2566.

This museum acknowledges the little-known fact that nearly a third of the Wild West cowboys—as well as many miners, farmers, legislators, newspaper reporters, and other pioneers—were African-American. What started as Paul Stewart's hobby is now recognized by the Smithsonian Institution as one of the most significant collections of African-American history in the West. The 35,000 items (some on display, some in storage) include photographs, saddles, guns, farm tools, and clothing. One display is about the "Buffalo Soldiers" (the term given to the black soldiers by Native Americans) who headed west after the Civil War. The displays reveal much about the lives of these Americans who helped shape the West.

Admission: $2 adults, $1.50 senior citizens, 75¢ youth 12–18, 50¢ children 11 and under.

Open: Wed–Fri 10am–2pm, Sat noon–5pm, Sun 2–5pm.

BUFFALO BILL'S GRAVE AND MUSEUM, on top of Lookout Mountain. Tel. 303/526-0747.

IMPRESSIONS

"When I walk down a Denver street, I always feel as if I were listening to a brass band."
—DABNEY OTIS COLLINS, 1917

This attraction draws Wild West fans to see memorabilia commemorating the famous frontier scout and showman. The museum is crammed with posters from the Wild West show, exhibits describing the Pony Express, guns, clothing, and more. It also has a permanent exhibit, "The Native American Gallery," dedicated to the Native Americans who performed in Buffalo Bill's show. There's a panoramic view of Denver from the nearby grave site.

Admission: $2 adults, $1.50 seniors, $1 children 6–12, free for children under 6.

Open: May–Oct daily 9am–5pm; Nov–Apr, Tues–Sun 9am–4pm. **Directions:** Take Exit 256 off I-70.

BYERS-EVANS HOUSE/DENVER HISTORY MUSEUM, 1310 Bannock St. Tel. 303/620-4933.

The historic Byers-Evans House, behind the Denver Art Museum, has been restored to the 1912–24 period and reflects the character of two of Denver's most important pioneer families. It was built by William N. Byers, who printed Denver's first newspaper, the *Rocky Mountain News,* on April 23, 1859, just six days after he arrived in the raw settlement. John Evans, the other owner of the house, came three years later to become Colorado's second territorial governor. Byers built the house in 1883 and sold it to the son of the governor six years later.

Housed in one wing, the Denver History Museum is a state-of-the-art encyclopedia of the city's early life. Visitors touch a video screen in any one of several kiosks to explore the Mile High City's past, following their own interests and making their own choices.

Admission: $2.50 adults, $2 seniors, $1 children 6–16.

Open: Byers-Evans House, Wed–Sun 11am–3pm. Denver History Museum, Wed–Sun 11am–4pm.

COLORADO HISTORY MUSEUM, 13th Ave. and Broadway. Tel. 303/866-4993.

The colorful story of the Old West and Colorado is illustrated through old photographs, dioramas of old forts and buffalo hunts, Native American artifacts, mining equipment, and other items on display. After looking at the special timeline encapsulating 150 years of Colorado's history, check out exhibits that put the dates in perspective—like the sod house, a Gold Rush–era log cabin, and a working rotary pump used by miners to extract underground ore. Special exhibits are mounted regularly.

Admission: $3 adults, $1.50 seniors and children.

Open: Mon–Sat 10am–4:30pm, Sun noon–4:30pm.

DENVER FIREFIGHTERS MUSEUM, 1326 Tremont Place. Tel. 303/892-1100.

In this museum showing how Denverites fought fires in earlier days, stroll past the 1909 fire truck and other old fire engines on your way to the upstairs restaurant. On your way out, through the former Firehouse No. 1 in downtown, ring a firetruck bell, watch a videotape about firefighting, and explore the other memorabilia, including firemen's clothes.

Admission: $2 adults, $1 children.

Open: Restaurant and museum, Mon–Fri 11am–2pm.

DENVER MUSEUM OF MINIATURES, DOLLS, AND TOYS, 1880 Gaylord St. Tel. 303/322-3704.

Adults and kids all love the elaborate dollhouses, displays of intricately detailed miniatures, and vintage-to-modern dolls and toys in this museum, which is on the upper level of the historic Pearce-McAllister Cottage, just west of City Park. The museum has both changing and permanent exhibits, plus special programs. The admission fee includes a tour of both the cottage and the museum.

Admission: $3 adults, $2 seniors, $1.50 children 2–16.

Open: Tues–Sat 10am–4pm, Sun 1–4pm.

FORNEY TRANSPORTATION MUSEUM, 1416 Platte St. Tel. 303/433-3643.

This is a fascinating graveyard of antique cars, carriages, steam engines, and rail cars. Transportation buffs will enjoy eyeing such vintage cars as a 1907 eight-passenger limousine with double running boards, a 1923 eight-passenger, six-wheel Hispano Suiza, Amelia Earhart's sporty Kissel Kar, Aly Khan's Rolls-Royce, and an original McCormick Reaper.

Admission: $4 adults, $2 teens, $1 children under 11.

Open: Mon–Sat 10am–5pm, Sun 11am–5pm. **Directions:** From I-25, take Exit 211 (West 23rd Avenue) and go east on Water St. half a mile to Platte Street. From downtown go west on 15th Street to Platte Street and turn left.

HIWAN HOMESTEAD MUSEUM, 4208 S. Timbervale. Tel. 303/674-6262.

This 17-room log cabin in suburban Evergreen exemplifies a relaxed style of summer-home living in its 1890–1930 period rooms. There are changing historical exhibits at this homestead and an active craft and school program. The museum is a 45-minute ride from downtown Denver.

Admission: Free.

Open: Tues–Sun noon–4pm (to 5pm in summer).

LITTLETON HISTORICAL MUSEUM, 6028 S. Gallup St. Tel. 303/795-3950.

There are two "living history" farms at this museum in suburban Littleton, a 25-minute drive from Denver, where you can see men and women in period costumes doing farm chores and cooking. The two farms, one dating from around 1860 and the other from about 1890, have a blacksmith shop where you can watch demonstrations of 19th-century blacksmithing; there's also a log school and an ice house. The main building has three galleries with changing exhibits on different aspects of the Littleton area and state history.

Admission: Free.

Open: Mon–Fri 8am–5pm, Sat 10am–5pm, Sun 1–5pm. **Directions:** Go south on Santa Fe Drive, turn left onto Belleview Avenue and right onto Windemere Street; drive south to Littleton Boulevard, turn left onto Littleton for two blocks, and then turn right onto Gallup Street.

MIZEL MUSEUM OF JUDAICA, 560 S. Monaco Pkwy. Tel. 303/333-4156.

The Mizel Museum features five changing exhibits a year which illuminate Jewish art, history, customs, and cultural heritage from around the world. The exhibits are accompanied by programs featuring speakers, films, tours, workshops, and symposia.

Admission: Free.

Open: Mon–Thurs 10am–4pm, Sun 10am–noon.

MUSEUM OF OUTDOOR ARTS, Greenwood Plaza Park

(offices at 6312 S. Fiddler's Green Circle), Englewood. Tel. 303/741-3609.

More than 50 intriguing pieces of art are placed in Greenwood Plaza Park, a museum without walls. It's a nice place to picnic. Call for free tour maps or to arrange a guided tour.

Admission: Park, free. Tour, $3 adults, $1 children.
Open: Daily, dawn–dusk.

MUSEUM OF WESTERN ART, 1727 Tremont Place. Tel. 303/296-1880.

The wonderful little Museum of Western Art, located in the Old Navarre Building, a one-time brothel and gambling hall across from the Brown Palace Hotel, is filled with stupendous visual images of the West. The outstanding permanent collection includes intricately detailed bronzes by Remington and Russell. The collection also includes paintings by Albert Bierstadt, Georgia O'Keeffe, and Thomas Moran, whose work helped convince Congress to institute a national park system. There are special exhibits in addition to the permanent collection. Call for the current schedule.

Admission: $3 adults, $1.50 students and seniors, free for children under 7.
Open: Tues–Sat 10am–4:30pm.

PEARCE-MCALLISTER COTTAGE, 1880 Gaylord St. Tel. 303/322-3704.

This pumpkin-yellow brick Dutch Colonial Revival home, just west of City Park, is representative of the style of living of upper-middle-class families from the early 1900s into the Roaring '20s. The "cottage," built in 1899, contains the Pearce family's original interior furnishings. Upstairs is the Denver Museum of Miniatures, Dolls, and Toys (see above for details). The admission fee includes a tour of the museum and the historic cottage.

Admission: $3 adults, $2 seniors and children 2–16.
Open: Tues–Sat 10am–4pm, Sun 1–4pm.

TRIANON MUSEUM AND ART GALLERY, 335 14th St. Tel. 303/623-0739.

At Tremont Place in downtown, the Trianon Museum houses a collection of 18th-century French art including paintings and furniture. There's a 60-key piano from around 1760, and a marble-and-gold *Poseidon* attributed to Cellini. The art gallery, where everything is for sale, has an eclectic collection, some of interest to serious collectors and other pieces for souvenir hunters.

Admission: $1 adults, free for children under 12.
Open: Mon–Sat 10am–4pm.

THE TURNER MUSEUM, 773 Downing St. Tel. 303/832-0924.

Located in a private home on Capitol Hill, on Downing Street between 7th and 8th Avenues, the Turner Museum is a privately owned collection of engravings and watercolors by the master impressionist painter J. M. W. Turner and by Thomas Moran, known for his western scenes, which helped convince Congress to create the national park system. The owners, Douglas and Linda Graham, have more than 3,000 works of art in their home. The nicest way to see the works is before or after a lovely meal prepared by the Grahams.

Admission: Tour, $7.50 per person. Meals, $10 breakfast, $12 lunch, $25–$50 dinner.

Open: Mon–Fri 2–5pm; other times by appointment.

PARKS, GARDENS & ZOOS

Denver, with more than 205 named parks within the city boundaries and 20,000 acres of park lands on nearby mountains, boasts the biggest city park and recreation system in America! The city even owns a ski resort: Winter Park. Within the city limits, visitors will find many places to picnic, play tennis or golf, or bike and jog on city-maintained pathways.

The best view of Denver's downtown skyline framed by the Rocky Mountains is from a bench in **City Park.** Bordered by Colorado Boulevard and York Street, and 17th and 26th Avenues, the park encompasses 487 acres of lawns, gardens, a lake with paddleboats, a public golf course, tennis courts, the zoo, and Denver's Museum of Natural History.

If you're in the downtown area and want a bit of green space, just walk to **Civic Center Park,** between the State Capitol and City and County Buildings, where the fountains and lawns are guarded by the *Bucking Bronco* statue.

In 1858 Denver was founded at the site of **Confluence Park,** at 15th Street and the South Platte River. Today there's a man-made river-running chute, grassy amphitheater, and brick-paved plaza at the site.

Washington Park has two lakes, a replica of Martha Washington's gardens at Mount Vernon, and lots of locals picnicking, walking, and jogging. The park is bordered on the southwest corner by Downing and Lousiana Streets.

DENVER BOTANIC GARDENS, 1005 York St. Tel. 303/ 331-4000, or 303/331-4010 for recorded information.

In the winter, strolling through the hothouse atmosphere of the Botanic Gardens will warm you up. When it's snowing outside, the glassed-in tropical conservatory is filled with orchids, bromeliads, and other exotic flowers. The Botanic Garden also has extensive grounds where both common and unusual plants are set in gardens and alongside pools and waterfalls. The Rock Alpine Garden displays thousands of mountain plants that thrive at high altitudes, and there's an authentic tea house in the Japanese Garden.

Admission: May–Sept, $4 adults, $2 children 6–15, free for children under 6; Oct–Apr, $3 adults, $1.50 seniors, $1 children 6–15, free for children under 6.

Open: Daily 9am–4:45; extended hours in summer and around the Christmas hols. **Closed:** New Year's and Christmas Days.

DENVER ZOO, in City Park at E. 23rd Ave. and Steele St. Tel. 303/331-4100.

Watch sea lions cavort underwater through a glass wall, or photograph the inhabitants of Bear Mountain, Bird World, Gorilla Habitat, and Monkey Island in their open habitats. But you'll also see snow leopards, native bighorn and Alaskan dall sheep, and the zoo's other 1,700 occupants in more traditional exhibits. City Park is home to both the zoo and the Denver Museum of Natural History, so it's a nice double-play (you might even finish the day with a ride in one of the swan boats on the lake in the park).

Admission: $4 adults, $2 seniors and children 6–15, free for children under 6.

Open: Summer, daily 10am–6pm; winter, daily 10am–5pm.

NEARBY ATTRACTIONS

ANHEUSER-BUSCH BREWERY, 2351 Busch Dr., Fort Collins. Tel. 303/490-4626.

The world's largest brewery has built a Clydesdale hamlet about 1¼ hours from Denver. Your kids will love watching the famous, enormous Clydesdale draft horses, and there's plenty of adult-oriented exhibits and a one-hour tour of the brewery for you. Because of the drive from Denver, you would do well to call ahead and check the tour schedule the day you intend to visit. Tours are available for the mobility impaired.

Admission: Free.

Open: Tours, daily 9:30am–5pm; Gift shop, daily 9:30am–6pm. **Closed:** Hols. **Directions:** Take I-25 north to Mountain Vista Drive (Exit 271) and turn right onto Busch Drive.

COLORADO STATE UNIVERSITY, off I-25, Fort Collins. Tel. 303/491-1101.

Combine a visit to Anheuser Busch with a tour of Colorado State University, learning center for more than 20,000 students in 167 degree programs. Colorado State, the state's only land-grant university, is in the mid-sized city of Fort Collins, approximately an hour's drive from Denver.

RED ROCKS PARK AND AMPHITHEATRE, on Hogback Rd. off the I-70 Morrison exit.

⭐ Take sturdy shoes, a blanket, and a picnic lunch so you can eat amid the towering red sandstone formations where the plains met the foothills 60–100 million years ago. The red, pink, and rust colors in the rock, which become intensified after a rainstorm, are from the iron oxide deposited in the sandstone. The 600-acre park includes a natural amphitheater where, courtesy of Mother Nature, the sounds of music bounce off 400-foot-high natural red sandstone side walls back at the audience. (Pay attention to the signs forbidding you to climb these walls, Creation Rock, and Ship Rock, as well as the other steep faces. There have been accidents when people ignored the warning.) Concerts range from such musicians as Dan Fogelberg to hard-rockers, and Denverites often arrive early for a picnic, especially if they don't have reserved seats (see "Denver Nights," below, for concert information). The 9,000-seat amphitheater, which faces Denver and the plains, is the site each spring for the annual Easter Sunrise Service. Note that the Red Rocks Trading Post, a gift and curio shop, has the only restrooms open during the day.

---

3. COOL FOR KIDS

Several of the attractions mentioned above will be of interest to children, such as the **Denver Zoo, Buffalo Bill's Grave and Museum,** the **Denver Firefighters Museum,** the dinosaurs at the **Denver Museum of Natural History,** the **Denver Museum of Miniatures, Dolls, and Toys,** and the famous **Clydesdale horses** at the Anheuser-Busch Brewery. Denver also has a number of museums and amusement areas that are enjoyable for kids of all ages.

During the summertime, take the kids on the **Platte Valley Trolley.** The 2½-mile round-trip ride on the open-air streetcar runs from Confluence Park, downtown, past the children's Museum and Mile High Stadium. During the summer tickets are available near Confluence Park. The trolley also runs for special fall events, such as Halloween. For more information, call 303/458-6255.

BIG FUN, 920 S. Monaco Pkwy. Tel. 303/369-8957.

Big Fun, a block south of Leetsdale Drive, is an indoor playground for kids 2–12. Climb through two stories of nets, tubes, tunnels, and slides and jump around on gigantic air mattresses. Paddle through ball pools or conquer Webbie Webbie—six levels of criss-crossed rubber bands. Big Fun has lots more, plus pizza to fill up hungry kids (and parents who have come along to join in the fun).

Admission: Free adults; $5.50 children weekdays, $6.50 weekends; $2.95 children under 2.

Open: Hours vary so call first (most of the winter it's Sun–Mon and Wed–Thurs 11am-7pm, Fri-Sat 10am-9pm).

CASA BONITA, 6715 W. Colfax Ave. Tel. 303/232-5115.

At Casa Bonita, in the JCRS Shopping Center, the younger children will be distracted and entertained, so you can rest your feet and take a breather from sightseeing. The nonstop action—divers plummeting into a pool near the 30-foot waterfall, mariachi bands, and puppet shows—should keep the children riveted for at least a while. If they're old enough to visit another part of the restaurant without you, let them make a trip through Black Bart's Cave and give them quarters for the video games in the arcade, while you enjoy a second cup of coffee. Most of the food is Mexican, although there are a few basic American dishes. You go through a cafeteria line, then carry your food to a table on one of the levels in this restaurant, which can hold up to 1,100 diners. The sopapillas, made throughout the day and served hot, with honey, at your table, are delicious. Meals run $6–$9, plus drinks (beer and wine are available).

Open: Daily 11am-9:30pm.

CELEBRITY SPORTS CENTER, 888 S. Colorado Blvd. Tel. 303/757-3321.

Ask Denver parents where they leave their older children for a few hours and most will point you toward the Celebrity Sports Center. Celebrity has giant water slides that circle part of the building; 80 bowling lanes; three arcade rooms with video, pinball, and arcade games; Krazy Kars (space-age bumper cars); and a 50-meter indoor swimming pool with three water slides. It's a terrific place to keep the younger children amused—but you should stay with them as they play. If you need a break, take advantage of the free supervised playroom for kids six months to 6 years (call for hours). There's no admission fee—activities are individually priced. During the summer there's an all-day pass that includes a game of bowling, swimming and slides, six game tokens, and a Krazy Kar ride.

Admission: Activities priced individually. Summertime, all-day pass available for $7.

Open: Sun–Thurs 8:30am-midnight, Fri-Sat 8:30am-2am.

COLORADO RAILROAD MUSEUM, 17155 W. 44th Ave. Tel. 303/279-4591.

If your kids enjoy trains, visit the Railroad Museum, a replica of an 1880-style railroad depot, in suburban Golden. The 50 old locomotives and railroad cars standing on narrow-gauge and standard-gauge tracks date from the 1870s. Rare old photos and memorabilia of the railroad era that generated the settlement and expansion of Colorado are displayed here.

Admission: $2.50 adults, $2 seniors, $1 children under 16.
Open: June–Aug, daily 9am–6pm; Sept–May, daily 9am–5pm.

DENVER CHILDREN'S MUSEUM, 2121 Crescent Dr. Tel. 303/433-7433.

"Hands on" is the rule in this museum. Your kids will race from one room to another learning about money in the banking exhibit, playing a newsmaker in the mini TV studio, and making a flag in the self-esteem exhibit. The "ballroom," filled with 80,000 plastic balls that kids jump into and toss around, is the most popular spot. Exhibits change frequently, and special events are scheduled throughout the year. There's a special hour for preschool-age children.

The museum's KidSlope is a year-round ski slope where kids can learn to ski. The mini-mountain even has a Coca-Cola Junior NASCAR race course. Call about lessons. Instruction and equipment rental is $3.

Admission: $3 adults, $4 children, $1.50 seniors over 60, free for children under 2. Free admission during Friday Night Live.

Open: Tues–Sun 10am–5pm, plus Fri 5:30–8pm for Friday Night Live. **Directions:** Take Exit 211 (23rd Avenue) off I-25, exit east to 7th Street, turn right on 7th Street, and turn right on Crescent Drive.

ELITCH GARDENS AMUSEMENT PARK, on W. 38th Ave. at Tennyson St. Tel. 303/455-4771, or 303/485-3745 TDD.

Elitch Gardens boasts three great roller coasters, including the nationally rated "Twister." Other fun rides include the Flume water ride (especially on hot days), the Sidewinder, the 100-foot Ferris wheel, and the carousel with hand-carved horses circa 1924. With a dozen other major rides, a 53-lane Skee Ball casino, games of skill, an 18-hole miniature golf course, and Kiddieland for "itty-bitty" children, kids of all ages will keep themselves entertained. Rest breaks come while watching musical entertainment and children's theater. If you don't get an unlimited pass you can buy individual ride tickets inside.

Admission: Gate admission and unlimited rides: for adults and children over 52 inches tall, $13 Mon–Fri, $14.75 Sat–Sun; for children age 4 and less than 52 inches tall, $10.50 Mon–Fri, $12.25 Sat–Sun; for children 3 and under, $5.50 Mon–Fri, $6.75 Sat–Sun. Gate admission only (rides additional), $7.50 adults Mon–Fri, $8 Sat–Sun; $5 seniors 55 and over; free for children 3 and under.

Open: Mid-Apr and May, Fri from 5pm, Sat–Sun from 10am; June–Labor Day, daily from 10am. **Bus:** RTD bus no. 38, along 38th Avenue from downtown.

FUNPLEX, 9670 W. Coal Mine Ave. Tel. 303/972-4344.

Whether they're in the mood for bowling, miniature golf, roller skating, or video games, Funplex, at Kipling Street, is the place to leave older kids for hours of fun, or to occupy younger kids with you as the chaperone. Funplex has more than 100 of the newest video and carnival games, as well as several billiard tables. The complex also houses 40 bowling lanes with open and league bowling, a Putters Park with two 18-hole miniature golf courses, rides for the younger kids, the Midway with carnival games, and Starport for roller skating. Local teens love the "Rock 'n Bowl" late-night sessions when they turn off the lights (except on the lanes) and play rock music. Hungry? Don't worry. There are several places to buy food. Special discounts are available for tours and large groups. The hours vary according to school schedules, so it's best to call before going.

Admission: Varies according to the activity, ranging from $2.50 to $4.50. Discount "fun money" books go for $8.75, $10.60, and $14.25.

Open: Summer, daily 11am–10pm; winter, hours vary, depending on school and holiday schedules.

HERITAGE SQUARE, on U.S. 40 in Golden. Tel. 303/279-2789.

This Victorian-style shopping complex has an entertainment center with bumper cars, go-karts, a small roller coaster, and an alpine slide open in the summer. The kids will enjoy the chair-lift ride to the top of the hill, and the ride down the alpine slide on a mini-toboggan with a brake. There are two slides, one for slower riders.

Heritage Square plans an annual Fourth of July celebration and several other events; call for specifics. There's no charge to enter the complex of specialty shops and restaurants, but there are admission fees to use the alpine slide and the other rides and games.

Admission: Varies according to ride: alpine slide, $4 per ride adults, $3 children 7–12; children 6 and under ride free with an adult.

Open: Rides, Memorial Day to Labor Day, Mon–Sat 10am–9pm, Sun 12–9pm; fall to spring, weekends, weather permitting.

KIDSPORT, near Concourse C in the main terminal at Stapleton Airport. Tel. 303/333-6507.

If your kids are antsy at the airport, take them to KidsPort and let them climb the walls (literally), or explore the globe, the world of travel, and other entertaining—and educational—exhibits. Kidsport has a baby playspace too. There will be a KidsPort at Denver International Airport.

Admission: $1 adults, $2 children; free for children under 2.

Open: Daily 9am–7pm.

LAKESIDE, at I-70 and Sheridan Blvd. Tel. 303/477-1621.

Lakeside is Denver's other, equally popular, amusement park. The Cyclone Coaster, Wild Chipmunk (another type of coaster), and Heart Flip are just a sampling of the 27 major rides. There are also 15 kiddie rides in a separate Kiddies Playland.

Admission: 75¢ gate admission; unlimited-ride pass, $6.95 Mon–Fri, $7.95 Sat–Sun and hols.

Open: May, Sat–Sun noon–11pm; June–Labor Day, Mon–Fri 6–11pm, Sat–Sun and hols noon–11pm. Kiddie Playland, Mon–Fri 1–10pm, Sat–Sun noon–10pm. **Closed:** Early Sept to Apr.

PARAMOUNT THEATRE, 1631 Glenarm Place. Tel. 303/534-8336.

The Paramount Theatre, in the heart of downtown just off the mall, has many special events, movies, and plays for children throughout the year. Call the box office (or Ticketmaster) for specifics.

TINY TOWN, 6249 Turkey Creek Rd., Morrison. Tel. 303/ 697-6829.

Little ones will love riding on the miniature coal-burning choo-choo that chugs along a track past a replica of Denver's first bank and mint, Fire Station #1, and dozens of other miniature buildings in Tiny Town. Creation of this one-sixth-size town started as one man's hobby around 1915, but his family and area residents have restored and built more than 100 buildings in recent years, because it's such a favorite with local kids.

Admission: $2 adults, $1 seniors and children 3–12, free for children under 3.

Open: Memorial Day Weekend–Sept, daily 10am–7pm; May and Oct, Sat–Sun 10am–5pm. **Closed:** Nov–Apr. **Directions:** Go west on Hampden Avenue (it becomes U.S. 285), drive (still on U.S. 285) through rugged Turkey Creek Canyon (worth the ride alone) on the four-lane highway, and turn left onto South Turkey Creek Road and go about half a mile.

WATER WORLD, 1800 W. 89th Ave. (entrance on 90th Ave. west of Pecos St.). Tel. 303/427-SURF.

On a steamy hot summer day, the best place in town to be is Water World in Federal Heights. This complex has two oceanlike wave pools, twisting water slides, inner-tube rapids, and lots of other action to keep you cool and the kids happy. There's also a small children's play area.

Admission: $13.50 adults, $12.50 children 4–12, free for seniors 60 and older and children under 4.

Open: Memorial Day–Labor Day, Wed and Fri 10am–9pm, Sat–Tues and Thurs 10am–6pm. **Closed:** Labor Day–Memorial Day.

4. ORGANIZED TOURS

For year-round tours that offer spectacular mountain scenery, try **Best Mountain Tours by the Mountain Men,** 3003 S. Macon Circle, in Aurora (tel. 303/750-5200). Destinations and daily availability vary, so call for information. Rates are $18 per person for gambling in Central City or Blackhawk, $30 per person for a half-day tour, and $50 per person for all-day tours. Private charters, for up to 14 people per van, are $250 a half day, $350 per van for a full day. Private gambling charters are available for $18 per passenger, (minimum six people). Passengers are picked up and dropped off at their hotels.

Gray Line Bus Tours & Charters (tel. 303/289-2841) runs a variety of excursions, including daily tours of either Denver or the Denver Mountain Parks, stopping at Red Rocks, Evergreen, and Buffalo Bill Cody's grave. The city tour is $16 per person; the mountain parks tour, $19 (when purchased together you'll save $3). Call for information about these trips, gambling excursions, and other tours. Tours leave from the Denver Bus Center, at 19th and Curtis Streets.

Two Wheel Tours (tel. 303/798-4601) offers half- and full-days bike tours of the Denver metropolitan area, and full-day tours in the mountains. The Denver area tours include half-day trips through Waterton Canyon, near Chatfield Reservoir; a ride on the Platte River Greenway from Chatfield to downtown Denver; and a "Denver City Highlights" tour which includes stops at the Molly Brown House, City Park, and Washington Park. Full-day tours take bicyclists to Mt. Evans, Vail Pass, or Squaw Pass for "downhill" tours (a van takes you uphill and you coast downhill); or to Summit county.

Half-day day trips cost $39.50–$59.50; full-day trips, $59.50–$89.50. The cost includes bicycle and helmet rental, and the tours are led by guides who are knowledgeable about the area's history, geology, and wildlife. All day trips include breakfast. Tours also include pickup and drop-off at your hotel.

WALKING TOUR 1 — DOWNTOWN'S
UPTOWN

Start: The corner of Larimer Street and 16th Street.
Finish: Right where you started.
Time: Allow 1½–2 hours, not including museum and shopping stops.
Best Times: Weekdays after the working crowd enters their offices.
Worst Times: Monday and holidays when the museums are closed.

Walking is a wonderful way to see and enjoy a city's idiosyncracies up close. If you want more in-depth knowledge about the buildings and sights on the downtown tours, stop at the visitors bureau and pick up a copy of the "Mile High Trail," a $1.50 booklet outlining six walking loops of downtown Denver.

A stroll around the uptown part of Denver's downtown reveals the high-energy business face of the city, and allows stops at some of the best museums. This tour includes a walk along parts of the 16th Street Mall, and stops at the Brown Palace, the Denver Art Museum, and the Capitol Building.

Begin at the corner of Writer Square and walk down 16th Street to the:

1. **Tabor Center,** on the 16th Street Mall between Larimer and Arapahoe Streets, is filled with shops, including two adult "toy" stores: Brookstone and Sharper Image. Be sure to walk upstairs and browse the vendors' carts in the bridge connecting the center's two buildings. The neighboring building is the:
2. **D & F Tower,** 1601 Arapahoe St., 325 feet tall and one of the Mile High City's most famous landmarks. It was inspired by the campanile in St. Mark's Square in Venice, and when completed was the tallest building west of the Mississippi. Continue down the mall to the:
3. **Ticket Bus,** at 16th and Curtis Streets, if you want to get tickets for any events, concerts, or plays.
   Now board the free shuttle bus and ride it to the end of the

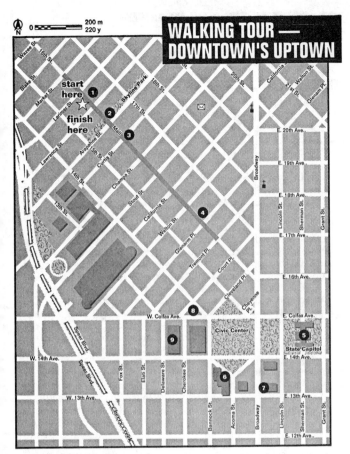

1 Tabor Center
2 D & F Tower
3 Ticket Bus
4 Paramount Theatre
5 State Capitol Building
6 Denver Art Museum
7 Voorhees Memorial and Fountain
8 Denver Convention and Visitor's Bureau
9 U. S. Mint

mile-long mall. As you go, notice the eclectic mix of buildings filled with stores. The mixture of architectural styles ranges from the ornamental Symes Building (820 16th St.) with its historical references such as egg and dart molding, to the Colorado Building (1615 California St.) with its mixtures of styles and art deco fir-tree frieze. If you look toward 17th Street, you'll see the sleek high-rise buildings that went up during Denver's energy boom in the 1970s and 1980s.

The next stop is the:

4. **Paramount Theatre,** 1623-41 Glenarm Place, the city's last movie palace which contains one of two operable dual-console Wurlitzer pipe organs in the country.

REFUELING STOP   The lively **Paramount Café** is set in the former lobby and is filled with movie memorabilia. The patio tables fill up when it's warm. An alternative choice is the adjacent **Goldie's Deli,** which has a yogurt machine.

When you're ready to continue your tour, get off at the end of the line, the Civic Center Bus Terminal. Turn left and walk down Broadway half a block to the corner of Colfax Avenue. The Civic Center Park will be to your right, and to your left will be the:

5. **State Capitol Building,** built in Federal Revival style and capped with a dome covered with 200 ounces of 24-karat gold leaf (see "More Attractions," above, for more information). Walk up the west-side steps to the marker that says you're one mile above sea level. Take a free tour of the building if you want, and head up the steps to the open-air viewing deck on the rotunda if you want a spectacular view of the mountains.
   Next, stroll across the green areas to the:

6. **Denver Art Museum,** a futuristic-looking fortress (see "The Top Attractions," above, for complete information). Take a look at the outstanding collection of Native American art and artifacts, and other parts of the museum's permanent collection. (Stop in the walled courtyard and see the Red Grooms sculpture.)
   Walk across the street to the:

7. **Voorhees Memorial and Fountain.** You'll get a terrific photograph of downtown Denver and the mountains if you put the *Bucking Bronco* statue, by Alexander Phimister Proctor, in the picture's foreground. On your left, the granite City and County Building, 1437 Bannock St., boasts one of the largest Christmas-light displays in the country at Christmastime. Return to Colfax Avenue and turn left for a stop at the:

8. **Denver Convention and Visitors Bureau,** at 225 W. Colfax Ave. There's a wealth of literature (including the "Mile High Trail" walking-tour booklet), and the staff is trained to answer your questions about where to go and what to see. Catercorner to the visitors bureau is the:

9. **U.S. Mint,** a "must see" stop on your tour. If the line is too long for your patience level, walk around the other side of the building and visit the gift shop which has exhibits, and numismatic items, coins, and more for sale. (See "The Top Attractions," above, for complete information.)
   Retrace your steps on Colfax Avenue and return to the Civic Center Bus Terminal.

REFUELING STOP   If it's tea time and you enjoy elegant surroundings, keep walking up Broadway to 17th Avenue and enter the **Brown Palace Hotel,** where tea is served every afternoon in the opulent lobby lounge capped by a nine-story atrium with a stained-glass ceiling. If you prefer a less fancy place, hop back on the 16th Street Mall shuttle and get off at the **Rock Bottom Brewery,** 1001 16th St.

Hop back on the shuttle and get off at Larimer Street, where you started. Stroll through Writer's Square, then call it a day.

WALKING TOUR 2 — LOWER
DOWNTOWN

Start: Larimer and 14th Streets.
Finish: Larimer Square.
Time: 1½–2 hours, not including stops.
Best Times: Anytime during the business day or weekend days.
Worst Times: When the galleries and boutiques are closed.

Lower downtown (or "LoDo," as the locals have nicknamed the area) is a vibrant section of the city where interesting shops, restaurants, and an increasing number of businesses are filling up renovated Victorian buildings and warehouses. This was once a deserted area at nighttime, but now loft apartments are being sold almost as fast as they're being built and folks are staying downtown to meet friends in the brewpubs or attend performances at the PLEX. Option for this tour: Hire a horse-drawn carriage to do the walking for you, while you do the looking.

1. **Larimer Square** was the one commercial block that the city of Denver had in 1858 (although it's not the original name), and it's the right place to start exploring historic lower downtown. From the corner of 14th Street and Larimer Street, head toward 15th Street, stopping to eye (and visit) the meticulously renovated Victorian buildings that house restaurants, specialty shops, and boutiques. The renovation of run-down Larimer Street in 1965, from shabby buildings that once housed bars and brothels, was the nudge needed to begin upgrading the entire district. Most of the buildings are brick or stone, because the use of wood was banned after an 1863 fire. As you explore this district, you'll notice that the mountains still frame many of LoDo's buildings, because city officials have insisted on restricting building heights here.
   On the south side of the street is the:
2. **Squash Blossom,** with its excellent assortment of western collectibles: quality Native American pottery, ranger belts, and lots of silver jewelry with inlaid turquoise and other stones.
   On the north side of the street, step into:
3. **The Market** and purchase an espresso at the counter and then browse this food emporium. Join the crowds reading papers or just whiling away time at the tables indoors or outdoors.
   Turn left on 15th Street, then right on Market Street. As you head north, peek in the windows of the public buildings, or walk through the public areas in a few of the buildings, for a look at the stunning way architects have combined contemporary design with historical detail.
   Turn left at 17th Street and stop in the historic:
4. **Hotel Oxford** and take a look at the art deco Cruise Lounge. This hotel has been a hostelry since the late 1800s.
   Back outside, visit the art gallery next door, then walk toward:
5. **Union Station,** built in 1881, where the trains roll through every day.

Turn right on Wynkoop and walk to 18th Street, noticing the:
6. **Beatrice Creamery Building,** at 1801 Wynkoop Street, considered one of the best examples of polychrome brickwork in the region. Today the renovated building, called the Ice House, is a design center. (Coors Field, home for Denver's new National League baseball team, the Colorado Rockies, is under construction two blocks north.)

Turn right onto 18th Street and you're ready for a:

REFUELING STOP At the **Wynkoop Brewery** you can sample the brews (buy a grouping of brews, each in a small tasting glass) and enjoy the ambience in Denver's oldest microbrewery (and that's not very old). Time it right and you can take a tour of the microbrewery. There's an upmarket billiard hall over the restaurant and loft apartments on the top floors.

A funky fueling stop for adults with kids (or those who love Miss Piggy and her relatives), **Hog Heaven,** at 1525 Blake Street, is just a few blocks away.

Outside the Wynkoop, head to the right on 18th Street and turn right onto:
7. **Wazee Street.** This section of LoDo contains about 20 art galleries and interesting shops in the old warehouses and factory buildings, including Robischon (1740 Wazee), Rule Modern and Contemporary (1736 Wazee), and Art for Living, Soho West (1730 Wazee).

Keep strolling down Wazee until you reach:
8. **The Elephant Corral,** 1444 Wazee St. The first cabin registered in the territory was erected on this site. By 1859 it housed a primitive log hotel and doubled as a freight station for livestock and supplies. Today it houses several elegantly decorated professional offices and companies behind 10-foot-high doors.

To end your tour, turn left on 14th Street and head back to Larimer Square.

5. SPORTS & RECREATION

SPECTATOR SPORTS

AUTO RACING There's drag racing at **Bandimere Speedway,** 3051 S. Rooney Rd., in the foothills community of Morrison (tel. 303/697-4870). The season runs from April through September.

BASEBALL Denver is in a state of euphoria because the city is getting its very own major-league baseball team: the **Colorado Rockies.** This new member of the National League plays its first game in the Mile High Stadium in April 1993. The new Coors Field is under construction and expected to open in 1995.

BASKETBALL The **Denver Nuggets** basketball team (tel. 303/893-6700 for ticket information) averages 40 home games each season in McNichols Arena, in the same sports complex as Mile High Stadium. Ticket prices run $8–$18.

DOG RACING Head to the **Mile-High Greyhound Park,** at Colorado Boulevard and 62nd Avenue (tel. 303/288-1591), for

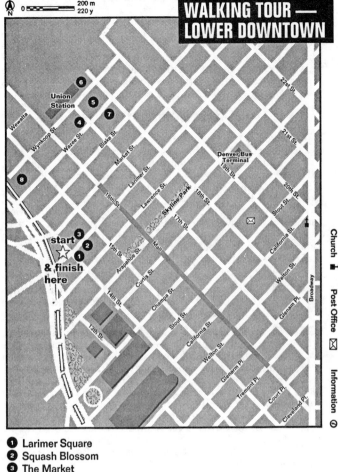

200 m
220 y

Union Station

Denver Bus Terminal

Skyline Park

start & finish here

Church ✝

Post Office ⊠

Information ☉

1. Larimer Square
2. Squash Blossom
3. The Market
4. Hotel Oxford
5. Union Station
6. Beatrice Creamery Building
7. Wazee Street art galleries
8. Elephant Corral

pari-mutuel greyhound racing June through February. Watch from the trackside dining room. General admission is $1; clubhouse admission, $3.

FOOTBALL The **Denver Broncos** (tel. 303/433-7466), of the National Football League, play their home games in Mile High Stadium, part of a sports complex at Exit 210B of I-25, at West 17th Avenue. Bronco fans have a nationwide reputation for being among the most avid supporters of a football team. With the exception of about 250 single seats (costing $19–$30), most home games are sold out well in advance. Occasionally there are single seats available the day of game, so call the box office. However, there's usually someone hawking tickets outside the main gates of the stadium on game day. If the weather's nice, take your chances—maybe you'll be lucky enough to get in and cheer for this NFL team, along with the other spectators being led by the Barrel Man, perhaps the team's most famous fan.

RECREATIONAL SPORTS

If you've come to Denver without gear for recreational activities, contact **Sports Rent.** This company rents everything from complete camping packages, mountain bikes, and canoes to sailboards, rollerblades, and exercise equipment. Sports Rent has two locations: 8761 Wadsworth Blvd., Arvada (tel. 303/467-0200), and 560 S. Holly St. (tel. 303/320-0222).

Daily guest passes are available at many of the 37 **recreation centers** around town. There are outdoor and indoor pools, fitness classes, weight rooms, and pickup basketball. For more information about what's available near your hotel, ask at the front desk or call Denver Parks and Recreation (tel. 303/964-2500). The daily guest fee for nonresidents is $4 for adults and $2 for youths 17 and younger.

BALLOONING To see the Front Range and the mountains while floating in a hot-air balloon, contact the **Life Cycle Balloon School,** 2450 S. Steele St. (tel. 303/759-3907).

BOATING & SWIMMING The **Cherry Creek Reservoir,** right in Denver, is a recreational area with bathing beaches at a lake that's open for boating and fishing, and miles of bike and jogging paths. For more information about using the park, contact the Cherry Creek State Recreation Area office (tel. 303/699-3860). You can rent bikes, sailboats, jet skis, and powerboats at the **Cherry Creek Marina** (tel. 303/779-6144). Arrangements may also be made for windsurfing or rollerblading rentals and instruction. The park is open year round, but the Cherry Creek Marina's season runs from April 1 to October 31.

You can also swim and boat at **Chatfield Reservoir** in the southwest metropolitan area.

FISHING There are more than 7,100 miles of streams and more than 2,000 reservoirs and lakes where you can drop a line or cast for fish in Colorado—but you'll need a license. For information about fishing licenses and fishing in local lakes and streams, contact **Uncle Milty's Tackle Box,** 4811 S. Broadway, Englewood, CO 80110 (tel. 303/789-3775); and for information about licenses, guide service, and fishing in higher mountain lakes and streams, contact **Flyfisher Ltd.,** 252 Clayton St., Denver, CO 80202 (tel. 303/322-5014).

GOLF Local chamber of commerce officials like to boast that Denverites can play golf more than 300 days a year because the sun shines so much, and even when it snows, very little sticks to the ground. There are several public golf courses: **City Park Golf Course,** East 25th Avenue and York Street (tel. 303/295-4420); **Harvard Gulch Golf Course** (par 3), East Iliff Avenue and South Clarkson Street (tel. 303/698-4078); **Kennedy Golf Course,** 10500 E. Hampden Ave. (tel. 303/751-0311), also with miniature golf on the premises; **Overland Golf Course,** South Santa Fe Drive and Jewell Avenue (tel. 303/698-4975); **Wellshire Golf Course,** 3333 S. Colorado Blvd. (tel. 303/692-5636); and **Willis Case Golf Course,** West 50th Avenue and Vrain Street (tel. 303/458-4877).

Greens fees for nonresidents at city courses are $16 for 18 holes, $10 for 9 holes, and $6 for the par-3 course. Call for hours, reservation of tee-off times, and to verify greens fees.

The 18-hole **Plum Creek Golf and Country Club,** 331 Players Club Dr., Castler Rock (tel. 303/688-2612), in the hill country 15 miles south of Denver, is open to the public.

HIKING & BACKPACKING You can explore the **Rocky Mountains,** but you'd better be properly prepared and equipped before venturing into the wilderness, even for an afternoon stroll. Call **EMS,** "the Outdoor Specialists," in the Villa Italia Shopping Center, West Alameda Avenue and South Wadsworth Boulevard in Lakewood (tel. 303/936-8612).

HORSEBACK RIDING You can take a guided ride at **Stockton's Plum Creek Stables,** 7479 W. Titan Rd., in suburban Littleton (tel. 303/791-1966), throughout the year. Guided rides, by reservation only, are $11 per rider; children must be at least 6 years old. Stockton's, located a 40-minute drive southwest of downtown near the Chatfield Reservoir, also offers barbecues, hayrides, winter sleighrides, and fishing.

JOGGING & BIKING Denver has more than 130 miles of off-road jogging and biking paths winding alongside streams and in parks throughout the metropolitan area. The front-desk clerk at your hotel will be able to tell you how to reach the section of the trail nearest you. There are 205 parks within the city, so there's plenty of green space for exercising outdoors.

You can rent bikes at **Cycle Logic,** 8936 W. Bowles Ave., Littleton (tel. 303/979-4868).

SKIING There are 25 downhill ski areas and many Nordic centers for cross-country skiers in this state, and several are located within a one- or two-hour drive of Denver. **Loveland Basin & Valley** (tel. 303/569-3203, or 303/571-5580 in Denver), **Winter Park** (tel. 303/726-5514, or 303/892-0961 in Denver), and **Eldora Mountain Resort** (tel. 303/440-8700) are the day-skiing areas closest to the city. At Loveland, one quad-chair, two triple-chair, double-chair lifts, and a poma lift access the 1,680-vertical-foot slopes. Winter Park has 20 lifts, including four high-speed quads, spread over the resort's adjacent peaks: Winter Park (2,220 vertical feet), Mary Jane (3,060 vertical feet), and Vasquez Ridge (1,214 vertical feet). Eldora's five double-chair lifts and a surface lift will get you to the 1,400-vertical-foot drop.

The **Denver Ski Lift** will transport you from your hotel to ski country for the day. Through the "Lift," you can also rent ski equipment and even winter clothing. For more information, call toll free 800/283-2754.

The Gart Brothers Ski Lift runs motorcoaches to some of the ski areas. Call the ski department at Gart Brothers (tel. 303/861-1122) for more information about the ski bus.

On weekends, ride the **Rio Grande Ski Train** (tel. 303/296-I-SKI) from downtown Union Station to Winter Park. After a two-hour ride through 34 tunnels, the mountains, on bridges over rivers, and through canyons, you'll arrive at the ski area in time for a full day on the slopes. The train leaves for the return trip to Denver as the lifts are closing.

For information about other ski areas in the state, contact **Colorado Ski Country USA**, 1560 Broadway, Suite 1440, Denver, CO 80202 (tel. 303/837-0793).

6. SAVVY SHOPPING

SHOPPING CENTERS

The premiere shopping address in Denver is the **Cherry Creek Shopping Center** (tel. toll free 800/424-6360), anchored by Lord and Taylor, Neiman-Marcus, Saks Fifth Avenue, and May D&F. The upscale mall ranked within the top 2% of shopping centers nationwide within a year of opening. More than 130 specialty shops include F. A. O. Schwarz, the Disney Store, Gucci, and Abercrombie & Fitch.

Adjacent **Cherry Creek North** boasts a collection of wonderful boutiques, galleries, restaurants, and sidewalk cafés strung along 1st, 2nd, and 3rd Avenues between University Boulevard and Steele Street. Store hours vary.

In the downtown area, you'll find specialty shops in **Writers Square,** between 15th and 16th Streets and Lawrence and Larimer Streets (tel. 303/628-9056).

Adjacent **Larimer Square,** the 1400 block of Larimer Street (tel. 303/534-2367), is a focal point of downtown activity. The crowds are a combination of visitors and locals, checking out merchandise in the shops and galleries, and filling up the restaurants, brewpub, and the Market tables, usually spilling out onto the sidewalk tables on warm days. The Victorian buildings here comprise the original Denver shopping district. The renovation and reemergence of Larimer Square has garnered national recognition for revitalization of a run-down downtown sector. Shops run the gamut from kitchenware at Williams-Sonoma to clothes at Laura Ashley or Ann Taylor and Native American art at the Squash Blossom. Store hours vary.

Tivoli Denver, at 9th and Larimer Streets (tel. 303/629-8712), is a wonderful-looking renovated brewery across the creek from Larimer Square. Although it fizzled in its original intent (to be a significant shopping center), Tivoli does house a 12-plex movie theater; Morton's of Chicago, an expensive steak house; the Boiler Room, a sports bar; Club Infinity, a dance club; and stores such as Fashion Bar and the Stage. Hours vary.

SHOPPING A TO Z

Both around town and in the nearby suburbs, Denver has thousands of shops just waiting for you. Here are some of my favorite shops, arranged by the type of merchandise they carry.

ANTIQUES

There's a strip of antiques shops on South Broadway. Some 40 shops are under one roof at **1298 South Broadway** (tel. 303/722-3359, 303/722-3358, or 303/722-3365). Shops in this mall deal in fine American and European hardwood furniture, American primitive and pine furniture, deco, nouveau, prints, lamps, stained glass, textiles, fine glass and china, and accessories. Hours are 10am to 5:30pm Monday through Saturday and noon to 5pm on Sunday.

COBWEB SHOPPE, 28136 Colo. 74. Tel. 303/674-7833.

The Cobweb Shoppe, in downtown Evergreen, a 40-minute drive from downtown Denver, has several dealers housing antiques, collectibles, jewelry and other unusual items. Open daily from 10am to 5pm.

ART & ARTISAN GALLERIES

There are many good galleries spread around town (also see "Southwestern Collectibles" and "Photographic Galleries," below). For the most complete list of current exhibits, check Friday's "Weekend" section in the *Denver Post*.

BROADWAY CENTRAL GALLERIES, between 9th and 10th Sts.

Broadway Central Galleries is a cluster of four galleries located in downtown Denver. The **Inkfish Gallery,** 949 Broadway (tel. 303/825-6727), specializes in museum-quality contemporary art in all price ranges. The **Alpha Gallery,** 959 Broadway (tel. 303/623-3577), features contemporary paintings and sculpture by regional and national artists. The **Joan Robey Gallery,** 939 Broadway (tel. 303/892-9600), features three-dimensional sculptures in a variety of media. **Brigitte Schluger Gallery—Arctic Art,** 929 Broadway (tel. 303/825-8555), features 20th-century American folk and outsider art, Eskimo carvings and prints, and African masks and artifacts, plus works by regional and national artists (closed Monday). Free parking is available on the corner of 9th Street and Broadway. Gallery hours vary slightly, but most are open Monday through Friday from 10am to 5pm and on Saturday from noon to 5pm.

CAROL SIPLE GALLERY, 1401 17th St. Tel. 303/292-1401.

This gallery represents regional and national artists. Open Monday through Friday from 11am to 5pm and on Saturday from noon to 4pm, or by appointment.

CIRCLE GALLERY, 221 Detroit St. Tel. 303/377-8706.

This gallery features contemporary and abstract artwork in all media by upcoming and internationally recognized artists and sculptors. Open Monday through Saturday from 10am to 6pm and on Sunday from noon to 5pm.

CLAY PIGEON, 601 Ogden St. Tel. 303/832-5538.

The Clay pigeon specializes in contemporary works in clay, featuring many porcelain and stoneware pieces. Open Tuesday through Friday from 10am to 6pm and on Saturday from 10am to 5pm.

EMMANUEL GALLERY, on the Auraria Campus, near 10th St. and Larimer St. Tel. 303/556-8337.

The Emmanuel Gallery, housed in an old stone Episcopal chapel which also served as a synagogue, presents contemporary art exhibits of well-known artists, plus campus faculty and student exhibitions. Open Monday through Friday from 11am to 5pm; call for additional hours, but closed during semester breaks.

FOOTHILLS ART CENTER, 809 15th St., Golden. Tel. 303/279-3922.

The Foothills Art Center runs a variety of exhibits, from weavings and sculpture to photography and mixed media. Call for hours and information about the current exhibits. Open Monday through Saturday from 9am to 4pm and on Sunday from 1 to 4pm.

GALLERY ONE OF WRITERS SQUARE, 1512 Larimer St. Tel. 303/629-5005.

Here you'll find an outstanding collection of paintings, graphics, and sculptures by internationally recognized artists, including Rothe, Erte, and Miró. Open Monday and Tuesday from 10am to 6pm, Wednesday through Saturday from 10am to 9pm and on Sunday from noon to 5pm.

KOHLBERG'S, 1720 Champa St. Tel. 303/292-4578.

A century-old business with a vast selection of antiques, jewelry and authentic Native American crafts. Open Monday through Saturday from 9am to 5:30pm.

THE KNOX GALLERIES, 1632 Market St. Tel. 303/820-2324.

Representational art by artists such as Mark Thompson and Kim English; and sculpture by George Lundeen, Glenna Goodacre, and others. Open Monday through Friday from 10am to 6pm and on Saturday from noon to 4pm.

MANOS, 101 Broadway. Tel. 303/778-8262.

Manos features folk art from Mexico, Guatemala, and Peru, as well as a few local artists. Open Tuesday through Saturday from 11am to 7:30pm and on Sunday from noon to 5pm.

MICHAEL GARMAN GALLERY, 8501 W. Bowles Ave., Littleton. Tel. 303/979-0999.

At South Wadsworth Boulevard, in the Southwest Plaza Shopping Center, the Michael Garman Gallery features intriguing sculptures and cityscapes of Americana. Open Monday through Friday from 10am to 9pm, on Saturday from 10am to 6pm, and on Sunday from 11am to 6pm.

MUDHEAD GALLERY, 555 17th St. Tel. 303/293-0007.

The selection of western and southwestern art includes Kachina dolls, pottery, Navajo rugs, bronzes, paintings, and jewelry. Open Monday through Friday from 9am to 6pm, on Saturday from 9am to 5pm, and on Sunday 10am to 4pm.

The Mudhead has a second location in the Brown Palace Hotel at 321 17th St. (tel. 303/293-9977), with similar hours.

NATIVE AMERICAN TRADING COMPANY, 1301 Bannock St. Tel. 303/534-0771.

This company across the street from the Denver Art Museum has an extensive collection of older Native American weavings, pots, baskets, paintings, jewelry, and artifacts. There are choices here for serious collectors as well as for novices. Open Monday through Friday from 10am to 5pm and on Saturday from 11am to 4pm.

ROBISCHON GALLERY, 1740 Wazee St. Tel. 303/298-7788.

There are choices for serious and beginning collectors at this gallery which specializes in modern, realist, and abstract art. There's an emphasis on artists from the southwestern and mountain states. Open Tuesday through Friday from 10am to 6pm and on Saturday from 11am to 5pm; on Sunday and Monday by appointment.

ROYCE GALLERIES, 2721 E. 3rd Ave. Tel. 303/333-1722.

This gallery features original graphics, lithographs, etchings, and serigraphs by such artists as Neiman and Doolittle. Open Monday through Friday from 10am to 6pm and on Saturday from 10am to 5pm.

SLOANE GALLERY OF ART, 1612 17th St. Tel. 303/595-4230.

Here you'll find paintings, sculptures, and lithographs by internationally known Russian artists. Open Tuesday through Saturday from noon to 8pm.

TAOS CONNECTIONS, 162 Adams St. Tel. 303/393-8267.

Located in Cherry Creek North, Taos Connections features regional and southwestern contemporary art. Open Monday through Friday from 10am to 6pm and on Saturday from 10am to 4pm.

TURNER ART GALLERY, 301 University Blvd. Tel. 303/355-1828.

This gallery displays contemporary and older American and European oils, antique botanicals, and Colorado landscapes. Open on Monday from 10am to 4pm and Tuesday through Saturday from 9am to 5:30pm.

BOOKSTORES

Many national bookstore chains have outlets in the Denver/Boulder area. **B. Dalton Bookseller** has 10 outlets, including one in the Tabor Center complex. **Waldenbooks** has 10 outlets, most in shopping malls. Barnes and Noble has four stores spread around the metropolitan area.

COLORADO HISTORY MUSEUM, 13th Ave. and Broadway. Tel. 303/866-4993.

The gift shop here has an extensive collection of books on local history. The museum has an excellent western research library. Open Monday through Saturday from 10am to 4:30pm and on Sunday from noon to 4:30pm.

COLORADO RAILROAD MUSEUM, 17155 W. 44th Ave., Golden. Tel. 303/279-4591.

The gift shop at this museum has an extensive collection of books about railroads. Open daily from 9am to 5pm.

HATCH'S, 2700 S. Colorado Blvd., in the University Hills Mall. Tel. 303/757-1028.

An excellent local chain of general-interest bookstores, there are four outlets owned by the company and a few franchise operations in the Denver/Boulder area. Most stores are open Monday through Friday from 9:30am to 9pm, on Saturday from 9:30am to 6pm, and on Sunday from noon to 5pm.

HERMITAGE ANTIQUARIAN BOOKSHOP, 290 Fillmore St. Tel. 303/388-6811.

Selling recent and antiquarian out-of-print books, Hermitage specializes in history and literature. Open Monday through Friday from 10am to 5:30pm, on Saturday from 10am to 5pm, and on Sunday from 11am to 4pm.

HUE-MAN EXPERIENCE, 911 Park Ave. W. Tel. 303/293-2665.

This is an ethnic bookstore with books by, for, and about African-Americans. Open Monday through Friday from 10:30am to 6:30pm and on Saturday from 10am to 5pm.

MUSEUM OF WESTERN ART, 1727 Tremont Place. Tel. 303/296-1880.

The museum has an impressive collection of books about western art and western artists. Open Tuesday through Saturday from 10am to 4:30pm.

OLD ALGONQUIN BOOKSTORE, 5900 E. Colfax Ave. Tel. 303/388-2224.

The Old Algonquin features used hardcover books. There are other used-book stores nearby. Open Monday through Saturday from 10am to 5pm and on Sunday from 10am to 4pm.

THE TATTERED COVER, 2955 E. 1st Ave. Tel. 303/322-7727.

⭐ On any given day this store has more than 400,000 books (115,000 titles) spread around the four floors. The magazine room, for example, has approximately 1,100 different titles. The Tattered Cover retains that old-fashioned atmosphere where readers are encouraged to browse and sit on comfortable chairs to read for a while. Each section, from Colorado history to psychology, is headed by specialists who can pull up the information or the name of the book you want on a computer. Open Monday through Saturday from 9:30am to 9pm and on Sunday from 10am to 6pm.

COLORADO PRODUCTS & SOUVENIRS

COLORADO PEDDLER, 15th St. at Lawrence St. Tel. 303/825-2932.

Located in Writers Square, the Peddler specializes in Colorado products made by more than 200 artisans around the state. Open Monday through Saturday from 10am to 6pm and on Sunday from noon to 5pm.

DEPARTMENT STORES

MAY D&F, 16th St. and Tremont Place. Tel. 303/620-9005.

Selling everything from gloves and T-shirts to pots and pans, there are several May D&F stores around the Denver area, most located in shopping malls. Open Monday through Saturday from 10am to 5pm.

DRUGSTORES

WALGREEN'S, 16th St. Mall at Stout St. Tel. 303/571-5316.

There are Walgreen drugstores all around the city; this location is downtown. Open Monday through Friday from 7am to 6:30pm, on Saturday from 8am to 6pm, and on Sunday from 11am to 5pm.

WATSON'S PHARMACY, 900 Lincoln St. Tel. 303/837-1366.

Watson's is an old-fashioned drugstore complete with a soda fountain, liquor store, and post office. Open Monday through Thursday from 9am to 11pm, on Friday from 9am to midnight, on Saturday from 10am to midnight, and on Sunday from noon to 9pm.

FASHION

ALL WEEK LONG OUTLET, A DIVISION OF EDDIE BAUER, INC., 750 16th Street Mall. Tel. 303/534-3050, or toll free 800/426-8020.

You'll find lots of excellent outdoor clothing and sporting gear for women at this Eddie Bauer store. Open Monday through Saturday from 9:30am to 6pm and on Sunday from noon to 5pm.

APPLAUSE, 2820 E. 3rd Ave., at Fillmore St. Tel. 303/321-7580.

Applause is filled with delightful, fine wearable art. You'll find an eclectic collection of clothing, accessories, jewelry, hand-painted furniture, and gifts. Open Monday through Saturday from 10am to 6pm.

BANANA REPUBLIC, 535 16th St. Tel. 303/595-8877.

The casual, private-label clothing for men and women ranges from rugged to refined looks. Accessories too. Open Monday through Saturday from 9:30am to 6pm and on Sunday from noon to 5pm.

FASHION BAR, 16th Street Mall. Tel. 303/620-9811.

The Fashion Bar, located downtown at Tremont Place, sells clothes for women and men in a wide price range. There are more than 20 Fashion Bars in Colorado, many located in malls. Open Monday through Saturday from 10am to 6pm.

MAX, 1411 Larimer Sq. Tel. 303/623-2888.

Max features women's sportswear with an ultra-contemporary look. Open Monday through Friday from 10am to 7pm, on Saturday from 10am to 6pm, and on Sunday from noon to 5pm.

GIFTS

COLORADO IN A BASKET, 2120 Grape St. Tel. 303/756-4778.

Stop here if you want to send a basket full of Colorado gifts and foods home to your friends. Open Monday through Friday from 9am to 5pm; Saturday call first.

GROCERIES

Safeway, King Soopers, and Albertson's are the main chains.

ALFALFA'S, 201 University Blvd. Tel. 303/320-0700.

If you're the type who wants to pick up specialty items and the "best" beef, fish, salads, fresh coffee beans, etc., head for Alfalfa's. You can put together a gourmet lunch to go, or just a sandwich, at the deli and bakery counters. Open Monday through Saturday from 8am to 10pm and on Sunday from 8am to 9pm.

JEWELRY

See "Southwestern Collectibles" for Touch of Santa Fe and the Squash Blossom, both of which carry wonderful silver jewelry (many pieces with stone inlays) made by Native Americans.

JOHN ATENCIO, 280 Detroit St. Tel. 303/377-2007.
This shop specializes in exquisite one-of-a-kind, handcrafted pieces of gold jewelry, many set with precious or semiprecious stones. Open Monday through Friday from 10am to 5:30pm and on Saturday from 10am to 5pm.

LUGGAGE

A. E. MEEK TRUNK AND BAG COMPANY, 1616 Stout St. Tel. 303/534-0770.
This company has an excellent selection of luggage, business cases, small leather goods, and interesting gifts, including many upscale items. Open Monday through Friday from 9:30am to 5:30pm and on Saturday from 10am to 4pm.

SOUTHWESTERN COLLECTIBLES

THE SQUASH BLOSSOM GALLERY, 1428 Larimer St. Tel. 303/572-7979.
Here you'll find an excellent collection of handmade silver jewelry by southwestern Native Americans, as well as crafts, fine art and folk art, furniture, artifacts, and gift items. Open Monday through Wednesday from 10am to 7pm, on Thursday and Friday from 10am to 9pm, on Saturday from 10am to 8pm, and on Sunday from noon to 5pm, with extended holiday hours.

TOUCH OF SANTA FE, 6574 S. Broadway, Littleton. Tel. 303/730-2408.
★ Whether you're a serious collector of Native American and southwestern collectibles, including art, pottery, and jewelry, or a tourist who wants to get an inexpensive but authentic piece, this is the place to visit. Potters range from Maria to Feather Woman, and jewelers include Ben Nighthorse and Kenneth Aguilar. The selection is the best in the Denver metropolitan area. Open Monday through Friday from 10:30am to 5:30pm and on Saturday from 10am to 5:30pm.

MALLS

AURORA MALL, East Alameda Ave. and S. Sable St., Aurora. Tel. 303/344-4120.
On the east side of Denver, the Aurora Mall has 136 stores on two levels. Anchors include Sears, J. C. Penney, and May D&F. Open Monday through Friday from 10am to 9pm, on Saturday from 10am to 7pm, and on Sunday noon to 6pm.

CINDERELLA CITY, W. Hampden Ave. and Broadway. Tel. 303/761-6800.
Located on the southwestern side of the city, this mall has several department stores and many specialty stores. Once the largest and best shopping on this side of the city, the mall still houses more than 120 stores, but far less than when opened. Open Monday through

Friday from 10am to 9pm, on Saturday from 10am to 6pm, and on Sunday from noon to 5pm.

THE SHOPS AT TABOR CENTER, 16th St. Mall at Lawrence St. Tel. 303/534-2141.

A complex with a mix of mostly upscale clothing, adult and kids' toys, books, shoes, and curio shops, there are 65 stores on three levels, including pushcarts and fast-food outlets. The Tabor Center is on the 16th Street Mall and connected to the Westin Hotel. Open Monday through Friday from 10am to 9pm, on Saturday from 10am to 6pm, and on Sunday from noon to 5pm.

SOUTHWEST PLAZA MALL, 8501 W. Bowles Ave., Littleton. Tel. 303/973-5300.

At South Wadsworth Boulevard at the southwest end of the metropolitan area, the popular Southwest Plaza Mall has 200 stores on two levels. Anchor stores are Joslins, May D&F, Sears, Montgomery Ward, and J. C. Penney. Open Monday through Friday from 10am to 9pm, on Saturday from 10am to 6pm, and on Sunday from 11am to 6pm.

WESTMINSTER MALL, U.S. 36 and Sheridan Blvd., Westminster. Tel. 303/428-5634.

This mall, on the north side of the metropolitan area, has 150 stores on one level. Anchors include Broadway Southwest, Joslins, May D&F, Mervyn's, and J. C. Penney. Open Monday through Saturday from 10am to 9pm and on Sunday from noon to 6pm.

VILLA ITALIA SHOPPING CENTER, W. Alameda Ave. and S. Wadsworth Blvd., Lakewood. Tel. 303/936-7424.

Villa Italia has 185 stores on two levels and a busy food court where you can get Japanese to barbecue. Anchors include May D&F, Joslins, Montgomery Ward, and J. C. Penney. Open Monday through Friday from 10am to 9pm, on Saturday from 10am to 6pm, and on Sunday from 11am to 5pm.

OFFICE SUPPLIES

COMPUTER RENTALS, 2422 S. Colorado Blvd. Tel. 303/782-0070, or toll free 800/437-0233.

You can come and use a wide range of equipment and software by the hour. The store also stocks computer equipment for delivery to local businesses and hotel guests. Open Monday through Friday from 8:30am to 5pm and on Saturday from 9am to 4pm.

OFFICE DEPOT, 600 E. Colfax Ave. Tel. 303/832-2582.

This warehouse-style office-supply store has a comprehensive range of office supplies and equipment at highly competitive prices. There are four Office Depot stores in the metro area. The other locations are 770 S. Colorado Blvd., Glendale (tel. 303/782-9400); 8525 E. Arapahoe Rd., Englewood (tel. 303/850-9800); and 1090 W. Hampden Ave. (tel. 303/761-9462). Open Monday through Friday from 8am to 7pm, on Saturday from 9am to 5pm, and on Sunday from 11am to 5pm.

PHOTOGRAPHIC GALLERIES

CAMERA OBSCURA, 1309 Bannock St. Tel. 303/623-4059.

The owner of Camera Obscura has a rotating photographic exhibit with prints by many world-famous photographers, including Ansel Adams, Henri Cartier-Bresson, and Annie Leibovitz. This outstanding gallery also displays works by lesser-known contemporary photographers. Open Tuesday through Saturday from 10am to 6pm and on Sunday from 1 to 5pm.

SPORTING GOODS

GART BROS. SPORTSCASTLE, 10th St. and Broadway. Tel. 303/861-1122.

There are several Gart Bros. stores in the metropolitan area, offering a complete line of equipment for most sports. Call the Sportscastle for the store nearest your lodging.

TELEPHONE RENTAL

RESORT CELLULAR, 6551 S. Revere Pkwy., Englewood. Tel. 303/792-2355, or toll free 800/932-6092.

If you "have to keep in touch," this company offers daily, weekly, and monthly cellular telephone rental service to visitors and conventioneers.

TOYS

CABOOSE HOBBIES, 500 S. Broadway. Tel. 303/777-6766.

Here you can watch model trains chug around the tracks and buy anything you want to set up your own railroad line. Open Monday through Friday from 9:30am to 6pm, on Saturday from 9am to 5:30pm, and on Sunday from noon to 5pm.

THE WIZARD'S CHEST, 2900 E. 2nd Ave. Tel. 303/321-4304.

You'll want to play around for hours at the Wizard's Chest, located in Cherry Creek, which specializes in toys for kids 10 and older. The costume department is fully stocked with complete outfits to professional stage makeup. Open Monday through Friday from 10am to 8pm, on Saturday from 10am to 5:30pm, and on Sunday from noon to 4:30pm.

WESTERN WEAR

MILLER STOCKMAN, 1600 California St. Tel. 303/825-5339.

Miller Stockman, downtown, has an excellent selection of cowboy boots, western wear, and both straw and felt cowboy hats. There are other Stockman stores around town. Open Monday through Friday from 10am to 8pm, on Saturday from 10am to 6pm, and on Sunday from noon to 5pm.

SHEPLERS, 8500 E. Orchard Rd. Tel. 303/773-3311.

There are a few Sheplers: This one is in the Denver Tech Center, and there's another at 10300 Bannock St., at 104th Avenue, west off I-25 in Northglenn (tel. 303/450-9999). Sheplers sells boots, cowboy hats, western shirts, belt buckles, and much more. Open Monday through Saturday from 10am to 9pm and on Sunday from 11am to 6pm.

WINE & LIQUOR

**APPLEJACK LIQUORS, 3320 Youngfield St., in the Apple-
wood Shopping Center, Wheat Ridge. Tel. 303/233-
3331.**
Located in the Applewood Shopping Center, Applejack Liquors
runs some of the best specials in town on liquor and wine. The huge
store has an extensive wine collection. Open Monday through
Thursday from 8am to 10pm, and on Friday and Saturday from 8am
to 11pm.

**ARGONAUT WINE AND LIQUOR, INC., 718 E. Colfax Ave.
Tel. 303/831-7788.**
The Argonaut also has excellent pricing. Open Monday through
Thursday from 8am to 10pm, and on Friday and Saturday from 8am
to 11:45pm.

**VINEYARD WINE SHOP, 261 Fillmore St., in Cherry Creek
North. Tel. 303/355-8324.**
Fine-wine buffs frequent the Vineyard Wine Shop. Open Monday
through Saturday from 9:30am to 6pm.

7. DENVER NIGHTS

Both daily newspapers, the **Denver Post** and the **Rocky Mountain News,** have special entertainment sections on Friday with
detailed listings of performances and special events. **Westword,** a
popular free weekly newspaper found in wire racks throughout the
city, also lists events. This paper often discusses the trendiest places
and happenings, and many of the "in" places advertise in its pages.
Up the Creek, another free weekly paper found in wire racks around
the city, has listings for events in the southern end of the metropolitan area.
You can purchase tickets for some events at the box office.
However, **Ticketmaster** (tel. 303/290-TIXS) has a lock on tickets
to most of the major concerts, plays, and other events in town until
the day of the program. There are Ticketmaster ticket centers (cash
only) at Gart Bros., Dave Cook Sporting Goods stores, Sound
Warehouse, and selected Budget Records & Tapes, or you can charge
tickets by phone. Be aware that Ticketmaster tacks on a hefty service
charge, which varies according to the base price of the ticket.
If you go to the English double-decker **Ticket Bus,** on the 16th
Street Mall at Curtis Street, you can purchase tickets (cash only) for
many live theater performances and any events also sold through
Ticketmaster. A board next to the bus lists the concerts, plays, and
other events for which tickets are available. Any half-price tickets for
productions are listed on a board. (Each event promoter decides if
half-price tickets will be sold, so they aren't available for many
performances). Ticket Bus hours are 10am to 6pm Monday through
Friday and 10am to 3pm on Saturday.

THE PERFORMING ARTS

Denverites have always loved the performing arts. In 1860, before the
city had a school or hospital, performances of *Macbeth* at a local

theater were sold out. Denver now boasts the second-largest performing complex in the nation! With 9,212 seats in nine theaters, the Denver Performing Arts Complex (DCPA) is second in capacity only to New York's Lincoln Center. And the community supports the events, plays, concerts, and other performances in the various venues in the PLEX (as locals call the DPCA), as well as in other theaters.

MAJOR PERFORMING ARTS COMPANIES
Classical Music

COLORADO SYMPHONY ORCHESTRA. Tel. 303/595-4388 or 303/98-MUSIC for information, or Ticketmaster at 303/290-8497 for tickets.

The musician-driven Colorado Symphony is in the black. A few years ago, the Denver Symphony Orchestra went bankrupt after several years of financial difficulties, and the musicians reorganized under the new name. In its first several seasons the new Colorado Symphony has successfully attracted audiences who might not have attended a classical music concert in the past. Innovative marketing, "bring a friend free" promotions, free concerts, and preconcert informative (and entertaining) discussions about the pieces to be played are among the techniques used to create a broader audience base. The majority of concerts are held in Boettcher Hall, a symphony-hall-in-the-round. During the summer some performances are held around the state. Check the local newspapers to see if there's a concert when you're in town.

Musicians of international caliber—from James Galway to Itzhak Perlman—perform in this city, either as soloists or with the symphony. Check the weekly arts calendar section of the local newspapers (on Friday) to see what classical music concerts are scheduled in the upcoming weeks.

Admission: Tickets, $8–$29.

DENVER CHAMBER ORCHESTRA, 1616 Glenarm Place, Suite 1360. Tel. 303/825-4911.

There are enough chamber music lovers in this area to support several chamber music series and individual concerts. Consult the local newspaper entertainment sections to see if there are any concerts scheduled during your visit. The Denver Chamber Orchestra brings in nationally acclaimed soloists for many concerts. Call for the schedule of concerts held at the Paramount Theatre, Trinity Church, and the Arvada Center for the Arts and Humanities. For tickets, call the Paramount box office (tel. 303/534-8336).

Admission: Tickets, $16.50.

Opera

OPERA COLORADO, 695 S. Colorado Blvd., Suite 20. Tel. 303/778-6464.

This company presents four performances in the fall and eight every spring, with internationally known singers in the lead roles. Write for information on the specific operas to be performed at Boettcher Hall, dates, and ticket prices.

Admission: Tickets, $15–$72.

CENTRAL CITY OPERA ASSOCIATION, 621 17th St., Suite 1601. Tel. 303/292-6700.

If you're in Colorado between late June and early August, head up

to Central City to see an opera in the restored Victorian Opera House, originally financed by the townspeople and built by miners, who were starved for "entertainment" in 1878. For a schedule of operas (all performed in English), dates, and ticket prices, contact the Central City Opera Association.
   Admission: Tickets, $19–$45.

Ballet

COLORADO BALLET, 999 18th St., Suite 1645. Tel. 303/ 298-0677.
This is the state's only professional ballet company. The group performs *The Nutcracker* in December, and several other ballets throughout the season.
   Admission: Tickets, $6–$43.

MAJOR CONCERT HALLS & ALL-PURPOSE AUDITORIUMS

ARVADA CENTER FOR THE PERFORMING ARTS, 6901 Wadsworth St. Tel. 303/431-3080, or 303/431-3939 for the box office.
   The Arvada Center hosts concerts, dance companies, speakers, and many other types of performances. Call for information about the current schedule.
   Admission: Ticket prices vary according to the production or performer.

DENVER CENTER FOR THE PERFORMING ARTS, 14th and Curtis Sts. Tel. 303/893-4100.
The "PLEX," as it's called by locals, covers four city blocks with buildings linked by the Galleria with its overhead glass arch. **Boettcher Hall** is the nation's first symphony-hall-in-the-round, home to the thriving Colorado Symphony and the place for performances by such world-class soloists as Itzhak Perlman and James Galway. The **Helen Bonfils Theatre Complex** is the permanent residence of the Denver Center Theater Company, a nationally acclaimed group which performs about a dozen plays each year. The theater building is composed of four stages: the **Stage,** the largest theater; the **Space,** a pentagonal arena; the **Source,** an intimate black box-style theater; and the **Cinema.**
   The 2,800-seat state-of-the-art **Temple Buell Theatre** opened in 1991 with a fully staged production of *Phantom of the Opera.* Each year a string of Broadway plays, from *Les Misérables* to *Miss Saigon,* are being brought to sell-out audiences by Robert Gardner/ Center Attractions. The Colorado Ballet and Opera Colorado's productions, and other musical and theatrical presentations, are staged here too. The adjacent renovated Auditorium Theater, also houses musical productions and other performances.
   The **Galleria** (tel. 303/623-6400), also located in the PLEX, takes the middle ground between dinner and classic theater, presenting pure entertainment in a cabaret-style setting. Long-running versions of musicals, like *Forever Plaid,* and comedies are put on in a 240-seat theater. The Theatre Café is next door.
   For information about events at the arts center, check the entertainment section of the local newspapers or call the arts center. Tickets are available through **Ticketmaster,** or call the center box office (tel. 303/893-4100) to charge tickets.

Admission: Ticket prices vary according to the production or performer.

FIDDLER'S GREEN, 6350 Greenwood Plaza Blvd. Tel. 303/741-5000 for concert information or 303/220-7000 for tickets.

This is an 18,000-seat amphitheater at the southeastern end of the metropolitan area (it's located just west of I-25 between Arapahoe and Orchard Roads). Performers range from INXS and Steve Winwood to Elton John and Tiffany. There are reserved bench seats and lawn tickets. The box office is open on show days from 10am to 9pm and tickets can be purchased here to avoid the Ticketmaster service charge.

Admission: Ticket prices vary according to performer or performance.

PARAMOUNT THEATRE, 1621 Glenarm Place. Tel. 303/825-4904 or 303/623-0106.

The historic downtown theater, with its gilded columns and walls, is the site for an eclectic collection of live performances, lectures, and films. Events range from the Gibson Jazz concerts to screenings of Warren Miller ski movies.

Admission: Ticket prices vary according to the production or the performer.

RED ROCKS, on Hogback Rd. north of Morrison. Tel. 303/694-1234.

Red Rocks, 12 miles west of Denver, is an 8,000-seat amphitheater set between dramatic 400-foot-high red sandstone rocks which wash the sound back at listeners. From May to September there's a concert series featuring top rock and contemporary musical performing artists. Call for more information or consult local newspaper listings.

Admission: Ticket prices vary according to performer.

THEATER

Denver has several local theater groups, such as the **Hunger Artists,** that only perform for a few weeks or months throughout the year. Check the entertainment sections of the local papers to see if any performances are scheduled while you're in Denver.

Dinner Theater

ASCOT DINNER THEATER, 9136 W. Bowles Ave. Tel. 303/971-0100.

This dinner theater presents Broadway hits, such as *Hello, Dolly* and *Dreamgirls,* and revues including *Salute to the Superstars* and Cole Porter's *Anything Goes.* The Ascot has a Las Vegas–style theater which holds 600.

Admission: $23.50–$32.50 for dinner and performance.

COUNTRY DINNER PLAYHOUSE, 6875 S. Clinton St., Englewood. Tel. 303/799-1410.

This playhouse presents Broadway hits and family entertainment throughout the year. Before the performance, guests enjoy a buffet dinner. Performances are Tuesday through Sunday evenings, and there are Saturday and Sunday matinees.

Admission: $17–$23 for dinner buffet and performance.

HERITAGE SQUARE MUSIC HALL AND DINNER THEA-

TER, on U.S. 40 in Heritage Sq., Golden. Tel. 303/279-7800.

If you want to hiss the villain tieing the heroine to the railroad tracks, and cheer the hero as he saves his true love, head to this theater. Guests start the evening with a buffet dinner, then move into the Victorian-style theater for a melodrama and a musical revue. The program changes every few months. A recent one, for example, was *Raider of the Lost Arms,* a playful parody on the adventures of "Louisiana Jones."

Admission: $10–$13.50 for show only, $18–$23 for buffet dinner and show.

THE CLUB & MUSIC SCENE
TEEN NIGHTCLUBS

Denver's legal drinking age is 21, but some clubs court teens 18 and older even though they're not allowed to drink. Most have cover charges, except on ladies' nights or other special evenings. Clubs where teens are welcome include **After the Gold Rush,** 5255 W. 6th Ave. (tel. 303/232-7874), and **Thirsty's,** 901 Wazee St. (tel. 303/571-4082).

COMEDY CLUBS

THE COMEDY WORKS, 1226 15th St. Tel. 303/595-3637.

This comedy club, located in Larimer Square, features national touring headline acts viewed on "The Today Show" and "Late Night with David Letterman." Headlining professionals appear Wednesday through Saturday; improvisational comedy and new talent gets a chance on Tuesday. (Wednesday is no-smoking night.) You must be 21 or older. Reservations are necessary.

Admission: $5 Sun–Thurs, $9 Fri–Sat, plus a two-beverage minimum.

GEORGE MCKELVEY'S COMEDY CLUB, 10015 E. Hampden Ave. Tel. 303/368-8900.

George McKelvey's has shows featuring headliners from the national circuit. Local talents get a chance to perform here too.

Admission: $5 Wed–Thurs and Sun, $7 Fri–Sat.

JAZZ & BLUES

In Denver you'll find live jazz at smoky bars to intimate lounges. Some places never or rarely have a cover charge; the cover charge at other nightspots varies according to the performer. The special entertainment sections in the Friday newspaper and *Westword* usually list who's playing where.

If you're lucky enough to be in town the night of a **Gibson Jazz** concert at the Paramount—go! The concerts are famous for teaming up some of the country's finest jazz musicians and putting them onstage for a jam session. (Each group is selected with an eye to blending certain talents and instruments.) Concerts are listed in the local newspapers around the time of the event.

BURNSLEY HOTEL, 1000 Grant St. Tel. 303/830-1000.

The lounge in this elegant hotel collects jazz fans on Friday and Saturday nights from 8:30pm to midnight. It tends towards soft jazz with a pianist and/or singer. Cocktails begin at $3.

Admission: Free.

EL CHAPULTEPEC, 1962 Market St. Tel. 303/295-9126.

The majority of top jazz names, and lots of up-and-comers drift in here to jam after their formal shows. The small bar is in a rough-looking neighborhood, but it's a popular place on weekends. There's jazz nightly from 8:30pm to 1:30am. Beer costs $2.75; cocktails begin at $4.

Admission: Free.

FALCONE'S RESTAURANT AND BAR, 1096 S. Gaylord St. Tel. 303/777-0707.

The house band, Alive on Arrival, is so popular with locals that they've been playing progressive jazz there for years. Jam sessions are Wednesday night, when locals can sit in with AOA. There's jazz Wednesday through Sunday from 8:30pm, and on Friday and Saturday from 9pm. Beer begins at $2; cocktails, at $2.25.

Admission: Free Sun and Wed–Thurs, $2 Fri–Sat.

THE WYNKOOP CABARET, 1634 18th St. Tel. 303/297-0920.

You'll find high-quality, cabaret-style entertainment and an occasional jazz performance at this club, tucked underneath the Wynkoop Brewery. It's open only for performances; call for the current schedule.

Admission: Varies according to the performers.

DANCE CLUBS/DISCOS

Nightclubs with dancing tend to go in and out of fashion quickly in Denver, so call before you head to a nightspot.

AQUA LOUNGE, 17th Ave. and Clarkston St. Tel. 303/832-FISH.

A DJ plays the dance music at this high-tech–looking dance spot. Guests flow between the dance floor and the pool tables. The happy hour buffet on Thursday and Friday from 4:30 to 9pm draws an eclectic crowd roughly ages 21–35 (more suits at happy hour). A late-night menu has light fare. Beer starts at $2.50; cocktails, at $2.50. It's open on Tuesday from 8pm to 2am, on Thursday and Friday from 4:30pm to 2am, and on Saturday from 8pm to 2am.

Admission: Varies.

CLUB INFINITY, 900 Auraria Pkwy., in Tivoli Denver. Tel. 303/534-0112.

A large place with a big dance floor and a contemporary gray-black decor, Club Infinity plays a variety of tunes, including hard rock, top-40 hits, and alternative music, usually on different evenings. All-you-can eat buffet dinners are set up Wednesday through Friday. There's dancing Tuesday through Saturday from 8pm to 2am.

Admission: Small cover charge, which includes the buffet when available.

COUNTRY/WESTERN

GRIZZLEY ROSE, 5250 N. Valley Hwy., off I-25 Exit 215. Tel. 303/295-1330.

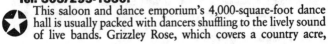 This saloon and dance emporium's 4,000-square-foot dance hall is usually packed with dancers shuffling to the lively sound of live bands. Grizzley Rose, which covers a country acre,

accurately bills itself as selling country-western fun, food, and dance. Once a warehouse, today the Grizzley Rose has that vast dance floor, replicas of storefronts lining two walls, billiards, souvenir shops, and the best people-watching in any of Denver's nightspots. Call for information about concerts; performers have included the Little River Band, the Nitty Gritty Dirt Band, and Willy Nelson. Ask about dance lessons and family days. Lunch and dinner can be ordered off the menu; happy hour includes a free buffet. The club is open Monday through Friday from 11am, on Saturday from 5pm, and on Sunday from 4pm.

Admission: Varies according to the band.

MIRAGE, 9555 E. Arapahoe Rd., Englewood. Tel. 303/790-1386.

You'll find western dancing nightly here, to tunes spun by a DJ. The place has three bars and one large dance floor. There are free line dances on Tuesday and couple dances on Thursday. Beer begins at $1.75; cocktails, at $2.25. Happy hour is Monday through Friday from 4 to 7pm. It's open Monday through Friday from 4pm to closing hour, on Saturday from 7pm to 2am, and on Sunday from 6pm to midnight.

Admission: Cover charge varies.

TRAIL DUST NORTH, 9101 Benton St., Westminster. Tel. 303/427-1446.

End the day with steak and a line dance or two—there's live music nightly. See Chapter 6, "Denver Dining," for more details about both Trail Dust steakhouses.

THE BAR SCENE

If you'd rather sit at a table than hop around a dance floor, head to the **Wynkoop,** 1624 18th St. (tel. 303/297-2700), a microbrewery and restaurant near Union Station. The brewpub's upscale billiards hall is a great place to hang out if you like to shoot pool. The historic art deco Cruise Room in **McCormick's** in the Oxford Hotel, at 1659 Wazee St. (tel. 303/825-1107), is an "in" urban spot with hungry drinkers because of the atmosphere and the great cocktail hour food specials. **Marlowes,** 511 16th St. (tel. 303/595-3700), is perennially trendy. You often have to fight your way through the crowd at the front bar in **Josephina's,** 1433 Larimer St. (tel. 303/623-0166), in Larimer Square, to get to the restaurant entrance. (See Chapter 6, "Denver Dining," for a complete description of the Wazee, the Wynkoop, McCormick's, Marlowe's, and Josephina's.)

The hottest gathering places in the city are at the downtown brewpubs. After work and into late evening the tables, both outside and in, fill rapidly at the Rock Bottom Brewery, Champions, and the Wynkoop. At any one, you'll be able to sample half a dozen brews, or more, in small sampler glasses for reasonable prices.

CHAMPIONS, 1442 Larimer St. Tel. 303/534-5444.

Located in a uniquely renovated old building in Larimer Square, the microbrewery and tables are spread over two floors, and the large patio dining area is set in a courtyard. Valet parking is available after 5pm. Beer begins at $2.10; sandwiches and entrees run $5.25–$10. Open daily from 11am to 2am.

MY BROTHER'S BAR, 2375 15th St. Tel. 303/455-9991.

Architects and postal workers share the space in My Brother's Bar, a place so casual that there's no name on the facade. Burgers and sandwiches run $4–$7. Beer starts at $1.50; cocktails, at $2.75. Open Monday through Saturday from 11am to 2am.

NO FRILLS GRILL, 7155 E. Hampden Ave. Tel. 303/759-9079.

This place has been jokingly—and accurately—described by one Denverite as "the fun college bar of your dreams." Beer begins at $1.10; cocktails, at $1.70. It's open daily from 11am to 2am, but closes earlier on weekdays if the crowd is light.

ROCK BOTTOM BREWERY, 1001 16th St. Tel. 303/534-7616.

Lots of dining area is wrapped around the glassed-in microbrewery, where folks are sampling the handcrafted beers like Red Rocks Red and Arapaho Amber. The patio area is set right on the 16th Street Mall for prime people-watching. There's live jazz some nights. Beers go from $3; Sandwiches and entrees run $6–$14. It opens daily at 11am; food is served till 11pm and last call is at 1:15.

MOVIES

There are dozens of movie theaters around the metropolitan area, including several multiplexes. Just look in the *Denver Post* or the *Rocky Mountain News* entertainment sections for current movie listings. The 12-screen **AML Tivoli**, 901 Larimer St. (tel. 303/790-4262) in Tivoli Denver is the major movie house in the downtown area. The **Mayan**, at 1st Avenue and Broadway (tel. 303/744-6796); the **Esquire**, at Sixth Avenue and Downing Street (tel. 303/733-5757); and **Chez Artiste**, 2800 S. Colorado Blvd. (tel. 303/757-7161), often offer foreign, critically acclaimed, and other avant-garde fare.

8. EASY EXCURSIONS FROM DENVER

There are lots of day trips into the mountains or to the plains cities of Boulder or Colorado Springs for travelers visiting the Mile High City. If you want a mix of scenic vistas and tourist attractions, head to Colorado Springs for the day. If you're into people-watching, visit Boulder's Pearl Street Mall. If heading down old mine shafts on guided tours and exploring remnants of the Wild West sound intriguing, head to Central City, Idaho Springs, or Georgetown. Travelers who like to view the countryside from a car, or hike in the high country, should visit Rocky Mountain National Park or Mount Evans. If you're traveling with young children in the car, just visit one mountain town and stop at the Buffalo Herd outlook and the Buffalo Bill Museum (see "More Attractions," above).

If you look at a map, you'll notice that most towns aren't too far off I-70, or too far from each other. I put together several trips with sights and attractions that easily fill a day, and give enough time for the traveler to enjoy everything without racing from town to town.

For example, I put Idaho Springs and Central City together, but you could just as easily visit Georgetown and Idaho Springs, or Georgetown and Central City, on the same day. Boulder and Central City (which has limited-stakes gambling), via the canyons and mountainous route through Nederland, is another interesting combination (see "Easy Excursions from Boulder" in Chapter 10 for directions). Shoppers will want to stop at the Silverthorne Discount Outlet Mall.

During the "mud season" in late spring, the melting snow in the mountains makes everything slushy. If you're heading into the mountains, take shoes that you can get muddy. The mountain peaks are beautiful to visit every season—whether it's summer, when the daytime temperatures often reach the 80s; fall, when golden-leaved aspens dot the mountainsides; or winter, when the ski lifts are running.

THE GOLD CIRCLE

Adults and children alike will enjoy this "gold circle" excursion, which follows scenic mountain roads to old mining towns.

Head out on U.S. 6 (6th Avenue Freeway) to Golden and continue approximately 12 miles west on U.S. 6, following the old railroad bed alongside a stream rushing its way through dramatic Clear Creek Canyon's sheer black rock walls. Turn right onto Colo. 119 for approximately 9 miles until you enter the "richest square mile on earth," the **Central City/Black Hawk National Historic District.** More than half a billion dollars in gold and other minerals has been mined here since the initial strike in 1859. Those smears of dirt that you can still see on the mountainside are called "trailings." This is what's left of the dirt miners hauled from the mine shafts when digging for gold. They spotlight the many abandoned mine shafts that dot the landscape. (*Warning:* Never walk near abandoned mine shafts and abandoned or old mine buildings which might house the entrance to old mines. The ground surrounding these holes is often unstable and might collapse. The Denver newspapers often have stories of someone who has ventured too close to these shafts and fallen in.)

You've entered the historic district when you see people panning for gold on the stream alongside the road and also when you see the Lace House, an 1860s house with an intricately filigreed Victorian facade (it's open for tours).

Turn left at the marked cutoff into **Black Hawk/Central City** and you're entering "gambling city," where casinos are set in buildings more than 100 years old. You can walk along streets once trod by miners, and head into the same saloons and stores, but now many house casinos with names like Bullwhackers, the Glory Hole, and the Gold Coin Saloon. Stop in at the Teller House to see the famous "Face on the Barroom Floor" (the woman's face was painted by *Denver Post* illustrator Herndon Dave in 1936)—and perhaps throw a few coins in slot machines on your way out.

It's rumored that the legend "The streets in America are paved with gold" started here in 1873, when local miners laid $20,000 worth of silver bricks as a sidewalk so President Grant wouldn't have to step in the mud. (Silver ingots were used because gold was "too common.") Flamboyant locals starved for entertainment built an opera house with hand-painted murals and a crystal chandelier in 1878. Edwin Booth and Fanny Barlow were among the performers who arrived in town during that era. Since the opera house was restored in 1932, Mae West, Lillian Gish, Helen Hayes, and Beverly Sills have all trod the stage floorboards (there's still an opera season every summer). Until the modern-day gold rush, visitors could still walk through an old mine and take a ride on a train driven by the largest original Colorado & Southern narrow-gauge steam locomotive for a narrated tour of the region. The train, which leaves from the depot in Central City every 45 minutes, runs over the original narrow-gauge track through the historic district, daily except Tuesday from late May to early September (call 303/582-5856 for more information). Things have changed dramatically in Central City since gambling was legalized, and the rush to open casinos has reached a fevered pitch. Many of the old tourist attractions have disappeared. You'll have to discover what's still available when you get there.

Our next stop is **Idaho Springs.** You can get there two ways. If heart-stopping steep hills and views thrill you, take the aptly named "Oh My God" dirt road through Virginia Canyon, which skirts cliffs and twists in hairpin turns to Idaho Springs. The faint-of-heart should backtrack on Colo. 119 to U.S. 6, turn west to reach I-70, and then head west four miles to Idaho Springs. This is the town where George Jackson netted $1,900 in gold dust the first week he mined his claim. Tour the Argo Gold Mill to learn how gold was extracted from ore-filled rocks. Ore from Clear Creek and Gilpin Counties was brought to this mill, which opened in 1913, through the Newhouse Tunnel just west of the mill. First the ore was assayed to determine its mineral content and the purchase price for the entire shipment was set. Next, the ore was crushed and ground by a special technique that exposed individual mineral particles. Finally, chemical and physical methods were used to obtain the actual gold. You can try gold panning here, perhaps sifting out a few flakes to take home as a souvenir. There are several casual restaurants (including a Beau Jo's) and saloons where you can have dinner before taking I-70 back to Denver.

THE SILVER BOOM & HIGH-COUNTRY TOWNS

GEORGETOWN Georgetown, about 40 miles west of Denver on I-70, became a boom town when someone discovered silver hidden in the black sand that the gold miners had cursed as a nuisance. Nicknamed the Silver Queen because of its precious ore, Georgetown today is the biggest of the three mining towns within an hour of Denver. And it's the only large mining town in this region that didn't have a major fire in the early years, so it's reasonably intact. The eye-catching steeples around town are on the top of firehouses, not churches, and the local department still wins the annual hose-cart races between mountain fire departments. The old Victorian buildings and rustic cabins house shops, restaurants, and antique stores.

The best way to learn about the silver boom is to ride the train chugging along the one-mile Georgetown Loop that encompasses much of the Georgetown–Silver Plume Mining District, a national historic landmark. From June to September, steam locomotives take tourists along the narrow-gauge track between the two towns. The grade from Georgetown to neighboring Silver Plume is so steep that the track snakes back and forth and even loops over itself on an

80-foot trestle at one point. You can get off the train at a midway stop for a one-hour guided walking tour of the Lebanon silver mine. It's a stop worth making. The train runs several times daily except Monday from early June through late September. There are no trains on Friday in June and September. (Call 303/670-1686 in Denver for more information.) Most of the parking is in Georgetown; however, anyone unable to climb long stairways must board at Silver Plume, two miles west of Georgetown off I-70's Exit 226.

The Silver Queen's streets are lined with shops filled with souvenirs, handcrafted items, and antiques. Walk along some of the side streets and stroll by the old firehouse, tour the restored Hamill House, or stop in the Hotel de Paris, which is now a museum.

From Georgetown, it's approximately 42 miles on the superhighway (I-70) back to Denver; however, you might choose to continue west at least to the Continental Divide.

THE CONTINENTAL DIVIDE If you head west on I-70, you'll reach the Eisenhower Tunnel. If you really want to see what the top of the world looks like (and if the weather is clear and the roads are dry), get off and head up, up, up over Loveland Pass. Stop at the Continental Divide, where—theoretically—you could tip a glass of water and the liquid that spills eastward will wind up in the Atlantic Ocean, while the water spilling over the western edge of the Divide will end up in the Pacific.

If you'd rather head through the Eisenhower Tunnel, a marvel of engineering that bores 1.7 miles through solid rock, it's all downhill from the opposite entrance to Dillon. Summit County, which encompasses Copper, Dillon, Frisco, Breckenridge, Silverthorne, and Keystone, is a high-altitude playground both summer and winter.

When it's warm outside, bicyclists zip down the bike/hike paths threading through the woods, or ride up trails on mountain bikes. Some hikers are trudging toward the peaks of 14,000-footers, while others prefer to take chair lifts uphill then walk back down. The tennis balls float higher on the courts set 9,000 feet above sea level, and the golf balls go farther on the mountain courses. Go fishing (if you have the proper license; see "Sports and Recreation," above) in the deep-blue, ice-cold Dillon reservoir or a mountain stream. Explore a ghost town or a gold barge, boats that dug up gold-flecked dirt from mountain streams.

A few ghost towns can be reached in regular cars, but four-wheel-drive vehicles are required to reach those towns on dirt roads in the backcountry. (You can take your own vehicle or sign up for guided tours in four-wheel-drive Jeeps.)

Visit one of the old gold barges, which dredged up the streambed with the front of the boat, pushed the mud and rock through machines on the boat to extract gold ore, then dumped the remaining debris rock alongside the stream. It took days for a gold boat to move a few hundred feet. There are no working gold barges left in Colorado, but a few are said to be operating in South America.

The shop-till-you-drop crowd makes a beeline for the Silverthorne Factory Outlet Mall, housing more than 50 stores. Outlets include Capezio, Evan-Picone, Gitano, J. Crew Factory Store, Liz Claiborne, Socks Galore, Van Heusen, and the Sunglass Broker.

During the winter, cross-country skiing to ghost towns, alpine skiing at three resorts, and snowmobiling toward the Continental Divide await visitors to Summit County, 75 miles west of Denver.

Sixty lifts, including two gondolas and 10 high-speed chairs, open up more than 4,800 skiable acres encompassing many powder bowls and 358 trails at four areas: Breckenridge, Copper Mountain, Keystone, and Arapahoe. Skiers stay in three resorts: Breckenridge, with hints of a Victorian past; Copper Mountain, with its AAA Four-Diamond lodging; and Keystone, where two gondolas lead to superb mountain-top dining and the Outback, a lift-serviced peak with off-piste-style skiing.

Allow an hour and a half for the return trip to Denver—more time if it's a Saturday or Sunday afternoon, especially during ski season.

ROCKY MOUNTAIN NATIONAL PARK

Once you've driven the 50-mile-long Trail Ridge Road that scrolls through Rocky Mountain National Park, the highest continuous highway in the world, you'll understand the lure of setting yourself on the tops of mountain peaks. Rocky Mountain National Park encompasses 405 square miles of mountains, including many snow-capped 14,000-footers, dotted with tiny high alpine lakes, and wildlife darting through colorful wildflower meadows. You cross the Continental Divide, a ridgeline stretching through the Rockies, at 12,183 feet above sea level. Chances are excellent you'll be able to throw a snowball, or at least see snow, even in the middle of summer. (Snowplows are needed to open up the road every spring.)

The best way to enjoy the park is to get out of your car and start walking. There are 400 miles of hiking trails in the park, but even a short hike on one of the flat trails will put you in the midst of the miniature wildflowers and stunted trees that cling to the mountain tundra.

Be aware that the driving loop from Denver, heading through the park and back via a different route, is a very long trip, as much as seven hours. Park officials suggest that you allow three hours to cover the 50-mile-long road inside the park, and even more time in the summer when it's bumper-to-bumper traffic on the 15-m.p.h. curves. I'd suggest heading up to the restaurant at 11,796 feet above sea level, having lunch, then turning around and going back down. (Or else you might spend the night in Estes Park, a popular summer-vacation spot, or in one of the resort towns on the opposite side of Rocky Mountain National Park, and drive back the next day.)

You can take the following loop from Denver to the park in either direction. Take I-25 to U.S. 36 through Boulder to Lyons; or you can take I-25 to Colo. 66 and turn west to Lyons. (The first route is better known, but some swear that the latter is faster because you don't have to go through the city of Boulder.) The scenic part of the ride begins at the tiny town of Lyons, with its antique shops. Next stop is the resort town of Estes Park, filled with restaurants, touristy shops, and lodges (call toll free 800/44-ESTES for the chamber of commerce). Stop at the visitor center to get a map of the park. The map outlines Trail Ridge Road, several spectacular outlook points, a number of hiking trails, and overnight camping areas.

After exploring the park, you might want to stay overnight in the Grand Lake area, the world's highest yacht anchorage, on the far side of the park. You can rent boats, swim, or go camping, horseback riding, and hiking in the mountains if you stay near Grand Lake, Granby, Silvercreek, or Winter Park (tel. 303/726-5587, or toll free

800/453-2525), a ski/summer resort with a network of mountain-biking paths. All these towns are on U.S. 40, the route to I-70 east, which leads back to Denver.

Before you reach I-70, U.S. 40 winds a very tightly curved path over the Continental Divide at Berthoud Pass, opening up some of the most dramatic scenery in the state. Even travelers with a fear of heights will enjoy this trip (between the gasps) as they negotiate the many curves. The road from the top of the pass (at 11,310 feet above sea level) down to the town of Empire offers breathtaking views of steep glacial bowls and mountainsides shorn of trees by avalanches. The actual length of this Denver–Rocky Mountain National Park driving loop is 216 miles, but you'll be crawling at very slow speeds while you sightsee inside the park and over Berthoud Pass.

GOLDEN, MOUNTAIN PARKS, RED ROCKS, BUFFALO BILL & EVERGREEN

This day trip stays closest to Denver, but will allow you to sample the high country and its mountain towns, and learn a little about one of the Wild West heros. If you only want to spend a few hours away from Denver, either head to Golden and the Coors Brewery, go antiquing in Morrison, or take the high alpine drive above Evergreen. (Golden and Morrison are both 20 minutes from downtown Denver; Evergreen is 30 minutes away.)

Take the Sixth Avenue Freeway (U.S. 6) into Golden and stop by the **Coors Brewery** for the free tour (see "The Top Attractions," above, for a complete description). History buffs might make a detour to the **Golden DAR Pioneer Museum,** 911 10th St. (tel. 303/278-7151), crammed with memorabilia from the early settlers' days. The town is home for the Colorado School of Mines, the nation's most prestigious school of mineral engineering.

To reach the **Buffalo Bill Museum** and his gravesite, return to the intersection of 19th Street and U.S. 6, cross U.S. 6, and stay on that winding road for approximately 4½ miles to the museum. The views of the plains are terrific as you climb Lookout Mountain. The museum offers a glimpse into William E. Cody's life and times, and it houses memorabilia of the Pony Express. (Buffalo Bill, when he was just 15, completed one of the longest Pony Express rides ever recorded.) See "More Attractions," above, for a description of the museum, prices, and hours.

Turn right out of the parking lot, follow Lookout Mountain Road to I-70 west, and start looking for the **buffalo.** With luck, you'll be able to capture on film the descendants of the 12 head of buffalo and the 14 head of elk received from Yellowstone National Park in 1914. The herd might be in the pastures on the north or south side of the highway. (They're fed in the north pasture during the winter.) If you don't see them, get on I-70 west and get off at the Chief Hosa exit, cross the highway, and drive up into Genessee Park and keep looking.

Get back on I-70 and head west to the next exit, El Rancho. Go south on Colo. 74, following the signs toward Bergen Park and Evergreen. After 2½ miles of winding road with spectacular scenic views, head west on Colo. 103 toward Squaw Pass. It's another scenic road, with pulloffs where you can photograph the vista of snow-capped mountains. Pristine blue **Echo Lake** is 9 miles up the highway. Stop for lunch and, if you brought your hiking shoes, try one of the trails. The 14-mile road from here to the summit of 14,264-foot **Mount Evans** is only open from June to Labor Day, and snow is a possibility even in July or August (take a jacket if you plan to drive to the top). Your ride on the highest paved road in North America is mainly above the tree line, opening up wide vistas of mountain peaks, and closeups of rare alpine flowers and 2,000-year-old bristlecones. When you head back down, turn south on Colo. 74 and head 5 miles into the center of **Evergreen,** a mountain community, with many residents who commute to Denver. Park your car in the center of town and check out some of the shops and galleries, like the Evergreen Art Gallery at 105 Main St. and the Cobweb Shoppe, an antiques/collectibles shop across the street. There are a few good, casual restaurants in the downtown area.

If you're tired or it's the end of the day, return to Denver via I-70. However, the loveliest loop is yet to come. From downtown Evergreen, take Colo. 74 in the opposite direction for a drive through the black rock-walled **Clear Creek Canyon** back to **Morrison.** (This is a daylight drive.) Tiny downtown Morrison is filled with antiques shops, so leave time to browse. Pick up a troll at the Morrison grocery (it's said if you name them, they'll safeguard your home). If it's close to lunch or dinnertime, stop at Tony Rigatoni's or the Morrison Inn, both located at the town's main intersection. Both are extremely popular restaurants and neither takes reservations, so you might have to wait for a table. (Some folks stroll around those shops that stay open later, while others relax in the lounges with a drink.) Tony Rigatoni's offers pizza and a variety of excellent fresh pastas, presented with close to "white glove" service by an attentive wait staff. The Morrison Inn serves Mexican food.

If it's daylight when you leave Morrison, follow the signs back to I-70, but stop at **Red Rocks Park,** located where those massive stands of red rocks are that you'll see on the left side of the road. It's a natural amphitheater where sounds bounce against the 400-foot-high walls and wash back at the audience. (See "More Attractions," above, for more information.)

BOULDER

Pearl Street Mall in this college town, home of the University of Colorado, is a fun place to people-watch, eat at an outdoor table, and shop away a few hours in the boutiques and galleries. See Chapters 8, 9, and 10 on Boulder for specific information about the city. A trip to Boulder, a stop to gamble in Central City (via Colo. 119 through Nederland), and a look at the Buffalo Bill Museum or Coors Brewery in Golden makes for an entertaining day.

COLORADO SPRINGS

Colorado Springs, 1¼ hours south of Denver along I-25, has been a resort town since the late 1800s. To learn why, read Chapters 11, 12, and 13 on this city. Exploring **Pikes Peak country,** anchored by this lovely city, takes many days. Look at the attractions in Chapter 13 and you'll easily make a list of stops that will fill up the day.

CHAPTER 8

GETTING TO KNOW BOULDER

The needle-sharp Flatirons form a mountain backdrop for this cosmopolitan city, situated 27 miles northwest of Denver. Boulder's residents are a mix of college students attending the University of Colorado (called CU by the locals); employees of the many computer, biotech, and research firms in the region; and people who just prefer a casual lifestyle. But whatever the reason for being here, most adults place a high premium on excellent schools for their kids and a high-quality entertainment and arts scene for themselves. "Hard bodies" are always in vogue in this city, and most of the people are into sports, especially hiking, biking, mountain climbing, and skiing. Boulder is home to many educational institutes besides CU: Naropa (a school offering an alternative approach to education) is located here, as is the School of Massage Therapy.

The nomadic Arapahoe tribespeople had been in the area that is now Boulder long before white settlers arrived, visiting primarily during the summer months before eventually moving to the Wyoming area. As with Denver and so many other Colorado cities, it was the Gold Rush that fueled the creation of the city of Boulder. In 1859 A. A. Brookfield and 60 other shareholders founded the Boulder City Town Company, laid out 4,044 lots, and tried to sell them to newcomers for $1,000 each. Evidently the price was too high—only 324 people had moved here by 1860. But Boulder continued to grow, albeit slowly. Primarily a support town for miners at the outset, Boulder later developed an agricultural base to feed the increasing population.

In 1861 the governor of Colorado Territory signed legislation to establish the territorial (later, the state) university, and Boulder began early lobbying to be the host site, at about the same time that the first schoolhouse in town was opened. The site was donated by Boulder in 1872, and in 1874 the legislature approved $15,000 in construction funds—if the Boulderites would match that sum. They did, and Old Main was built to house the entire university, from the single classroom to the president's living quarters.

In the mid-1860s an intense rivalry flared up between Boulder and the neighboring town of Valmont as each tried to be the preeminent town in the region. The rivalry culminated in a "newspaper war," which ended only when Boulderites stole the other town's hand press and put the rival newspaper out of business.

The arrival of the railroad in 1879 brought a population boom and the number of Boulder residents jumped to 3,000.

Around the turn of the century, Boulder, like other cities along the Front Range, purchased land for parks, including the eastern slope of Flagstaff Mountain (80 acres). The growing city then convinced the federal government to add 1,800 neighboring acres of mountainsides and canyons. Today the Boulder Mountain Parks System encompasses 9,000 acres of land, ensuring a permanent backdrop of untouched mountain beauty for local residents.

By 1908 the city population had risen to 10,000, including many residents who evidently did not approve of "demon rum." Boulder became a "dry" town 13 years before Prohibition, and it took 15 elections to start the liquor flowing again. The economy slumped through the Depression years but picked up again in the 1940s and '50s, during which time new laws were enacted permitting the sale of liquor by the drink (bars) and so-called 3.2 beer (beer containing not more than 3.2% alcohol, sometimes called "near beer").

Today this city of 85,000 people is thriving, with a diverse industrial base that includes many research, computer, biotechnology, and high-tech firms, and a state university that occupies a 600-acre downtown campus. The Boulder campus of the University of Colorado, part of a four-campus system that ranks 11th among public universities in the U.S. receiving public research funding, has 22,000 undergraduate and graduate students from every state and more than 70 foreign countries.

1. ORIENTATION

If you keep in mind that the mountains are always on the west side of the city, you won't have any trouble finding your way around Boulder.

ARRIVING

BY PLANE Most visitors arriving by plane land at **Denver's Stapleton International Airport** and take ground transportation to Boulder. (After October 29, 1993, visitors should be arriving at the new Denver International Airport.) For all the details on airlines and fares, see "Getting There" in Chapter 2. And for information on just about anything at Stapleton—flight schedules and connections, parking, ground transportation—call toll free 800/AIR-2-DEN. (This number is expected to be transferred to Denver International when it opens.) **Boulder Municipal Airport** (tel. 303/440-7065) is used for private and business aircraft, but no major airlines. There's a 41,000-foot paved runway that can accommodate single- and twin-engine propeller planes.

From Stapleton International Airport, a **taxi** to Boulder will cost approximately $36, but it can be split among several riders; there's a taxi stand outside the lower doors of the airport terminal. The **Boulder Airporter** (tel. 303/321-3222) is an airport van service. The fare from local hotels or the University of Colorado campus is $9.50, and door-to-door service from private homes is $12.

BY TRAIN There is no passenger train service to Boulder.

However, there is passenger service from both coasts to Denver, from which ground transportation is available to Boulder. See "Getting There" in Chapter 2 for more train information.

BY BUS   The buses of the **Greyhound/Trailways** bus lines (tel. 303/292-6111) stop at the RTD Terminal at 14th and Walnut Streets in downtown Boulder.

There are express RTD buses (tel. 303/299-6000 for schedule information) to Boulder from both downtown Denver and Stapleton International Airport; the fare is $2.50 per person one way (exact change is required).

BY CAR   The most direct driving route from Denver is I-25 north to U.S. 36 toward Boulder. Drivers coming from the west on I-70 should take I-70 to the Morrison/Golden exit (Exit 259) and follow U.S. 40 north to U.S. 6; turn left on U.S. 6 north, which leads to Colo. 93 north, which in turn runs directly into Boulder. Those arriving from the east on I-70 should follow I-70 to I-25 north (Exit 274) and then U.S. 36 (Exit 217) to Boulder. If you're driving into the area from the east or west on I-80, take I-80 to Cheyenne and then I-25 south to Colo. 52 west (Exit 235) to the Longmont Diagonal (Colo. 119), which runs southwest into Boulder. If you're coming from the south on I-25, take I-25 through Denver to U.S. 36 north (Exit 217) to Boulder.

TOURIST INFORMATION

The **Boulder Chamber of Commerce,** 2440 Pearl St., Boulder, CO 80302 (tel. 303/442-1044), has staff ready to answer your questions. Maps, brochures, and general information about the city and its attractions and restaurants are available. It's open on Monday from 9am to 5pm and Tuesday through Friday from 8:30am to 5pm (closed Saturday and Sunday). A **visitor center** on the Davidson Mesa overlook on U.S. 36 provides free information, Memorial Day to Labor Day, daily from 9am to 4pm.

The **Stapleton Information Center,** located between Concourses C and D at Stapleton International Airport, is a booth where visitors can get information about Denver and Colorado. Brochures are always available, and the booth is staffed daily from 8am to 5pm. **Colorado Ski Country USA** also maintains a booth at Stapleton during the winter months, with literature and information about the different ski areas in the state.

CITY LAYOUT

Boulder's numbered streets run parallel to the mountains, beginning with 3rd Street and increasing in number to the east. (Other cities in Boulder County use the same grid, so you'll find 124th Street, for example, in Broomfield.) The low-numbered addresses begin on the west side of town and increase to the east. For example, 1110 Spruce St. is eight blocks from the city line, which nudges the mountains. This pattern gives the city half a grid to work with, so there is no need for "east" or "west" designations.

The north and south halves of the grid are defined by a line that begins at the intersection of Broadway and Ash Street and runs east on Ash to the Boulder–Denver Turnpike (U.S. 36), continuing on the turnpike to South Boulder Road and extending east on South Boulder Road beyond the city limits. Everything south of this line has "south" in the address. However, most addresses to the north of that line do *not* have a "north" designation. The city streets north of downtown are ordered alphabetically—Alpine, Balsam, Cedar, and so on. Boulder Airport is in the northeast corner of town.

MAIN ARTERIES & STREETS The **downtown** area, centered on the Pearl Street Mall, is rather small compared to Denver's. It extends roughly from 9th to 18th Streets (east-west) and from Pine Street to Arapahoe Avenue (north-south). Just southeast of the downtown area, to the east of Broadway, is the University of Colorado campus.

The **main north-south thoroughfares** are Broadway (Colo. 93 in the southern part and Colo. 7 in the northern), Folsom Avenue (which runs from the CU campus north), 28th Street (U.S. 36), and the Foothills Parkway (Colo. 157). The **major east-west cross streets** include Iris Avenue (in the north), Valmont Road (east of Folsom Avenue), Pearl Street (of which four downtown blocks are a pedestrian mall closed to traffic), Canyon Boulevard (which extends from the foothills east to 28th Street), Arapahoe Avenue (which becomes Arapahoe Road east of 28th Street), Baseline Road (which heads east to I-25), and South Boulder Road.

The main route to and from Denver is U.S. 36, which becomes 28th Street in Boulder. The primary route to and from Golden is the Foothills Highway (Colo. 93), which becomes Broadway in Boulder. The Longmont Diagonal (Colo. 119) stretches northeast from 28th Street at the north end of Boulder toward the town of Longmont.

Note: Don't confuse the Foothills Parkway (Colo. 157), which runs north-south from the Longmont Diagonal (Colo. 119) to U.S. 36 along the east side of the city, with the Foothills Highway (Colo. 93), which runs up from Golden and becomes Broadway in the western part of Boulder.

STREET MAPS Maps of the city and state are available at the Boulder Chamber of Commerce, 2440 Pearl St., Boulder, CO 80302 (tel. 303/442-1044). Members of the **American Automobile Association** can get free maps from the local office at 1933 28th St. (tel. 303/442-0383). You can also get city maps at many hotels.

NEIGHBORHOODS IN BRIEF

Boulder has several neighborhoods, from historic Mapleton Hill to the much newer Gun Barrel section, site of many high-technology companies and industrial operations.

Mapleton Hill This historic section of downtown, encompassing Pine, Spruce, and Mapleton Streets west of Broadway, has a wealth of Victorian-era buildings.

University Hill West of the CU campus (west of Broadway), University Hill is a largely residential area teeming with students living in boarding, sorority, and fraternity houses.

The Canyons There are spectacular mountain houses up in Left Hand, Sunshine, Coal Creek, and Boulder Canyons, west of town.

Shanahan Ridge This high-rent district pushes against Devil's Thumb, a huge rock outcropping where housing ends and the open land begins.

Table Mesa This middle-class neighborhood is west of South Broadway and south of South Boulder Road.

Gun Barrel   This northeast sector of the city is the site for many high-technology companies and home to Celestial Seasonings, the tea manufacturer.

2. GETTING AROUND

BY PUBLIC TRANSPORTATION (BUS)   The **Regional Transportation District** (RTD) (tel. 303/299-6000 for route and schedule information, 303/299-6700 for other customer-service matters) runs the buses that service metropolitan Denver, Boulder, and some foothills communities. In Boulder, bus fare is 60¢ for adults and children aged 6 and older—there are no senior-citizen or off-peak-hours discounts (bus fares are higher in Denver). There is express RTD bus service to Denver (both downtown and Stapleton International Airport) from the Boulder bus terminal at 14th and Walnut Streets; the fare is $2.50 per person one way.

BY TAXI   There are no taxi stands and taxis won't stop for you on the street, so you'll have to call **Boulder Yellow Cab** (tel. 303/442-2277). In town, the fare is $2 for the first mile and $1.20 for each additional mile; out-of-town fares are $1.20 per mile.

Visitors can arrange for airport transfers, in-town limousine service, or trips to mountain resorts. Call **Boulder Limousine Service,** 1800 30th St. (tel. 303/449-5466), or **Rocky Mountain Limousines, Inc.,** 1050 Walnut St., Suite 212 (tel. 303/444-2777).

BY CAR   Several major car-rental agencies are represented in Boulder, including **Avis,** 4800 Baseline Rd. in the Meadows Shopping Center (tel. 303/499-1136); **Budget Rent-a-Car,** 1345 28th St., at the Clarion Hotel (tel. 303/341-2277); **Hertz,** 1760 14th St. (tel. 303/443-3520); and **National,** 2960 Center Green Court S. (tel. 303/442-5110). For information on state driving regulations and on renting a car in Denver, see "Getting Around" in Chapter 4.

Parking   Rates at the city's downtown parking lots are 25¢ per hour for the first three hours and $1 for each additional hour. Some downtown merchants will validate these parking tickets. Metered parking on the street is also available, which requires nickels, dimes, and quarters. Outside downtown it's usually possible to park in free parking lots or on side streets.

ON FOOT   Boulder is a small enough city to walk around, and many residents do it regularly.

FAST   BOULDER

Some of the information given in the "Fast Facts: Denver" section in Chapter 4 also applies to Boulder, including area codes, climate, liquor laws, road conditions, telephones, time zone, and tipping. The items below are specific to Boulder.

Babysitters   The front desk or concierge at your hotel may well be able to provide information on babysitters. The hourly cost may vary by day and time, as well as by the age of your children, and there may be an additional charge for transportation. Boulder's child-care referral service (tel. 303/441-3180), open daily from 8am to 5pm, can also help.

Banks   Banking hours vary, but most banks are open Monday through Friday from 9am to 5pm. Drive-through services at some banks start as early as 7am and stay open until 6pm. Rocky Mountain BankCard System's automated Plus System (tel. toll free 800/THE-PLUS for locations) is available at more than 600 automated teller machines in the metropolitan area. Many hotels will cash checks for guests.

Barbershops/Beauty Salons   If you need a haircut or a trim, go to Fresh Hair, 1738 Pearl St. (tel. 303/449-8160), or Supercuts in the Crossroads Mall, 1600 28th St. (tel. 303/449-6901).

Business Hours   Store hours vary widely in Boulder. The Crossroads Mall is open Monday through Friday from 10am to 9pm, on Saturday from 10am to 6pm, and on Sunday from noon to 5pm.

Currency and Exchange   Foreign-currency-exchange services are available at the Affiliated National Bank, at the corner of North Broadway and Canyon Boulevard (tel. 303/442-6770).

Dentists/Doctors   For dental and medical referrals, call Prologue (tel. 303/443-2584).

Emergencies   Dial 911 for police, ambulance, and fire emergencies (for non-emergency police assistance, call 303/441-4444). The Poison Control Center number is 303/629-1123. For State Patrol emergencies, call 303/239-4501.

Eyeglasses   The Boulder Optical Company, at 1928 14th St. (tel. 303/442-4521), has a lab on the premises. Crossroads Optical, 3013 Walnut St. in Walnut Garden (tel. 303/443-9555), also has rush service available for some glasses, depending on the lenses.

Fax Machines   Most print and copy shops, and many hotels, have fax services. Kinko's, at 1717 Walnut St. (tel. 303/449-7100), is open 24 hours.

Hospitals   Emergency care is available at Boulder Community Hospital, 1100 Balsam Ave., at North Broadway (tel. 303/440-2037).

Laundry/Dry Cleaning   If your hotel doesn't have laundry service, ask at the front desk for a reliable dry cleaner or the location of the nearest laundry. Dependable Cleaners is located in the Village Shopping Center on Folsom Avenue south of Canyon Boulevard (tel. 303/443-0290). Duds 'n Suds, at 2317 30th St. in the Crossroad Commons (tel. 303/440-WASH), has a drop-off service.

Libraries   Anyone can use the local libraries, but a local card is needed to check out material. The main library is at 9th Street and Canyon Boulevard (tel. 303/441-3100); it also has copy machines for public use (at a charge). The library is open Monday through Thursday from 9am to 9pm, on Friday and Saturday from 9am to 6pm, and on Sunday from noon to 6pm.

Newspapers   The *Boulder Daily Camera* is the city's main newspaper. Weekend events are covered in the Friday entertainment section; the Sunday "Calendar" lists events for the upcoming week. The *Denver Post* and the *Rocky Mountain News* are the metropolitan region's major local papers. The "Weekend" pull-out in Friday's *Denver Post* and the "Happenings" section in Friday's *Rocky Mountain News* list weekend events, movies, shows, museums, and restaurants. *Boulder* magazine, which comes out three times a year and is free, lists seasonal events and information about the arts, restaurants, shops, and nightlife.

Pharmacies   There are pharmacies at many King Soopers and Safeway grocery stores. Jones Drug and Camera Center, at 1370 College Ave. (tel. 303/443-4420), offers free delivery. The Medical Center Pharmacy is located in the Boulder Medical Center, 2750 N. Broadway (tel. 303/440-3111).

Photographic Needs   C.P.I. Photo, 1600 28th St., in the Crossroads Mall (tel. 303/442-3033), offers one-hour service on color-print film. Amaranth Photographic Laboratories, at 2540 Frontier Ave. (tel. 303/443-2550), is a custom lab.

Post Office   The main post office is located downtown at the corner of 15th and Walnut Streets (tel. 303/938-1100).

Radio   Local radio stations include KBCO (1190 AM and 97.3 FM) and KBOL (1490 AM), which play contemporary music, and KGNU (88.5 FM), which programs a variety of musical styles. You can also tune in many Denver stations.

Religious Services   Most religious faiths are represented in Boulder. Among those active in town are Catholic, Jewish, Baptist, Southern Baptist, Seventh-Day Adventist, Christian Science, Church of Christ, Church of Jesus Christ of Latter-Day Saints (Mormon), Episcopal, Lutheran, Jehovah's Witnesses, Methodist, Pentecostal, and Presbyterian. Check the *Yellow Pages* for a complete listing of houses of worship.

Safety   Whenever you're traveling in an unfamiliar city, stay alert. Be aware of your immediate surroundings. Wear a moneybelt, and don't sling your camera or purse over your shoulder. This will minimize the possibility of your becoming a victim of crime. It's your responsibility to be aware and be alert even in the most heavily touristed areas. Boulder is generally a safe city, although walking alone at night along the Boulder Creek path is not recommended.

Shoe Repairs   A & V Shoe Repair, 637D S. Broadway (tel. 303/494-5054), does some repairs quickly. Action Shoe Repair, 2709 Arapahoe Ave. (tel. 303/440-3737), also offers fast service on some repairs.

Taxes   The city sales tax is 6.66%. There's also a hotel tax of 9.4% added to the room rate.

Television   Denver's stations on channels 2, 4 (NBC), 7 (CBS), and 9 (ABC) are aired in Boulder. PBS is on channel 6.

Useful Numbers   The Rape Crisis hotline number is 303/443-7300, accessible 24 hours, seven days a week. For Travelers Aid call 303/832-8194.

3. NETWORKS & RESOURCES

FOR STUDENTS   The University of Colorado student union is in the University Memorial Center (tel. 303/492-6161), at the corner of Broadway and Euclid. The student union houses the Alferd (not

Alfred) Packer Grill, a popular eating and gathering place for students.

The Youth Services Office, City of Boulder, is at 2160 Spruce St. (tel. 303/441-4357).

FOR GAY MEN & LESBIANS   The Boulder Queer Collective has a recording with information on gay, lesbian, and bisexual groups, events, and activities (tel. 303/449-8623).

The Lesbian, Bisexual, and Gay Community Office Alliance (tel. 303/492-8567) is located in Room 28 in the basement of CU's University Memorial Center. When school is in session, hours are Monday through Friday, 11am to 1pm.

FOR WOMEN   The YWCA (tel. 303/443-0419) provides counseling and women's services.

FOR SENIORS   Many tourist attractions, movie theaters, and restaurants offer senior-citizen discounts; ask before paying admission. Call **Boulder Senior Services** (tel. 303/441-3148) for more information about senior activities in this city. The **West Boulder Senior Center** is located at 909 Arapahoe Ave. and the **East Boulder Senior Center** is located at 5660 Sioux Dr.

CHAPTER 9

BOULDER ACCOMMODATIONS & DINING

Although Boulder is a comparatively small city, it can boast of plentiful lodging and dining choices in all price ranges and in a variety of styles.

1. BOULDER ACCOMMODATIONS

The following accommodations range from deluxe to nothing-special-but-clean. (Beware: There are some run-down properties near the university that you might want to avoid; those are not listed here.) No-smoking rooms and units accessible to the disabled are available at most hotels. The listing is divided into two general categories—"Expensive" and "Moderate/Inexpensive." "Expensive" means a double room will run $90–$140 per night; "Moderate/Inexpensive" means one will run about $40–$90. The quoted rates should be considered approximate price ranges, since many hotels have a wide variety of rates for the same room, depending on the time of year you're booking. Most rates do *not* include the 9.4% hotel tax that will be added to the cost of your room.

In addition to the hotels and motels listed below, you'll also find several **bed-and-breakfast inns** around Boulder. Some business people, as well as vacationers, prefer the more informal surroundings, and several of these B&Bs are quite elegant.

Finally, for those who travel in their home, the **Colorado Campground and CabinResort Association** (303/499-9343) directory lists several campgrounds and ranches in the Boulder area. You can also contact the Boulder Mountain Lodge (tel. 303/444-0882) and the U.S. Forest Service (tel. 303/444-6600).

EXPENSIVE

The quality of expensive accommodations at the most expensive hotels in this town is comparable to that of similar lodgings in major cities like nearby Denver—but the prices in Boulder are much lower!

HOTELS

THE BROKER INN, 555 30th St., Boulder, CO 80303. Tel. 303/444-3330, or toll free 800/338-5407. Fax 303/444-6444. 116 rms. A/C TV TEL

$ Rates: $95 single; $105 double. Ask about their corporate rate. AE, DC, MC, V. **Parking:** Free.

The Broker is popular with businesspeople but it's also in a good location if you're the parent of a University of Colorado student. The rooms boast brass beds and comfortable leather lounge chairs. It's comfort without flash in these rooms with paneled and wallpapered walls. Some rooms have steam showers and some suites have whirlpool tubs.

Dining/Entertainment: The Gazebo Lounge is the place for a quiet drink. Bentley's Lounge, once a swimming pool and patio, is now a lively indoor bar. On weekends, advance reservations are needed at the popular Boulder Broker Restaurant (see "Boulder Dining," below, for a description).

Services: Room service, free newspaper Mon–Fri.

Facilities: Outdoor pool (open in summer), access to nearby health club.

CLARION HARVEST HOUSE HOTEL, 1345 28th St., Boulder, CO 80302. Tel. 303/443-3850, or toll free 800/545-6285, or 800/CLARION, the Clarion chain's national reservations number. Fax 303/443-1480. 270 rms. A/C TV TEL

$ Rates: $93–$110 single; $113–$143 double. Ask about corporate rates for VIP Tower rooms, and weekend specials which run $59–$84 per room. Children 18 and younger stay free in parents' room. AE, DC, DISC, MC, V. **Parking:** Free.

The Clarion has three towers with rooms wrapped around acres of gardens, lawns, and patios. The hotel, a 10-minute walk from the university, was gutted and rebuilt four years ago. The VIP Tower rooms are handsomely furnished units with desks (including calculators), two telephones, free snack packs, bathrobes, and hairdryers. But the real reason for staying in this tower is the use of the Executive Travelers Club, a suite of rooms that look as if they've been moved intact from a private club. The club concierge will help with anything from restaurant reservations to hiring a limousine or sending a fax. Relax on one of the couches in the library, make business calls, then grab a book or watch the news on the big-screen television. There are complimentary hors d'oeuvres and cocktails every afternoon, and desserts and after-dinner drinks can be ordered. There's a private meeting room available on a first-come, first-served basis, and a board room can be reserved for a fee.

The spacious rooms in the other wings of the hotel contain either two double beds or a king-size bed, a comfortable chair, and a desk. Rooms in the south wing have an Aztec decor, with navy and rose accents, while rooms in the west wing have a southwestern theme with pastel colors. Staying in these rooms, you'll have all the comforts of a luxurious hotel, but none of the trimmings you get in the VIP Tower.

Dining/Entertainment: Breakfast, lunch, and dinner are served in the Bistro, specializing in American cuisine. Etched glass dividers separate the dark wood tables in this simply decorated but lovely restaurant. Lunch entrees average $6, dinner entrees $12–$17.

Champs Lounge sports bar serves light fare, including hot and cold sandwiches, hors d'oeuvres, and snacks, from 11am to 2am. Prices range from $3 to $7. Champs throws parties both before and after university football games as well as around the time of the local volleyball tournaments.

HOMEWOOD SUITES, 4950 Baseline Rd., Boulder, CO 80303. Tel. 303/499-9922, or toll free 800/CALL-HOME. Fax 303/499-6706. 112 suites. A/C TV TEL
$ Rates (including breakfast): $102–$131 suites. Rates are lower for longer stays; ask about weekend rates. AE, CB, DC, DISC, MC, V. **Parking:** Free.

Homewood Suites' comfortable accommodations come with separate living and sleeping areas, a kitchen equipped with microwave and dishes, two televisions, and a videocassette player. Some suites have fireplaces.
   Services: Complimentary cocktail hour Mon–Fri, electronic messaging system, computer jacks.
   Facilities: Workout room, swimming pool, 24-hour mini-convenience store, executive business center.

HOTEL BOULDERADO, 2215 13th St., Boulder, CO 80302. Tel. 303/442-4344, or toll free 800/433-4344. Fax 303/442-4378. 160 rms, 29 suites. A/C TV TEL
$ Rates: $99–$139 single. Each additional person $12 extra. AE, DC, DISC, MC, V. **Parking:** Free.

Guests at this centrally located hotel step back in time when they stay in the old section, built in 1909. Travelers who prefer a modern decor opt for rooms in one of the hotel's newer additions. No two rooms are alike in this fascinating old Victorian building, and the creaky old elevator is extravagantly designed. All the rooms have modern conveniences and a Victorian decor, with rich woodwork, coordinated floral wallpapers, and draperies. The bathrooms have hairdryers. The newer additions have dark paneling and solid, comfortable furniture in both the public areas and the rooms. The rooms are spacious, with patterned carpets and wallpaper. Some suites have a minibar.
   Dining/Entertainment: The hotel has three restaurants and cocktail lounges. The mezzanine lounge, under the stained-glass ceiling over the central public areas, is a popular local meeting place. Winston's Seafood Grill and Bar, specializing in fresh fish and prime rib, is on the main floor. The Steak Joint is located on the hotel's lowest level, next to the Catacombs Bar.
   Services: Room service, fresh flowers.
   Facilities: Access to nearby health club.

RESIDENCE INN–BOULDER, 3030 Center Green Dr., Boulder, CO 80301. Tel. 303/449-5545, or toll free 800/331-3131. Fax 303/449-2452. 128 suites. A/C TV TEL
$ Rates (including continental breakfast): $109 studio; $129 penthouse suite. Reduced rates available for stays of a week or longer. Pets $5 per night. AE, DC, DISC, MC, V. **Parking:** Free.

Staying here is like moving into a private apartment. The hotel, located off the Foothills Parkway at Valmont Road, is a member of Marriott's Residence Inn chain and consists of studios and penthouse suites in a group of low-rise town homes. In the studios the bed is against the back wall, with the front section set up as a tiny living room wrapped around a fireplace and a full kitchen. The two-story penthouse suites with vaulted ceilings have a sitting room (with a Murphy bed) on the main floor, which can be closed off by a curtain from the living room, kitchen, and bathroom; there's a second bedroom in an upstairs open loft and a bathroom at the top of the stairs. The compound has landscaped walkways, and the staff is friendly and helpful, which keeps many guests coming back.

Dining/Entertainment: The Gatehouse contains a pleasant, oversize living room where guests staying in the town homes gather each morning for the complimentary continental breakfast. After a rough work—or vacation—day, guests return for the happy hour that's offered Monday through Friday from 5 to 7pm. Fresh coffee and free newspapers are always available. During the summer there's a free outdoor barbecue on Wednesday.

Services: If you leave a shopping list, the staff will buy your groceries. Complimentary coffee and newspapers are always available at the Gatehouse.

Facilities: Pool with heated whirlpool; courts for handball, basketball, and volleyball.

BED & BREAKFASTS

BOULDER VICTORIA, 1305 Pine St., Boulder, CO 80302. Tel. 303/938-1300. Fax 303/938-1435. 7 rms (all with bath). A/C TV TEL

$ Rates (including continental breakfast): $88–$138 single or double; $153 White-Dyroff Suite. AE, MC, V.

This upscale B&B is set in the historic Dwight Nicholson house, built in the late 1870s. Rooms are furnished with period antiques and canopy beds, and some rooms have private porches, steam showers, or fireplaces. Continental breakfast (which may be served in your room) and afternoon tea and evening port come with the room.

BRIAR ROSE BED AND BREAKFAST INN, 2151 Arapahoe Ave., Boulder, CO 80302. Tel. 303/442-3007. 9 rms (all with bath).

$ Rates (including continental breakfast): $65–$95 single; $80–$105 double. Children 5 or younger stay free in parents' room. AE, DC, MC, V. **Parking:** Free.

At this centrally located, English-style B&B, each bedroom is decorated differently, with antique furniture, fresh or dried flower arrangements, and handmade feather comforters. Close the door to one of the two rooms with fireplaces and you'll think you've stepped into the bedroom of a wealthy aristocrat from the Victorian era. Light a fire in the morning and request the continental breakfast in your room. There are five rooms in the red-brick main house and rooms in a carriage house across the courtyard (the upstairs carriage-house rooms are larger). Four rooms have air conditioning.

PEARL STREET INN, 1820 Pearl St., Boulder, CO 80302. Tel. 303/444-5584, or toll free 800/232-5949. Fax 303/444-6494. 7 rms (all with bath). A/C TV TEL

$ Rates (including breakfast): $93–$103 single; $103–$123 double. Ask for corporate and weekly rates. AE, MC, V. **Parking:** Free.

The cozy Pearl Street Inn, located three blocks from the Pearl Street pedestrian mall, has individually furnished bedrooms, each with private bath and fireplace. Most of the rooms overlook the courtyard. Wine and afternoon tea are served, and nightly turn-down service and a room-service menu are offered.

MODERATE/INEXPENSIVE

HOTELS

ARAPAHOE LODGE, 2020 Arapahoe Ave., Boulder, CO 80302. Tel. 303/449-7550. 52 rms. A/C TV TEL
$ Rates: Sept–May, $42–$51 single; $51–$63 double. June–Aug, $45–$55 single; $54–$66 double. AE, DC, DISC, MC, V. **Parking:** Free.

The Arapahoe Lodge is tucked away in a quiet residential section but within walking distance of theaters, shopping centers, the university, and downtown. The motel has attractively decorated oversize rooms, from standard to deluxe, most with queen-size beds. There's an indoor pool, a hot tub, and a sauna.

BEST WESTERN GOLDEN BUFF, 1725 28th St., Boulder, CO 80301. Tel. 303/442-7450, or toll free 800/999-BUFF. Fax 303/442-8788. 112 rms & suites. A/C TV TEL
$ Rates: $62–$80 single; $72–$80 double. Ask about rates for long stays. AE, DISC, MC, V. **Parking:** Free.

The rooms at this motel, located across the street from Boulder's biggest shopping mall, have king- or queen-size beds, oversize tubs, and refrigerators. The rooms, in blends of brown and beige, have plush carpeting and attractive desks, side tables, and headboards with a woven-wood design. The suites are often reserved long-term by people relocating to the area. There's a heated outdoor pool and the

---

Ⓕ FROMMER'S COOL FOR KIDS: HOTELS

The Clarion *(p. 158)* A good place to stay with the kids, especially in the summertime. the Clarion has a nice swimming pool and lots of nearby green space, and it's next to the Creekside Path and within walking distance of the Crossroads Mall.

Foot of the Mountain *(p. 162)* There's lots of space for the kids to get rid of high energy, and since you're staying in a log cabin, you won't have to worry about too much noise for the person overhead or underneath. Across the street is a lovely park with a playground, as well as the Creekside Path.

The Residence Inn *(p. 159)* Because it's more like a town-home complex than a formal hotel, children may feel they're in more comfortable surroundings. With a full kitchen in each unit, snack time is never a problem.

Holiday Inn *(p. 163)* At the inn's "Holidome," kids can use the pool and play inside even when the weather is bad.

casual, independently owned Bluff restaurant, open for breakfast, lunch, and dinner.

BOULDER INN, 770 28th St., Boulder, CO 80303. Tel. 303/449-3800, or toll free 800/233-8469, or 800/528-1234 for Best Western Central Toll-Free Reservations. Fax 303/449-3800. 95 rms. A/C TV TEL

$ Rates (including continental breakfast): $45–$77 single; $50–$84 double. Children 16 and younger stay free in parent's room. Ask about senior-citizen discounts. AE, DC, DISC, MC, V. **Parking:** Free.

The Boulder Inn is within walking distance of the university and has comfortable, clean rooms furnished with extra-long beds; king- and queen-size beds are also available. The inn has an outdoor pool, indoor sauna and hot tub, and a 24-hour switchboard. There are banquet and meeting-room facilities available for up to 75 people.

THE COURTYARD BY MARRIOTT, 4710 Pearl East Circle, Boulder, CO 80301. Tel. 303/440-4700, or toll free 800/321-2211. Fax 303/440-8975. 147 rms & suites. A/C TV TEL

$ Rates: $75 single; $85 double. Children 12 and under stay free in parents' room. AE, DC, MC, V. **Parking:** Free.

Located at the intersection of the Foothills Parkway and Pearl Street, about 10 minutes from the university and 15 minutes from downtown, the Courtyard is a small, informal hotel for business travelers and vacationers alike. Both the regular bedrooms and the one-bedroom suites have either a king-size bed or two double beds, and the suites have mini-refrigerators. Rooms are equipped with television, faucets for boiling water and instant coffee, and an extra-long telephone extension cord so that you can use the telephone while sitting at the desk or lying on the couch. If you want a no-smoking room, request it when you make a reservation because they fill up rapidly.

The rooms in this three-story hotel are wrapped around a courtyard with a swimming pool. The lobby and lounge area have couches, chairs, and tables, and two meeting rooms seat up to 25 people. The full-service restaurant, decorated with richly hued wood beams and trim, is separated from the lobby area by leaded-glass dividers. The hotel has no room service, but the restaurant (closed Friday and Saturday nights) will pack meals to go. There's also an indoor swimming pool, a whirlpool, and an exercise room.

DAYS INN, 5397 S. Boulder Rd., Boulder, CO 80303. Tel. 303/499-4422, or toll free 800/325-2525. Fax 303/949-0269. 74 rms. A/C TV TEL **Transportation:** Hourly shuttle service to/from the Denver airport.

$ Rates (including continental breakfast): $54–$64 single; $59–$69 double. AE, MC, V.

Just off the Table Mesa exit of U.S. 36, this Days Inn has the comfortable rooms one expects from this chain. Guests get free local phone calls and there's a restaurant/lounge.

FOOT OF THE MOUNTAIN, 200 Arapahoe Ave., Boulder, CO 80302. Tel. 303/442-5688. 18 rms. TV TEL

$ Rates: $35–$50 single; $40–$55 double. AE, DISC, MC, V.

This lodge is a grouping of log cabins located in a beautiful, quiet setting just five minutes from downtown. Set against a hillside overlooking a city park and a stream, these weathered log cabins with pine-paneled interiors are ideal for travelers who don't want to pay for pools and restaurants. Amenities include cable television, a refrigerator, coffee, and free local telephone calls.

HIGHLANDER INN, 970 28th St., Boulder, CO 80303. Tel. 303/443-7800, or toll free 800/525-2149. Fax 303/443-7800, ext. 155. 71 rms & suites. A/C TV TEL
$ Rates: $53–$60 single; $57–$71 double; $68–$86 suite. Ask about rates for longer stays. AE, DC, MC, V. **Parking:** Free.
Situated near the university, the Highlander Inn has both standard rooms and suites. A clean, pleasantly decorated motel, it's a good buy for the money, especially the apartment suites and family units with kitchenettes. There's an outdoor seasonal pool, and pets are welcome, too.

HOLIDAY INN, 800 28th St., Boulder, CO 80303. Tel. 303/443-3322, or toll free 800/HOLIDAY. Fax 303/443-0397. 165 rms. A/C TV TEL
$ Rates: $63–$77 single; $73–$87 double. AE, DC, DISC, MC, V. **Parking:** Free.
This Holiday Inn, within walking distance of the university, is a comfortable, reasonably priced motel. The compact rooms, most of which overlook the sprawling pool in the atrium, are decorated in yellow and green. Oliver's Food and Spirits, the glass-walled restaurant overlooking the atrium, is open daily for all meals. Oliver's Pub is a popular after-work watering hole. There's also a games room and an exercise room.

LAZY-L MOTEL, 1000 28th St., Boulder, CO 80303. Tel. 303/442-7525, or toll free 800/424-1115. 53 rms & suites. A/C TV TEL
$ Rates: $45 single; $55–$65 double; $65–$95 suite for up to six. AE, DC, DISC, MC, V. **Parking:** Free.
The Lazy-L is right across the highway from the university campus. There's a playground and laundrette on premises.

A BED & BREAKFAST

THE MAGPIE INN, 1001 Spruce St., Boulder, CO 80302. Tel. 303/449-6528. Fax 303/449-6528 (after pickup, press 1, then 1). 5 rms (all with bath). A/C TV TEL
$ Rates (including continental breakfast): $68–$108 single or double. AE, MC, V.
Built in 1899, the Magpie Inn is conveniently located in Boulder's Mapleton Hill historic district, a block from the busiest section of the Pearl Street Mall. Rooms are charmingly decorated with traditional Victorian flare, each by a different local decorator. Two rooms have fireplaces, and two rooms are connected by a sitting room with a balcony overlooking the city. Freshly brewed coffee, continental breakfast, and afternoon sherry come with the room.

2. BOULDER DINING

The number and variety of good restaurants in a town this size is not surprising if you consider Boulder's cosmopolitan population. Many

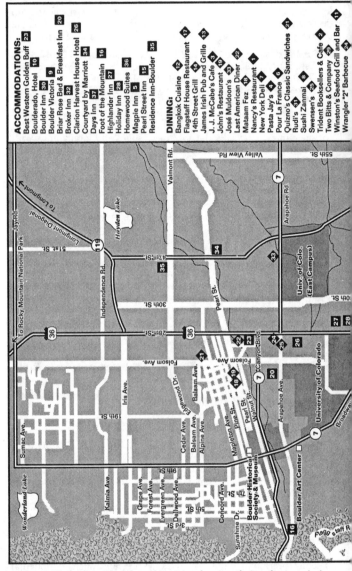

ACCOMMODATIONS:
Best Western Golden Buff 23
Boulderado, Hotel 10
Boulder Inn 30
Boulder Victoria 9
Briar Rose Bed & Breakfast Inn 20
Broker Inn 32
Clarion Harvest House Hotel 34
Courtyard by Marriott 16
Days Inn 37
Foot of the Mountain 27
Highlander Inn 28
Holiday Inn 36
Homewood Suites 5
Magpie Inn 15
Pearl Street Inn 35
Residence Inn-Boulder

DINING:
Bangkok Cuisine 12
Flagstaff House Restaurant 17
14th Street Grill 4
James Irish Pub and Grille 13
J. J. McCabe's Cafe 3
John's Restaurant 19
José Muldoon's 43
Last American Diner 48
Mataam Fez 7
Nancy's Restaurant 1
New York Deli 6
Pasta Jay's 21
Pour La France 31
Quizno's Classic Sandwiches 8
Rudi's 2
Swensen's 29
Sushi Zanmai 11
Trident Booksellers & Cafe
Two Bitts & Company
Winston's Seafood Grill and Bar
Wrangler "2" Barbecue

of the residents have fled from big cities, leaving their urban anxieties behind but bringing with them their sophisticated tastes. Add to them some 22,000 hungry college students plus the folks who are genuinely qualified to display a "Colorado Native" bumper sticker, and you have the makings of a community that frequently eats out and demands diverse cuisine.

Of Boulder's 200 or so restaurants, listed here are the long-time local favorites, several acclaimed by restaurant critics, and some of my favorites. I've arranged the restaurants into price categories: "Very

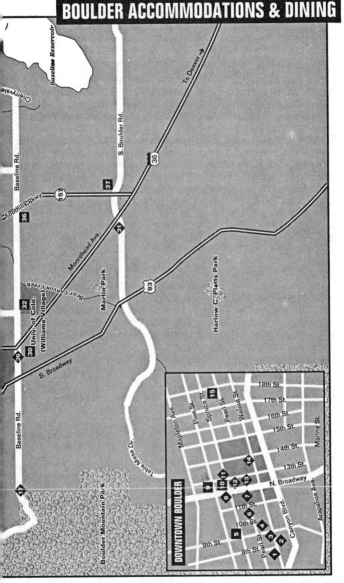

Expensive," where a complete meal will cost more than $35; "Expensive," $22–$35; "Moderate," $10–$21; and "Budget," less than $10. (Remember that you can turn a moderate restaurant into an expensive one by loading up on drinks, appetizers, and dessert.)

Keep in mind that many of the finer restaurants in this city change their menus several times a year, so some dishes described in this book might not be available when you visit. Also note that the credit and charge cards accepted are listed "as of the moment." See

"Frommer's Smart Traveler: Restaurants" in Chapter 6 for money-saving hints.

VERY EXPENSIVE

FLAGSTAFF HOUSE RESTAURANT, 1138 Flagstaff Rd. Tel. 303/442-4640.

Cuisine: FRENCH/CONTINENTAL. **Reservations:** Recommended.

$ Prices: Appetizers $8–$12; main courses $23–$38. AE, DC, MC, V.

Open: Dinner only, Sun–Thurs 6–10pm, Fri–Sat 5–10pm.

The Flagstaff House is an elegant, attractive glass-and-wood building built into the side of Flagstaff Mountain, just a 10-minute drive from downtown. The view from the restaurant is by itself worth the ride up the winding mountain road, for you can see out over Boulder and the surrounding flatlands, hundreds of feet below. The elegant candlelit dining room with glass walls allows you to soak up the dramatic view. The glassed-in terrace is open during the winter.

The menu changes nightly, but you might begin your meal with choices like lobster, smoked salmon, and lump crab with wasabe vinaigrette; pâté of duck; or wild mushrooms and Brie. The main courses might include ruby-red trout and scallops, rack of Colorado lamb, and a selection of game. Save room for desserts like chocolate soufflé with espresso ice cream. If you don't want to have dinner, you can have drinks on the terrace during the "alpenglow hour" or just coffee, perhaps after an evening at the theater or a concert at Chautauqua. The wine cellar contains over 23,000 bottles and more than 1,000 varieties.

GREENBRIAR, 8735 N. Foothills Hwy. Tel. 303/440-7979.

Cuisine: CONTINENTAL. **Reservations:** Recommended Fri–Sun. **Directions:** Take the Jamestown exit off U.S. 36, about 7½ miles north of Boulder.

$ Prices: Appetizers $6.75–$12.75; main courses $14.75–$24.75. AE, DC, MC, V.

Open: Dinner daily 5–10pm; brunch Sun 11am–2:30pm.

Greenbriar resembles a roadside country inn as its guests dine at tables lit by oil lamps. Start off with bourbon barbecued bison, steak tartare, or oysters. Entrees include such traditional dishes as filet mignon and filet of salmon and such innovative fare as lobster Caesar salad and venison grenadine. Ask for a table in one of the rooms with a fireplace or the book-lined walls. During the summer, cocktails are served on the flagstone patio by the flower garden. The desserts—like chocolate-soufflé cake and apple-blackberry crisp—are rich and wonderful.

JOHN'S RESTAURANT, 2328 Pearl St. Tel. 303/444-5232.

Cuisine: ECLECTIC. **Reservations:** Not required.

$ Prices: Appetizers $2.50–$5; main courses $13.50–$20. AE, DC, MC, V.

Open: Dinner only, daily 6pm–9:30pm.

Many local residents swear that John's might just be the best restaurant in town; it's also rated highly by restaurant critics. John's, which seats only 30 people, is in a cottage a few steps below street level. There's a regular menu plus eight or nine nightly specials, featuring classic dishes of France, Spain, the Italian provinces, and North America. The chef serves up such dishes as filet mignon (perhaps prepared with cream and brandy), fresh salmon, lobster ravioli, and paella Valenciana. Dinners come with soup, salad, and vegetable. Dessert choices change frequently. One favorite: deliciously rich Chocolate Intensity, prepared with raspberries and crème à l'anglaise.

EXPENSIVE

GOLD HILL INN, Mapleton Ave., Gold Hill. Tel. 303/443-6461.
  Cuisine: CONTINENTAL. **Reservations:** Recommended. **Directions:** Take Mapleton Avenue 10 miles west of Boulder.
  $ Prices: Six-course dinner $20. No credit cards.
  Open: Dinner only, Wed–Mon 6–10pm. **Closed:** Nov–Apr.
The rustic Gold Hill Inn, set on a mountainside above Boulder, is a secret jealously guarded by those who have eaten there. The menu changes nightly, but could include roast lamb, Glasgow roast beef, or snapper Vera Cruz.
  If you want to spend the night, there are nine rooms in the Bluebird Lodge with queen-size beds and antique furnishings.

MATAAM FEZ, 2226 Pearl St. Tel. 303/440-4167.
  Cuisine: MOROCCAN. **Reservations:** Recommended.
  $ Prices: Five-course dinner $21.75. AE, DC, MC, V.
  Open: Dinner only, Sun–Thurs 6–9:30pm, Fri–Sat 6–10pm.
Eating with your fingers is polite at Mataam Fez, where you sit on cushions on the floor around a low table. The food, prepared from traditional recipes, includes such dishes as lamb with artichokes, lemon, and olives; and Cornish hens with honey and almonds. Belly dancers perform Thursday through Sunday, and there's live music on Wednesday.

TWO BITTS & COMPANY, 2690 Baseline Rd. Tel. 303/494-8972.
  Cuisine: AMERICAN. **Reservations:** Recommended.
  $ Prices: Appetizers $3–$6.25; main courses $9.95–$18.95; lunch $4.95–$8.25. DC, MC, V.
  Open: Lunch Tues–Sat 11am–3pm; dinner Tues–Sat 5–9pm.
Currently one of the best and most popular restaurants in Boulder, this charming bistro is run by a couple who own a catering business. The menus change monthly, and the food is billed as "varied American cuisine." For lunch, you might choose a combination salad plate consisting of spicy Thai chicken salad; smoked salmon, cucumber, and dill pasta salad; and cheese tortellini. Sandwiches have a special flair, such as turkey and pepper jack cheese with mayonnaise and Dijon mustard. On the dinner menu you might find oven-roasted sea bass with Szechuan pepper crust, chicken mole with black beans and polenta, or grilled veal chop. Leave room for such outrageous desserts as fresh fig pizza with mascarpone and raspberry zinfandel syrup, bittersweet chocolate tart with raspberry

sauce, and warm apple-spice cake with maple ice cream and caramel sauce. Two Bitts also features a wine sampler: three types of wine with approximately three ounces per glass.

MODERATE

BANGKOK CUISINE, 2017 13th St. Tel. 303/440-4830.
Cuisine: THAI. **Reservations:** Not required.
$ **Prices:** Appetizers $2.50–$5.95; main courses $4.25–$5.95 at lunch, $5–$9.95 at dinner. AE, MC, V.
Open: Lunch Mon–Fri 11:30am–3pm; dinner Mon–Fri 5–10pm, Sat–Sun noon–10pm.

Located half a block south of the Hotel Boulderado, this Thai restaurant offers traditional dishes, including steamed rice with cashew chicken and Thai fried rice with beef, pork, or chicken. The Thai chef also prepares several tasty daily specials.

14TH STREET GRILL, 1400 Pearl St. Tel. 303/444-5854.
Cuisine: AMERICAN. **Reservations:** Not required.
$ **Prices:** Appetizers $2.50–$4.95; main courses $3.50–$15.50. DISC, MC, V.
Open: Mon–Thurs 11am–10pm, Fri–Sat 11am–11pm, Sun 5–10pm.

At this casual restaurant, diners on the outdoor patio can watch their pizzas being cooked in the wood-burning oven behind the counter. You can also get pasta, rôtisserie chicken, and sandwiches.

HARVEST RESTAURANT AND BAKERY, 1738 Pearl St. Tel. 303/449-6223.
Cuisine: HEALTH FOOD. **Reservations:** Not required.
$ **Prices:** Appetizers $3–$6; main courses $3–$10. AE, MC, V.
Open: Daily 7am–10pm.

This is a large, busy restaurant specializing in producing "the healthiest food around." Open for breakfast, the Harvest serves omelets, biscuits and gravy, scrambled tofu, and hot seven-grain cereal. Lunch and dinner items include sandwiches on whole-grain bread, healthy salads, Mexican food, and soups.

JAMES IRISH PUB AND GRILLE, 1922 13th St. Tel. 303/449-1922.
Cuisine: IRISH. **Reservations:** Not required.
$ **Prices:** Appetizers $4–$6.25; main courses $5–$5.50 at lunch, $9–$14 at dinner. AE, DC, MC, V.
Open: Daily 11am–11pm (pub, daily 11am–2am).

Will it surprise you to know that you can get corned beef and cabbage, Cornish pastry, and hearty soups in this popular, classic Irish pub? But you can also order giant salads and overstuffed sandwiches. Drink specials can be had during the happy hour, Monday through Thursday from 4 to 7pm. On weekend nights, sip a mug of Irish coffee while listening to live Irish music.

J. J. MCCABE'S CAFE, 945 Walnut St. Tel. 303/449-4130.
Cuisine: AMERICAN. **Reservations:** Not required.
$ **Prices:** Appetizers $1.95–$6.60; main courses $4–$12.95. AE, DC, DISC, MC, V.
Open: Mon–Fri 3:30am–2am; breakfast Sat–Sun 10am–2pm.

Ⓕ FROMMER'S COOL FOR KIDS: RESTAURANTS

The Last American Diner *(p. 169)* This place is always a hit because of the skating serving staff.

Swensen's *(p. 171)* It's got hot-fudge ice-cream sundaes and a generally "kid-friendly" menu.

J. J. McCabe's *(p. 168)* Down-home with hearty, inexpensive American food, this is the kind of place where kids climb around inside the booths and you needn't worry about their being on their best behavior.

Quizno's Classic Sandwiches *(p. 172)* Kids can munch on overstuffed subs and watch sports on the TV. It's also a good place to pick up food for a family picnic.

J. J. McCabe's on the mall serves fat burgers, hefty sandwiches, and fresh seafood (like half a pound of broiled or fried shrimp for $6.95) in the large, open dining room. It's a down-home place where the kids can climb on benches in the wooden booths and you don't have to make sure they're on their best behavior. There's a bar, pool tables, and a dance floor, with live entertainment nightly.

JOSÉ MULDOON'S, 1600 38th St. Tel. 303/449-4543.
   Cuisine: MEXICAN. **Reservations:** Not required.
$ Prices: Appetizers $3–$6; main courses $3–$7 at lunch, $4–$11 at dinner. AE, MC, V.
   Open: Lunch Mon–Sat 11am–3pm; dinner Sun–Thurs 5–10pm, Fri–Sat 5–11pm; brunch Sun 10am–2pm; happy hour Mon–Fri 3–7pm.
José's is equally popular as a watering hole and a place to eat. The menu has a full range of Mexican and southwestern entrees made with blue corn and black beans. At lunch or dinner diners can build their own tostadas, tacos, and burritos.

THE LAST AMERICAN DINER, 1955 28th St. Tel. 303/ 447-1997.
   Cuisine: AMERICAN. **Reservations:** Not required.
$ Prices: Breakfast $2.85–$7.50; sandwiches/salads $2.75–$5.95; dinners $4.95–$10.50. MC, V.
   Open: Mon–Thurs 6:30am–midnight, Fri 6:30am–3am, Sat 8am–3am, Sun 8am–midnight.

Ⓢ Waiters and waitresses on roller skates glide over to your table leaving malts, shakes, burgers, or the Blue Plate Special on your table. Slip some change into the jukebox and listen to a couple of nostalgic '50s tunes while you sample the meatloaf plate, a turkey burger, or fresh Rocky Mountain trout. Wrap up your meal with homemade cherry pie. There's a children's menu as well.

NANCY'S RESTAURANT, 825 Walnut St. Tel. 303/449-8442.
   Cuisine: CONTINENTAL. **Reservations:** Recommended for dinner.

$ Prices: Light fare $6.95–$9.75; dinners $13.95–$17.95. AE, MC, V.
Open: Breakfast/lunch daily 7:30am–2pm; dinner Tues–Sat 5:30–9pm.

You can get a moderately priced dinner or an expensive one at Nancy's, depending on what you order and when you go. The less expensive early-evening dinners, served from 5:30 to 6:30pm, include such entrees as steak, chicken breast piccata, and fresh fish, and come with soup or salad and vegetables. The regular dinner menu contains offerings like beef medallions dijonnais, veal Genovese (sautéed with vegetables in a light pesto and white wine sauce), and quail pêche (braised with peach brandy and sage), as well as fresh fish, filet mignon, and pastas.

Nancy's, which also has seating on the patio, serves breakfast and lunch as well. Breakfast means delicious omelets and quiche, lox and cream cheese on a bagel, and waffles; each costs between $3.50 and $6.75. Lunch items include entrees, sandwiches, and salads, and average $6. Nancy's sells its own retail items, including honey, jellies, and flavored vinegars.

NEW YORK DELI, 117 Pearl St. Tel. 303/449-5161.

Cuisine: DELI. **Reservations:** Not required.
$ Prices: Appetizers $1.95–$4.75; sandwiches/salads $3.75–$6.95; dinner deli platters $10.50–$16.95; main breakfast courses $2.50–$6.75. AE, MC, V.
Open: Sun–Thurs 8am–9pm, Fri–Sat 8am–10pm.
This deli on the mall is a slice of New York, complete with the hubbub of noisy diners crammed into booths and tables. The extensive menu boasts every kind of deli item imaginable—just a few are bagel sandwiches, lox, eggs and onions, blintzes, and, of course, kosher deli pickles. There's free delivery with an order of $5 or more.

PASTA JAY'S, 925 Pearl St. Tel. 303/444-5800.

Cuisine: ITALIAN. **Reservations:** Not required.
$ Prices: Appetizers 75¢–$4.95; sandwiches and main courses $3.75–$7.95; pizzas $6.50–$11.50. MC, V.
Open: Daily 11am–11pm.

It's worth the wait for a table in this old house that's been turned into a very popular restaurant. Although the owner is Polish, the tasty pastas and pizzas are definitely Italian. In addition to standards like spaghetti with meat or fresh marinara sauce, there are daily specials with imaginative variations—jumbo shells stuffed with fresh basil, spinach, ricotta, and meat; and ravioli stuffed with various cheeses, walnuts, and spices. The garlic bread, loaded with garlic and accented with a touch of onion, is outstanding! The desserts are downright sinful.

RUDI'S, in the South Creek Shopping Center, 4720 Table Mesa Dr. Tel. 303/494-5858.

Cuisine: NATURAL FOODS. **Reservations:** Not required.
$ Prices: Appetizers $4–$7.75; main courses $9.50–$18. MC, V.
Open: Lunch Mon–Fri 11:30am–2:30pm; dinner Sun–Thurs 5:30–9:30pm, Fri–Sat 5:30–10pm; southwestern brunch Sat–Sun 8am–2:30pm.
The tables at Rudi's, a small storefront restaurant at the south end of town, are usually occupied by health-conscious diners and those who

like gourmet vegetarian dishes. Rudi's cooks use purified water for cooking and service, hormone-free natural beef, and range-fed chicken. Dishes range from masala dosa (curry stuffed in brown rice cakes) and spanakopita to Moroccan chicken with apricots and pepper steak sauté.

SUSHI TORAH, 2014 10th St. Tel. 303/444-2280.

Cuisine: JAPANESE. **Reservations:** Accepted only for dinner.
$ Prices: Appetizers $3.50–$10; main courses $4–$16. AE, MC, V.
Open: Lunch Tues–Fri 11:45am–2pm; dinner Tues–Sat 5–10pm.

This reasonably priced, tiny restaurant just off the mall specializes in sushi (and has a sushi bar) but also offers tempura and other Japanese dishes.

SUSHI ZANMAI, 1221 Spruce St. Tel. 303/440-0733.

Cuisine: JAPANESE. **Reservations:** Not required.
$ Prices: Appetizers $2.80–$5.80; main courses $9.80–$13.80. AE, MC, V.
Open: Lunch Mon–Fri 11:30am–2pm; dinner daily 5–10pm.

My friends who live in Boulder swear that this restaurant has the best sushi bar in town. Some diners come just to watch the Japanese chef flashing his knives as he slices, dices, and cooks your dinner with style on the hibachi steak table. Happy hour is from 5 to 6:30pm and all evening on Sunday when sushi is $1.25 per piece.

SWENSEN'S, in the Arapahoe Village Shopping Center, 2525 Arapahoe Ave. Tel. 303/443-9631.

Cuisine: AMERICAN/ICE CREAM. **Reservations:** Not accepted.
$ Prices: Appetizers $1.55–$2.95; main courses $3–$6. AE, MC, V.
Open: Sun–Thurs 11am–10pm, Fri–Sat 11am–11pm.

Banana splits, ice-cream sodas, and other fanciful concoctions are served up at the old-fashioned ice-cream parlor. Casual and popular with families, Swensen's also offers burgers, chicken, soup, salads, and sandwiches.

WILDERNESS PUB AT THE BOULDER BEER CO. TASTING ROOM, 2880 Wilderness Place. Tel. 303/444-8448.

Cuisine: AMERICAN. **Reservations:** Not required.
$ Prices: Appetizers $1.75–$4.95; main courses $3.95–$6.25. MC, V.
Open: Mon–Sat 11am–10pm.

Stop at the Wilderness Pub after finishing up one of the free tours of this modern microbrewery. (Tours are at 11am, 2pm, and 5pm.) The pub features burgers, bratwurst, fish and chips, fresh soups, and salads. You can get the brewery's beers on tap or in bottles.

WRANGLER "2" BARBECUE, 1675 28th St. Tel. 303/447-0223.

Cuisine: BARBECUE. **Reservations:** Not required.
$ Prices: Appetizers $2.50–$4.25; meals $4–$18.50. AE, DC, MC, V.
Open: Sun–Thurs 11:30am–10pm, Fri–Sat 11:30am–11pm.

The pork and beef ribs, chicken, sausage, and steak are barbecued with sauce prepared from a recipe taken from the Figure "2" Ranch in Texas. Swordfish, spicy shrimp, and large sandwiches are also available at this casual place.

BUDGET

THE FALAFEL KING, 1314 Pearl St. Tel. 303/449-9321.
 Cuisine: MIDDLE EASTERN. **Reservations:** Not required.
$ Prices: Meals $2–$6. No credit cards.
 Open: Mon–Thurs 10:30am–8pm, Fri–Sat 10:30am–9pm, Sun 11:30am–7pm.

The Falafel King offers a range of Mediterranean specialties, including falafel, gyros, spinach pastry, dolmades, and moussaka, as well as salads, combo sandwiches, and baklava. You can eat inside, or you can bag it and find a bench on the mall and people-watch.

THE FALAFEL MAN, in the Crossroads Mall, 1700 28th St. Tel. 303/442-2888.
 Cuisine: MIDDLE EASTERN. **Reservations:** Not required.
$ Prices: Meals $2–$5. No credit cards.
 Open: Mon–Fri 10am–9pm, Sat 10am–6pm, Sun noon–5pm.

When I'm in a hurry but want fresh, tasty food, I go to the Falafel Man in the Crossroads Mall. At this booth in the food court you can order falafel, gyros, moussaka, matzoh-ball soup, fresh salads, sandwiches, or baklava. Seating is available in the food court.

MUSTARD'S LAST STAND, 1719 Broadway. Tel. 303/444-5841.
 Cuisine: AMERICAN. **Reservations:** Not required.
$ Prices: $1.75–$6. No credit cards.
 Open: Mon–Fri 10am–9pm, Sat 11am–9pm, Sun noon–7pm.

The business crowd and students rub shoulders as they line up for an all-beef hot dog on a steamed poppyseed bun with a choice of trimmings, including sauerkraut and dill pickles. Burgers, sandwiches, meatless soy franks, and fresh-cut fries are also available. Sit inside or out on the patio.

POUR LA FRANCE, 1001 Pearl St. Tel. 303/449-3929.
 Cuisine: FRENCH. **Reservations:** Not required.
$ Prices: Appetizers $2.75–$5.50; bistro cuisine $4.95–$7.25. MC, V.
 Open: Mon–Sat 7am–midnight, Sun 8am–11pm.

Quiche, sandwiches on crisp French bread or flaky croissants, pastries to drool over, and good coffee keep people returning to this European-style café. Soups, salads, and pissaladières (gourmet pizza from the south of France) are offered in addition to the daily specials. Beer and wine are available. The patio is a popular spot on nice days.

QUIZNO'S CLASSIC SANDWICHES, 601 S. Broadway. Tel. 303/494-5360.
 Cuisine: SUBS. **Reservations:** Not required.
$ Prices: Subs $3.50–$9. AE, MC, V.
 Open: Daily 10am–9pm.

Quizno's has delicious, oversize fresh subs—classic Italian, tuna, and vegetarian among others—made to order on regular or whole-wheat rolls. Beer and wine are available. Dine in and watch sports on the TV or call ahead for take-out.

This Quizno's is located in the Table Mesa Shopping Center in the "E" storefront. There branches are located in the Gunbarrel section, at 6525 Gunpark Dr. (tel. 303/530-4920); and on the mall at 1136 Pearl St. (tel. 303/449-3366).

SPECIALTY DINING

HOTEL DINING

BOULDER BROKER INN RESTAURANT, in the Boulder Broker Inn, 555 30th St. Tel. 303/449-1752.

 Cuisine: LIGHT CONTINENTAL. **Reservations:** Recommended; call at least a week ahead for Fri–Sun reservations.

$ Prices: Full dinners $18–$34. AE, DC, MC, V.

 Open: Lunch daily 11am–2pm; dinner daily 5–10pm; brunch Sun 10am–3pm.

If you can't make it much past the seemingly bottomless bowl of fresh shrimp that's served with every full meal, you can always ask for a doggy bag and take the rest back to your room for a late-night snack. Choose among entrees such as Rocky Mountain trout, veal picatta, duck, prime rib, and beef Wellington, the house specialty. There's an extensive salad and dessert bar offered at lunchtime on weekdays. The Broker Inn has a relaxed atmosphere in its three dining rooms, with prints and stained-glass panels adorning the dark paneled walls. Nightly music in Bentley's Lounge.

WINSTON'S SEAFOOD GRILL AND BAR, in the Hotel Boulderado, 2215 13th St. Tel. 303/442-4560.

 Cuisine: SEAFOOD. **Reservations:** Not required.

$ Prices: Appetizers $4.95–$7.95; main courses $10.95–$21.95; sunset dinners $8.50–$12. AE, DC, MC, V.

 Open: Breakfast Mon–Fri 6:30–10:30am; lunch daily 11am–2pm; dinner daily 5–10pm; brunch Sun 7am–2pm.

Located in the original dining room (circa 1909) of the Hotel Boulderado, Winston's has large square windows topped by old-fashioned fan-shaped stained glass that offer a view of the street action, but without the noise. The dinner menu includes seafood specials, which change nightly, as well as lamb chops, Malaysian chicken, prime rib, and lobster (most nights).

COFFEEHOUSES

Pour La France (see "Budget," above) is a popular spot for espresso or cappuccino.

TRIDENT BOOKSELLERS & CAFE, 940 Pearl St. Tel. 303/443-3133.

 Cuisine: COFFEE & PASTRY. **Reservations:** Not required.

$ Prices: Coffee, espresso, pastry $1–$4. MC, V.

 Open: Mon–Fri 6:30am–11pm, Sat 7am–11pm, Sun 7:30am–11pm.

Book lovers gravitate to this cafe, where you can buy a good read in the delightfully cluttered used-book store occupying half the building. At the counter in the next room, you can have tea, espresso, or cappuccino and pastry while you enjoy your book.

CHAPTER 10

WHAT TO SEE & DO IN BOULDER

Boulder is so close to Denver—just a 30-minute drive away—that all of that larger city's many attractions are easily available to you (see Chapter 7 for details). But Boulder is very much its own community, with its own list of things to see and do—sights, museums, amusements, special events, sports, shopping, and nightspots. In this chapter I've covered the highlights, but you're sure to discover more things of interest on your own.

SUGGESTED ITINERARIES

IF YOU HAVE ONE DAY Mix up the order to fit your mood, but either visit the National Center for Atmospheric Research and allow time for a stroll along the paths, or visit the Leanin' Tree Museum and Celestial Seasonings at the other end of town. (Advance reservations are suggested for visiting Celestial Seasonings because space is limited.) Plan on lunchtime, a people-watching stroll, and window-shopping at the Pearl Street Mall, followed by a drive through the University of Colorado campus. On a nice day, either don walking shoes or rent a bike and join the locals on the Boulder Creek Path.

IF YOU HAVE TWO DAYS Spend your first day as outlined above. On the second day, if part or all of Trail Ridge Road is open (from late spring through early fall), visit Rocky Mountain National Park. If not, visit Estes Park and/or Central City/Blackhawk—especially if you're a gambler.

IF YOU HAVE THREE DAYS Spend the first two days as suggested above. On Day 3, tour the Boulder Brewery and visit the University of Colorado Museum in Henderson. Or if you enjoy biking or hiking and the weather is amenable, spend the day in Eldorado Canyon or try some of the off-road biking trails.

1. THE TOP ATTRACTIONS

THE PEARL STREET PEDESTRIAN MALL.

Starting out as just another downtown renovation project, the four-block-long Pearl Street Mall has won national acclaim from urban-planning experts because it has turned into a gathering center for strolling, shopping, bumping into friends, and people-watching. Day and evening, you'll find just about everyone—

browsers and shoppers, families, businesspeople, CU students—walking past the many intriguing shops, trendy boutiques, galleries, and outdoor dining patios. There are plenty of entertainers as well—mimes, a piano player (who moves his instrument to the mall each morning), and other musicians. Begin your stroll at either end of the landscaped mall, which stretches along downtown Pearl Street from 11th to 15th Streets. Stores lining the mall are a blend of locally owned businesses, art galleries, and such major chains as Esprit, Ann Taylor, Pendleton, and Banana Republic.

NATIONAL CENTER FOR ATMOSPHERIC RESEARCH (NCAR), at the end of Table Mesa Dr. Tel. 303/497-1174.

Perched atop Table Mesa in southwestern Boulder, the dramatic pink sandstone building that houses the center was designed by the renowned architect I. M. Pei. You can walk through the mesa lab on a self-guided tour to see how NCAR scientists study everything from the oceans to insects in order to better understand the workings of the earth's atmosphere. The facts brought out should intrigue even visitors who are not particularly interested in the sciences, because the information deals with the weather and other subjects that affect our daily lives. There's a free guided tour at noon some days; call the number above for the current list of scheduled tours and a description of what's available to NCAR visitors. Exhibits, some interactive, show how the NCAR uses satellites, weather balloons, computers that simulate the globe's climate, and even solar research to understand wind shear, the "greenhouse effect," and other mysteries of our atmosphere. The mesa lab has two huge CRAY computers and two art galleries. NCAR also has some of the most pleasant easy-walking paths in the region. Leave time for a stroll around the mesa along paths weaving through the 380-acre mesa site, past grazing deer and stands of trees edging the sheer slabs of rocks called the Flatiron Mountains. One trail is handicapped-accessible.

Open: Mon–Fri 8am–5pm, Sat–Sun and hols 9am–3pm.

CELESTIAL SEASONINGS, 4600 Sleepytime Dr. Tel. 303/530-5300.

The corporate headquarters for Celestial Seasonings, which makes 45 herb and black teas, is one of Boulder's most popular tourist stops. Started by 19-year-old Mo Siegel and friends, who gathered wild herbs around Boulder, Celestial Seasonings grew into a major business that helped revolutionize the tea industry. It was eventually bought out by Kraft, Inc., but management bought the company back from Kraft in 1988, and today Celestial Seasonings is the largest herb-tea manufacturer in the U.S. (It also produces traditional teas.) Visitors taking the free 30-minute tour of the production facility learn how the herbs are cleaned and the tea is bagged and shipped, while all the time inhaling the rich aromas of cinnamon, clove, and other spices in the various teas. After the tour, visitors may browse the gift shop, picking up boxes of the various teas. (Be sure to check out the bargain bin for some close-to-giveaways on damaged tea boxes filled with perfectly good tea!) On a hot day, you'll notice many folks keep returning to the pots of iced teas to "sample." Visitors may lunch in the company's cafeteria, Monday through Friday from 11:30am to 1:30pm.

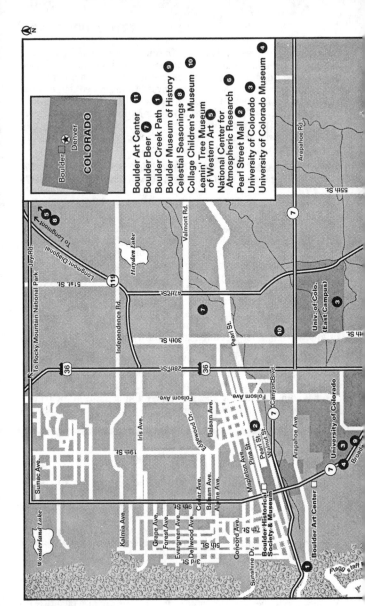

Admission: Free.

Open: Tours (on a first-come, first-served basis), Mon–Thurs at 11am and 1pm. Reservations are strongly recommended, and required for groups of six or more. Children must be 5 years or older to go on the tours; one adult per two children required for ages 5–8.

THE UNIVERSITY OF COLORADO.

Wear comfortable shoes to explore the 600-acre CU campus (locals never say "UC"), located east of Broadway just a few blocks

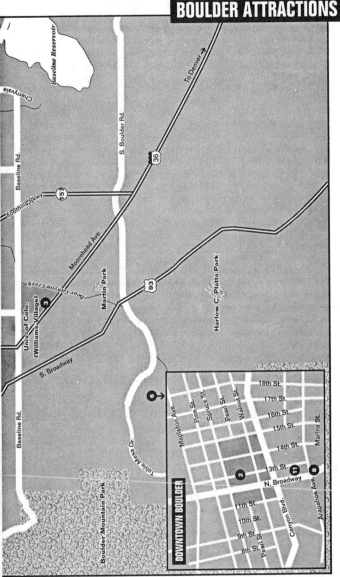

south of downtown. Here you can visit Old Main, the original building erected in the 1870s that once housed the entire university. The Heritage Center, on the third floor of Old Main (tel. 303/492-6329), houses memorabilia documenting the history of the university (it's open Tuesday through Friday from 10am to 4pm, and before and after every home football game). The Norlin Library, the largest research library in the state, has extensive holdings of American and English literature, and also houses a significant collection of western memorabilia and rare books. At the University of Colorado Museum in the Henderson Building (see "More Attractions," below) you'll learn more about the American Southwest.

Free campus tours are given Monday through Friday, starting at the Admissions Office (tel. 303/492-6301) in the Regents Building.

BOULDER BEER, 2880 Wilderness Place, off Valmont Rd. Tel. 303/444-8448.

If you're curious about the way beer is brewed in a microbrewery, take one of the free 25-minute tours and taste samples at the Boulder Brewery, located in a contemporary building near the Boulder Airport. The tours through this modern brewery with its shining copper vats are timed so that you can have lunch or dinner in the Wilderness Pub, a casual restaurant overlooking the bottling area. To put the production capacity in perspective, this microbrewery makes approximately 100 kegs a day, while the Coors Brewery in Golden turns out approximately 300,000 kegs an hour!

Admission: Free.

Open: Tours, Mon–Sat at 11am, 2pm, and 5pm.

2. MORE ATTRACTIONS

BOULDER ART CENTER, 1750 13th St., between Arapahoe Ave. and Canyon Blvd. Tel. 303/443-2122.

A multi-arts facility, the art center features contemporary local, state, and national artists in the two exhibition galleries. The center also has live performances of music, dance, poetry readings, and other art forms.

Admission: $2 nonmembers, $1.50 students and seniors.

Open: Tues–Fri 11am–5pm, Sat 8am–5pm, Sun noon–4pm.

BOULDER MUSEUM OF HISTORY, 1206 Euclid Ave., at 12th St. Tel. 303/449-3464.

Set in a lovely French château-style stone mansion, this museum is a window into Boulder's past. The exhibits are set up in the elegant rooms of the Harbeck House, with Italian tile fireplaces. A "cottage" built by a New Yorker who even lugged out west a richly colored Tiffany stained-glass window (which lights up the stairway landing today), it's rich in eccentricities. In the kitchen there's a woman bending over the old-fashioned stove, while a young girl sits at the table making cookies (they're both human-size dolls). A rare round ice refrigerator, an apple peeler, and other implements on the counters hint at the work involved when the Victorian-age cooks made meals. The exhibits change several times a year, because the historical society has collected more than 35,000 photographs and objects, including clothing, toys, and tools, used by Boulder residents as early as the 1860s. The museum has a large clothing collection, including some exquisitely beaded 1920s dresses, as well as one of the best quilt collections in the state. There's a Victorian fair every summer; call for the date.

Admission: $1.

Open: Tues–Sat noon–4pm.

UNIVERSITY OF COLORADO MUSEUM, in the Henderson Bldg. on the CU campus. Tel. 303/492-6892.

DID YOU KNOW . . . ?

- The Flatiron Mountains were named by the pioneer women for the way they reminded them of the flat irons they used for ironing.
- Astronaut Scott Carpenter named his space capsule *Aurora 7* because he grew up in Boulder on the corner of Aurora and 7th Streets.
- Chief Niwot placed a friendly curse on those who gaze upon the beautiful Boulder Valley: They must surely return.
- Locals claim that there are more used-book stores in Boulder per capita than any other city in the country.
- Boulderites love to eat out—the city has more than 200 restaurants!
- The Hotel Boulderado was named after Boulder and Colorado so that guests would never forget where they stayed.
- Boulder is one of the few cities with a "trout condo," located in Boulder Creek.

This museum features the natural history and anthropology of the Southwest. The exhibits include a display of Southwest Anasazi pottery, and a collection of Pueblo, Navajo, and Spanish colonial antique textiles.

Admission: Free.

Open: Mon–Fri 9am–5pm, Sat 9am–4pm, Sun 10am–4pm.

LEANIN' TREE MUSEUM OF WESTERN ART, 6055 Longbow Dr. Tel. 303/530-1442.

There's a wonderful collection of western art hidden in the upstairs museum in the corporate headquarters of Leanin' Tree, the world's largest publisher of western-art greeting cards. The gallery is crammed with intricately detailed, realistic paintings and bronzes of cowboys riding horses and herding cattle, Native Americans in battle, and other scenes from the Wild West era. The works, all by established contemporary western artists, include several award-winning pieces from the National Academy of Western Art and Cowboy Artists of America. Artists featured include Gordon Snidow, Howard Fogg, Charlie Dye, Bill Moyers, John Hampton, and Earle E. Heikka. Many of the works have been reproduced on the company's greeting cards for sale in the downstairs shop.

Admission: Free.

Open: Mon–Fri 8am–4:30pm, Sat on a limited basis (call for more information).

3. COOL FOR KIDS

COLLAGE CHILDREN'S MUSEUM, 2065 30th St., in Aspen Plaza, opposite the Crossroads Mall. Tel. 303/440-9894.

Tots to fifth-graders will enjoy the hands-on exhibits. The museum has an art express area, a dress-up section, a shadow room, and changing exhibits.

Admission: $2 per person, $7 maximum per family; children under 2, free.

Open: Wed 2–5pm, Thurs–Sat 11am–5pm, Sun 1–5pm.

OTHER ATTRACTIONS & ACTIVITIES

At the **Boulder Creek Observatory,** on the Boulder Creek Path behind the Clarion Harvest House, the younger ones can feed the huge trout (special food is available from vending machines) swimming at eyeball level behind a special glass barrier built at this section of the free-flowing Boulder Creek. Admission is free.

There are also **Kids' Fishing Ponds,** on the Boulder Creek Path, stocked by the Boulder Fish and Game Club, open only to children under the age of 12. The ponds are on the south bank and the alternative pedestrian path behind the Highland School building, now an office complex, between 6th and 9th Streets.

During the summer the **Boulder Parks and Recreation Department** (tel. 303/441-3400) plans many activities for children, including dance and theater performances in the parks. Call for more information.

In addition, the **Buffalo Bill Museum** in Golden, the **Denver Children's Museum,** and **amusement parks** in and around Denver will keep your children happily occupied. For details on these Denver attractions, see "Cool for Kids" in Chapter 7.

4. TOURS

There are no organized tours of Boulder, but for a **self-guided walking tour** of the Victorian buildings in the historic Mapleton Hill section, you can get a map at the Boulder Chamber of Commerce, 2440 Pearl St. (tel. 303/442-1044). The houses described on the map are a veritable architecture lesson.

Several companies operating out of nearby Denver—**Gray Line Bus Tours & Charters, Best Mountain Tours by the Mountain Men,** and **Two Wheel Tours**—offer regularly scheduled tours of Denver, the mountain parks, and other sights, and some will arrange tours custom-made to your interests. For details, see Chapter 7.

5. SPORTS & RECREATION

BIKING   Bike paths thread the city. The **Boulder Creek Path** runs for nine miles across Boulder and up into Boulder Canyon, while the city's longest trail is the **East Boulder Trail,** which can be picked up between 75th and 95th Streets on Arapahoe Road at the Teller Farm Trailhead. The **Foothills Trail** goes 7.3 miles from Wonderland Lake to 51st Street, just north of the Boulder Reservoir.

To get a copy of the **Boulder Bicycling Map** ($3) showing bicycle routes, contact the Boulder Chamber of Commerce (tel. 303/442-1044). If you're interested in off-road biking, ask for the **Front Range Boulder Biking Guide** to off-road Boulder County bicycling.

You can rent a bike at **Cycle Logic,** 2525 Arapahoe Ave. (tel. 303/443-0061), or **Doc's Ski and Sports,** 629 S. Broadway (tel. 303/499-0963), in Table Mesa Center, on the Boulder Bike Path. Average rates are $4 per hour, $12–$18 per day, and $30 per weekend.

If you plan on riding at night, you must carry a light on the front of your bicycle.

CLIMBING The sheer sandstone **Flatirons** are famous among mountain climbers worldwide because of their degree of climbing difficulty. Just aim a pair of binoculars at the mountainside on a nice day and chances are good that you'll see someone climbing. The steep cliffsides in **Eldorado Canyon** are often challenged by climbers, too.

If you're interested in climbing, contact **Boulder Mountaineer** (tel. 303/442-8355) or the **International Alpine School** (tel. 303/494-4904).

FISHING Licenses are needed to fish in Colorado's lakes and streams. Contact the **Colorado Division of Wildlife,** Department of Natural Resources, 6060 Broadway, Denver, CO 80216 (tel. 303/297-1192 or 303/291-7535), for information.

You can get fishing licenses at **Mcguckin Hardware,** 2525 Arapahoe Ave., Boulder (tel. 303/443-1822).

GOLF There are several golf courses open to the public, including the **Flatirons Golf Course** (18 holes), 5706 Arapahoe Ave. (tel. 303/442-7851), operated by the city. Other courses include **Haystack** (9 holes and a driving range), 5877 Niwot Rd. (tel. 303/530-1400); **Lake Valley** (18 holes and a driving range), five miles north of Boulder on Neva Road, east of U.S. 36 (tel. 303/444-2114); and **Coal Creek Golf Course** (tel. 303/666-7888). Average rates for these courses for 9- or 18-hole games are $8.50–$12.50 weekdays, $10–$16.50 weekends.

HIKING, JOGGING & RUNNING There are more than 30 miles of jogging paths in Boulder and more than 100 miles of hiking trails in the park system, with trailheads at Chautauqua Park, Flagstaff Mountain, the National Center for Atmospheric Research, and Eldorado Springs, among other places. For a copy of the **Boulder Mountain Park Trail Map** ($3), which lists the length of trails and classifies trails by degree of difficulty, contact the Boulder Chamber of Commerce, 2440 Pearl St. (tel. 303/442-1044).

The **Boulder Creek Path,** which snakes back and forth over Boulder Creek, runs from one end of town to the other, past ponds with geese, fish, and ducks, a sculpture park, and gardens. The path is used as a pedestrian shortcut through town, and by walkers, bicyclists, and joggers. A stroll on this path is one of the nicest ways to get a real feel for this city. Two of the most popular jogging trails are the **Mesa Trail** above Chautauqua Park, which begins at Bluebell Shelter, and **Dakota Ridge,** on Mapleton Avenue west of Boulder Memorial Hospital.

Hikers will find some of the most spectacular scenery in **Eldorado Canyon State Park,** a few miles south of town. One of the trailheads is at a narrow slash in the multitoned red-rock mountainside, and the path wends upward. Information about this difficult trail is listed in the Boulder Mountain Park Trail Map.

HORSEBACK RIDING There are plenty of riding trails threading the mountains. For information about hourly rides and trail rides, call **Bar A Stables** (tel. 303/499-0258). For information about trail rides, unguided rides, breakfast rides, and pack trips, call the **Peaceful Valley Lodge and Guest Ranch** (tel. 303/440-9632).

HUNTING For more information about the elk, antelope, and deer seasons, call the **Colorado Division of Wildlife** (tel. 303/

291-7529). It's also possible to hunt other big game—including black bear, mountain lion, and moose—at certain times during the fall.

SAILBOARDING   Beach Street, 1521 Pearl St. (tel. 303/444-2333), offers sailboard rentals and instruction at the Boulder Reservoir.

SKIING   The **Eldora Mountain Resort** (tel. 303/440-8700) is 21 miles from Boulder, and on the city bus line. Five chairs and a surface lift open up 1,400 vertical feet of mountainside; equipment rentals are available. The other Front Range areas, including Loveland, Keystone, Arapahoe, Breckenridge, and Copper, are all within a two-hour drive.

SOARING & GLIDING   The **Cloud Base,** at Boulder's Municipal Airport (tel. 303/530-2208), offers scenic flights and instruction.

SWIMMING   The **Boulder Parks and Recreation Department** has two outdoor pools and three indoor pools. There's also a beach and swimming at Boulder Reservoir. Call 303/441-3412 for more information.

6. SAVVY SHOPPING

SHOPPING CENTERS

The most entertaining place to shop is the **Pearl Street Pedestrian Mall** and its surrounding streets. For details, see "The Top Attractions," above.

If you're more interested in buying basics, try the huge **Crossroads Mall** (tel. 303/444-0722), located between 28th and 30th Streets off Arapahoe Road, which has more than 150 stores. Besides the anchoring chains like Sears, J. C. Penney, Fashion Bar, Montgomery Ward, May D&F, and Mervyn's, the mix of specialty stores offers everything from fine jewelry to stationery and toys. On a rainy day, locals get their exercise by walking around the marked "Walker's Track," which starts next to the C.P.I. One-Hour Photo shop. Stalls in the food court offer choices from Chinese to fresh salads, and there are at least half a dozen restaurants elsewhere in the mall.

There are several **other shopping centers** in the section of town roughly bordered by Folsom Avenue, 30th Street, Arapahoe Avenue, and Pearl Street. There's also a shopping area on Broadway near Table Mesa Drive, at the south end of town.

SHOPPING A TO Z

ART GALLERIES

Lots of galleries are located on, or just off, the Pearl Street Mall, and many have free maps listing most of the downtown galleries. Hours tend to change seasonally, so call ahead.

BOULDER ARTS & CRAFTS CO-OP, 1421 Pearl St. Tel. 303/443-3683.

On the Pearl Street Mall, this co-op representing local artists working in all media is filled with both decorative and usable art, including jewelry, handmade clothing, leather bags, stained glass, blown glass, and carved wooden boxes. Open in summer, Monday through Saturday from 10am to 9pm and on Sunday 11am to 6pm; in winter, Monday through Saturday from 10am to 6pm and on Sunday from 11am to 6pm.

MACLAREN/MARKOWITZ GALLERY, 1011 10th St. Tel. 303/449-6807.

Just off the mall, this gallery features contemporary and southwestern paintings, sculpture, folk art, and New Guinea artifacts. Open Monday through Wednesday from 10am to 5:30pm, on Thursday and Friday from 10am to 9pm, on Saturday from 10am to 5:30pm, and on Sunday from noon to 5pm.

MUSTARD SEED GALLERY, 1932 14th St. Tel. 303/447-8626.

At this gallery, just off the mall, you'll find displays of both contemporary and traditional paintings, pottery, art glass, photographs, and jewelry. Open Monday through Saturday from 10am to 5pm and on Sunday from 1 to 4pm.

WHITE HORSE GALLERY, 1218 Pearl St. Tel. 303/443-6116.

Located on the mall, the White Horse has an outstanding collection of Native American fine art, including paintings, prints, Kachinas, jewelry, pottery, weavings, and baskets. Open Monday through Saturday from 9:30am to 9pm and on Sunday from 11:30am to 6pm.

BOOKSTORES

In addition to the bookstores listed below, there's a **B. Dalton Bookseller** at 2700 Arapahoe Ave. (tel. 303/447-8718), and both a **Hatch** (tel. 303/444-5990) and a **Waldenbooks** (tel. 303/442-8557) in the Crossroads Mall, 1600 28th St.

THE BOOKWORM, 2850 Iris Ave. Tel. 303/449-3765.

The Bookworm, in the Diagonal Plaza, is a popular used-book store. It also sells some new titles.

BOULDER BOOKSTORE, 1107 Pearl St. Tel. 303/447-2074.

With books spread over four floors, this is the place to go if you're looking for unusual or serious literature. And you can get coffee, espresso, and light meals at the attached Bookend Café.

There's another Boulder Bookstore at 2525 Arapahoe Ave. (tel. 303/443-2942).

COLORADO BOOK STORE, 1111 Broadway. Tel. 303/442-5051.

College students frequent this well-stocked store, at College Avenue on the hill, for new and used books and textbooks.

TRIDENT BOOKSELLERS AND CAFE, 940 Pearl St. Tel. 303/443-3133.

Close to the west end of the pedestrian mall, Trident has an eclectic collection of books in an old building. After you purchase a book, you can walk through the inside doorway into the café, buy a pastry and an espresso, then sit and read. The bookstore is open daily from 10am to 11pm; the café, Monday through Friday from 6:30am to 11pm, on Saturday from 7am to 11pm, and on Sunday from 7:30am to 11pm.

GIFTS

APPLAUSE, 1123 Pearl St. Tel. 303/442-7426.

This store, located on the mall, has a unique collection of wearable art. You'll find everything from socks to dresses and jewelry to children's clothes, much of it hand-painted. Hand-painted furniture is sold, too. Open Monday through Wednesday from 10am to 6pm, Thursday through Saturday from 10am to 9pm, and on Sunday from noon to 5pm.

ECOLOGY HOUSE, 1441 Pearl St. Tel. 303/444-7023.

Located on the mall, Ecology House is a treasure house of sculptures, books, jewelry, T-shirts, and other gifts and trinkets—all featuring an environmental theme. Part of the proceeds are donated to environmental causes. Open daily from 10am to 8pm.

INTO THE WIND, 1408 Pearl St. Tel. 303/449-5356.

Located on the mall, Into the Wind has an extravagant collection of colorful kites and windsocks. Open Monday through Saturday from 10am to 6pm and on Sunday from noon to 5pm.

TOPAZ GEM & MINERAL, 942 Pearl St. Tel. 303/447-0600.

This store has an interesting collection of rocks, minerals, and jewelry. Open Monday through Saturday from 9:30am to 5:30pm and on Sunday from noon to 5pm.

GROCERIES

ALFALFA'S, 1651 Broadway. Tel. 303/442-0997.

Alfalfa's is an "upscale" grocery store with everything from out-of-season fresh fruit to fresh pasta. There's an excellent deli that's also a popular take-out lunch stop.

SPORTING GOODS

CHIVERS SPORTS, 2000 30th St. Tel. 303/442-2493.

Chivers specializes in ski, tennis, swim, and soccer gear.

GART BROS. SPORTING GOODS, 2525 Arapahoe Ave. Tel. 303/449-6180.

Gart Bros. has equipment for all types of sports. There's another Garts at 3320 28th St. (tel. 303/449-9021).

WINE & LIQUOR

BOULDER WINE MERCHANT, 2690 Broadway. Tel. 303/443-6761.

This store has a solid wine collection for all tastes.

LIQUOR MART, 1750 15th St. Tel. 303/449-3374.

Here you'll find a large selection of discounted wine and liquor.

7. BOULDER NIGHTS

For information about local stage and musical presentations, check the Friday entertainment section or the Sunday "Calendar" in the *Boulder Daily Camera* for news of upcoming events. In addition, the Friday "Weekend" section of the *Denver Post* and the Friday entertainment section of the *Rocky Mountain News* both list many events in Boulder. And, of course, Denver's nightlife is only a 20- to 40-minute drive down U.S. 36.

THE PERFORMING ARTS

There's an exciting blend of programming in the historic and renovated **Chautauqua Auditorium,** 900 Baseline Rd. (tel. 303/422-3282), and the Community House in historic Chautauqua Park, which opened on July 4, 1898. The mix includes the Colorado Music Festival, a film series, and the award-winning Chautauqua Summer Festival, which brings nationally known performers to Boulder. Head to a Chautauqua performance early enough to have lunch or dinner at the historic Chautauqua Dining Hall.

MUSIC FESTIVALS & SERIES

ARTIST SERIES, Macky Auditorium Concert Hall, on the University of Colorado campus. Tel. 303/492-8008, or 303/492-6309 for the box office.

This annual series, brings in such international artists as Isaac Stern, Dave Brubeck, and the Royal Philharmonic Orchestra of London. Many emerging and regional artists also perform during the subscription series at the Macky Auditorium and in free concerts off the campus.

BOULDER BACH FESTIVAL, P.O. Box 1896, Boulder, CO 80306. Tel. 303/494-3159.

This annual April event is dedicated to the music of J. S. Bach. In addition to orchestral, choral, and chamber performances, the weekend includes public lectures and children's concerts.

BOULDER PUBLIC LIBRARY CONCERT SERIES, at the Library Auditorium, 1000 Canyon Blvd. Tel. 303/441-3100.

Local, regional, and national artists perform in concert. The emphasis is on classical music, but there are a few jazz performances and children's concerts.

COLORADO MUSIC FESTIVAL, at the Chautauqua Auditorium. Tel. 303/499-1397 for ticket information.

This festival is an international ensemble composed of principal musicians from leading orchestras. Performances at the Chautauqua Auditorium are under the direction of conductor Giora Bernstein. Every summer the festival chooses an annual humanities project, which includes a series of special concerts with a central theme along with relevant lectures, symposia, films, and exhibits.

ORCHESTRAS

BOULDER PHILHARMONIC ORCHESTRA, Macky Audito-

rium Concert Hall on the University of Colorado campus. Tel. 303/492-8423, or 303/492-6309 for the box office.

A community orchestra that performs year round, it often brings in world-famous artists like the Canadian Brass and violinist Nadia Salerno-Sonnenberg.

UNIVERSITY OF COLORADO COLLEGE OF MUSIC, Campus Box 301, Boulder, CO 80309. Tel. 303/492-6352.

Performances by faculty and students are scheduled throughout the year.

DANCE

There are several local dance groups that perform regularly. Check the newspaper to see if a performance is scheduled while you're in town.

COLORADO DANCE FESTIVAL, P.O. Box 356, Boulder, CO 80306. Tel. 303/442-7666.

Usually held in June, this festival is a combination of performances, classes, and workshops exploring many areas of dance. Most of the workshops and classes are held in the University Theater on campus, and the performances are held in the Irey and University Theaters.

THEATER FESTIVALS

COLORADO SHAKESPEARE FESTIVAL, University of Colorado, Campus Box 261, Boulder, CO 80309. Tel. 303/492-1527.

For the last 32 summers this festival has drawn crowds from all over the country for productions of the Bard's plays. Company members include nationally known actors. Performances are held from late June through mid-August in the Mary Rippon Outdoor Theater at the university.

THEATER HOUSES

BOULDER'S DINNER THEATER, 5501 Arapahoe Ave. Tel. 303/449-6000.

This theater puts on productions of such popular Broadway musicals as *Show Boat* and *Paint Your Wagon*. The evening starts with a sit-down dinner in this cabaret-style theater. After you've been served, the waiters and waitresses become the actors and singers. Performances are Tuesday through Sunday evenings, and Sunday afternoon.

Admission: Dinner and show, $23 Tues–Thurs evening and Sun matinee, $27 Fri, $31 Sat.

BOULDER THEATER, 2032 14th St. Tel. 303/444-3600 for concert information, or 303/444-3601 for ticket information and sales.

Big-name acts to children's theater go on stage at the historic art deco Boulder Theater. Check the local newspaper for schedules when you are in town.

Admission: Ticket prices vary according to performer.

FOX THEATRE, 1135 13th St. Tel. 303/447-0095.

This converted movie theater is now the venue for live music performances, childrens' theater, and more. Performers booked are a mix of local and national talent.

THE BAR & CLUB SCENE

The nights and hours for live music vary, so call beforehand. Cover charges vary too, but the average is $3.

TWO FAVORITES

BOULDER CITY LIMITS, 484 Diagonal, at 47th St. and Longmont Diagonal. Tel. 303/444-6666.

This is Boulder's big country-western bar. There's live music on Thursday, Friday, and Saturday, and you can shoot pool for free on Tuesday.

WEST END TAVERN, 926 Pearl St. Tel. 303/444-3535.

A very trendy bar, it has been voted in local polls as the "best neighborhood bar" since it opened five years ago. The rooftop is the busiest place on nice afternoons and evenings, and jazz and blues notes waft through the crowd during the week.

OTHER CHOICES

Other places include **Tulagi's,** 1129 13th St. (tel. 303/442-1369), a casual college bar offering live music several nights each week; **Boulder Express,** 2075 30th St. (tel. 303/443-8162), where the canned music keeps people dancing; and **Potter's,** 1207 Pearl St. (tel. 303/444-3100), another popular meeting place and dance spot, has six big-screen televisions.

The atmospheric **Mezzanine Lounge,** in the historic Boulderado Hotel at 13th and Spruce Streets (tel. 303/442-4344), is a great place to chat with friends over live background music. Sip a yard of English ale at **Pearl's,** 1125 Pearl St., on the mall (tel. 303/443-4548), while listening to a live jazz band.

Champs, in the Clarion Harvest House Hotel, 1345 28th St. (tel. 303/443-3850), is a busy sports bar with six televisions, a games room, and a two-acre garden out in the back, while at **J. J. McCabe's Café,** 945 Walnut St. (tel. 303/449-4130), you'll find pool tables.

MOVIES

There are many commercial movie theaters in Boulder. For information about the **International Film Series,** the **Travel Film Series,** and the **Macky Auditorium Film Center Series,** call 303/492-8423. For information about the **Boulder Public Library Film Series,** call 303/441-3100.

---

8. EASY EXCURSIONS FROM BOULDER

It's easy to explore rustic mountain towns and posh ski resorts, sample city life in Denver, and even drive down to Colorado Springs when you're staying in Boulder. For a full description of these day trips, turn to "Easy Excursions from Denver" in Chapter 7. The touring information provided in that chapter works well for anyone staying in Boulder, with a few slight route adjustments. The scenic ride to and through Rocky Mountain National Park is actually shorter, because most Denverites go through Boulder on their way to Estes Park. However, plan on an extra 40 minutes of driving time to visit Colorado Springs, because you'll have to take U.S. 36 to I-25, through Denver and on down to Colorado Springs.

If you want to take the Gold Circle trip, which leads to old mining (now gambling) towns, or the Silver Boom and High Country Towns trip, you can slide into the loops in two ways. From Boulder, you could take Colo. 93 south to Golden and get on the I-70 expressway. But the most scenic route is through Boulder Canyon and the mountain town of Nederland. Head west out of town on Canyon Boulevard (Colo. 119) into the canyon, then drive past Boulder Falls and into Nederland. From Nederland, you'll follow the signs to Central City, which means staying on winding Colo. 119.

If you want a day trip hugging the plains, you can visit Golden, Evergreen, and even scenic Mount Evans by driving south on Colo. 93 to Golden and picking up the described loop.

GETTING TO KNOW COLORADO SPRINGS

Pikes Peak country has been a hot tourist spot since the late 1800s. Colorado City, the original town founded at the base of Pikes Peak, was a raucus frontier town populated by miners, cowboys, and other travelers heading into the mountains on foot or by the narrow-gauge railway climbing up to the gold fields at Cripple Creek. It was eventually absorbed by its more sober neighbor, Colorado Springs, perched on a plain 6,035 feet above sea level. Today, several of the remaining buildings in the Old Colorado City Historic District house boutiques, galleries, and restaurants.

Civil War hero Gen. William Palmer actually founded Colorado Springs as "Little London," for genteel folks. He fell in love with the region while researching a route for a Kansas Pacific Railroad line that was to go from the Missouri River to California. When Palmer's recommendation to lay track through this region was rejected in 1869, he decided, in 1871, to make his fortune by building a north-south line from Denver to Texas. He understood that building a city alongside the Denver and Rio Grande Railroad tracks ensured passenger traffic, and he envisioned the city as a "model of good taste and refinement."

Wealthy Easterners and the sons of the English gentry showed up in the late 1800s, bringing their pastimes of polo and cricket. But the mood was sober in Colorado Springs, in stark contrast to neighboring Colorado City. That city flourished as upright citizens visited in search of more libertine pursuits, including the imbibing of liquor, illegal in their home town. Palmer's plan went further awry as settlers raised havoc while riding through on their way to the rich gold mines around Cripple Creek.

However, the area was permanently enshrined in American folklore in 1895, after a tourist named Katharine Lee Bates rode up to the top of Pikes Peak in a wagon drawn by horse and burro. After returning to Colorado Springs, she composed the lyrics for the classic song "America the Beautiful."

Around the turn of the century, wealthy miners erected mansions in the north end of town, parks were laid out, and hotels like the Antlers and the Cliff House in nearby Manitou Springs went up. Tuberculosis victims slept on the sun porches of homes along the broad streets (built wide so that General Palmer could turn his four-in-hand carriage without having to back up) and bathed in the mineral waters in nearby Manitou Springs. But by 1909 the stream of

Cripple Creek gold dwindled to a trickle, and residents with an eye to the future turned to real estate and tourism for a living. So in 1915 a road for automobiles was laid down extending to the top of Pikes Peak, and in 1918 the elegant Broadmoor Hotel was opened and soon became a fashionable summer-long stop for the rich. By 1920 the city was reportedly the wealthiest per capita in the country.

Since then Colorado City has become a military stronghold. Camp (now Fort) Carson was constructed in the 1940s, Peterson Air Force Base was established in 1952, and the U.S. Air Force Academy opened at the north end of town in 1954. And three years later the headquarters for NORAD (the North American Aerospace Defense Command), the nuclear missile strike early-warning system for the United States and Canada, was founded here. The city also supports a thriving arts community and a symphony, several colleges, and the U.S. Olympic Training Center. It's home to 281,140 people, with some 397,000 in the metropolitan area. The major industries, besides tourism, are space technology, computers and electronics, and printing and publishing. Proving it's still a tourist draw, the region attracts approximately 4.2 million visitors every year.

1. ORIENTATION

ARRIVING

BY PLANE   Many airlines offer direct flights or connections (more than 100 flights per day) to **Colorado Springs Airport,** situated at the east end of the city. A new $39.5 million terminal is currently under construction that will allow the airport to accommodate 2.4 million passengers yearly, almost double the number who used it in 1992. The terminal is scheduled to open in fall 1994.

If you can't get a direct flight or a decent connection to Colorado Springs, route through Denver's Stapleton International Airport (see "Orientation" in Chapter 4 for complete information).

Air Carriers   Airlines flying into Colorado Springs include **American Airlines** (tel. 719/632-7760, or toll free 800/433-7300), **America West** (tel. 719/630-0737, or toll free 800/228-7862), **Continental** (tel. 719/473-7580, or toll free 800/525-0280), **Delta** (tel. 719/633-5560, or toll free 800/221-1212), **Mesa** (tel. 719/591-6211), **Trans World Airlines** (tel. 719/599-4400, or toll free 800/221-2000), and **United Airlines** (tel. toll free 800/241-6522). At this time, TWA has a direct flight to and from St. Louis, American Airlines has a direct flight to and from Dallas, America West has direct flights to and from Phoenix and Las Vegas, and Delta has direct flights to and from Salt Lake City and Dallas. If you can't route through one of these cities, you must route through Denver.

Ground Transportation   Limousine service between the Colorado Springs and Denver airports is available through the **Airporter** (tel. 719/578-6232) in Denver, 719/599-0505 in Colorado Springs). The fee is approximately $25 from airport to airport, plus an additional $10 for a hotel dropoff or pickup.

BY TRAIN   No passenger trains stop in Colorado Springs. The nearest Amtrak station is in Denver, and you must fly or take ground transportation from that city (see "By Plane," above).

BY BUS **Greyhound/Trailways** bus lines (tel. 719/635-1505, or toll free 800/531-5332 for route, fare, and schedule information) has a terminal in Colorado Springs at 327 S. Weber St.

BY CAR The main route into Colorado Springs from the north or south is **I-25**, which runs along the eastern slope of the Rockies from just north of Cheyenne, Wyoming, through Colorado, and south as far as El Paso, Texas. **U.S. 24** is the major east-west route to Colorado Springs (if you're driving into town from the east, the highway becomes Platte Avenue; it's Cimarron Street on the west end of town.) If you're heading cross-country from the east on I-70, you can take Exit 359 onto U.S. 24. If you're traveling eastward through the Rockies on U.S. 50, you might try **Colo. 115** as a scenic shortcut to Colorado Springs.

TOURIST INFORMATION

The **Convention and Visitor Bureau Visitor Information Center,** 104 S. Cascade Ave., Suite 104, in the downtown Sun Plaza building (tel. 719/635-7506, or toll free 800/DO-VISIT), is open Monday through Friday from 8:30am to 5pm and Saturday and Sunday from 9am to 3pm during the summer (Memorial Day through Labor Day), and Monday through Friday from 8:30am to 5pm during the winter. The staff is ready to answer visitors' questions and offers free itinerary planning. Maps, general information about the city, and brochures on attractions and restaurants are also available. There's free parking on Colorado Avenue; those with campers can park one block west.

Further information about this region can be obtained through the **Fun Fone Events Line** (tel. 719/635-1723) or by contacting the **Pikes Peak Country Attractions Association,** 354 Manitou Ave., Manitou Springs, CO 80829 (tel. 719/685-5894).

CITY LAYOUT

It's easy to find your way around central Colorado Springs. The main north-south artery is **I-25**, which runs through the middle of the city. The **downtown** area is laid out in a classic grid pattern, roughly bounded by Wahsatch Avenue to the east, Cimarron Street to the south, I-25 to the west, and Uintah Street to the north. The major north-south downtown thoroughfares are Nevada Avenue, Cascade Avenue, and Tejon Street, all lined with stores and restaurants. Outside the core business area, large Victorian houses and other older homes line many of the wide avenues. Colorado College is located at the north end of the downtown area. **Old Colorado City** is to the west of I-25, connecting with the downtown area on **Colorado Avenue** (Bus. U.S. 24). Outside the grid pattern the streets twist and curve according to the terrain.

MAIN ARTERIES & STREETS The **major north-south thoroughfares** are (from east to west): I-25, Nevada Avenue (U.S. 87/85), Hancock Avenue (which becomes the Hancock Expressway in the southern part of town), Union Boulevard, North and South Circle Drives, Academy Boulevard (Colo. 83), and Powers Boulevard.

The **main east-west streets** are (from north to south): Woodmen Road, Austin Bluffs Parkway (which becomes Garden of the Gods Road west of I-25), Fillmore Street (and Constitution Avenue in the eastern part of town), Uintah Street, Platte Avenue (U.S.

24 and Colo. 4), Cimarron Street (and its extension, Airport Road), Fountain Boulevard (which leads to the airport), and Lake Avenue (the westward extension of South Circle Drive).

STREET MAPS   Maps of the city and state are available at the Convention and Visitor Bureau Visitor Information Center, 104 S. Cascade Ave., Suite 104, Colorado Springs, CO 80903 (tel. 719/635-7506, or toll free 800/DO-VISIT). Members of the **American Automobile Association** can get free maps from the office at 3325 N. Carefree Circle (tel. 719/591-2222). City maps are also available at many hotels.

NEIGHBORHOODS IN BRIEF

Old Colorado City   Site of the original town at the base of Pikes Peak, Colorado City is now a historic district housing an eclectic collection of shops, art galleries, and restaurants centered on Colorado Avenue (Bus. U.S. 24) from 24th to 28th Streets.

Rockrimmon   This well-to-do section of the city features luxury houses on wooded lots and Briargate, a fast-growing middle-class community. It's near the U.S. Air Force Academy, which is itself a self-contained community, at the northern edge of town.

The Broadmoor Area   This lovely older residential section, which pushes against Cheyenne Mountain, surrounds the Broadmoor Hotel and Resort at the end of Lake Avenue in southwestern Colorado Springs.

Southeastern Colorado Springs   The Peterson Air Force Base and Colorado Springs Airport are the main features of this end of town.

Manitou Springs   Centuries ago the Ute and Arapahoe tribes were drawn to the mineral waters flowing from the earth on the flank of Pikes Peak; more contemporary tourists discovered them beginning in the 1870s (you can still test the mineral waters today). Today, neighboring Manitou Springs, adjacent to Colorado Springs, has a main street lined with arts-and-crafts boutiques and souvenir shops. The surrounding streets are lined with well-preserved Victorian homes and mansions. Many of the region's tourist attractions, including Cave of the Winds, Pikes Peak Cog Railway, the Manitou Cliff Dwellings Museum, and Miramont Castle, are located here.

2. GETTING AROUND

BY PUBLIC TRANSPORTATION [BUS]   **Colorado Springs Transit Management, Inc.** (tel. 719/475-9733 for route and schedule information), operates buses only Monday through Saturday from 6:15am to 6:15pm—so plan on taking taxis in the evening and on Sunday.

In Colorado Springs, the bus fare for adults is 60¢ for intown routes and 75¢ for routes that go outside the city limits. Children 12–18 pay 40¢ on school days and 60¢ on Saturday and holidays, children 6–11 pay 25¢, and youngsters 5 and under ride free with a fare-paying adult. Senior citizens and the handicapped pay 25¢.

Transfers are free, but exact change is needed for all fares. There's express service from the Chapel Hills Mall in the northern metropolitan sector into downtown in the morning and a return trip in the afternoon.

From Memorial Day through Labor Day the **Jolly Trolley** circles between downtown Colorado Springs and the Pikes Peak Cog Railway depot, stopping in Old Colorado City and Manitou Springs. An all-day pass costs $3 for "stop anywhere" privileges on the trolleys.

BY TAXI & LIMOUSINE You'll find a taxi stand outside the airport terminal, and the doorkeepers at major hotels have quick access to cabs, but you'll have to order one yourself anywhere else in the city. Call **Yellow Cab** (tel. 719/634-5000). Fares are $3 for the first mile and $1.35 for each additional mile. There's a 40¢ charge for each extra passenger over age 12.

Visitors can arrange for limousine service in the city or surrounding areas from **Western Limousine,** 1615 Kodiak Dr. (tel. 719/520-5754).

BY CAR Major rental agencies with booths at the airport or shuttle service to car centers include **Avis** (tel. 719/596-2751, or toll free 800/331-1212), **Budget Rent-A-Car** (tel. 719/574-7400, or toll free 800/262-RENT), **Dollar Rent-A-Car** (tel. 719/591-6464, or toll free 800/800-4000), **National** (tel. 719/596-1519, or toll free 800/CAR-RENT), and **Hertz** (tel. 719/596-1863, or toll free 800/654-3131).

I have discovered that **Enterprise Rent-a-Car** (tel. 719/574-2800 in Colorado Springs East, or toll free 800/325-8007) is a good company to rent from if you can work within their hours. Most of their cars are less than a year old, have low mileage, and cost comparatively less. Drivers get unlimited mileage within Colorado.

Parking There are meters on most of the downtown streets, so have nickels, dimes, and quarters handy (25¢ should buy you an hour of parking). Garages and lots in the downtown area cost approximately $1 per hour. Outside downtown it's usually possible to park in free parking lots or on the side streets.

Driving Rules For information on state driving regulations, and driving in winter in the mountains, see "Getting Around" in Chapter 4.

ON FOOT It's easy to get around downtown Colorado Springs on foot. However, you'll need to take buses or have a car to move around the city and visit the various attractions.

FAST *COLORADO SPRINGS*

Some of the information given in "Fast Facts: Denver" in Chapter 4 also applies to Colorado Springs; this includes climate, clothing, health tips, liquor laws, telephones, and tipping. The items below are specific to Colorado Springs.

Airport   See "Orientation," above.

American Express   The office (719/636-3871) is at 818 Tejon St. To report a lost or stolen card, dial toll free 800/528-4800.

Area Code   The telephone area code for Colorado Springs is 719.

Babysitters   The front desk or concierge at your hotel may well be able to provide information on babysitters. ABC Baby Sitting Agency (tel. 719/635-4229) charges by the hour and by the child.

Banks   Banking hours vary, but most banks are open Monday through Friday from 9am to 4pm. The Rocky Mountain BankCard System's automated Plus System (tel. toll free 800/THE-PLUS for locations) is available at a number of locations in the Colorado Springs metropolitan area. In addition, many hotels will cash checks for guests.

Barbershops/Beauty Salons   A popular choice is the Viva Salon, 3645 Star Ranch Rd. (tel. 719/579-8482), in the Broadmoor area. You can also try Wavelengths Salon, 110 E. Kiowa St. (tel. 719/471-9110).

Business Hours   Store hours vary widely. Most of the malls are open Monday through Friday from 9:30 or 10am to 9pm closing at 5 or 6pm on Saturday. Many malls open between 11am or noon and close at 5 or 6pm on Sunday.

Currency Exchange   Three of the major banks will change certain types of foreign currency. Try the Affiliated National Bank (tel. 719/471-5000), the Colorado National Bank (tel. 719/473-1333), or the Norwest Bank (tel. 719/636-1361 downtown).

Dentist   For 24-hour dental referrals, call the Colorado Springs Dental Society Emergency and Referral Service (tel. 719/598-5161). The answering service number is 719/473-3168.

Doctor   For medical referrals, call the Colorado Springs Doctors Exchange (tel. 719/632-1512) or the Memorial Hospital Physician Referral (tel. 719/475-5226). The Colorado Springs Medical Center, with five offices, offers 24-hour emergency physician coverage. The central facility is at 209 S. Nevada Ave. (tel. 719/475-7700).

Emergencies   Dial 911 for police, ambulance, and fire emergencies; for non-emergency police assistance, call 719/632-6611. For the Colorado State Patrol call 719/635-3581. Poison control information can be obtained through the Rocky Mountain Poison Control Center (tel. 719/630-5333, or toll free 800/332-3073). Care and Share (for transient people who need food and shelter) can be reached at 719/528-6767.

Eyeglasses   You can replace lost or broken glasses in about an hour, in many cases, at the Pearle Vision Center in the Chapel Hills Mall, 1710 Briargate Blvd. (tel. 719/598-3427), or at the Pearl Vision Express in the Citadel Mall, 750 Citadel Dr. E. (tel. 719/550-0300).

Fax Machines   Most print and copy shops, and many hotels, have fax services. There's a Kinko's Copies at 214 E. Pikes Peak Ave. (tel. 719/633-6683).

Hospitals   For emergency service, head to St. Francis Hospital, 825 E. Pikes Peak Ave. (tel. 719/636-8850 for the emergency room); Penrose Hospital, at 2215 N. Cascade Ave. (tel. 719/630-5333 for the emergency department); Penrose Community Hospital, 3205 N. Academy Blvd. (tel. 719/591-3216 for the emergency department); or Memorial Hospital, 1400 E. Boulder St. (tel. 719/475-5221 for the emergency and trauma center).

Laundry/Dry Cleaning   If your hotel doesn't have a

laundry service, ask at the front desk for a reliable cleaners or the location of the nearest laundry. There are four One Hour Cleaners in Colorado Springs. The ones at 1859 S. Nevada Ave. (tel. 719/473-1597), at 2322 N. Wahsatch Ave. (tel. 719/634-3166), and 1608 N. Academy Blvd. (tel. 719/596-3646) offer one-hour service Monday through Friday from 8am to 6pm and on Saturday from 8 to 11am. The branch at 2823 Dublin Blvd. (tel. 719/593-7617) offers "in by 9am, out by 4pm" service.

Libraries Anyone can use the local libraries, but a local card or a Colorado Library Card is needed to check out material. The main library is located at 20 N. Cascade Ave. (tel. 719/531-6333). There are copy and fax machines.

Lost Property If you have lost something of value, call the front desk at your hotel and call the city police (tel. 719/632-6611).

Newspapers The *Gazette Telegraph* is the city's largest daily paper. The "Lifestyle" section, and "Scene" on Fridays, lists weekend events, movies, shows, museums, and restaurants. You can also get Denver's daily papers—the *Denver Post* and the *Rocky Mountain News*. The *Cheyenne Edition* is a weekly newspaper. *Springs* magazine, a free monthly publication distributed in wire racks around the city, covers the entertainment scene and runs ads from many of the current "in" restaurants and nightclubs.

Pharmacies There are pharmacies at many King Soopers and Safeway grocery stores. There are several Walgreens pharmacies, including one at 28 S. Tejon St. (tel. 719/634-3742).

Photographic Needs Try 50-Minute Photo, 6902 N. Academy Blvd. (tel. 719/598-6412), in the Woodmen Valley Shopping Center off I-25.

Post Office The downtown post office is at 201 E. Pikes Peak Ave. (tel. 719/570-5343), and there are many other branches. Call 719/570-5339 for postal information. The branch at 3655 E. Fountain Blvd. (tel. 719/570-5377) has a late-evening pickup.

Radio There are more than a dozen local AM and FM radio stations. KILO (94 FM) and KKFM (96 FM) are hard rock; KVUU (99.9 FM) and KKLI (106.3 FM) are adult contemporary; KKCS (101.9 FM and 1460 AM), KKHI (105.5 FM), and KRDO (1240 AM) are country; KCME (88.7 FM) is classical; KRDO (95.5 FM) is easy listening; and KVOR (1300 AM) is all news.

Religious Services Religious faiths are well represented in this town. St. Mary's Catholic Cathedral, 22 W. Kiowa St. (tel. 719/636-2345); Temple Shalom, 1523 E. Monument St. (tel. 719/634-5311); and First Southern Baptist Church, 1409 Palmer Park Blvd. (tel. 719/633-4625), all welcome visitors. Look under "Churches and Synagogues" in the *Yellow Pages* for a complete listing.

Safety Whenever you're traveling in an unfamiliar city, stay alert. Be aware of your immediate surroundings. Wear a moneybelt, and don't sling your camera or purse over your shoulder. It's your responsibility to be alert even in the most heavily touristed areas.

Shoe Repairs If you need shoe repairs, go to Woodmen Valley Shoe Repair, 6976 N. Academy Blvd. (tel. 719/599-0031) in the Woodmen Valley Shopping Center; or Westside Boot & Shoe Repair, 615 W. Colorado Ave. (tel. 719/471-1081).

Taxes Sales tax varies according to the city and county. The combined state and local sales tax in Colorado Springs is 6.5%. The hotel tax to be added to the room rate is 8.5%.

Television   The major television stations are Channels 5 (PBS), 8 (NBC), 11 (CBS), and 13 (ABC); Channel 21 (KXRM) is Fox, an independent station; and cable is available at most hotels.

Time   Colorado Springs is on Mountain Standard Time, two hours behind Eastern Standard, one hour behind Central Standard, and one hour ahead of Pacific Standard.

Useful Telephone Numbers   For road conditions call 719/635-7623.

Weather   For weather information dial 719/596-1116.

3. NETWORKS & RESOURCES

FOR THE DISABLED   For disability information and referral call toll free 800/255-3477.

FOR STUDENTS   Students will find peers around the Colorado College campus on Cache La Poudre and Uintah St., and around Poor Richard's Pizza Restaurant, 324½ N. Tejon St., and the nearby coffeehouse.

FOR GAY MEN & LESBIANS   Contact the Gay and Lesbian Community Center of Colorado, 1245 E. Colfax Ave., Denver (tel. 303/831-6268).

FOR WOMEN   The Women's Resource Agency can be reached at 719/471-3170. The Center for Prevention of Domestic Violence has a hotline (tel. 719/633-3819).

FOR SENIORS   Many tourist attractions, movie theaters, and restaurants offer senior-citizen discounts. Ask before paying the admission fee. Contact the Colorado Springs Senior Center (tel. 719/578-6808) for a list of places offering senior discounts.

COLORADO SPRINGS ACCOMMODATIONS & DINING

Although much smaller than Denver, Colorado Springs offers a surprising range of accommodations and restaurants at all price levels, suitable for all types of travelers. In this chapter I've chosen some of the best buys, which offer the most for the money.

1. COLORADO SPRINGS ACCOMMODATIONS

It doesn't take long to drive from one end of Colorado Springs to the other—just 20 minutes, unless you get caught in rush-hour traffic. Furthermore, since the city's attractions are spread all over, price and style—rather than location—will most likely be the primary concern for travelers selecting accommodations. Therefore, I've listed the accommodations by price: "Very Expensive" means a double room will cost more than $200 per night; "Expensive," $75–$140; "Moderate," $45–$74; and "Budget," less than $44. Most of the hotels listed below offer corporate rates and have no-smoking and handicapped-accessible rooms. Remember to ask for any other special rates.

In addition to the hotels and motels listed below, you'll find other kinds of accommodations in and around Colorado Springs. Bed-and-breakfast inns and homes are increasingly popular with travelers. I have listed several here, including a mansion set high on a hillside overlooking the city. A referral and reservations service, **Bed & Breakfast Inns of Colorado,** offers a number of lodging choices along the Front Range, from rooms in ordinary family homes to mini-castles, Victorian inns, and Tudor mini-mansions. For a copy of the listings booklet, send a self-addressed business-size envelope and $3 to Bed & Breakfast Inns of Colorado, 1102 W. Pikes Peak Ave., Colorado Springs, CO 80904.

For those who travel in their home, the **Colorado Campground and CabinResort Association** directory lists several campgrounds and ranches in the Colorado Springs area. See "Longer-

Term Stays and Camping" in Chapter 5, for further details. It may also be helpful to refer back to Chapter 5 for the money-saving hints in "Frommer's Smart Traveler: Hotels."

The rates quoted below should be considered general price ranges, since many hotels have a wide variety of rates for the same type of room, depending on the time of year. Most rates do *not* include the 8.5% hotel tax that will be added to your bill. Prices were accurate at press time but are, as always, subject to change.

VERY EXPENSIVE

BROADMOOR HOTEL, 1 Lake Ave. (P.O. Box 1439), Colorado Springs, CO 80901. Tel. 719/634-7711, or toll free 800/634-7711. Fax 719/577-5700. 544 rms, 60 suites. A/C MINIBAR TV TEL

$ Rates: $135–$175 single or double; $220–$1,700 suites. DC, DISC, MC, V. **Parking:** Free.

The Broadmoor Hotel has had a Mobil five-star rating since 1960 and an AAA five-diamond rating since 1976, both of which accurately reflect the high level of service and amenities. This 3,000-acre resort serves simultaneously as business hotel, busy conference center, luxury vacation resort, and one of the country's most popular golf hideaways. The Broadmoor, which opened in 1918, has accomplished the difficult feat of retaining an old-world ambience while offering guests contemporary activities. If you're not staying here, stop by for a meal and take a look.

The luxurious guest rooms and suites are located in three buildings: the pale-pink stucco Broadmoor Main, opened in 1918; an addition called Broadmoor South; and a separate building called Broadmoor West. All rooms are lavishly decorated, with plush carpeting, striped wallpaper, prints on the walls, separate vanity tables with chairs, and terrycloth robes in the bathrooms. However, the style of each building is distinct. Broadmoor Main has an Italian Renaissance decor with hand-worked frescos and bas-reliefs on the ceilings, stairs, and arches. The nine-story Broadmoor South, built in 1962, is part of the main building but has a more modern look. Broadmoor West, across the small lake from the main building, has elegant public rooms filled with Oriental art dating back to the Ming and T'sing Dynasties.

If you want old-world elegance, reserve a room in Broadmoor Main or the wings. They come in different sizes and shapes, ranging from small twin rooms and tower rooms with decks to lakeside suites or corner suites with closets large enough to hold a crib. There are several deluxe suites in which many U.S. presidents have stayed.

Although the original hotel opened in 1918, the amenities are modern, thanks to a major multi-million-dollar renovation in recent years. The Broadmoor claims to staff two or more employees for each guest room.

Dining/Entertainment: The hotel has eight restaurants: Charles Court, decorated to resemble an English country manor house (see "Colorado Springs Dining," below); the Penrose Room, an elegant Edwardian room; the Tavern Room, for informal dining with entertainment; the Garden Room, a tropical restaurant with delicious salads; the Golden Bee, a reconstructed 18th-century English pub; Julie's Restaurant (open summer only), serving continental breakfasts, light lunches, and a late-night menu; the Golf Club Dining

Room, serving breakfast, lunch, and dinner; and the South Golf Club Dining Room, offering lunch during summer only.

Services: The Broadmoor runs the Bee Bunch Children's program during the summer months. For a fee, children 5–12 can go to a kids' camp from 9am to 4pm and from 6 to 10pm, including lunch and/or dinner. Activities are arranged by age groups and are well thought out. While the younger group might go swimming, have paddleboat races, and use the playground, the older kids attend a golf clinic and swim. Another day, everyone goes to the zoo, attends a tennis clinic, or plays croquet. Evenings are for movies and indoor ice skating.

Facilities: Convention hall, Broadmoor World Arena (for ice skating), three 18-hole golf courses, three heated pools (two seasonal), 12 tennis courts (four covered), squash courts, bike rentals, an exercise room, and a parcourse fitness circuit. Mark Cross, Pappagallo, Montaldo, and several other shops are tucked in various buildings. There's so much to do here that the Broadmoor publishes a weekly pamphlet outlining your choices.

EXPENSIVE

HOTELS

ANTLERS DOUBLETREE, 4 S. Cascade Ave., Colorado Springs, CO 80903. Tel. 719/473-5600, or toll free 800/528-0444. Fax 719/389-0259. 290 rms, 13 suites. A/C TV TEL

$ Rates: Weekdays, $105–$125 single; $115–$135 double; $150–$850 suite. Weekends, $49–$99 single or double. AE, CB, DC, DISC, ER, JCB, MC, V. **Parking:** $4 per day.

A high-rise hotel in the heart of downtown, the Antlers has been completely refurbished in an upscale manner and taken over by the Doubletree chain. It's a true big-city hotel, both in amenities and styling—but you'll find one of the Doubletree chain's trademark fat chocolate-chip cookies waiting when you walk into your room. The rooms are decorated in quiet tones of beige, tan, and green. Guests on the concierge floor get a continental breakfast, afternoon hors d'oeuvres, and upgraded amenities. Some suites have minibars.

Dining/Entertainment: A lively brewpub, Judge Baldwin's Brewing Company features casual fare. Palmers Restaurant, just off the lobby, has breakfast and lunch buffets; the dinner menu features regional cuisine. The lobby lounge has piano music.

Services: Room service, courtesy airport shuttle.

Facilities: Health club with indoor lap pool, whirlpool, and aerobic and weight-training stations; gift shop; newsstand; hair salon.

CHEYENNE MOUNTAIN CONFERENCE RESORT, 3225 Broadmoor Valley Rd., Colorado Springs, CO 80906. Tel. 719/576-4600, or toll free 800/428-8886. Fax 719/576-4186. 216 rms & suites. A/C MINIBAR TV TEL

$ Rates (including 3 meals/day): $150–$265 single, $230–$390 double. (Rates vary according to season.) Call at least 10 days in advance for special packages, which include golf and other activities. Holiday rates are also available. AE, DC, DISC, MC, V. **Parking:** Free.

This hotel is a sprawling complex with rooms and suites clustered in low, natural-wood buildings spread around the property. There are three types of rooms: standard rooms with king-size beds, parlor suites with two queen-size beds and a connecting sitting room, and bilevel suites. Accommodations are comfortable but not plush. The suites with cream walls and blond-wood furniture have minibars in the living room, robes, and an additional sink in the bedroom. Every guest room has a private deck.

Dining/Entertainment: There are two restaurants in the main building and a third at the country club. Remington's is a small gourmet restaurant. Tables in the earth-tone room are set on different levels so that most diners have wonderful views of Cheyenne Mountain. The cavernous Mountain View Dining Room, with a vaulted ceiling and plentiful seating, features elaborate buffets. There's also a lounge and a billiards room.

Services: Room service, business service center.

Facilities: 18-hole golf course; fully equipped health club; four outdoor pools and one indoor pool; 18 tennis courts (6 indoors); racquetball and handball courts; small lake with fishing, sailing, and swimming.

COLORADO SPRINGS MARRIOTT HOTEL, 5580 Tech Center Dr., Colorado Springs, CO 80919. Tel. 719/260-1800, or toll free 800/228-9290. Fax 719/260-1492. 302 rms, 8 suites. A/C TV TEL **Directions:** Take Exit 147 (Rockrimmon Boulevard) off I-25.

$ Rates: $120 single; $130 double; $230–$300 suite. Ask about weekend packages and corporate rates. Children 18 and under stay free in parents' room. AE, MC, V. **Parking:** Free.

When this Marriott opened in the northwestern end of town, it filled a niche: It offers individual businesspeople, vacationers, and groups full-service hotel amenities and flexible conference facilities. The nine-story, red-brick hotel has color-coordinated guest rooms decorated in soft green, rose, and mauve tones. All rooms are accessible only by computer-coded cards, and the concierge floor has restricted elevator access. Although guests staying on that floor must check in at the main desk, they can get a concierge's assistance during the day, a complimentary continental breakfast in the private lounge each morning, and complimentary hors d'oeuvres at the honor bar in the lounge each afternoon. Guests are provided with hairdryers and robes. Some suites have minibars.

The view of Pikes Peak is spectacular from the hotel. The stunning two-story lobby has seating areas set apart from the entrance and check-in areas by rectangular brick pillars and ledges holding decorative vases and glass artworks.

Dining/Entertainment: Gratzi's, a sophisticated casual restaurant with glass walls offering a view of Pikes Peak, is set behind the bar. The food is good and well priced. There's a conventional breakfast menu, but order the breakfast buffet, which has a mix of cereals, fresh fruits, eggs, and side dishes and is priced about the same as if you'd ordered juice, coffee, and eggs. Gratzi's specializes in fresh seafood and fresh pasta with innovative sauces for lunch and dinner.

Cahoots, a sports bar, has a loaded hors d'oeuvres bar during the "hungry" happy hour. Chat's, a lobby piano bar, is a comfortable place to unwind after work.

Services: Room service, concierge, valet parking.

Facilities: Indoor and outdoor pools, whirlpools, sauna, health club, 18 tennis courts, squash and racquetball courts.

EMBASSY SUITES HOTEL, 7290 Commerce Center Dr., Colorado Springs, CO 80919. Tel. 719/599-9100, or toll free 800/362-2779. Fax 719/599-4644. 207 suites. A/C TV TEL **Transportation:** Free shuttle service to and from the airport. **Directions:** Take the Woodmen Road exit off I-25.

$ Rates: $99 for one person. Each additional adult $10 extra. Children 12 and under stay free in parents' room. Ask about lower weekend rates. AE, DC, MC, V. **Parking:** Free.

Each suite in this hotel on the north side of town has a living room in addition to the private bedroom, which is on a par with the quality of single guest rooms at similarly priced hotels. The living rooms contain a sofa bed, dining area, wet bar, microwave oven, and mini-refrigerator. The bedroom has a vanity sink and the bathroom is off the living room.

The suites overlook a vast atrium with waterfalls, pools surrounded by greenery, and exotic birds in cages.

Dining/Entertainment: The Polo Club Bar & Grill, at one end of the atrium, is open for lunch, dinner, and Sunday brunch. There's another dining area at the other end where guests get a full cooked-to-order breakfast each morning, and can enjoy a two-hour complimentary cocktail party each afternoon.

Services: Room service.

Facilities: Swimming pool, Jacuzzi, steam room, and sauna open 24 hours; golf privileges at a nearby course.

HEARTHSTONE INN, 506 N. Cascade Ave., Colorado Springs, CO 80903. Tel. 719/473-4413, or toll free 800/521-1885. 23 rms (21 with bath, 2 with shared bath). A/C **Directions:** From I-25, get off at Unitah Street (Exit 143); travel east to the third stoplight and turn right onto Cascade Avenue for seven blocks.

$ Rates (including breakfast): $70–$120 single; $80–$130 double. AE, MC, V. **Parking:** Free.

If you like a bed-and-breakfast atmosphere but want the privacy of a larger place, stay at this charming inn, a 10-minute walk from downtown. The adjoining Victorian buildings, which were gutted and rebuilt, were once a private home and a neighboring boarding house for tuberculosis patients. Each room in the inn has a different decor and personality, and all are furnished with antiques and color-coordinated linens. Rooms are named, rather than numbered, to reflect their personalities. The Solarium, for example, is a corner room with a private sitting porch hidden from passersby by wooden latticework. The Library has a queen-size bed with an open carved-walnut headboard, an ornate tiled fireplace with an oak mantel and built-in bookcases, and a comfortable reading chair. The Loft has inset keyhole dormers overlooking the street, a queen-size iron-and-brass bed in the main room, a slanted ceiling, and a child's bed in an alcove. Three rooms have private porches, and three have working fireplaces. Because the two connected houses have several different levels, usually there are no more than three or four rooms opening off the same hallway, so you have a good deal of privacy. Room prices include a gourmet breakfast, with homemade breads, served in the dining room each morning. No smoking is allowed anywhere inside the inn. There are two telephones in private alcoves, plus a few cellular phones available at an additional per-minute charge.

RADISSON INN COLORADO SPRINGS NORTH, 8110 N. Academy Blvd., Colorado Springs, CO 80920. Tel. 719/598-5770, or toll free 800/333-3333. Fax 719/598-3434. 200 rms. A/C TV TEL **Transportation:** Free shuttle to/from the airport. **Directions:** Take Exit 150A off I-25.

$ Rates: $75–$90 single; $80–$100 double. AE, DC, DISC, MC, V. **Parking:** Free.

The Radisson is located at the northernmost end of the city. Its rooms are wrapped around a giant atrium adorned with plants. The Garden Terrace Room (open for three meals daily), the Atrium Terrace Bar, several seating areas, a pool, and a whirlpool are all inside the atrium. There's a sauna and an exercise room nearby.

Dining/Entertainment: The Garden Terrace restaurant is for casual dining, and there's a piano bar in the atrium lounge.

Services: Room service, courtesy airport shuttle, golf privileges at Pine Creek Golf Course.

Facilities: Fitness center, indoor pool and whirlpool.

RED LION HOTEL, 1775 E. Cheyenne Mountain Blvd., Colorado Springs, CO 80906. Tel. 719/576-8900, or toll free 800/547-8010. Fax 719/576-4450. 299 rms. A/C TV TEL **Transportation:** Free shuttle service to/from the airport. **Directions:** Take Exit 138 off I-25.

$ Rates: $79–$109 single; $89–$119 double. Winter weekends, $69 single or double per night with advance reservations. AE, DC, DIS, MC, V. **Parking:** Free.

At the south end of the city, the deluxe Red Lion has rooms spread around a plant-filled atrium. The large rooms, with double sinks, are attractively decorated in deep-rose and beige tones.

Dining/Entertainment: The atmosphere is electric in Maxi's Lounge, a dark, noisy bar with a happy hour starting at 5pm weekdays; it has live entertainment Tuesday through Saturday evenings in the summer, and Friday and Saturday only in winter. Maxi's restaurant, with its soft armchairs, candlelit tables covered with rose tablecloths, and high banquette booths, is popular with locals and reservations are recommended. Entrees, which range from $18 to $29, include steaks, salmon, veal, and rack of lamb. The Red Lion also has the more casual Atrium Coffee Shop, which offers cheaper early-bird specials from 5 to 7pm. Complimentary coffee is available each morning in the lobby Quiet Bar, which is also a relaxing place for later in the day.

Services: Free shuttle to/from the airport and a nearby shopping mall.

Facilities: Weight room with a full complement of exercise machines, indoor/outdoor pool; access to the Gleneagle Golf Club.

RESIDENCE INN, 3880 N. Academy Blvd., Colorado Springs, CO 80917. Tel. 719/574-0370, or toll free 800/331-3131. Fax 719/574-7821. 96 rms. A/C TV TEL

$ Rates (including continental breakfast): $103 studio; $134 penthouse suite. Ask about corporate rates and reduced rates for longer stays and weekends. AE, DC, MC, V. **Parking:** Free.

Located on the northeast side of town, the Residence Inn is another member of the Marriott chain of condo-style hotels. Guests stay in units that look more like private suites than hotel rooms. In the studios the bed is set against the back wall and the front section of the room has a full kitchen and a tiny living room area in front of a fireplace. The two-story penthouse suites with vaulted ceilings have a sitting room (with a Murphy bed) on the main floor, which can be closed off with a curtain from the living room, kitchen, and bathroom. There's a second bedroom upstairs in an open loft and a bathroom at the top of the stairs. Pets are allowed.

Dining/Entertainment: Social hour Mon–Fri, 5pm–7pm, with free drinks and hors d'oevres.

Services: Complimentary grocery-shopping service.

Facilities: Sport court, hot tub, outdoor seasonal pool, laundry facility.

BED & BREAKFASTS

RED CRAGS, 302 El Paso Blvd., Manitou Springs, CO 80829. Tel. 719/685-1920. 6 rms (all with bath).
$ Rates: $75–$150 single or double. MC, V.
This huge, elegant old Victorian mansion, set on a bluff with two acres and ponds with ducks, has six rooms on the upper floors. They vary from the Teddy Roosevelt Room, which comes with a huge fireplace and private deck, to a charming fourth-floor two-bedroom suite with breathtaking views. The public rooms include a solarium and a lovely living room with a fireplace.

RED STONE CASTLE, Manitou Springs, CO 80829. Tel. 719/685-5663 or 719/685-5070. 1 suite. **Directions:** Call for directions.
$ Rates (including full breakfast): $85 single; $120 double. Each additional person $25 extra.
The owners of the historic Red Stone Castle, perched high on the mountainside, have turned the third floor into a one-of-a-kind B&B: Inspiration Suite. Set atop this home made with Manitou red sandstone 1½ feet thick, the apartment is all curves and windows with great views. There's a turret sitting room with rounded walls, two bed chambers with queen-size beds (closed off from each other visually but not by complete walls), and a bathroom with an extra-long antique clawfoot tub.

MODERATE

HOTELS

COMFORT INN, 8280 Colo. 83, Colorado Springs, CO 80920. Tel. 719/598-6700, or toll free 800/228-5150. Fax 719/598-3443. 104 rms, 5 suites. A/C TV TEL **Directions:** Take Exit 150A off I-25.
$ Rates (including continental breakfast): $54 single; $59 double. AE, DC, DISC, MC, V. **Parking:** Free.
This Comfort Inn, located next to the Air Force Academy, provides comfortable rooms with televisions. A whirlpool and an outdoor pool are available for guest use.

DRURY INN, 8155 N. Academy Blvd., Colorado Springs, CO 80902. Tel. 719/598-2500, or toll free 800/325-8300. Fax 719/598-2500. 118 rms. A/C TV TEL **Directions:** Take Exit 150A off I-25.
$ Rates (including continental breakfast): Oct. 1–May 22, $40–

FROMMER'S COOL FOR KIDS: HOTELS

Broadmoor Hotel *(see page 198)* Kids 5–12 will enjoy attending the Broadmoor's summer program, with activities like tennis and swimming that are lively and arranged by age groups.

Residence Inn *(see page 202)* It resembles a condominium development, so its safer for kids to walk around and play at the sports court, with its basketball hoop and seasonal swimming pool.

Embassy Suites *(see page 201)* Both parents and kids love this place. The suites have private bedrooms, so kids sleep in the living room—with their own TV. There's an indoor pool, and a full breakfast is included in the room rate.

El Colorado Lodge *(see page 204)* Kids don't have to be as quiet as in a regular hotel room, because they are staying in cabins. Outside, there's plenty of room to run around and play without getting near a street.

Silver Saddle Motel *(see page 205)* Bring your own movies and the kids can watch them on the motel's "family channels."

$42 single, $46–$48 double. May 23–Sept 30, $59 single, $69 double. AE, MC, V. **Parking:** Free.

The guest rooms are typical of this chain, which offers some of the nicest rooms in the moderate price range. Guest services include free local telephone calls.

EL COLORADO LODGE, 23 Manitou Ave., Manitou Springs, CO 80829. Tel. 719/685-5485, or toll free 800/782-2246. 25 units. A/C TV TEL **Directions:** Take the Manitou Avenue exit off U.S. 24 and turn left onto Manitou Avenue.

$ Rates: $38.50–$83.50 per cabin.

Adobe-style cabins create a pleasant ambience for vacationers. Most of the units, which house one to seven guests, have beamed ceilings and fireplaces; eight have kitchenettes. El Colorado has a large outdoor pool, a shuffleboard area, and a basketball court.

GARDEN OF THE GODS MOTEL, 2922 W. Colorado Ave., Colorado Springs, CO 80903. Tel. 719/636-5271, or toll free 800/637-0703. 28 rms. A/C TV TEL **Directions:** From I-25 take Exit 141 (U.S. 24) and go west to 26th Street; turn right two blocks and turn left on Colorado Avenue.

$ Rates: $38.50–$65.50 single or double. Winter rates approximately 30% lower. AE, DISC, MC, V.

A "mom and pop," nonchain motel, the Garden of the Gods has a small indoor heated pool. You can walk to several restaurants.

HAMPTON INN, 7245 Commerce Center Dr., Colorado

Springs, CO 80919. Tel. **719/593-9700,** or toll free 800/HAMPTON. Fax 719/598-0563. 127 rms. A/C TV TEL **Directions:** Take Exit 149 off I-25.

$ **Rates** (including continental breakfast): $42–$48 single; $48–$56 double. Slightly higher in summer. AE, MC, V. **Parking:** Free.

The Hampton Inn is the best buy in the moderate range for value-conscious travelers and businesspeople on strict expense accounts who want a conventional hotel. The rooms at this nationwide chain are neither chintzy nor plush. They are comfortable and decorated with attractive, solid double or king-size beds, dressers, desks, and comfortable chairs. Rooms have a single double bed, two double beds, a king-size bed, or a king-size bed and a sofa bed. At the Hampton Inn on the north side of town, there's an indoor swimming pool, remote-control TV, and hairdryers in the bathrooms. Fax and photocopier service are available 24 hours.

There's also a southside Hampton Inn at 1410 Harrison Rd., Colorado Springs, CO 80919 (tel. 719/579-6900), one block west of I-25 off Exit 138. Room rates are $55 single, $60 double.

LE BARON, 314 W. Bijou St., Colorado Springs, CO 80905. Tel. 719/471-8680, or toll free 800/477-8610. Fax 719/471-0894. 245 rms, 1 suite. A/C TV TEL **Directions:** Get off I-25 at the Bijou Street exit and go west.

$ **Rates:** $65 single; $75 double; $225 suite. 25% discount for senior citizens. AE, DC, DISC, MC, V.

The price is a steal for the quality of the rooms, perhaps because of the hotel's location—on the far side of the expressway from downtown (although still within walking distance). The Bijou 314 restaurant is off the lobby, which has a nice seating area around a fireplace. The hotel has a heated pool and gazebo in the inner courtyard, an exercise room, and courtesy airport shuttle service.

QUALITY INN, 555 W. Garden of the Gods Rd., Colorado Springs, CO 80907. Tel. 719/593-9119, or toll free 800/292-9119. Fax 719/260-0381. 159 rms. A/C TV TEL

$ **Rates** (including continental breakfast): $67 single; $73 double. Children 17 and under stay free in parents' room. Corporate rates available. AE, DC, MC, V. **Parking:** Free.

The Quality Inn is a good choice for the budget-conscious traveler. The rooms have either double or king-size beds, and separate desk areas. Breakfast is served each morning in the Quality Clubroom, a large living room with wingback chairs and couches near the check-in desk. Complimentary coffee, tea, and juice are always available. The inn has a heated outdoor pool and laundry facilities. It's located on the north side of town just off the highway, a few minutes' walk from a Village Inn and a Hungry Farmer, making it easily accessible to inexpensive meals.

SILVER SADDLE MOTEL, 215 Manitou Ave., Manitou Springs, CO 80829. Tel. 719/685-5611, or toll free 800/S-SADDLE. 54 rms & suites. A/C TV TEL **Directions:** Take U.S. 24 to the Manitou Avenue exit and go right; the motel is across from the city park.

$ **Rates:** $39.50–$79.50 single or double; $69.50–$104.50 two-bedroom suite. Rates may be higher on holiday weekends. AE, DISC, MC, V.

You'll find comfortable rooms here, and 12 of them have hot tubs! Amenities include a large, heated seasonal swimming pool, outdoor hot tubs, in-room coffee, and free reservation service for area attractions. Bring your VCR tapes, or rent them nearby, and the Silver Saddle will play them through your television on one of its closed-circuit channels.

BED & BREAKFASTS

ONALEDGE, 336 El Paso Blvd., Manitou Springs, CO 80829. Tel. 719/685-4265. 2 rms, 2 suites (all with bath). A/C **Directions:** Take U.S. 24 west to Manitou Avenue, go west on Manitou Avenue for two blocks and turn right on Mayfair Street; go to the top of the hill to El Paso Boulevard and Onaledge will be directly in front of you.

$ Rates (including breakfast): $70–$75 single or double; $100–$120 suite. AE, DISC, MC, V.

This smashingly gorgeous English Tudor stone mansion has trimmings like copper hardware and a copper fireplace hood, two player pianos, hardwood floors, and eight natural rock terraces outside. The rooms and suites in this home are opulently decorated: The Craftwood Room has a brass bed and wicker furniture; the Onaledge Room, off the public common area, has large windows framing Pikes Peak; the Rockledge has a king-size canopy bed and a hot tub for two; and the Fireplace Suite has a private hot tub. Breakfast is served on one of the patios when it is warm outside.

TWO SISTERS INN, 10 Otoe Place, Manitou Springs, CO 80829. Tel. 719/685-9684. 4 rms (2 with bath, 2 with shared bath) in the main house, honeymoon cottage (with bath). **Directions:** Go west on Manitou Avenue and turn left onto Otoe Place.

$ Rates (including full breakfast): $52 single or double with shared bath, $65 single or double with bath; $80 honeymoon cottage.

The Two Sisters Inn is a charmingly decorated Victorian home just a few steps from Manitou Spring's main street. There are four cozy bedrooms, all odd angles and fetchingly decorated, in the main house, and a private honeymoon cottage with a featherbed. One bathroom has a clawfoot tub. On warm days, breakfast is served in the garden. This is a no-smoking inn.

BUDGET

BUDGET INN, 1440 Harrison Rd., Colorado Springs, CO 80906. Tel. 719/576-2371. 43 rms. A/C TV TEL **Directions:** Take Exit 138 off I-25 at the south end of town.

$ Rates: Apr 15–Oct 15, $43.95 single; $48.95 double. Oct 16–Apr 14, $31–$36 single or double. MC, V. **Parking:** Free.

The Budget Inn epitomizes the concept of clean, cheap lodging. Most of the rooms in this motel have two double beds, although two rooms have king-size beds.

MOTEL 6, 3228 N. Chestnut St., Colorado Springs, CO

80907. Tel. 719/520-5400, or 505/891-6161, the Motel 6 central reservations number. 84 rms. A/C TV TEL **Directions:** Take Exit 145 (Fillmore Street) off I-25 and drive a block west to Chestnut Street.

$ Rates: $25 single; $31.50 double. AE, MC, V. **Parking:** Free. This Motel 6, on the northwest side of the city, has a year-round pool. Located six miles south of the Air Force Academy, it's close to downtown and an easy drive to many tourist attractions.

---

2. COLORADO SPRINGS DINING

Nouveau California to Tex-Mex—you can find it all in Colorado Springs, and there are plenty of good restaurants in all price ranges. As I did with hotels, I've listed restaurants by price: "Very Expensive" indicates that a complete meal will cost more than $40 per person; "Expensive," $20–$35; "Moderate," $10–$20; and "Budget," less than $9. (If you're on a tight budget, try one of the luxury choices at lunchtime, when prices are lower.)

Keep in mind that many of the finer restaurants in this city change their menus several times a year, so some dishes described in this book might not be available when you visit. The credit and charge cards accepted at restaurants are listed "as of the moment."

VERY EXPENSIVE

BRIARHURST, 404 Manitou Ave. Tel. 719/685-1864.
   Cuisine: AMERICAN/INTERNATIONAL. **Reservations:** Recommended.
$ Prices: Appetizers $4.50–$7.50; main courses $10.50–$29.95. AE, MC, V.
   Open: Dinner Mon–Sat from 6pm, with last seating at 9:30pm.
Elegance is the watchword at the Briarhurst, a lovely 1876 manor in Manitou Springs that's owned by the chef. Entrees range from steak Diane and homemade fettuccine with seafood sauce to a vegetarian platter to shrimp and scallops dijonnaise. You can also order chateaubriand bouquetière or rack of Colorado lamb. Try the fixed-price ($15.95) Grazer's Menu: any three items selected from appetizers, soup, salads, or dessert. Adventuresome eaters might enjoy the fixed-price ($17) International Showcase dinner, featuring cuisines from different countries.

LA PETITE MAISON, 1015 W. Colorado Ave. Tel. 719/ 632-4887.
   Cuisine: FRENCH. **Reservations:** Recommended.
$ Prices: Appetizers $3.50–$5.25; main courses $11.95–$18.50. AE, DC, DISC, MC, V.
   Open: Dinner only, Tues–Sat 5–10pm.
Locals say that this restaurant is the right place to celebrate special occasions. Inside this bright-blue Victorian house, the chef prepares contemporary country French cuisine, including such imaginative dishes as rib eye of veal with wild mushrooms and

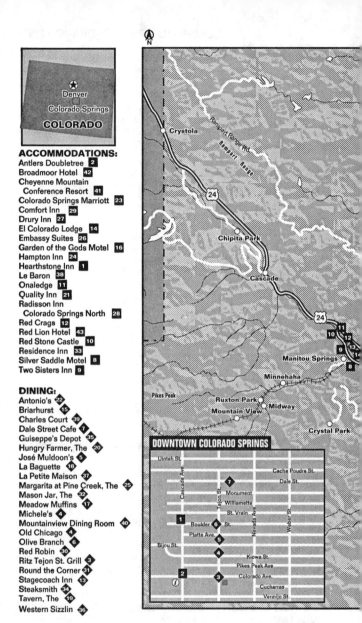

sherry and sautéed lean duck breast with peppercorns and brandy. Dinners include a green salad and the chef's selection of accompaniments. The early-evening menu, served from 5 to 6:30pm, runs $7.50–$13.95.

EXPENSIVE

THE MARGARITA AT PINE CREEK, 7350 Pine Creek Rd.,

COLORADO SPRINGS
ACCOMMODATIONS & DINING

50 yards north of the Embassy Suites. Tel. 719/598-8667.
Cuisine: GOURMET CONTINENTAL. **Reservations:** Recommended.
$ Prices: Dinners average $22; "lite" dinners $16; lunch $6.50. AE, DC, CB, MC, V.
Open: Lunch Tues–Fri 11:30am–2:30pm; dinner Tues–Sat 6–8:30pm.

⭐ Arrive in time and you might be lucky enough to get a table with a view of the sun setting over Pike's Peak at this wonderful restaurant with southwestern decor. Tables inside the white stucco building rest on tile floors, and some nights a harpsichord player creates lightly tinkling background music. But you come for the food, course after course of exquisitely prepared food creatively laid out on your plate. The menu changes weekly and includes a mix of classic and ethnic dishes, built on fresh fish, veal, pasta, lamb, steak, and duckling. Entrees are served with appetizer, soup, salad, bread, vegetables, and dessert. A six-course Mexican meal is served Tuesday through Friday nights.

STEAKSMITH, 3802 Maizeland Rd. Tel. 719/596-9300.
Cuisine: STEAK/SEAFOOD. **Reservations:** Recommended.
$ Prices: Appetizers $3.50–$5.50; main courses $11.95–$21.75. AE, DC, MC, V.
Open: Dinner only, Mon–Sat 5:30–10pm, Sun 4–9pm.

Despite its name, locals come to Steaksmith for the seafood as well. The prime rib is especially popular with locals, although the menu lists a dozen other cuts of prime, aged beef. Imaginatively prepared seafood entrees, including items like fresh fish, shrimp, scallops, and Alaskan king crab, change daily. Meals at this casually elegant restaurant include a choice of rice, fries, pasta, or baked potato, and salad bar or soup of the day. Grazers should eye the appetizer menu.

MODERATE

ANTONIO'S, 301 Garden of the Gods Rd., one block east of I-25 on Northpark Dr. Tel. 719/531-7177.
Cuisine: ITALIAN. **Reservations:** Recommended.
$ Prices: Appetizers $3.95–$5.95; main courses $6.95–$15.95. AE, MC, V.
Open: Lunch Mon–Fri 11:30am–2pm; dinner daily 5–10pm.

Two cousins of Sicilian descent—one a restaurateur from Buffalo, N.Y., and the other a chef who worked in New York City and Las Vegas—run Antonio's. They dish out large portions of pasta, so you shouldn't go away hungry. Dig into a plate of spaghetti with meat

---

Ⓕ FROMMER'S COOL FOR KIDS: RESTAURANTS

Red Robin (see p. 215) At this popular joint, kids can devour mouth-watering burgers topped with almost anything they want.

Western Sizzlin (see p. 216) With a games room, an ice-cream-sundae buffet, and inexpensive food, you can't go wrong!

Meadow Muffins (see p. 214) Kids can explore the collection of original movie props, signs, and assorted oddities on the walls while they wait for their "Jiffy burgers" or other fun food.

sauce or tortellini filled with broccoli, pine nuts, and prosciutto and smothered in cream or tomato sauce. Or you might try the veal marsala or veal saltimbocca, or one of the house specialties, such as linguine vongole (with clams in red or white sauce). Lighter fare includes vegetable lasagne or spinach salad. There's a children's menu, too. The Mediterranean decor and hanging plants create a comfortable, casual setting. Live Italian opera on Sunday night.

DALE STREET CAFE, 115 E. Dale St. Tel. 719/578-9898.
   Cuisine: AMERICAN NOUVELLE. **Reservations:** Not required.
$ Prices: Appetizers $2.25–$4.25; main courses $5–$9.50. MC, V.
   Open: Mon–Thurs 11:30am–9pm, Fri–Sat 11:30am–9:30pm.
This isn't a health-food restaurant, but according to the owners the emphasis is on healthful food. The menu lists a variety of pastas, Mediterranean pizzas, salads, and fish, all creatively prepared. The soups are made from scratch. Highlights of the menu include linguine pesto; fettuccine Willa, with "whitefish" crab, madeira, and cream; Coho salmon with fresh red-pepper sauce; fresh trout with capers in wine sauce; and naturally fed Colorado chicken with mustard sauce or lemon-lime butter. How about Neapolitan pizza with fresh tomato, basil, and garlic, or five-cheese pizza? Salads include niçoise, spinach, chicken dijonnaise, and seafood. The same menu is used at lunch and dinner, but might change according to the season. There are no red-meat dishes.

The decor fits the style of the food: informal yet stylish, from the wood tables and ice-cream chairs to the watercolors on the walls and the chamber music in the background. The café is set in a Victorian house with deep-lavender trim and dining room windows with stained-glass inserts. There's a full bar and an outdoor patio.

GUISEPPE'S DEPOT, 10 S. Sierra Madre St. Tel. 719/635-3111.
   Cuisine: ITALIAN. **Reservations:** Not required.
$ Prices: Appetizers $1.25–$2.95; main courses $4.75–$13.95. AE, DC, DISC, MC, V.
   Open: Sun–Thurs 11am–10pm, Fri–Sat 11am–11:45pm.
You can get a sumptuous meal at this old-train-station-turned-Italian-restaurant, located one block west of the Antlers Hotel. The glass ticket windows still line one side of the long room where passengers once arrived loaded down with luggage. Today photos of trains line the walls that surround booths and tables covered with red-checked tablecloths. In the dining room overlooking the tracks, trains chug by as diners eat rolls warmed and buttered before being brought to the table.

Guests can find everything from chef Darden's special baked lasagne to fried chicken to lobster tails. You can also order overflowing plates of spaghetti, stone-baked pizza topped with anything from pepperoni to pineapple, T-bone or New York steak, prime rib, and a wide selection of hot and cold sandwiches.

THE HUNGRY FARMER, 575 Garden of the Gods Rd. Tel. 719/598-7622.
   Cuisine: AMERICAN. **Reservations:** Not required.
$ Prices: Appetizers $3.95–$5.50; main courses $9.95–$16.50. AE, CB, DC, DISC, MC, V.

Open: Lunch Mon–Fri 11:30am–2pm; dinner Mon–Sat 5–10pm, Sun noon–9pm.

At this restaurant, waitresses in granny-style dresses serve you in rooms where bales of hay hang from the ceiling and corn husks decorate the walls. The family-style meals include the "bottomless bucket" of soup, corn on the cob, potatoes, and muffins. If you have room for a main dish, you can choose among fried shrimp or the catch of the day, light salads, veal Oskar, chicken Kiev, prime rib, and steak. The farm specialties include country-fried steak, barbecued ribs, and liver and onions.

If you have to wait for seating, visit Granny's Parlour, where you can nibble on cheese and sip a glass of complimentary wine. There's music in the Still, the larger bar with high bar stools around cocktail tables, but the atmosphere is cozier in the Study, a small bar with couches.

JOSÉ MULDOON'S, 222 N. Tejon St. Tel. 719/636-2311.

Cuisine: MEXICAN. **Reservations:** Not required.
$ Prices: Appetizers $3.75–$4.75; main courses $4.50–$6.25 at lunch, $4.50–$9 at dinner. AE, MC, V.
Open: Lunch Mon–Sat 11:30am–4pm; dinner Mon–Sat 5–10pm, Sun 4–10pm; brunch Sun 10:30am–3pm.

Although this restaurant is on one of Colorado Springs's busiest streets, once you step inside you'll feel as if you've been transported to New Mexico. Scenes of the Southwest and pictures of Native American pueblos decorate the walls. During the summer the patio is the most popular place to sit in this big, bustling restaurant. All the classic Mexican and southwestern dishes—enchiladas, fajitas, and chimichangas—are available at lunch and dinner. There's even a make-your-own tostada bar. The lunch menu lists several salads, while steaks and chicken meals are served up for dinner. There's live entertainment Tuesday through Saturday from 9:30pm to 1:30am. Bar food is available until 1am.

José Muldoon's has a second restaurant and equally popular watering hole at 1600 38th St. (tel. 719/449-4543). Stoke up on the all-you-can-eat Mexican buffets at lunch and dinner. Happy hour is from 3 to 7pm.

OLD CHICAGO, 118 N. Tejon St. Tel. 719/634-8812.

Cuisine: ITALIAN. **Reservations:** Accepted only for parties of six or more.
$ Prices: Appetizers $2.50–$4.50; pasta bar $7.25; main courses $4.50–$9.50. AE, MC, V.
Open: Lunch Mon–Sat 11am–3pm; dinner Mon–Thurs 5–10pm, Fri–Sat 5–11pm, Sun noon–10pm.

The $7.95 pasta bar is the biggest draw at Old Chicago, a restaurant decorated with memorabilia from the Windy City. The problem of choosing among the 110 available brands of beer, including 25 on tap, keeps the discussion moving in the tavern area. If you complete the 10-beer "World Beer Tour," you get your name inscribed in the "Hall of Foam." You can order deep-dish pizzas, sandwiches, or salads off the menu while in the bar, or head for the pasta bar. The homemade linguine, spaghetti, and fettuccine can be topped with six different sauces. The waiters will give you the daily list of sauces, which could include pesto, shrimp and lobster, cioppino, white or red clam, mushroom, artichoke, and four-cheese, as well as the not-so-unusual marinara and bolognese. The soup and salad selection is good, including basil chicken and primavera salad with minestrone soup. Chocoholics should save room for the Kahlúa fudge brownie, topped with ice cream and hot fudge, or a giant chocolate-chip cookie. Everything on the menu, with the exception of the pasta bar, is served at all hours to diners seated on stools around the high cocktail tables in the long tavern area at the front of the restaurant.

Old Chicago has a second location at the north end of the city: 7115 Commerce Center Dr. (tel. 719/593-7678).

OLIVE BRANCH, Boulder St. at Tejon St. Tel. 719/475-1199.
   Cuisine: NOUVELLE AMERICAN. **Reservations:** Accepted only for parties of six or more.
$ Prices: Main courses $3–$8. AE, MC, V.
   Open: Breakfast Mon–Sat 7–11am; lunch Mon–Sat 11am–3pm; brunch Sun 9am–2pm.

This restaurant, open only for breakfast and lunch, is billed by the owners as "an adventure in healthful dining." House specialties include quiche (the variety changes daily), chicken marsala, and stir-fry. Its reputation for great vegetarian food came from dishes like the vegetable Noel—fresh sautéed vegetables over wild rice with a creamy sauce and three melted white cheeses (you can also get it with chicken). Breakfast choices run the gamut from yogurt pancakes to Spanish omelets.

There's another Olive Branch restaurant at Vickers Drive and Academy Boulevard (tel. 719/593-9522), which is open for dinner. Appetizers run $2.25–$4.95; main courses, $4.50–$8.95.

RITZ TEJON ST. GRILL, 15 S. Tejon St. Tel. 719/635-8484.
   Cuisine: CONTEMPORARY AMERICAN. **Reservations:** Not required.
$ Prices: Appetizers $2–$6; main courses $6–$14; lunch $3.95–$7.50. AE, MC, V.
   Open: Daily 11am–10pm.

"Puttin' on the Ritz" in this town means stepping into this art deco restaurant and nightspot. The marble counters and slick tile floor, the two-story-high ceilings where fans swirl lazily, the glass-block walls, and the salmon-colored pleated shades on the lamps lighting the large horseshoe bar are reminiscent of the 1920s. The menu changes several times a year; however, the basic theme is new American cuisine. Entrees include such imaginative dishes as black-bean ravioli with goat cheese and chorizo sauce and fried chicken with garlic mashed potatoes and sage gravy. Some other choices are steak prepared five different ways, pizzas, and sandwiches.

STAGECOACH INN, 702 Manitou Ave. Tel. 719/685-5815.
   Cuisine: CONTINENTAL. **Reservations:** Not required.
$ Prices: Appetizers $3–$4; main courses $4.95–$6.50 at lunch, $9–$17 at dinner. DISC, MC, V.
   Open: Dinner daily 5–9:30pm; brunch Sun 11am–2pm.

You can get a good meal at the rustic Stagecoach Inn, a historic stagecoach stop on Fountain Creek in Manitou Springs. Entrees include duck Bigarde, roasted rabbit, filet of salmon, onion-smothered steak, and vegetarian stagecoach.

BUDGET

LA BAGUETTE, 2417 W. Colorado Ave. Tel. 719/577-4818.

Cuisine: FRENCH. **Reservations:** Not accepted.

$ Prices: Sandwiches and pastries $1–$5; bistro dinners $4.95–$9.50. No credit cards.

Open: Mon 7am–6pm, Tues–Sat 7am–9pm, Sun 8am–5pm.

⭐ 🅢 The aroma of baking French bread envelops you when you walk through the door of this French café. Step up to the counter and order a continental breakfast, choosing a plain croissant or one of the fruit-filled ones, juice, and coffee or espresso. At lunchtime you can get onion soup, croissant sandwiches, and fruit and cheese plates. French bistro dinners—cheese fondue, fettuccine, and chicken—are available Tuesday through Saturday.

THE MASON JAR, 5050 N. Academy Blvd. Tel. 719/598-1101.

Cuisine: AMERICAN. **Reservations:** Accepted only for special occasions or for large groups.

$ Prices: Appetizers $3–$3.30; main courses $4.90–$11; light portions $4.90–$6.90. DISC, MC, V.

Open: Summer, daily 11:30am–9:30pm. Winter, Sun–Thurs 11:30am–9pm, Fri–Sat 11:30am–9:30pm.

🅢 The casual coffee-shop atmosphere at this spot, where drinks are served in mason jars, is toned up by the fireplace. It's a good place for families, because less expensive "lighter" portions are available for small eaters and children. Chicken fried steak, pork chops, steak, prime rib, fried chicken, fried shrimp, catfish, and halibut are all on the menu. Regular meals include soup or salad, coleslaw, potato, and biscuits or bread. The "Half Pints" menu for ages 8 and under includes $2.90 meals.

There's another Mason Jar at 2925 W. Colorado Ave. (tel. 719/632-4820). Hours may vary slightly. Both restaurants have liquor licenses.

MEADOW MUFFINS, 2432 W. Colorado Ave. Tel. 719/633-0583.

Cuisine: AMERICAN. **Reservations:** Not accepted.

$ Prices: Appetizers $1.70–$4.60; burgers and sandwiches $4.50–$5. MC, V.

Open: Daily 11am–10:30pm (bar 11am–2am).

⭐ The irreverent attitude at this restaurant is best described on the menu (which can be folded and mailed): "World famous for fun, frivolity, frolic, and the best burgers this side of the Brooklyn Bridge. No Horses served at main bar." The truth is, you'll get your Jiffy burger (peanut butter, bacon, and jack cheese on a beef patty), Oink & Cheese, or spicy buffalo wings fairly quickly, unless the place is packed. But you'll want to wander around this multilevel restaurant while waiting for your food just to explore the grab bag of original movie props, signs, and other oddities hanging from the ceiling and tacked to the wooden walls. Check out the sled from *Dr. Zhivago,* and a torpedo. If you come in the evening, try to grab seats around one of the high, log-slab bar tables overlooking the dance floor. You can get burgers, sandwiches, hot dogs, and a range of salads.

MICHELLE'S, 122 N. Tejon St. Tel. 719/633-5089.
   Cuisine: AMERICAN/ICE CREAM. **Reservations:** Not accepted.
   $ Prices: Sandwiches and burgers $3.50–$4.95; ice cream $1.10–$5.20. AE, CB, DC, DISC, MC, V.
   Open: Mon–Thurs 9am–11pm, Fri–Sat 9am–midnight, Sun 10:30am–11pm.

The locals go to Michelle's to gorge themselves on ice-cream sundaes, although you can get a meal, too. Choices include sundaes, sodas, and such creations as the American Beauty (two scoops of ice cream, strawberries, bananas, sugar wafers, nuts, and a cherry), a dessert croissant (with two scoops of vanilla ice cream, hot fudge, nuts, whipped cream, and a cherry), and the Pikes Peak Surprise (elevation 13 inches—any flavor). Ten of you could share a flaming Mount Olympus for $34.50!

If you must eat lunch or dinner first, the menu also lists a variety of hot and cold sandwiches, more than half a dozen types of burgers, and homemade chili. Michelle's also has a breakfast menu with omelets averaging $4.25 and full breakfasts (eggs, toast, potatoes, and bacon or sausage) averaging $3.50.

There's another Michelle's at the Citadel Mall, 750 Citadel Dr. E. (tel. 719/597-9932).

RED ROBIN, 3680 Citadel Dr. N. Tel. 719/597-2473.
   Cuisine: AMERICAN. **Reservations:** Not required.
   $ Prices: Appetizers $3.25–$4.95; main courses $3.95–$9.95. AE, DISC, MC, V.
   Open: Mon–Thurs 11am–11pm, Fri–Sat 11am–1am, Sun 11am–10pm.

The Red Robin is a member of a chain of "burger and spirits" emporiums that consistently have mouth-watering burgers surrounded by big steak fries. Some folks order a plain or cheeseburger, but my favorite is the more elaborate avocado burger, with guacamole, bacon, Swiss cheese, and red onion. You can get burgers topped with mushrooms, Tex-Mex trimmings, teriyaki sauce, wine sauce, or barbecue sauce; you can get the same treatment on a grilled chicken breast. The salads are large, but don't be daunted, because the vegetables are so fresh and delicious. Try the stir-fried chicken-and-vegetables salad, the Cobb salad, or the El Taco Salad. Red Robin also serves fajitas (including a Cajun-style version) and sandwiches.

The Red Robin is a popular spot, so arrive early if you don't want to wait. If you do have to wait, check out the list of exotic cocktails—it's as long as the main menu. If you have a child along, ask for a "cookie magic," a non-alcoholic drink that tastes like an Oreo cookie topped with ice cream.

There's another Red Robin restaurant at the Chapel Hills Mall, 1410 Jamboree Dr. (tel. 719/598-2473).

ROUND THE CORNER, 5079 N. Academy Blvd. Tel. 719/593-8278.
   Cuisine: AMERICAN. **Reservations:** Not required.
   $ Prices: Appetizers $1.50–$3; main courses $2.50–$6.25. MC, V.
   Open: Daily 11am–10pm.

This is a member of a chain that has eliminated a lot of the hassles in family and fast-food dining, without sacrificing the quality of the food. You sit down at the table, read the menu, then pick up the telephone at your table and order (no waiting for waiters). When your meal is ready, the telephone rings and you walk to the counter to pay and pick up.

Hamburgers, cooked to your specifications, come plain or loaded with toppings like bleu-cheese dressing, bacon, hickory sauce, guacamole, sour cream, cheese, and green pork chili. The menu is extensive. There's soup and a variety of salads, chicken and chopped sirloin steak platters, and more than a dozen varieties of sandwiches. You can also get big baskets of fries (plain or with chili cheese) or french-fried onion rings, and deep-fried cheese sticks or mushrooms.

WESTERN SIZZLIN, 221 S. 8th St. Tel. 791/633-8000.
   Cuisine: AMERICAN. **Reservations:** Not accepted.
$ Prices: Dinner $4–$10; kid's plate $2. AE, MC, V.
   Open: Sun–Thurs 11am–9pm, Fri–Sat 11am–10pm.

Not to be confused with the chain restaurant "Sizzler," this locally popular cafeteria-style restaurant won't let you go away hungry. In addition to steak, the price includes potatoes, Texas toast, and the ice-cream-sundae bar. The salad bar has tacos, fried chicken, and tasty fried apple sticks, as well as garden greens.

SPECIALTY DINING

HOTEL DINING

CHARLES COURT, in the Broadmoor Hotel, 75 Elpomar Rd. Tel. 719/634-7711.
   Cuisine: CONTEMPORARY AMERICAN. **Reservations:** Recommended.
$ Prices: Appetizers $6.50–$12.50; main courses $19–$39. DISC, MC, V.
   Open: Breakfast daily 7–10:30am; dinner Sun–Fri 6:30–9:30pm, Sat 6–9:30pm.

At Charles Court, in Broadmoor West at the Broadmoor Hotel, waiters refold your cloth napkin into a decorative shape if you leave the table during the meal. Need I say more about the quality of the service? The decor isn't elaborate, but the room's rich wood trim, fine china with the Broadmoor insignia, and the soft white cloths exude charm and elegance.

You'll find that the presentation of food and the service are as important as taste in this award-winning restaurant. The menu changes regularly, but you might find bacon-and-leek vichyssoise or game bird consommé with aged sherry for starters. Move onto crisp Colorado mountain bass with caramelized sweet onion in a whole-herb lobster broth, the roast rack of Colorado lamb with peach-mint compote, or pepper steak flambé à la Charles. Ask about the fixed-price Harvest Menu. If you go with a group of two or more, consider sharing desserts because you're going to have a terrible time choosing between the fresh berries with the light, very tasty French vanilla sauce and the soufflés. Jacket and tie required for men.

MOUNTAIN VIEW ROOM, in the Cheyenne Mountain Conference Resort, 3225 Broadmoor Valley Dr. Tel. 719/576-4600.
   Cuisine: AMERICAN. **Reservations:** Not required.
$ Prices: Dinner buffet $18.50 adults, $9.25 children 5–12; soup-

and-salad buffet $9.95; dessert buffet $5.25. AE, DC, DISC, MC, V.
Open: Dinner only, daily 5–10pm.

You can eat all you want at the America's Harvest nightly buffet in this resort restaurant. The choice of dishes changes nightly, as the chefs explore regional foods. Guests dine in a large, vaulted room with glass windows looking out at lovely vistas. (Call before going. When the hotel isn't full, they may serve only à la carte off the menu.)

THE TAVERN, in the Broadmoor Hotel, 1 Lake Ave. Tel. 719/634-7711.
    Cuisine: STEAK. **Reservations:** Not required.
$ **Prices:** Appetizers $6.50–$9.50; main courses $14.75–$27.50. DC, MC, V.
    Open: Daily 11:30am–11pm.

The Tavern is the Broadmoor's five-star "informal" restaurant. Original Toulouse-Lautrec lithographs line the wall in the main room of the Tavern. Although there are other restaurants here, offering fancier surroundings and more elaborate menus, the informal atmosphere in the Tavern's main room, and in the foliage-filled, sunlit Garden Room, is very relaxing. Well-cut and aged beef and prime rib are house trademarks. If you're not a meat lover, try Rocky Mountain trout, or rôtisseried chicken or duck.

AFTERNOON TEA

The **English Connection,** 124 N. Nevada Ave. (tel. 719/632-9060), is a small downtown restaurant that serves a classic English high tea with quiche, finger sandwiches, and pastries Monday through Saturday from 2 to 4pm for $5.95 per person. Prepare to blow your day's calorie count on the goodies in the pastry case. Choices can range from pumpkin or Mandarin orange cheesecake to raspberry trifle. You can also get lunch, including soup and salad, sandwiches, and quiche of the day. You can choose omelet fixings at breakfast. It's open for breakfast Monday through Saturday from 7 to 11am and for lunch Monday through Saturday from 11am to 3pm and on Sunday from 8am to 1pm. AE, MC, V.

There's a second location at 1601 S. Tejon St. (tel. 719/632-3277) for meals and catering. Hours are different.

The **British Home Shoppe,** 323 N. Tejon St. (tel. 719/520-5444), was opened by a woman who wanted a place to meet her compatriots. You can get a full tea here, including scones with clotted cream, and sandwiches. Desserts include English favorites such as trifle and fruit crumble. If you have a yen for a Cornish pastie, bangers, or toad-in-the-hole, head here for lunch. Reservations are advisable for lunch or tea. The front of the shop is stocked with English-made goods for sale. It's open Tuesday through Saturday; lunch is served from 11:30am to 2:30pm and tea is served from 2:30 to 5pm. AE, MC, V.

LATE-NIGHT/24-HOUR DINING

THE WAFFLE HOUSE, 755 Fillmore St. Tel. 719/475-2726.
    Cuisine: AMERICAN. **Reservations:** Not accepted.
$ **Prices:** Main courses $1.55–$7.55. No credit cards.
    Open: Daily 24 hours.

For the best, fastest pecan (or plain) waffles in town, and a decent cup of coffee, go to the Waffle House, located just west of I-25. You can get breakfast 24 hours a day in this narrow restaurant with a long counter, a few booths, and a row of chairs against the wall for hungry people waiting in line for a seat. Lots of waffle irons behind the counter ensure fast action on your order. Steak and eggs, sandwiches, burgers, chef's salad, and steak and chicken dinners are also available.

WHAT TO SEE & DO IN COLORADO SPRINGS

Colorado Springs has been a fashionable tourist stop since the late 1880s. Natural formations such as Pikes Peak, the Garden of the Gods, and the Cave of the Winds lured both wealthy Europeans and Easterners back then and are still drawing camera-sporting vacationers today. Add modern-day attractions like the U.S. Air Force Academy, the ProRodeo Hall of Fame and the Museum of the American Cowboy, and the Manitou Cliff Dwellings—not to mention special events, sports and recreational activities, and nightlife—and you can come up with an itinerary that can take weeks to cover. You'll have to get picky here, unless you're visiting for several weeks.

SUGGESTED ITINERARIES

IF YOU HAVE ONE DAY Visit the U.S. Air Force Academy, then drive through Garden of the Gods and stroll along its paths for a closer look. Lunch in Old Colorado City and explore the shops, then head for Seven Falls. If you have both energy and time left over and you're interested in rodeos, visit the ProRodeo Hall of Fame and the Museum of the American Cowboy. If you have children, visit the Ghost Town or the Hall of the Presidents Living Wax Studio instead of exploring Old Colorado City.

IF YOU HAVE TWO DAYS Spend Day 1 as outlined above. On your second day, head for the summit of Pikes Peak, either by the auto road or on the cog train. On your way, stop in Manitou Springs and visit either the Cave of the Winds or the Cliff Dwellings Museum. If you have children with you, stop at the Buffalo Bill Wax Museum in Manitou Springs and North Pole/Santa's Workshop. End the day with dinner at the Flying W Ranch.

IF YOU HAVE THREE DAYS Spend your first two days as suggested above. Spend the third day in Cripple Creek, a gold-rush-town-turned-gambling-mecca where many of the casinos are set in old saloons. In and around the gambling halls, you can still find remnants of the Old West. Tour the Molly Kathleen Mine and take a ride past picturesque mining ruins on the narrow gauge train.

ATTRACTIONS:

American Numismatic
  Association Money Museum **2**
Broadmoor, The **20**
Cave of the Winds **8**
Colorado Springs
  Fine Arts Center **1**
Colorado Springs
  Pioneer Museum **4**
Garden of the Gods **9**
Hall of Presidents **16**
Manitou Cliff
  Dwellings Museum **7**
May Natural History Museum **22**
McCallister House **3**
Miramont Castle **6**
Museum of the
  American Cowboy **13**
Nikola Tesla Museum **18**
North American Aerospace
  Defense Command (NORAD) **21**
Pikes Peak Cog Railway **5**
Seven Falls **19**
U. S. Air Force Academy **11**
U. S. Olympic Training Center **14**
Van Briggle Art Pottery **15**
Western Museum of
  Mining and Industry **12**
White House Ranch
  Living Historic Site **10**
World Figure Skating Hall
  of Fame and Museum **17**

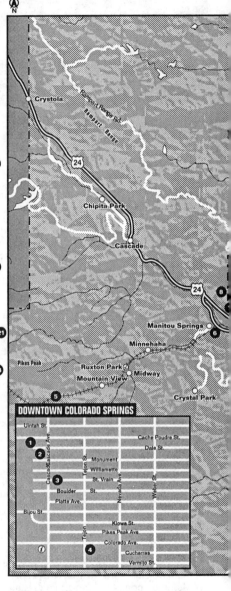

IF YOU HAVE FOUR DAYS OR MORE Spend Days 1–3 as
discussed above. On your fourth day, if you're mildly athletic, spend
the day hiking or biking around the Colorado Springs area. If
you're in good shape and can handle hiking at heights, challenge
one of the hiking trails that climb up the mountainsides. If it's spring
or summer, book a raft trip. (While most raft companies won't
take small children, the senior citizens I've rafted with love "float
trips.")

COLORADO SPRINGS ATTRACTIONS

U.S. Air Force Academy

Pikeview

Vista Grande

Park Vista Estates

Glen Eyrie

Garden of the Gods Rd.

Van Buren St.

Constitution Ave.

Galley Rd.

Platte Ave.

Airport Rd.

Fountain

Skyway

Cheyenne Blvd.

Lake Ave.

Colorado Springs Municipal Airport

Broadmoor

Airport ✈

Information ⊙

1. THE TOP ATTRACTIONS

PIKES PEAK

"Pikes Peak or Bust!" was the motto that kept settlers moving
their wagon trains westward over the plains during the 1880s.
Today visitors drive up the 14,110-foot-high mountain in cars,

ride up on the cog railway, and occasionally even hike up to the summit.

The views are awesome if you drive up the well-maintained 19-mile gravel **Pikes Peak Hwy.** It's a fantastic drive, but not a trip for travelers with a fear of heights. The toll road starts a few miles past the town of Manitou Springs at 7,400 feet elevation and climbs 7,000 feet higher, often above the cloud line, until it reaches the peak. There's a spectacular 360° view at the top, encompassing the snow-capped peaks of the nearby Collegiate Range and the plains stretching eastward. On a clear day you can even see the Sangre de Cristo Mountains in southern Colorado and northern New Mexico, 100 miles to the south.

Allow at least two to three hours for the round-trip and stops at a few of the overlook areas to take photos and watch the mountain sheep. The Glen Cove restaurant and souvenir shop is 11 miles up the road. At the summit, you'll find a visitor center, restaurant, and curio shop.

The Pikes Peak Hwy. starts at Cascade, where the toll road meets U.S. 24. In summer (June 10–Labor Day) it's open to uphill traffic daily from 7am to 6:30pm, and in spring and fall (May–June 9 and from Labor Day until snow starts falling, closing the road) it's open daily from 9am to 3pm. The toll is $5 for adults and $2 for children 6–11 (children 5 and under enter for free). For more information, contact the City of Colorado Springs Department of Transportation, Pikes Peak Highway Division, P.O. Box 1575, Mail Code 431, Colorado Springs, CO 80901 (tel. 719/684-9383).

If you'd rather let others do the driving while you do the looking, hitch a ride on the **Pikes Peak Cog Railway.** The Swiss-made cars crawl up the 46,000 feet of track from the railroad station in Manitou Springs through forests of aspen and green pines, past the barren stretches above the 11,578-foot tree line, to the mountain's summit. The cog railway operates May through October, weather permitting. Eight round-trips are scheduled daily from early June through late August, but during May, September, and October the schedule depends on the weather. Round-trip fares are $19.90 for adults, $9 for children 5–11, and free for children 4 and under sitting on a parent's lap. Advance reservations are strongly recommended, and since the mountain weather is so erratic, always call ahead to confirm your reservations and verify that the train is running. Even if it's 100° in Colorado Springs, take along a jacket or sweater, because it could be chilly at the summit.

Note: Those who have cardiac or respiratory problems should not take this trip.

For tickets and additional information, contact the Cog Railway Depot, P.O. Box 1329, Colorado Springs, CO 80901 (tel. 719/685-5401). To reach the depot, take U.S. 24 (Exit 141 off I-25) toward Manitou Springs and exit at the signs to Cog Railway and Manitou Springs; then take Manitou Avenue to Ruxton Avenue, turn left, and go one mile to the depot.

Automobile buffs plan trips to Colorado Springs around the **Pikes Peak Auto Hill Climb,** the nation's second-oldest auto race, held every July 4. Racing legends from Bobby and Al Unser to Mario Andretti and Parnelli Jones vie for first place as they speed around the 156 turns on the gravel road heading skyward. Admission is $15 per person; children 12 and under attend for free. For practice dates, contact the Pikes Peak Auto Hill Climb, 135 Manitou Ave., Manitou Springs, CO 80829 (tel. 719/685-4400).

If you miss the annual race, visit the **Race Car Museum,** 135 Manitou Ave. in Manitou Springs (tel. 719/685-5996), filled with race cars and memorabilia from past races. The museum is open Memorial Day through Labor Day, daily from 9am to 5pm. Admission is $3 for adults; children 12 and under, free.

CAVE OF THE WINDS, on U.S. 24, six miles west of Colorado Springs. Tel. 719/685-5446.

Tourists have been spelunking in the Cave of the Winds since 1881. The first groups to explore these underground caverns carried candles and were encouraged to take stalactites home as souvenirs, but today you can only look at the beautiful natural-stone formations.

The fascinating 40-minute "Discovery Tour" takes visitors along well-lighted concrete or smooth stone walkways. You'll see massive limestone canopies overhead, delicate crystal flowers growing on the walls, and intricate stone formations. The tour, which traces the trail of the original explorers, John and George Pickett, is for all ages and levels of fitness.

The two-hour "Wild Tour" is for comfortably clad, athletically fit adults who want to scramble through narrow tunnels and explore some of the darkest portions of the caverns. This chance to go exploring is offered three times daily in the summer and by reservation only in the winter. Take a sweater along, because it's always cool underground.

Kids and adults will enjoy the laser-light show played on the canyon wall nightly from May 1 to September 15. The images spread a half mile across and 15 stories high!

Admission: Cave of the Winds, $8 adults, $4 children 6–15, free for children 6 and younger; laser show, $5 adults, $3 children 6–15, free for children under 6.

Open: Cave of the Winds, winter, daily 10am–5pm; summer, daily 9am–9pm. One laser show nightly May 1–Sept 15.

GARDEN OF THE GODS, off U.S. 24.

Use your imagination as you wander through the red sandstone rock formations sculpted by wind, rain, and erosion into kissing camels, dragons, and other fantastic shapes. Take an easy walk or go on a longer hike on trails winding past rich red rock framing snow-covered Pikes Peak and other equally exhilarating scenes.

The Trading Post, an adobe-style building, houses a restaurant, a gift shop, and a southwestern art gallery where you can purchase Navajo rugs, Santa Clara pottery, and Kachinas. The visitor center, open from early June to Labor Day, houses exhibits showing the geology and history of the park.

Admission: Free.

Open: Daily 8am–8pm. **Directions:** Take U.S. 24 to the Ridge Rd. exit, then turn north.

U.S. AIR FORCE ACADEMY, off I-25. Tel. 719/472-2555.

The Air Force Academy is Colorado's most popular "man-made" attraction. Opened in 1958, the academy has provided the U.S. Air Force with highly trained officers since the 206 members of the first class of cadets were commissioned as second lieutenants in June 1959.

When you visit, enter via the North Gate for a leisurely six-mile drive, past the earth-bound B-52 poised as if it's in flight, to the visitor center. Keep a sharp eye for deer crossing the road as you drive toward the steep spires of the Ramparts Range, which towers over the academy's main campus. If the guard at the gate doesn't give you a self-guided tour map, pick up one at the Barry Goldwater Air Force Visitor Center, the best place to start your visit. Step into the theater for the short movie explaining the "Academy experience," then look at the exhibits on the academy's history and cadet life. You can also take one of the free one-hour guided tours of the main campus that leave from the visitor center. The high note of the tour is the cadet chapel, with its 17 aluminum spires that soar 150 feet skyward. Whatever your religious beliefs, a few minutes in one of the sanctuaries in this architecturally stunning nondenominational chapel (there are separate Protestant, Catholic, and Jewish sanctuaries, as well as an "all faiths" room) is an experience not to be missed. Protestant and Catholic chapel services are open to visitors. Other sights include the classroom buildings and the planetarium, with shows open to the public some days.

Admission: Free.

Open: Academy Visitor Center, daily 9am–5pm. Chapel services open to public Sun at 9am and 11am. **Directions:** Take Exit 156B off I-25.

2. MORE ATTRACTIONS

MUSEUMS & GALLERIES

AMERICAN NUMISMATIC ASSOCIATION MONEY MUSEUM, 818 N. Cascade Ave. Tel. 719/632-2646.

If you like to look at coins, tokens, medals, and paper money, this is the place. The museum boasts the largest collection west of the Smithsonian. The exhibits include the workshop of former U.S. Mint Chief Engraver Gilroy Roberts (who made the obverse of the John F. Kennedy half dollar), looking as if he had just stepped away from work for a minute. There's a tactile display of coins designed for the visually impaired.

Admission: $1 adults, 50¢ students 10–17 and seniors over 65, free for members and children under 10.

Open: Mon–Fri 8:30am–4pm.

COLORADO SPRINGS FINE ARTS CENTER, 30 W. Dale St. Tel. 719/634-5581.

The Fine Arts Center is home for the Fine Arts Museum and the Taylor Museum, the Bemis Art School, and a theater for the performing arts. The permanent collection in the **Fine Arts Museum** includes works by Georgia O'Keeffe, John James Audubon, and John Singer Sargent. The **Taylor Museum** galleries feature sandpaintings and Native American and Hispanic artifacts from the Southwest. During the summer, you can lunch at a restaurant set up on the porch.

DID YOU KNOW . . . ?

- The air at the top of Pikes Peak (14,110 feet) has only half the oxygen found at sea level.
- In 1893 Katherine Lee Bates, a visiting professor at Colorado College, wrote the words to "America the Beautiful" after a wagon ride to the summit of Pikes Peak. Woodrow Wilson was on the same wagon trip.
- Colorado Springs is known as the "space capital of the world," with more space-related agencies and military space commands than anywhere else.
- The structures inside Cheyenne Mountain that house the North American Aerospace Defense Command (NORAD) are supported on 1,319 springs, weighing half a ton each, to protect the delicate electronic equipment inside from shock.
- Shredded wheat was first made in the 1890s by the Colorado Springs Cereal Food Company.
- At sunrise, the shadow of Pikes Peak extends as far as 50 miles to the west.

Admission: $2.50 adults, $1.50 seniors and students 13–21, $1 children 6–12, free for children under 6.

Open: Tues–Fri 9am–5pm, Sat 10am–5pm, Sun 1–5pm.

COLORADO SPRINGS PIONEER MUSEUM, 215 S. Tejon St. Tel. 719/578-6650.

The region's history is on display in both permanent and changing exhibits at the Pioneer Museum. You've seen the courtroom in this museum on "Perry Mason" television episodes.

Admission: Free.

Open: Mon–Sat 10am–5pm, Sun 1–5pm.

MANITOU CLIFF DWELLINGS MUSEUM, five miles west of Colorado Springs on U.S. 24. Tel. 719/685-5242.

Most of the ruins of cliff dwellings hugging the sides of Phantom Cliff Canyon are real, though they're made from stones moved from their original sites by archeologists in the early 1900s, who saw the original dwellings being plundered. This museum has some excellent examples of the dwellings ancient Native American tribes built at the base of, or on ledges on the side of, massive cliffs in the Southwest. If you've never been to Mesa Verde or Canyon de Chelly, this museum is a good place to learn about the Native Americans who lived during the Great Pueblo period, A.D. 1100–1300. Even the (labeled) cactus and trees are indigenous to those regions. Created by archeologists in the early 1900s, the museum also has a small collection of artifacts and exhibits of the period of the basket-makers, ancestors of the cliff dwellers. The collection is housed in a pueblo that exemplifies the architecture of the Taos Pueblo tribe in New Mexico. Native American folk dancers perform during the summer.

Admission: $4 adults, $3 seniors, $2 children 7–11, free for children 6 and under.

Open: Apr–May and Sept–Oct, daily 9am–5pm; June–Aug, daily 10am–6pm.

Closed: Nov–Mar.

MAY NATURAL HISTORY MUSEUM, 710 Rock Creek Canyon. Tel. 719/576-0450, or toll free 800/666-3481.

You get two museums for the price of one here. The **Natural History Museum** contains a significant collection of some 7,000 unusual invertebrates and giant tropical insects collected from jungles worldwide. On display are grotesque beetles as well as beautiful butterflies. The **Museum of Space Exploration** houses photographs taken by planetary spacecraft, including *Voyager II*.

Admission: $4 adults, $2 children under 13.

Open: May–Sept, daily 9am–5pm. **Closed:** Oct–Apr. **Directions:** Head four miles southwest of the city limits on Nevada Avenue (Colo. 115) and look for the giant beetle outside.

MCALLISTER HOUSE, 423 N. Cascade Ave. Tel. 719/635-7925.

History buffs can get a sense of what life was like in Colorado Springs during the late 1800s when they tour the house that belonged to Henry McAllister, one of the town's founders. Guided tours through the house, which contains some of the original furnishings, effectively brings that era and the family's lifestyle alive.

Admission: $2 adults, $1 students and seniors, 75¢ children 6–16.

Open: May–Aug, Wed–Sat 10am–4pm, Sun noon–4pm; Sept–Apr, Thurs–Sat 10am–4pm.

MUSEUM OF THE AMERICAN COWBOY, 101 Pro Rodeo Dr. Tel. 719/593-8847 or 719/593-8840.

The hard life of a cowboy is documented in this museum. Start with the multimedia theater presentation that takes you for a historical "walk" through the early West. A tour of Heritage Hall traces the development of ropes, saddles, boots, and other cowboy

---

FROMMER'S FAVORITE COLORADO SPRINGS EXPERIENCES

A Visit to Simpich Character Dolls Chat with the craftspeople in their work rooms as they create by hand exquisite dolls, using tiny brushes to paint on eyes and other detail.

Lunch at the Colorado Springs Fine Arts Center Sitting on the porch on a hot day while cooled by the shade of the buildings' stone walls and a breeze through the trees will unwind the most frazzled tourist. The view of Pikes Peak alone is worth the price of the meal. Open summers only.

Exploring Colorado City Unlike many cities' historic sections that have been gussied up for tourists and overflow with souvenir shops, this section of town has a number of truly intriguing shops.

The Cadet Chapel at the U.S. Air Force Academy No matter what your religious beliefs, spending a few quiet moments on a bench in the main chapel of this unusual building, with its view of the soaring Ramparts Mountains filling the windows, is a memorable experience.

gear throughout the last 100 years. In another theater, you and the kids will find your hearts in your throats as you watch a Brahma bull ride—viewed from atop the bull. The last stop here is the **Pro Rodeo Hall of Fame,** honoring rodeo greats. During the summer there's an outdoor mini-rodeo arena where you can chat with a rodeo clown and eye a Brahma bull and a bronco.

Admission: $5 adults, $2 children 5–12, free for children under 5.

Open: Memorial Day–Labor Day, daily 9am–5pm; winter, daily 9am–4:30pm. **Closed:** New Year's, Easter, Thanksgiving, and Christmas Days.

NIKOLA TESLA MUSEUM, 17 E. Las Vegas St. Tel. 719/ 475-0918.

In 1899, eccentric inventor Nikola Tesla, in an attempt to "broadcast" electricity, set up a 50-foot diameter coil that generated 10 million volts of electricity and 135-foot-long lightning bolts. The thunder was heard as far away as Cripple Creek, and his experiment ruined the Colorado Springs electrical generator, causing a citywide black-out. Today, Tesla is called the father of alternating current, and his Tesla coil (a hollow-core transformer) laid the groundwork for every broadcasting system from radio to radar, and for medical magnetic resonance imaging (MRI).

A group of Tesla fans founded this museum to rekindle the enthusiasm for science and research that was so vibrant early in the 20th century. You'll see one million volts of raw power unleashed, light bulbs without wires, and ongoing experiments on the cutting edge of technology.

Admission: Free.

Open: Sept–May, Mon–Sat 10am–6pm; Jun–Aug, Mon–Sat 10am–6pm, Sun 11am–4pm.

NORTH AMERICAN AEROSPACE DEFENSE COMMAND (NORAD), inside Cheyenne Mountain. Tel. 719/554-6826.

NORAD is the United States' and Canada's warning system against a nuclear missile strike. Set inside Cheyenne Mountain, the buildings are supported on 1,319 springs, weighing half a ton each, to protect the delicate electronic equipment inside from shock. Tours of this complex are offered, but it's very difficult to get a reservation. Call the tour hotline number listed above for a lengthy explanation of who can come and when, and how to make a reservation. Parties of 1–15 people may only sign up for Saturday tours, and larger groups may only go on Monday and Friday. You should apply at least six months in advance.

WESTERN MUSEUM OF MINING AND INDUSTRY, off I-25. Tel. 719/488-0880.

Here you can relive Colorado's colorful mining past and see how miners timbered, drilled, blasted, mucked, and moved ore from the mine to the stamp mill. Temporary exhibits interpret modern mining issues and concerns. You can even try panning for gold yourself.

Admission: $4 adults, $3.50 seniors and students 13 or older, $1.50 children 5–12, free for children under 5.

Open: Mar–Nov, Mon–Sat 9am–4pm, Sun noon–4pm; Dec–Feb, by appointment only. **Closed:** Major hols. **Directions:** Take Exit 156A off I-25; the museum is across from the North Gate of the Air Force Academy.

WHITE HOUSE RANCH LIVING HISTORY SITE, at the White House Ranch on Gateway Rd. Tel. 719/578-6777.

This site, at the east entrance to the Garden of the Gods park, gives visitors a sense of the way Coloradans lived during the homestead period (1868), the working ranch period (1895), and the estate period (1907). The White House Ranch has a nature trail for the blind.

Admission: $3 adults, $2 seniors over 55, $1 children 6–12.

Open: Early June to Labor Day, Wed–Sun 10am–4pm; Labor Day–Christmas, Sat 10am–4pm, Sun noon–4pm. **Closed:** Christmas to early June.

WORLD FIGURE SKATING HALL OF FAME AND MUSEUM, 20 1st St. Tel. 719/635-5200.

This museum, sponsored by the United States Figure Skating Association, is a repository for costumes, skates, medals, and memorabilia of several famous skaters. The walls are lined with paintings and other art dealing with skating; there's also a library.

Admission: Free.

Open: Jun–Aug, Tues–Sat 10am–4pm; Sept–May, Mon–Fri 10am–4pm.

OTHER ATTRACTIONS

FLORISSANT FOSSIL BEDS NATIONAL MONUMENT, 14 miles west of Woodland Park. Tel. 719/748-3253.

At the Florissant Fossil Beds, you'll see intricately detailed fossilized plants and insects, and giant petrified sequoia stumps. It's a fascinating look at what was once a temperate lake in prehistoric times. The visitor center has fossil displays and interpretive programs providing information and history on the fossils and geology of the area. There's an 1878 homestead and scenic trails at this 6,000-acre national monument.

Admission: $2 per person; $4 per family.

Open: Summer, daily 8am–7pm; winter, daily 8:30am–4pm.

Directions: Take U.S. 24 35 miles west to Florissant; at the town center, turn south on Teller County Road No. 1 and go for half a mile.

HALL OF PRESIDENTS, 1050 S. 21st St. Tel. 719/635-3553.

At the Hall of Presidents, one block south of U.S. 24, you see how Gen. George Washington must have looked when crossing the Delaware River on that freezing Christmas night in 1773. Displays include more than 100 life-size wax figures of presidents, first ladies, and other famous people. The Fairyland area, with characters from favorite storybooks, is a hit with youngsters.

Admission: $4 for anyone 12 and older, $2 children 6–11, free for children under 6.

Open: Apr–May, daily 9am–5pm; June–Aug, daily 9am–9pm; Sept–Oct, daily 9am–5pm; Nov–Mar, call for hours.

MIRAMONT CASTLE, Ruxton Ave., Manitou Springs. Tel. 719/685-1011.

Built by a wealthy French Catholic priest, the 46-room Miramont Castle is located two blocks off Manitou Avenue in Manitou Springs. With nine distinctly different styles of architecture, this is an interesting stop if you like to poke around old homes. Few of the rooms have 4 corners (the chapel has 8 sides and another room has 16), and the drawing room boasts a gold ceiling and a massive sandstone fireplace. There's also a warren of tiny rooms on the top floor. This Victorian mansion, formerly the home of Father Francolon, a missionary in the Southwest, and his mother, has been a sanitorium and an apartment house, and is now a project of the Manitou Springs Historical Society. In a building alongside the house is a marvelous model-railroad museum where intricately detailed model trains chug around a room-size set of miniature tracks. There's a tea room and soda fountain open for lunch inside the castle. Proceeds benefit the continuing restoration of the castle.

Admission: $2.50 adults, $1 children 6–12, free for children under 6.

Open: House and museum, Memorial Day–Labor Day, daily 10am–5pm; Sept–May, daily 1–3pm. Tea room and soda fountain, daily 11am–4pm. **Closed:** Easter, Thanksgiving, and Christmas Days.

PIKES PEAK VINEYARD AND WINERY, 3901 Janitell Rd. Tel. 719/576-0075.

If you've never seen how wine is made or participated in a wine tasting, this is a fun way to spend an hour. The smell of fermenting wine permeates the air as you drive up to this small winery. The wine, which is distributed mainly in Colorado, is made from a blend of French-American hybrid grapes grown behind the winery and in other midwestern states. During the short tour visitors learn how grapes are crushed, stemmed, aged in tanks or in oak and steel casks, and then bottled and hand-corked. The tour fee can be applied toward purchase of a bottle of wine.

Admission: $2 tour and wine-tasting.

Open: Oct–Mar, Mon–Fri by appointment, Sat 11am–4pm; Apr–Oct, Mon–Sat 11am–4pm.

SEVEN FALLS, in South Cheyenne Canyon, off Cheyenne Blvd. Tel. 719/632-0765.

City dwellers will especially enjoy the car ride past the towering Pillars of Hercules, where the canyon narrows to a width of 42 feet. Drive slowly to appreciate the unusual rock formations and lush foliage surrounding cascading waterfalls. Or, if you prefer, slip on some comfortable shoes and walk up the 265 steps to the Eagle's Nest platform for a view of the waterfall tumbling 300 feet down the granite mountainside in seven distinct leaps. (You may also opt for the express elevator waiting to take you uphill through the mountain.) The canyon is illuminated with colored lights from mid-May through mid-September.

Admission: Daytime, (including elevator ride), $4.50 adults, $2 children 6–12, free for children 5 and under; after 5pm, $5.75 adults, $3 children 6–12.

Open: June–Labor Day, daily 8am–10:15pm; spring and fall, closes a little earlier; in winter, call for hours. **Directions:** Head west on Cheyenne Boulevard.

U.S. OLYMPIC TRAINING CENTER, 1750 E. Boulder St. Tel. 719/578-4618 for the visitor center or 719/578-4644 for the tour hotline.

Each year approximately 14,000 of America's top amateur athletes take turns training at the 36-acre U.S. Olympic Training Center. As you tour the Sports Center, with its five gymnasia and weight-training quarters, 400-meter track and Super Turf–covered field for soccer and field hockey, shooting range, and nearby 7-Eleven Velodrome, you'll see some of the nation's best amateur athletes in training. Seventeen of the 38 national governing bodies for Olympic sports have their headquarters here. Of the U.S. athletes who participated in the 1984 Olympic games, 47% of the gold medalists, 40% of the silver medalists, and 63% of the bronze medalists trained at the center.

Admission: Free.

Open: Tours, Mon–Sat 9am–4pm, Sun noon–4pm. **Directions:** Go one block north on Union Boulevard off U.S. 24 East.

VAN BRIGGLE ART POTTERY, 600 S. 21st St. Tel. 719/633-7729.

The tour begins with a demonstration of throwing the potter's wheel and ends in the showroom, where you can browse and purchase Van Briggle pieces, noted for their clear, colorful glazes and graceful lines. The company was founded at the turn of the century by Artus Van Briggle, a famous designer for Rookwood Pottery in Cincinnati, Ohio. After he died in 1904, his widow commissioned the gifted architect Nicholas Van den Arend to create a lasting monument to her husband, the result of which is the striking building at 300 W. Uintah St.

Admission: Free.

Open: Apr–Oct, Mon–Sat 8am–5pm; Nov–Mar, call for hours.

---

3. COOL FOR KIDS

Some of the places listed below might be more fun for your children than for you. However, several of the attractions listed above can be enjoyed by the entire family: The **Pro Rodeo Hall of Fame and Museum of the American Cowboy,** the **Manitou Cliff Dwellings Museum, Seven Falls,** and the **Hall of Presidents** wax museum appeal to all ages.

COLORADO SPRINGS CHILDREN'S MUSEUM, 750 Citadel Dr., in the Citadel Mall. Tel. 719/574-0077.

Kids can broadcast their own radio show, create people-size bubbles, and paint or draw at the art table in this nonprofit museum located in the mall upstairs next to Mervyn's.

Admission: 50¢ for everyone over age 2.

Open: Wed–Fri 10am–3pm, Sat 10am–5pm, Sun 1–5pm.

BUCKSKIN JOE, off U.S. 50. Tel. 719/275-5149.

More than 20 westerns have been filmed at this Old West theme park about an hour southwest of Colorado Springs. Such stars as John Wayne and James Arness were immortalized swaggering down the main street here. Mock fights are staged around the 27 buildings that children can explore. Take a wagon ride or head into the backcountry on horseback. Panning for gold, mine tours, and magic shows are offered as well.

Admission: $6 adults, $4.25 children 4–11, free for children 3 and younger.

Open: Apr–May, some weekends; June–Aug, daily 9am–8pm;

Sept–Oct, 10am–6pm; Nov–Mar, call for the shorter hours. **Directions:** Take Colo. 115 south, then U.S. 50 west; it's a one-hour drive from Colorado Springs.

BUFFALO BILL WAX MUSEUM, 404 Manitou Ave., Manitou Springs. Tel. 719/685-5900.

Davey Crockett, Wyatt Earp, and Kit Carson are just a few of the 32 heroes and villains posing permanently in this museum.

Admission: $3 adults, $1.50 children 6–16, free for children under 6.

Open: Apr, daily 9am–6pm; May–Aug, daily 8am–6pm; Sept, daily 9am–5pm. **Closed:** Oct–Mar.

CAREFREE HIGHWAY GO-KART PARK, 3445 E. Platte Ave. Tel. 719/591-8778.

Kids from 9 to 90 will enjoy racing around the tracks at the Go-Kart Park. The speeds vary at the four tracks. There's also Aeroball (basketball on a trampoline), a video arcade, and an ice-cream shop.

Admission: $1.50 per ride on junior speedway, $1 for toddler park ride, $2.25 for all other rides.

Open: Summer, Mon–Fri 11am–11pm, Sat 10am–11pm, Sun noon–10pm; the rest of the year, call for seasonal hours.

CHEYENNE MOUNTAIN ZOO, Cheyenne Mountain Zoo Rd. Tel. 719/475-9555.

Kids will love a stroll through this zoo perched on the side of Cheyenne Mountain, south of the Broadmoor Hotel. All the familiar animals are here—Siberian tigers, lions, black leopards, elephants, and giraffes. There's a colorful antique carousel with vintage, hand-carved horses. Zoo admission includes a look at the Will Rogers Shrine of the Sun, a tall stone structure that provides a panoramic view of the surrounding countryside. The shrine, built in 1937 and dedicated to the beloved American humorist, contains a pictorial biography of Rogers.

Admission: $5.50 ages 12 and older, $4.50 seniors, $3 children 3–11, free for children under 3.

Open: Summer, daily 9am–6pm; winter, daily 9am–5pm.

FLYING W RANCH CHUCKWAGON SUPPERS, Flying W Ranch Rd. Tel. 719/598-4000, toll free 800/748-3999.

The Flying W Ranch is a lot of fun. In the summertime the evening starts with a stroll through the old western town, a dozen buildings—from a dance hall to a general store—that have been restored and filled with authentic furnishings and memorabilia from the late 1800s and early 1900s. Although the Flying W feeds up to 1,400 hungry diners barbecue beef and trimmings each night, cafeteria style, the actual wait for food isn't very long because the dinner lines are well organized. After dinner, the Flying W Wranglers, an enthusiastic group of performers, grab guitars and banjos and let loose with music that keeps your toes tapping and a string of yarns about the Old West that keeps you laughing. If it's raining, the dinner is indoors.

During the wintertime, you can dine in the steak house and then enjoy the western show.

Admission: Summer, supper and show, $12 adults, $6 children 8 and younger; winter, steak dinner and show, $17 per person.

Open: Summer, the western town opens at 4:30pm, dinner starts at 7:15pm, and the show begins around 8:30pm; winter, two seatings, one at 5pm and another at 8pm. **Directions:** Drive a quarter mile north of Garden of the Gods Road on 30th Street, then go west one mile on Flying W Ranch Rd.

GHOST TOWN, U.S. 24 West and 21st St. Tel. 719/634-0696.

Colorado's gold-rush days are brought to life when you stroll through this indoor ghost town. The general store, the Wells Fargo office, a Victorian home, and a western saloon are full-size, but under one roof (it's a great rainy-day stop). You can run your fingers over the keys of the player piano, play the nickelodeon, and watch early movies. Car buffs should know that they'll find a 1903 Cadillac and Franklin D. Roosevelt's official bulletproof limousine here. Ghost Town is next door to the Van Briggle Art Pottery.

Admission: $3.75 adults, $1.50 children 6–16, free for children under 6.

Open: Summer, Mon–Sat 9am–6pm, Sun 1–6pm; call for specific season dates and shorter off-season hours.

MANITOU WATER SLIDE, 327 Manitou Ave., Manitou Springs. Tel. 719/685-5867.

On a hot day, get wet riding down the water slide. Once you've cooled off, try a round of miniature golf or explore the Miracle House where gravity seems to play tricks on you.

Admission: $4 per person for 10 rides, $8 for unlimited rides; golf, $2 per person; Miracle House, $1 per person.

Open: Memorial Day weekend to Labor Day, daily 10am–8pm (golf until 11pm). **Closed:** Early Sept to early June.

NORTH POLE/SANTA'S WORKSHOP, on U.S. 24, 10 miles west of Colorado Springs. Tel. 719/684-9432.

At the North Pole/Santa's Workshop, you can take your kids for a spin around a Christmas tree, ride the *Enterprise* shuttle, and take a train ride around Santa's workshop. Of course, there are many workshops where busy elves have readied early Christmas gifts. The admission fee includes unlimited rides, all shows (including the magician), and, of course, the right to whisper your Christmas wishes into Santa's ear.

Admission: $7.95 people aged 2–59 for unlimited rides and magic show, $3 seniors over 59, free for children under 2.

Open: Mid-May to May 31, daily 9am–5pm; June–Aug, daily 9:30am–6pm; Sept–Dec 24, Fri–Tues 10am–5pm. **Closed:** Christmas to mid-May.

4. ORGANIZED TOURS

Pikes Peak Tours, 3704 W. Colorado Ave. (tel. 719/633-1181, or toll free 800/345-8197), is the main tour operator in the region, offering a variety of tours from May through October. Day tours include a four-hour bus trip up Pikes Peak, a tour of the Air Force Academy and the Garden of the Gods, and a rafting trip. Every evening during the summer there's a tour to the Cave of the Winds and Seven Falls. Tours cost $15–$50 per person.

Challenge Unlimited, 204 S. 24th St. (tel. 719/633-6399, or toll free 800/798-5954), offers an array of outdoor adventures. Bike tours range from half-day tours of the Air Force Academy to a ride along the Ramparts. This company also offers a Pikes Peak "downhill" (only) ride.

5. SPORTS & RECREATION

SPECTATOR SPORTS

AUTO RACING   The annual **Pikes Peak Auto Hill Climb,** held every July, is a world-famous race that attracts the royalty of race-car drivers as they head up the challenging 12.42-mile gravel road—with 156 curves—to the summit. Call 719/685-4400 for more information.

BASEBALL   The **Sky Sox,** a triple-A farm team of the expansion Colorado Rockies—Denver's new major-league baseball team—plays ball at Sky Sox Stadium, 4385 Tutt Ave., from April to August. Tickets for both afternoon and evening games are $5.50 for adults, $5 for children ages 14 and under, for box seats; and $3.50 for adults, $3 for seniors and children ages 14 and under, for general admission. For game dates, call 719/597-1449.

DOG RACING   From April to September you can wager on the dogs in action at **Rocky Mountain Greyhound Park,** 3701 N. Nevada Ave. (tel. 719/632-1391, or toll free 800/444-PAWS). There's live racing Wednesday through Saturday starting at 7:30pm, and afternoon racing on Sunday, Monday, Wednesday, and Saturday at 1pm.

FOOTBALL   The **Falcons,** the U.S. Air Force Academy football team, play several home games in the fall. For game dates and ticket information, call 719/472-1895.

RECREATIONAL SPORTS

There are more than 110 **city parks** around town, administered by the Colorado Springs Park and Recreation Department. There are exhibits of Colorado wildlife, slide shows, and the trailheads for self-guiding nature trails at **Bear Creek Nature Center,** 245 Bear Creek Rd., at 26th Street (tel. 719/520-6387).

BACKPACKING   For information, renting mountain bikes or camping equipment, books, and maps of the area, contact **Grand West Outfitters,** 3250 N. Academy Blvd. (tel. 719/596-3031). Also, see "Hiking," below.

BIKING   You can pick up a copy of the **Colorado Area Bicycle Access Map** at the Convention and Visitor Bureau Visitor Information Center, 104 S. Cascade Ave., Suite 104 (tel. 719/635-7506), in the downtown Sun Plaza building. Ask about paths running along Monument Creek, from the north to the south end of the city.

FISHING There are plenty of great fishing spots, including Prospect Lake and the streams around Colorado Springs, but you need a license. Licenses can be purchased at most local sporting-goods stores.

For a license and/or information about fishing in the area, contact **Angler's Covey, Inc.,** 917 W. Colorado Ave., Colorado Springs, CO 80904 (tel. 719/471-2984). This fly-fishing shop has guide services for half- and full-day trips.

You can also get information about licenses and regulations from the **Hunting and Fishing Division** of the Colorado Division of Wildlife (tel. 719/473-2945).

GOLF There are several municipal golf courses open to visitors. For tee-off reservations, greens fees, and other information, contact the **Patty Jewett Municipal Golf Course** (27 holes), 900 E. Espanola St. (tel. 719/578-6825); **Valley Hi Municipal Golf Course** (18 holes), 610 S. Chelton Rd. (tel. 719/578-6926); the **Pine Creek Golf Club** (18 holes), 9850 Divot Trail (tel. 719/594-9999); and the **Cimarron Hills Golf Course,** 1850 Tuskegee Place (tel. 719/597-2637). There's a driving range at the Valley Hi course.

HIKING This region is threaded with hiking paths. There are several hiking trails in the **Garden of the Gods** that open onto spectacular scenery. The 12-mile **Barr Trail** to the top of Pikes Peak is popular with experienced hikers who can handle the change in altitude.

For information about hiking trails in the area, call the **U.S. Forest Service** (tel. 719/636-1602). Also, see "Backpacking," above.

HORSEBACK RIDING The **Academy Riding Stables of Colorado Springs,** 4 El Paso Blvd. (tel. 719/633-5667), offers one- and two-hour riding tours through the Garden of the Gods. The **Mark Reyner Stables,** 3254 Paseo Rd. (tel. 719/634-4173), offers rides through Palmer Park.

HUNTING For information about hunting, call the **Hunting and Fishing Division** of the Colorado Division of Wildlife (tel. 719/473-2945).

You can get hunting licenses at many sporting-goods stores, including **Blicks Sporting Goods** (tel. 719/636-3348) downtown.

For information about hunting before you arrive, contact the **Colorado Division of Wildlife,** 6060 Broadway, Denver, CO 80216 (tel. 303/297-1192).

RAFTING White-water rafting down Colorado's rivers is legendary. You can choose a float trip over mostly ripple-free waters or a rugged outing where you're sure to get wet when the raft bounces against rocks in the rapids. Prices vary, but expect to spend about $28 for a 30- to 45-minute float trip, a low of $47 for a half-day trip up to a high of $85 for a full-day trip, depending on the rafting company and the location of the trip. The best months to raft are mid-May through mid-July. Many of the trips are run on the Arkansas River through Brown's Canyon or the Royal Gorge. Private transportation is necessary, because the starting points for the different raft trips are between one and two hours from the city.

For more information, contact **River Runners,** 11150 U.S. 50, Salida, CO 81201 (tel. 719/539-2144, or toll free 800/525-2081); or

Arkansas River Touring, P.O. Box 1032-P, Buena Vista, CO 81211 (tel. 719/395-8949, or toll free 800/332-RAFT).

SKIING   With a 1,160-foot vertical drop, **Monarch** is 120 miles away. Call toll free 800/332-3668 for more information.

The Front Range ski areas off I-70, including **Keystone, Copper, Breckenridge, Winter Park,** and **Vail,** are approximately 110–145 miles away and most can be reached by either spectacularly scenic mountain roads or superhighways.

SWIMMING   There is swimming at the indoor **Municipool,** 270 Union St. (tel. 719/578-6634). Admission is $2 for adults 18 and over and $1 for children 17 and under.

TENNIS   There are more than 110 city parks around town, and many have tennis courts. Contact the **Colorado Springs Park and Recreation Department** (tel. 719/578-6640) for more information.

6. SAVVY SHOPPING

There are many specialty shops in the downtown region. **Old Colorado City,** on Colorado Boulevard between 24th and 28th Streets, is lined with specialty shops and galleries. Main Street in **Manitou Springs** has several crafts shops and galleries, and there are several expensive shops at the Broadmoor Hotel.

SHOPPING A TO Z
ART & CRAFT GALLERIES

COLORADO SPRINGS ART GUILD/GALLERY, 2501 W. Colorado Ave., Suite 206. Tel. 719/389-0303.
This gallery is a showcase for local and regional artists. The gallery hosts a variety of open exhibits.

COMMONWHEEL ARTIST CO-OP, 102 Canon Ave., Manitou Springs. Tel. 719/685-1008.
Commonwheel is a cooperative and the exhibit space features work by 40 local artists and craftspeople.

FLUTE PLAYER GALLERY, 2501 W. Colorado Ave. Tel. 719/632-7702.
The Flute Player features Southwest Native American art, including Hopi Kachinas and paintings, Pueblo pottery, and Navajo rugs.

HAYDEN-HAYES GALLERY, at the Broadmoor Hotel, 1 Lake Ave. Tel. 719/577-5744.
This gallery features representational art in an eclectic mix of style, media, and content.

MICHAEL GARMAN GALLERY, 2418 W. Colorado Ave. Tel. 719/471-9391.
The Michael Garman Gallery displays sculptures by the owner, who captures wonderful bits of Americana and urban life.

POTTERY BY PANKRATZ, 366 2nd St., Monument. Tel. 719/481-3108.

Located off I-25's Exit 161 in Monument (toward Denver), this gallery features creative and functional tableware, vases, and sculptures.

SQUASH BLOSSOM/COGSWELL GALLERY, 2531 W. Colorado Ave. Tel. 719/632-1899.

This gallery specializes in southwestern art, including works by R. C. Gorman, Tom Owen, Frederick Prescott, and Jean Richardson.

BOOKSTORES

There are **Waldenbook** outlets in the Citadel Mall (tel. 719/597-4038) and the Chapel Hills Mall (tel. 719/594-9187). There are three **B. Dalton Bookseller** stores, including one in the Chapel Hills Mall (tel. 719/594-6800). All are open during regular mall hours, usually Monday through Friday from 10am to 9pm, on Saturday from 10am to 5pm, and on Sunday from noon to 5pm.

THE BOOKSELLERS JLM, 1526 S. Nevada Ave. Tel. 719/635-4020.

This is a general-interest bookstore with a strong children's section. Open Monday through Saturday from 10am to 6pm and on Sunday from noon to 4pm.

CHINOOK BOOKSHOP, 210 N. Tejon St. Tel. 719/635-1195, or toll free 800/999-1195.

This is a good full-service bookstore, with a fine Colorado section and an excellent section of globes and maps. Open Monday through Friday from 9:30am to 6pm, on Saturday from 9:30am to 5:30pm, and on Sunday from noon to 4pm.

FOUR CORNERS BOOKSHOP, 119 E. Bijou. Tel. 719/635-4514.

A large used-book shop with a very helpful and knowledgeable staff. Open daily from 9:30am to 7pm.

MCKINZEY-WHITE BOOKSELLERS, 8005 N. Academy Blvd. Tel. 719/590-1700.

Mckinzey-White, in front of the Chapel Hills Mall, is the town's largest general bookstore. Open Monday through Friday from 9:30am to 9pm, on Saturday from 9am to 6pm, and on Sunday from 11am to 6pm.

POOR RICHARD'S, 320 N. Tejon St. Tel. 719/578-0012.

Poor Richard's is a large depository of used books, in 164 categories, popular with both locals and Colorado College students. Open daily from 10am to 8pm.

DEPARTMENT STORES

There are several **K Mart** discount stores, including one at 3020 N. Nevada Ave. (tel. 719/471-3555). Around town are also two **Mervyn's** department stores, one in the Citadel Mall (tel. 719/596-8484) and the other in the Chapel Hill Mall (tel. 719/531-9000).

GIFTS

SIMPICH CHARACTER DOLLS, 2413 W. Colorado Ave. Tel. 719/636-3272.

This store features exquisite handmade dolls. Visitors are allowed to wander through the workrooms and watch craftspeople creating the dolls. Open Monday through Saturday from 10am to 5pm.

THE SWISS MISS SHOP, 8545 U.S. 24 W., Cascade. Tel. 719/684-9679.
   One mile west of the Pikes Peak/North Pole turnoff is a large shop featuring gifts and collectibles, such as wood carvings, Hummel figurines, Royal Doulton china, and traditional European gifts like music boxes, beer steins, and cuckoo clocks. Open May 15 to Labor Day, Monday through Saturday from 10am to 6pm and on Sunday from 9am to 6pm; the rest of the year, Monday through Saturday from 10am to 5pm and on Sunday from 1:30 to 5pm; closed Sunday January to March.

MALLS/SHOPPING CENTERS

There are two major malls in Colorado Springs: the Citadel and Chapel Hills Mall. The **Citadel,** 750 Citadel Dr. E., on the east side of the city at Academy Boulevard and Platte Avenue, has more than 175 stores, including May D&F and specialty shops. Open daily from 10am to 9pm. The **Chapel Hills Mall,** 1710 Briargate Blvd. in the north end of town at Academy and Briargate Boulevards. Open Monday through Friday from 10am to 9pm, on Saturday from 10am to 6 or 7pm, and on Sunday from noon to 6pm.

SPORTING GOODS

There are several **Gart Bros.** outlets in the city, including one at 3921 Palmer Park Blvd. (tel. 719/574-1400). The two **Blicks** outlets are located at the Citadel Mall, 750 Citadel Dr. E. (tel. 719/591-6435), and downtown at 119 N. Tejon St. (tel. 719/636-3348).

WESTERN WEAR

MILLER STOCKMAN, in the Citadel Mall, Academy Blvd. and Platte Ave. Tel. 719/574-1520.
   Miller Stockman, on the lower level of the mall, stocks western wear, including Tony Lama, Justin, Stetson, and Levis.

COWTOWN BOOT COMPANY, 5166 N. Academy Blvd. Tel. 719/598-1960.
   This is the place for handmade cowboy boots.

WESTERN WEARHOUSE, 5506 N. Academy Blvd. Tel. 719/590-9711.
   The Western Wearhouse stocks everything you need to dude up like a cowboy.

7. COLORADO SPRINGS NIGHTS

THE PERFORMING ARTS
MUSIC & DANCE

Both national and local productions are staged at the **Pikes Peak Center,** 190 S. Cascade Ave. (tel. 719/520-SHOW).

Every summer, the **Colorado Opera Festival** (tel. 719/473-0073) presents productions in English, featuring nationally known singers.

The **Colorado Springs Symphony Orchestra** (tel. 719/633-4611) offers series of classical, pop, and youth concerts.

THEATER COMPANIES

Theatreworks (tel. 719/593-3232), a regional theater that's part of the University of Colorado at Colorado Springs, produces five shows each season. Theatreworks also puts on free Shakespeare in the Park performances every summer.

DINNER THEATER

GOLD BAR ROOM THEATER, in the Imperial Hotel, 123 N. 3rd St., Cripple Creek. Tel. 719/689-2922.

Even if you head to Cripple Creek for gambling, take time out to cheer the heroine and hiss the villain during a melodrama at the Gold Bar Room Theater in the historic Imperial Hotel. Some theatergoers watching an evening performance choose to spend the night in the renovated turn-of-the-century hotel (with modern conveniences), rather than driving home along the mountain roads late in the evening. Room rates range from $45 to $55 per night. June through September, plays are presented twice daily, Tuesday through Saturday at 2pm and 8:30pm and on Sunday at 1pm and 4:30pm; no performances on Monday.

Admission: Tickets, $7–$9.

IRON SPRINGS CHATEAU, 444 Ruxton Ave., Manitou Springs. Tel. 719/685-5104 or 719/685-5572.

You can boo the rotten guys and cheer the heroes during melodramas at the Iron Springs. Evenings begin with an all-you-can-eat family-style meal, followed by a melodrama during which the audience is encouraged to respond to the actors' antics, and sing along during the vaudeville-style olio that follows.

Admission: Show only, $9.50; dinner and show, $18 adults, $10 children 10 and younger. Ask for group and senior citizen rates.

THE BAR & CLUB SCENE

The **Ritz Grill,** 15 S. Tejon St. (tel. 719/635-8484), is home for downtown rhythm and blues, while ragtime sing-along piano entertainment draws a cheerful crowd to the **Golden Bee,** at the Broadmoor, 1 Lake Ave. (tel. 719/634-7111).

There's dancing at **Maxi's,** in the Red Lion, 1775 E. Cheyenne Mountain Blvd. (tel. 719/576-8900), and at the Sheridan North, 8110 N. Academy Blvd. (tel. 719/598-5770).

The crowds at **Old Chicago,** 118 N. Tejon St. (tel. 719/634-8812) and 7115 Commerce Center Dr. (tel. 719/593-7678), come to sample the 114 different types of beers available in bottles and on tap. **Cahoots,** in the Marriott, 5580 Tech Center Dr. (tel. 719/260-1800), is a sports bar. **Dublin Down,** 1850 Dominion Way (tel. 719/528-1704), has jazz, and there are large-screen TVs for sports fans. **Murphy's Tavern,** 2729 N. Nevada Ave. (tel. 719/634-9196), draws all types of folks.

You'll find both local and big-time rock and heavy-metal acts on stage at **Rock 'N' Roll,** 840 Arcturus Dr. (tel. 719/444-0144), but some folks come for the pool tables. **The Deluxe Tavern,** 2510 E. Bijou St. (tel. 719/577-4324), is a great choice for local rock bands. (Cover charge only $1.) **Cowboys,** 3900 Palmer Park Blvd. (tel. 719/596-1212), is a gathering spot for country-western music lovers. If you don't know how to line dance or swing, stop in Tuesday for free lessons. National performers are featured here from time to time. Call for a schedule.

There are two **Corner Pocket Billiard Lounges** where you can shoot pool and enjoy a full-service bar plus food. The lounges at 3780 E. Boulder St. (tel. 719/596-9516) and 3430 N. Academy Blvd. (tel. 719/596-9790) open at 11am.

For an evening of laughter, head to **Jeff Valdez' Comedy Corner,** 1305 N. Academy Blvd. (tel. 719/591-0707).

MOVIES

There are more than 20 movie screens at three theater complexes around the intersection of South Academy Boulevard and Platte Avenue.

Kimball's Cinema, 324 N. Tejon St. (tel. 719/578-8206), shows first-run foreign films as well as films by independent American filmmakers. It's next door to an espresso bar, a bookstore, and a pizzeria.

8. EASY EXCURSIONS FROM COLORADO SPRINGS

Cripple Creek, the Royal Gorge, and Denver are all within easy reach of Colorado Springs and offer a wide range of experiences. You can learn about the gold-mining era and head underground to explore a mine shaft in Cripple Creek, or you may just want to try your luck gambling at the town's many casinos. If you like scenic vistas and can handle the heights, visit the Royal Gorge, which has some of the country's most spectacular scenery. And, of course, Denver is where you'll find plenty of big-city attractions.

CRIPPLE CREEK   To get to Cripple Creek, take U.S. 24 up Ute Pass to the Continental Divide and then head south on Colo. 67 to Cripple Creek. The ride takes you around the western side of Pikes Peak over an all-weather road that clings to the cliffs and delivers spectacular mountain views. In the summer, if you're willing to travel on a winding gravel road, take Gold Camp Road (County Rd. 4), which follows the old Short Line Railroad bed. When Teddy Roosevelt visited Cripple Creek, he described his trip up the Short Line as "scenery that bankrupts the English language."

The discovery of gold in Poverty Gulch in 1891 put Cripple Creek (so named after a cow that a rider was chasing fell, tripping the horse, which threw the rider, resulting in broken bones for all three) on the map. By 1896 there were more than 10,000 people living in the region, in spite of two major fires that destroyed much of the town. Brick buildings replaced the debris and the population grew to more than 25,000 by 1900, including the many miners needed to extract ore from the nearly 500 mines operating in the region. The avenues were lined with banks, department stores, schools, churches, and homes. Five newspapers were published, two opera houses were built, and there was even a stock exchange. However, as the gold veins were tapped and subsequently ran dry, the population dwindled until fewer than 5,000 people were left in the town by 1920. During World War II the town was practically deserted, and many residents from the nearby flatlands pulled down buildings for the lumber, which was scarce at that time.

But a few years ago **limited-stakes gambling** was legalized, and it literally changed the face of the town. The main street, Bennett Avenue, is now lined with casinos, with many tucked away in the old buildings. Gamblers move from one gambling parlor to the next, carrying paper buckets filled with coins. You'll find gaming tables and machines set into a variety of buildings, from ones restored to resemble a western saloon to some decked out in Las Vegas–style glitz. The names range from the Golden Horseshoe and Madame June's, to the Brass Ass (burros wandered through the town's streets for many years). Just walk down the main street and step through the open doors.

It's still possible, though, to see remnants of the Old West. Go underground in the **Mollie Kathleen Gold Mine,** where you'll descend 1,000 feet. The **Cripple Creek District Museum** houses mining memorabilia, including machinery, maps, and ore samples. In between pulling slot machine handles, you can catch a matinee or evening performance of a melodrama in the theater at the **Imperial Hotel,** on 3rd Street. The **Old Homestead Parlour House,** on Myers Avenue, is the only house still standing in the infamous red-light district, and is open for tours.

For years many of the miners walked out of their homes in town and hitched a ride to work on the **Cripple Creek–Victor Narrow Gauge Railroad.** They would step off the train, walk across the road, and go underground into the mine. Take a ride on the train, behind the 15-ton iron horse steam engine, or drive the loop through the mining district. If you'd rather drive the approximately six-mile-long Cripple Creek–Victor loop, ask for a copy of the **self-guided tour map** of the Cripple Creek district. Plan on spending 45 minutes to an hour, depending on how many times you stop to look and take photographs.

The sheet describing the trip details the many mines you'll pass, and tells about the town of **Victor.** This town hasn't changed much in years (and you can't gamble here). Take a close look at some of the old buildings on the main street, once the second-largest concentration in the district, and stop by the **Victor Trading Company & Manufacturing Works,** 114 S. 3rd St. (tel. 719/689-2346). There you'll find everything from brooms to business cards being made with antique equipment.

Be sure to stay away from abandoned mine shafts or an abandoned building that might contain a mine opening. The ground could collapse and you could fall hundreds of feet. At least once or twice a year the local newspapers report such an incident.

It's a wonderful drive to Cripple Creek, but you do have the option of taking one of the "gamblers" shuttles that several companies run to and from Colorado Springs. Ask at the front desk of your lodging property for more information. The **Cripple Creek Express** (tel. 719/630-0542) is one such company. If you want to catch an evening performance of a melodrama at the Imperial Hotel, consider reserving one of the refurbished rooms with modernized amenities.

THE ROYAL GORGE   The world's highest suspension bridge is strung across the Royal Gorge over the Arkansas River flowing swiftly 1,053 feet below. To reach the gorge, take I-25 south to Colo. 115, drive south to U.S. 50, and then head west to Cañon City. (It's approximately 47 miles to Cañon City and another 8 to the Royal Gorge.)

Once there, you can drive or walk across the bridge, but there are several other ways you can enjoy the scenery. Step into the 35-passenger aerial tram that glides on wires over the gorge. If you'd rather walk along the Arkansas River looking up at the bridge, take a ride on the world's steepest inclined railway, which runs from the canyon rim to the bottom. The **Royal Gorge Scenic Railway** offers 30-minute trips along the canyon rim on a narrow-gauge train. Tickets are $4.50 for adults and $3.50 for children 4–11. There are also rafting and riding companies operating in this region.

The Royal Gorge is a tourist-oriented operation: There's a theater with a multimedia show, a playground for kids, and a pizza parlor. The admission price ($8.50 for adults and $6.50 for children 4–11) includes all rides, shows, and attractions. Exact hours change according to the season, but the complex is open year round during daylight hours. For more information, contact **Royal Gorge Bridge,** P.O. Box 549, Cañon City, CO 81215 (tel. 719/275-7507).

DENVER   You could make a dozen trips to the Mile High City and do something different each day. See Chapter 7 to learn more about such top attractions as the U.S. Mint, the Denver Art Museum, and the Museum of Natural History. In normal traffic, the ride to downtown Denver takes approximately 1¼ hours.

INDEX

GENERAL INFORMATION

SIGHTS & ATTRACTIONS

DENVER & ENVIRONS

Note: *indicates author's favorite.

BOULDER

COLORADO SPRINGS & ENVIRONS

ACCOMMODATIONS

DENVER

AIRPORT

Comfort Inn (M), 59
Courtyard Marriott (M), 59
Days Hotel (M), 59
Drury Inn (M), 59–60
Embassy Suites Denver Airport Hotel (E), 57–8
Hampton Inn (M), 60
Motel 6, 38th Avenue (B), 60
Motel 6, 39th Avenue (B), 60
Red Lion Hotel (E), 58
Stouffer Concourse Hotel (E), 58–9
Travelers Inn (B), 60–1

DOWNTOWN

Brown Palace Hotel (VE*), 45–7
Burnsley Hotel (E), 49–50
Cambridge Hotel (VE*), 47–8
Castle Marne (B&B*), 65
Central YMCA (B), 53
Comfort Inn (M), 52
Denver Marriott–City Center (VE), 48
Executive Tower Inn (E*), 50
Holiday Inn Denver Sports Center (M), 52
Hotel Denver (M), 52
Hyatt Regency (VE), 48–9
Melbourne Hotel (B), 53
Metropolitan Suites (A), 66
901 Penn House (A), 67
Oxford Hotel (E), 50
Queen Anne Inn (B&B), 65–6
Radisson Hotel (E), 51
Ramada Inn (M), 52–3

Victoria Oaks Inn (B&B), 66
Westin Hotel (VE), 49

NORTH, WEST & SOUTHWEST

Comfort Inn (M), 54
Days Inn (M), 54–5
Denver Marriott West (E), 53–4
Doubletree Hotel (E), 54
Hampton Inn (M), 55
La Quinta (M), 55–6
Motel 6, Sixth Avenue (B), 56
Motel 6, Thornton (B), 56
Motel 6, Wheat Ridge (B), 56
Regency Hotel (M), 56
Valli-Hi Motel Hotel (B), 56–7
White Swan Motel (B), 57

SOUTH, SOUTHEAST & THE TECH CENTER

Cherry Creek Inn (M), 63
Denver South Residence Inn (M), 63–4
Denver Tech Courtyard (M), 63
Embassy Suites (E), 61
Hampton Inn Denver/Aurora (M), 64
Hyatt Regency Tech Center (E), 61–2
Loews Giorgio Hotel (E), 62
Many Mansions (A), 66–7
Motel 6–Denver South (B), 64
Scanticon (E), 62
Sheraton (E), 62–3
Travelers Inn (B), 64

BOULDER

Arapahoe Lodge (M), 161
Best Western Golden Buff (M), 161–2
Boulder Inn (M), 162
Boulder Victoria (B&B*), 160
Briar Rose Bed and Breakfast Inn (B&B), 160
Broker Inn (E), 158
Clarion Harvest House Hotel (E), 158–9
Courtyard by Marriott (M), 162
Days Inn (M), 162

Foot of the Mountain (M$), 162–3
Highlander Inn (M), 163
Holiday Inn (M), 163
Homewood Suites (E), 159
Hotel Boulderado (E), 159
Lazy-L Motel (M), 163
The Magpie Inn (B&B), 163
Pearl Street Inn (B&B), 160–1
Residence Inn–Boulder (E), 159–60

COLORADO SPRINGS

Antlers Doubletree (E), 199
Broadmoor Hotel (VE*), 198–9
Budget Inn (B), 206
Cheyenne Mountain Conference Resort (E), 199–200
Colorado Springs Marriott Hotel (E), 200
Comfort Inn (M), 203
Drury Inn (M), 203–4
El Colorado Lodge (M*), 204
Embassy Suites Hotel (E), 201
Gaden of the Gods Motel (M), 204
Hampton Inn (M$), 204–5

Hearthstone Inn (E*), 201
Le Baron (M$), 205
Motel 6 (B), 206–7
Onaledge (B&B*), 206
Quality Inn (M), 205
Radisson Inn Colorado Springs North (E), 202
Red Crags (B&B), 203
Red Lion Hotel (E), 202
Red Stone Castle (B&B), 203
Residence Inn (E), 202–3
Silver Saddle Motel (M), 205–6
Two Sisters Inn (B&B), 206

KEY TO ABBREVIATIONS: B = Budget; E = Expensive; M = Moderate; VE = Very expensive; A = Apartment rental; B&B = Bed & Breakfast; * = Author's favorite; $ = Super-value choice.

Please Send Me the Books Checked Below.
FROMMER'S COMPREHENSIVE GUIDES
(Guides listing facilities from budget to deluxe,
with emphasis on the medium-priced)

	Retail Price	Code		Retail Price	Code
☐ Acapulco/Ixtapa/Taxco 1993–94	$15.00	C120	☐ Jamaica/Barbados 1993–94	$15.00	C105
☐ Alaska 1990–91	$15.00	C001	☐ Japan 1992–93	$19.00	C020
☐ Arizona 1993–94	$18.00	C101	☐ Morocco 1992–93	$18.00	C021
☐ Australia 1992–93	$18.00	C002	☐ Nepal 1992–93	$18.00	C038
☐ Austria 1993–94	$19.00	C119	☐ New England 1993	$17.00	C114
☐ Austria/Hungary 1991–92	$15.00	C003	☐ New Mexico 1993–94	$15.00	C117
☐ Belgium/Holland/Luxembourg 1993–94	$18.00	C106	☐ New York State 1992–93	$19.00	C025
☐ Bermuda/Bahamas 1992–93	$17.00	C005	☐ Northwest 1991–92	$17.00	C026
☐ Brazil 1993–94	$20.00	C111	☐ Portugal 1992–93	$16.00	C027
☐ California 1993	$18.00	C112	☐ Puerto Rico 1993–94	$15.00	C103
☐ Canada 1992–93	$18.00	C009	☐ Puerto Vallarta/Manzanillo/Guadalajara 1992–93	$14.00	C028
☐ Caribbean 1993	$18.00	C102	☐ Scandinavia 1993–94	$19.00	C118
☐ Carolinas/Georgia 1992–93	$17.00	C034	☐ Scotland 1992–93	$16.00	C040
☐ Colorado 1993–94	$16.00	C100	☐ Skiing Europe 1989–90	$15.00	C030
☐ Cruises 1993–94	$19.00	C107	☐ South Pacific 1992–93	$20.00	C031
☐ DE/MD/PA & NJ Shore 1992–93	$19.00	C012	☐ Spain 1993–94	$19.00	C115
☐ Egypt 1990–91	$15.00	C013	☐ Switzerland/Liechtenstein 1992–93	$19.00	C032
☐ England 1993	$18.00	C109	☐ Thailand 1992–93	$20.00	C033
☐ Florida 1993	$18.00	C104	☐ U.S.A. 1993–94	$19.00	C116
☐ France 1992–93	$20.00	C017	☐ Virgin Islands 1992–93	$13.00	C036
☐ Germany 1993	$19.00	C108	☐ Virginia 1992–93	$14.00	C037
☐ Italy 1993	$19.00	C113	☐ Yucatan 1993–94	$18.00	C110

FROMMER'S $-A-DAY GUIDES
(Guides to low-cost tourist accommodations and facilities)

	Retail Price	Code		Retail Price	Code
☐ Australia on $45 1993–94	$18.00	D102	☐ Israel on $45 1993–94	$18.00	D101
☐ Costa Rica/Guatemala/Belize on $35 1993–94	$17.00	D108	☐ Mexico on $50 1993	$19.00	D105
☐ Eastern Europe on $30 1993–94	$18.00	D110	☐ New York on $70 1992–93	$16.00	D016
☐ England on $60 1993	$18.00	D107	☐ New Zealand on $45 1993–94	$18.00	D103
☐ Europe on $45 1993	$19.00	D106	☐ Scotland/Wales on $50 1992–93	$18.00	D019
☐ Greece on $45 1993–94	$19.00	D100	☐ South America on $40 1993–94	$19.00	D109
☐ Hawaii on $75 1993	$19.00	D104	☐ Turkey on $40 1992–93	$22.00	D023
☐ India on $40 1992–93	$20.00	D010	☐ Washington, D.C. on $40 1992	$17.00	D024
☐ Ireland on $40 1992–93	$17.00	D011			

FROMMER'S CITY $-A-DAY GUIDES
(Pocket-size guides with an emphasis on low-cost tourist accommodations and facilities)

	Retail Price	Code		Retail Price	Code
☐ Berlin on $40 1992–93	$12.00	D002	☐ Madrid on $50 1992–93	$13.00	D014
☐ Copenhagen on $50 1992–93	$12.00	D003	☐ Paris on $45 1992–93	$12.00	D018
☐ London on $45 1992–93	$12.00	D013	☐ Stockholm on $50 1992–93	$13.00	D022

FROMMER'S WALKING TOURS
(With routes and detailed maps, these companion guides point out the places and pleasures that make a city unique)

	Retail Price	Code		Retail Price	Code
☐ Berlin	$12.00	W100	☐ Paris	$12.00	W103
☐ London	$12.00	W101	☐ San Francisco	$12.00	W104
☐ New York	$12.00	W102	☐ Washington, D.C.	$12.00	W105

FROMMER'S TOURING GUIDES
(Color-illustrated guides that include walking tours, cultural and historic sights, and practical information)

	Retail Price	Code		Retail Price	Code
☐ Amsterdam	$11.00	T001	☐ New York	$11.00	T008
☐ Barcelona	$14.00	T015	☐ Rome	$11.00	T010
☐ Brazil	$11.00	T003	☐ Scotland	$10.00	T011
☐ Florence	$ 9.00	T005	☐ Sicily	$15.00	T017
☐ Hong Kong/Singapore/ Macau	$11.00	T006	☐ Thailand	$13.00	T012
			☐ Tokyo	$15.00	T016
☐ Kenya	$14.00	T018	☐ Venice	$ 9.00	T014
☐ London	$13.00	T007			

FROMMER'S FAMILY GUIDES

	Retail Price	Code		Retail Price	Code
☐ California with Kids	$18.00	F100	☐ San Francisco with Kids	$17.00	F004
☐ Los Angeles with Kids	$17.00	F002	☐ Washington, D.C. with Kids	$17.00	F005
☐ New York City with Kids	$18.00	F003			

FROMMER'S CITY GUIDES
(Pocket-size guides to sightseeing and tourist accommodations and facilities in all price ranges)

	Retail Price	Code		Retail Price	Code
☐ Amsterdam 1993–94	$13.00	S110	☐ Miami 1993–94	$13.00	S118
☐ Athens 1993–94	$13.00	S114	☐ Minneapolis/St. Paul 1993–94	$13.00	S119
☐ Atlanta 1993–94	$13.00	S112	☐ Montreal/Quebec City 1993–94	$13.00	S125
☐ Atlantic City/Cape May 1993–94	$13.00	S130	☐ New Orleans 1993–94	$13.00	S103
☐ Bangkok 1992–93	$13.00	S005	☐ New York 1993	$13.00	S120
☐ Barcelona/Majorca/ Minorca/Ibiza 1993–94	$13.00	S115	☐ Orlando 1993	$13.00	S101
☐ Berlin 1993–94	$13.00	S116	☐ Paris 1993–94	$13.00	S109
☐ Boston 1993–94	$13.00	S117	☐ Philadelphia 1993–94	$13.00	S113
☐ Cancun/Cozumel/ Yucatan 1991–92	$ 9.00	S010	☐ Rio 1991–92	$ 9.00	S029
☐ Chicago 1993–94	$13.00	S122	☐ Rome 1993–94	$13.00	S111
☐ Denver/Boulder/ Colorado Springs 1993–94	$13.00	S131	☐ Salt Lake City 1991–92	$ 9.00	S031
			☐ San Diego 1993–94	$13.00	S107
☐ Dublin 1993–94	$13.00	S128	☐ San Francisco 1993	$13.00	S104
☐ Hawaii 1992	$12.00	S014	☐ Santa Fe/Taos/ Albuquerque 1993–94	$13.00	S108
☐ Hong Kong 1992–93	$12.00	S015	☐ Seattle/Portland 1992– 93	$12.00	S035
☐ Honolulu/Oahu 1993	$13.00	S106	☐ St. Louis/Kansas City 1993–94	$13.00	S127
☐ Las Vegas 1993–94	$13.00	S121			
☐ Lisbon/Madrid/Costa del Sol 1991–92	$ 9.00	S017	☐ Sydney 1993–94	$13.00	S129
☐ London 1993	$13.00	S100	☐ Tampa/St. Petersburg 1993–94	$13.00	S105
☐ Los Angeles 1993–94	$13.00	S123	☐ Tokyo 1992–93	$13.00	S039
☐ Madrid/Costa del Sol 1993–94	$13.00	S124	☐ Toronto 1993–94	$13.00	S126
			☐ Vancouver/Victoria 1990–91	$ 8.00	S041
☐ Mexico City/Acapulco 1991–92	$ 9.00	S020	☐ Washington, D.C. 1993	$13.00	S102

Other Titles Available at Membership Prices
SPECIAL EDITIONS

	Retail Price	Code		Retail Price	Code
☐ Bed & Breakfast North America	$15.00	P002	☐ National Park Guide 1993	$15.00	P101
☐ Bed & Breakfast Southwest	$16.00	P100	☐ Where to Stay U.S.A.	$15.00	P102
☐ Caribbean Hideaways	$16.00	P005			
☐ Marilyn Wood's Wonderful Weekends (within a 250-mile radius of NYC)	$12.00	P017			

GAULT MILLAU'S "BEST OF" GUIDES
(The only guides that distinguish the truly superlative from the merely overrated)

	Retail Price	Code		Retail Price	Code
☐ Chicago	$16.00	G002	☐ New England	$16.00	G010
☐ Florida	$17.00	G003	☐ New Orleans	$17.00	G011
☐ France	$17.00	G004	☐ New York	$17.00	G012
☐ Germany	$18.00	G018	☐ Paris	$17.00	G013
☐ Hawaii	$17.00	G006	☐ San Francisco	$17.00	G014
☐ Hong Kong	$17.00	G007	☐ Thailand	$18.00	G019
☐ London	$17.00	G009	☐ Toronto	$17.00	G020
☐ Los Angeles	$17.00	G005	☐ Washington, D.C.	$17.00	G017

THE REAL GUIDES
(Opinionated, politically aware guides for youthful budget-minded travelers)

	Retail Price	Code		Retail Price	Code
☐ Able to Travel	$20.00	R112	☐ Italy	$18.00	R125
☐ Amsterdam	$13.00	R100	☐ Kenya	$12.95	R015
☐ Barcelona	$13.00	R101	☐ Mexico	$11.95	R016
☐ Belgium/Holland/ Luxembourg	$16.00	R031	☐ Morocco	$14.00	R017
☐ Berlin	$13.00	R123	☐ Nepal	$14.00	R018
☐ Brazil	$13.95	R003	☐ New York	$13.00	R019
☐ California & the West Coast	$17.00	R121	☐ Paris	$13.00	R020
☐ Canada	$15.00	R103	☐ Peru	$12.95	R021
☐ Czech and Slovak Republics	$15.00	R124	☐ Poland	$13.95	R022
☐ Egypt	$19.00	R105	☐ Portugal	$16.00	R126
☐ Europe	$18.00	R122	☐ Prague	$15.00	R113
☐ Florida	$14.00	R006	☐ San Francisco & the Bay Area	$11.95	R024
☐ France	$18.00	R106	☐ Scandinavia	$14.95	R025
☐ Germany	$18.00	R107	☐ Spain	$16.00	R026
☐ Greece	$18.00	R108	☐ Thailand	$17.00	R119
☐ Guatemala/Belize	$14.00	R010	☐ Tunisia	$17.00	R115
☐ Hong Kong/Macau	$11.95	R011	☐ Turkey	$13.95	R027
☐ Hungary	$14.95	R118	☐ U.S.A.	$18.00	R117
☐ Ireland	$17.00	R120	☐ Venice	$11.95	R028
			☐ Women Travel	$12.95	R029
			☐ Yugoslavia	$12.95	R030